PEOPLE, MARKETS, GOODS:
ECONOMIES AND SOCIETIES IN HISTORY

Volume 15

Women and the Land, 1500–1900

PEOPLE, MARKETS, GOODS:
ECONOMIES AND SOCIETIES IN HISTORY

ISSN: 2051-7467

The interactions of economy and society, people and goods, transactions and actions are at the root of most human behaviours. Economic and social historians are participants in the same conversation about how markets have developed historically and how they have been constituted by economic actors and agencies in various social, institutional and geographical contexts. New debates now underpin much research in economic and social, cultural, demographic, urban and political history. Their themes have enduring resonance – financial stability and instability, the costs of health and welfare, the implications of poverty and riches, flows of trade and the centrality of communications. This paperback series aims to attract historians interested in economics and economists with an interest in history by publishing high quality, cutting edge academic research in the broad field of economic and social history from the late medieval/ early modern period to the present day. It encourages the interaction of qualitative and quantitative methods through both excellent monographs and collections offering path-breaking overviews of key research concerns. Taking as its benchmark international relevance and excellence it is open to scholars and subjects of any geographical areas from the case study to the multi-nation comparison.

PREVIOUSLY PUBLISHED TITLES IN THE SERIES
ARE LISTED AT THE BACK OF THIS VOLUME

Women and the Land
1500–1900

Edited by
Amanda L. Capern, Briony McDonagh
and Jennifer Aston

THE BOYDELL PRESS

First published 2019
The Boydell Press, Woodbridge

ISBN 978-1-78327-398-0

The Boydell Press is an imprint of Boydell & Brewer Ltd
PO Box 9, Woodbridge, Suffolk IP12 3DF, UK
and of Boydell & Brewer Inc.
668 Mt Hope Avenue, Rochester, NY 14620–2731, USA
website: www.boydellandbrewer.com

A catalogue record for this book is available
from the British Library

Index compiled by James Helling

Contents

List of Illustrations vii
List of Contributors ix

Introduction: Women, Property and Land
Briony McDonagh, Amanda L. Capern, Jennifer Aston and Hannah Worthen 1

1. Women, Work and Land: The Spatial Dynamics of Gender Relations in Early Modern England 1550–1750
Amanda Flather 29

2. Spinsters with Land in Early Modern England: Inheritance, Possession and Use
Judith Spicksley 51

3. Becoming Anne Clifford
Jessica L. Malay 77

4. The Heiress Reconsidered: Contexts for Understanding the Abduction of Arabella Alleyn
Amanda L. Capern 100

5. From Magnificent Houses to Disagreeable Country: Lady Sophia Newdigate's Tour of Southern England and Derbyshire, 1748
Jon Stobart 127

6. On Being 'fully and completely mistress of the whole business': Gender, Land and Estate Accounting in Georgian England
Briony McDonagh 149

7. Negotiating Men: Elizabeth Montagu, 'Capability' Brown and the Construction of Pastoral
Stephen Bending 176

8. Women's Involvement in Property in the North Riding of Yorkshire in the Eighteenth and Nineteenth Centuries
Joan K. F. Heggie 201

9. Invisible Women: Small-scale Landed Proprietors in Nineteenth-century England
Janet Casson 226

10. More than Just a Caretaker: Women's Role in the Intergenerational Transfer of Real and Personal Property in Nineteenth-century Urban England, 1840–1900
Jennifer Aston 244

Afterword
Amy Louise Erickson 267

Select Bibliography 277
Index 283

Illustrations

Figures

1. Bequests of land to daughters by Lincoln fathers, 1559–1693 62
2. Landholding by spinsters, 1545–1700 63
3. Changes in landholding by spinsters, 1545–1700 64
4. Differential livestock and landholding by spinsters in Chester, Durham, Norfolk and Lincolnshire, 1545–1700 70
5. Changes in livestock holding in four jurisdictions over the seventeenth century 73
6. Proportion of single women involved in formal lending with land, 1545–1700 74
7. A page from the ledgers of Elizabeth Prowse 163

Tables

1. Distribution and coverage of the documents in the spinster will sample, 1545–1700 55
2. Female landowners keeping accounts and featured in the text 157
3. Breakdown of datasets by line, gender and unique transactions 207
4. Breakdown of datasets by period, gender and unique people 211
5. Breakdown of female datasets by marital status and unique females 212
6. Breakdown of datasets by township and gender 216

7. Breakdown of female datasets by marital status and type of transaction, 1885–89 218

8. Breakdown of unique female participation by type of transaction, 1885–89 219

9. Breakdown of women-to-women transactions by year and marital status 221

10. Breakdown of female wills by marital status 223

11. Women's plot ownership across the four regions 232

12. Comparative regional analysis of the ownership of plots by subgroups of women owners 232

13. Women's ownership categories and marital status 234

14. Marital status of testators by sex 256

15. Content of last will and testament by sex 259

16. Values of male and female estates 264

Contributors

Jennifer Aston is a Senior Lecturer in Modern British History at Northumbria University. Her research focuses on gender and small business ownership, bankruptcy and English law. After completing an ESRC funded PhD at the University of Birmingham, she held the EHS Eileen Power Research Fellowship at the Institute of Historical Research. She spent three years at Oxford as Research Associate on the ESRC funded 'Victorian Professions' project and one year at the University of Hull as Research Associate in the Gender, Place and Memory Research Cluster. She has several articles on women's property ownership and her first monograph, *Female Entrepreneurship in Nineteenth-Century England: Engagement in the Urban Economy* was published in 2016. She is currently co-editing *Female Entrepreneurs in the Long Nineteenth Century: A Global Perspective*, which will be published by Macmillan in 2020.

Stephen Bending is Professor of Eighteenth Century Literature and Culture at the University of Southampton. His publications include *Green Retreats: Women, Gardens and Eighteenth-Century Culture* (2013), *A Cultural History of Gardens in the Age of Enlightenment* (2015), and *The Writing of Rural England, 1500-1800* (2003). He is editor of *Women's Travel Writings in Revolutionary France* (2008) and has published numerous articles on eighteenth-century gardens and landscape. He is general editor of the Chawton House Library series, which publishes modern editions of eighteenth-century women's novels, travel writing and memoirs. He is currently working on the related projects *Pleasure Gardens and Problems of Pleasure in Britain, France and North America, 1660-1830* and *Women in Retreat: American Landscapes, 1750-1835*.

Amanda L. Capern is a Senior Lecturer in Early-Modern Women's History, University of Hull. She is author of *The Historical Study of Women: England, 1500-1700* (2010) and co-editor of *Women, Wealth and Power* (2007). She was specialist sub-editor of the modern edition of Mary Hays' *Female Biography* (2013/14), is co-editor of the book series *Gender and History* (Palgrave/ Macmillan International) and editor of *The Routledge History of Women in Early Modern Europe* (forthcoming). She has published widely on early-modern women, including recent essays on female prophets and religious writers. Her recent research is on gender, debt and family litigation. She is currently a Leverhulme Trust research fellow (2019-2020) working on a monograph on women's and family finances and litigation in early-modern society.

Janet Casson completed a DPhil at the University of Oxford in 2013 on 'Women and Property: A Study of Women as owners, lessors and lessees of Plots of Land in England during the Nineteenth Century as revealed by the Land Surveys carried out by the Railway, Canal and Turnpike Companies'. Her statistical study of women's ownership of land in nineteenth-century England was published as a chapter in *Large Datasets in Economic History* (2013). She has subsequently carried out case studies of over 600 individual women landowners. She has taught, been an economic consultant and is current Honorary Treasurer of the charitable library, Business Enterprise Heritage Trust.

Amy Louise Erickson is University Lecturer in British Economic and Social History 1500-1750 in the History Faculty of the University of Cambridge. She is in the Cambridge Group for the History of Population and Social Structure. Her research interests lie in historical feminist economics, ranging from control of assets (*Women and Property in Early Modern England,* 1993), through sustainable economies (*The Marital Economy in Scandinavia & Britain 1400-1900*, 2005), to employment rates ('Married women's occupations in eighteenth-century London', *Continuity & Change* 2008) and entrepreneurship (articles in *History Workshop Journal* 2011, 2014, and *Eighteenth-Century Life*, 2018). She is also interested in how and by whom history is told (*Generations of Women Historians*, 2018).

Amanda Flather is Lecturer in History at the University of Essex. She has broad interests in the social and cultural history of early modern England and her research focuses principally on gender relations, with particular emphasis on the history of the organisation of social space in England between the mid-sixteenth and eighteenth centuries. She is the author of *Gender and Space in Early Modern England* (2007) and has published a number of articles and essays on the influence of gender on space and its use, including 'Gender and the Organization of Sacred Space in Early Modern England, c. 1580-1640' (2015) and 'Space, Place and Gender: The Sexual and Spatial Division of Labour in the Early Modern Household' in *History and Theory* (2013).

Joan K. F. Heggie is a Research Fellow in History at Teesside University. Her research focuses on Teesside's industrial past and her oral histories with former steelworkers are exhibited in 'Steel Stories' at Kirkleatham Museum (2019-20). Other interests include women's history, women's relationships to and with property, and the life and art of Viva Talbot, a wood engraver (1900-83). She curates exhibitions of Talbot's work and her biography of Talbot appears in G. Batho, & A. Roberts (eds.), *Durham Biographies, Volume Seven*. Other publications include *Middlesbrough's Iron & Steel Industry* (2013) and 'The British Steel Archive Project: forging new kinds of partnerships to preserve significant business archives, *Business Archives: Principles and Practice* (2009).

Jessica L. Malay is Professor of English Renaissance Literature at the University of Huddersfield. She is the editor of *Anne Clifford's Great Books of Record* (2015) and also *Anne Clifford's Autobiographical Writing, 1590-1676* (2018). She has written widely on early-modern culture including domestic violence, sibylline prophecy and women's writing and space. Most recent publications include 'Elizabeth Hardwick's Material Negotiations' (2019). She is at present leading a Leverhulme research project exploring early-modern autobiography through civic court records: *Autobiographical Acts in Seventeenth Century England, Scotland, Wales and New England*.

Briony McDonagh is a Senior Lecturer in Historical Geography at the University of Hull. She has published widely on the medieval and early modern British landscape, on women's histories and on the historical geographies of enclosure, property, protest and the law. Her book, *Elite Women and the Agricultural Landscape, 1700–1830* (2017), won the Joan Thirsk Memorial Prize and Women's History Network Book Prize. She is co-editor of *Remembering Protest in Britain since 1500* (2018) and *Hull: Culture, History, Place* (2017). She is Chair of the Historical Geography Research Group, co-editor of *Historical Geography* (University of Nebraska Press) and 2019 President of the British Science Association's Geography Section.

Judith Spicksley is Lecturer in Economic History at the Wilberforce Institute, University of Hull. She is the editor of *The Business and Household Accounts of Joyce Jeffreys, Spinster of Hereford, 1638-1648* (2012). Other publications include *Women, Wealth and Power* (2007), as co-editor. She is interested in the lives of never-married women and questions of social worth and debt and has published widely in the area, including 'Women, "Usury" and Credit in Early Modern England: The Case of the Maiden Investor', *Gender and History* (2009). She has held a Leverhulme Trust Fellowship 2018-2019 and is currently working on a book from that project on debt and slavery in the *longue durée*.

Jon Stobart is Professor of History at Manchester Metropolitan University. His research has explored the spaces and practices of retailing and consumption in eighteenth-century England and more recently has focused on the country house as a site of consumption, examining processes of supply and the ways in which material culture was constructed around shifting priorities of taste, wealth, pedigree and comfort. Recent publications include *Consumption and the Country House* (2016), *Travel and the British Country House* (2017), and *Comfort and the Home in Western Europe* (2019) and multiple articles, including 'Making the Global Local? Overseas Goods in English Rural Shops, c. 1600-1760' in *Business History* (2017).

Hannah Worthen is a Post-Doctoral Research Associate in the Gender, Place and Memory research cluster at the University of Hull. She was awarded her AHRC funded PhD in 2017 from the University of Leicester in collaboration with The National Archives on 'The experience of war widows in the mid-seventeenth century'. She researches the experiences of widows who petitioned in defence of property and is the author of 'Supplicants and Guardians: The Petitions of Royalist Widows during the Civil Wars and Interregnum, 1642–1660', *Women's History Review*, 26:4 (2017). A joint article with Amanda Capern and Briony McDonagh, 'Gender, Property and Succession in the Early Modern-English Aristocracy: The Case of Martha Janes and her Illegitimate Children' has been accepted by *Women's History Review*.

Introduction

Women, Property and Land

BRIONY MCDONAGH, AMANDA L. CAPERN, JENNIFER ASTON AND HANNAH WORTHEN

In this book, we examine the pre-history of gendered property relations in the modern world, focusing on the four hundred year period between roughly 1500 and 1900. More specifically, the book is about how gender shaped opportunities for and experiences of owning property. The focus is especially on land, residential buildings and commercial property, but livestock, commons and personal property also feature. This project has been driven by an explicitly feminist agenda: we are deliberately seeking to challenge the idea that the existence of patriarchal property relations – including the doctrine of coverture and gendered inheritance practices – meant that property was concentrated almost exclusively in male hands. Here we tell a different story: of significant levels of female landownership and how women's desire to own property and manage its profits and landscapes led to emotional attachments to land and the willingness and determination to fight for the right to legal title. The intention here is to reveal to as full an extent as possible – through both quantitative and qualitative interdisciplinary methodologies – the story of female inheritance of property and its transmission through women's hands. While recognising that everything from law to social custom and practice privileged men in early modern society, we argue that the story of land was the story of women's lives too and that the history of land and property cannot be told without their inclusion.

This book asserts that using gender as a lens complicates and nuances the history of land and property. It forces a reconsideration of the history of the aristocracy and landed gentry, much of which is still framed within the model of masculine genealogies first provided in the nineteenth century by Burke's *Peerage* and *Landed Gentry*. These histories of land and its relationship to the state led to exceptionally male-dominated historiographies of economic and political change for a century after.[1] Against this backdrop of male genealogical concerns, women who inherited and managed land were consistently painted in the literature as exceptional. Histories of heiresses offered the classic supplement to the norm, or the addition that does not alter the whole, while biographies of individual female landowners always hinted at the exotic.[2] This book argues for the reverse: for the mainstreaming of women in histories of land and state. Elizabeth Talbot, countess of Shrewsbury – the 'Elizabethan dynast' – and Lady Anne Clifford, countess of Pembroke, Dorset and Montgomery – romanticised by one biographer as the 'proud northern lady' – have, of course, loomed large in past historiography, strengthening the idea that landed women were out of the ordinary and something exceptional.[3] It is only now that their stories are being presented differently. Jessica Malay's work writes Clifford fully into the politics of land and state and Barbara Harris's *English Aristocratic Women* has demonstrated how vital female business management and familial networks were to English family life, the politics of patronage and social structure.[4] In this book we aim to shift this familiar picture even further, to create new and unexpected patterns that will alter the social, economic, political and environmental histories of England from the early modern period to the cusp of the modern age.

The history of women's property rights, title and access to land and real estate is also important to our understanding of contemporary gendered

1 For example, John Habakkuk's *Marriage, Debt and the Estates System* (Oxford and New York, 1994) was largely predicated on the idea of the landed estate based on male lineage. For histories that offered a narrative of the high-road to civil war between opposing male political classes, see R. H. Tawney's 'The Rise of the Gentry, 1558-1640', *Economic History Review* 11:1 (1941), 1-38 and the debate in Lawrence Stone, 'The Anatomy of the Elizabethan Aristocracy', *Economic History Review* 18:1 (1948), 1-53 and Hugh Trevor-Roper, 'The Elizabethan Aristocracy: An Anatomy Anatomized', *Economic History Review* New Series, 3:3, 279-98. The debate was summarised by J. H. Hexter, 'Storm over the Gentry', in *Reappraisals in History* (London, 1961), 117-62.

2 Joan Wallach Scott, 'Gender: A Useful Category of Historical Analysis', *American Historical Review* 91:5 (1986), 1053–75; Hilary Thomas, '"With this ring": The Importance of the Heiress in the Descent of Three Glamorgan Estates', *Morgannwg* 49 (2005), 67–78; Ann Marie Curtis, 'An Accidental Heiress: The Life and Times of Anna Maria Hunt of Mollington Hall (1771–1861)', *Cheshire History* 50 (2010–11), 50–9; D. E. Jenkins, 'Mary Brocksopp (1811–1835): A Minor North Derbyshire Heiress', *Derbyshire Miscellany* 13:4 (1993), 103–8; Angélique Day, 'Marie Angélique de la Cherois: Life of a Huguenot Heiress, 1700–1771', *The Huguenots and Ireland: Anatomy of an Emigration*, eds C. E. J. Caldicott, H. Gough and Jean-Paul Pittion (Glendale, CA, 1987), 377–97.

3 David Durant, *Bess of Hardwick: Portrait of an Elizabethan Dynast* (London, 2000); Martin Holmes, *Proud Northern Lady: Lady Anne Clifford 1590–1676* (Chichester, 1984).

4 Jessica L. Malay, *Anne Clifford's Autobiographical Writing 1590–1676* (Manchester, 2018) and *Anne Clifford's Great Books of Record* (Manchester, 2015). See also Jessica Malay, this volume. Barbara Harris, *English Aristocratic Women, 1450–1550: Marriage and Family, Property and Careers* (New York and Oxford, 2002).

experiences of property and landownership at a global scale. This is not least because patriarchal property relations enshrined in the English common law were exported across the world via British colonialism. Today, the structures of capitalism spread across the globe to intersect with multiple legal systems resulting in gender inequalities over land and property. We argue that this book is centrally important at this juncture. It provides historical explanations for the long history of economic inequality experienced by English women at a time when interest in the politics of land and property ownership is undergoing a public and critical resurgence. This interest is not confined to England or Great Britain. In the Anglophone world of the United States, Canada, Australia and New Zealand, the bursting of the North American subprime mortgage bubble in 2007 has had wide and deep consequences including the global financial crisis that has so dramatically affected ownership of and access to land and residential property. Land values have risen dramatically in recent years so that land accounted for 51 per cent of the United Kingdom's net worth in 2016. This has been a boon primarily to large landowners and rentiers, while at the same time the unaffordability of housing means many people are struggling just to get onto the property ladder.[5] Campaign groups like Generation Rent, PricedOut and Empty Homes lobby for better and more affordable housing and fewer long-term empty properties, yet successive UK governments seem unable to fix the problem, and they freely admit this. As one historian recently put it, the housing crisis is 'the new "land question" of the modern era'.[6]

Access to land and residential property is, therefore, one of the big political topics of the early twenty-first century. Yet, there has been relatively little consideration of the ways that gender might shape access to and experience of property ownership. In part, this is because we know relatively little about the gendering of property ownership in contemporary Britain, even whilst it is clear that women are disproportionately affected by the recent housing crises in the United Kingdom and elsewhere. Not only does the gender pay gap mean that women spend more of their earnings on rent, but changes to housing benefit – of which women make up nearly two-thirds of claimants – and cuts to domestic violence services have hit women in the UK particularly hard.[7] Women frequently carry a double burden: if alone raising children,

5 Phillip Inman, 'UK's wealth rises as land values soar by £450bn in a year', *The Guardian*, 29 August 2018, available at https://www.theguardian.com/business/2018/aug/29/uks-wealth-rises-as-land-values-soar-by-450bn-in-a-year, accessed 26 June 2019.

6 Michael Tichelar, *The Failure of Land Reform in Twentieth-Century England. The Triumph of Private Property* (London, 2018), p. 3.

7 'Housing is a women's issue: the facts', *The Guardian*, 6 March 2017, available at https://www.theguardian.com/housing-network/2017/mar/06/housing-womens-issue-international-womens-day; accessed 7 September 2018; Housing and Gender: Briefing from the UK Women's Budget Group on the impact of changes in housing policy since 2010 on women,

then there is no second income to put towards extortionately high rents, but they are also disadvantaged by the pay gap, part-time work and poor provision of affordable childcare services. In the United States, three-quarters of those living in affordable housing are women, a situation which results from long-standing structural inequalities in society. Women live in poverty at higher rates than men and comprise 60 per cent of the minimum-wage workforce and more than 70 per cent of the 'tipped' workforce.[8] The latter is particularly striking, not least because it is becoming a more prevalent feature of the British labour market where the set minimum wage is lower than in the United States and is especially discriminatory towards people under the age of twenty-five.

Clearly, women's access to and ownership of property in the present day is disadvantaged compared with that of men. Crucially, however, this is *not* a modern phenomenon and this edited collection provides the contextualisation necessary to tackle this inequality. In this introductory chapter, we do three things. Firstly, we offer an overview of the growing body of literature on two key themes relating to women and property, namely: women, property and the law in early modern England; and women, work and business in the seventeenth, eighteenth and nineteenth centuries. In doing so, we both signal the breadth and depth of emerging research on these themes and provide historiographical context for the individual chapters in the book. Secondly, we explore the issue of women's property in the here-and-now in more detail, arguing that understanding the historical context of the relationships between women and property ownership is central to explaining the present day situation. Thirdly, we briefly introduce the chapters that follow, drawing out the key themes and findings, challenges and approaches that cross and connect them, as well as highlighting important future research directions.

Women, property and the law in early modern England

Histories of property, of the aristocracy and of agricultural and landscape change all say remarkably little about women as the owners of land and other real property. As Nancy Wright and Margaret Ferguson put it, much of the scholarship on early modern law 'assumes that women cannot be theorised as subjects [i.e. owners] of property and, as a result, are not subjects for

November 2017, available at https://wbg.org.uk/wp-content/uploads/2017/11/housing-pre-budget-nov-2017-final.pdf, accessed 7 September 2018.

8 'A Gender Lens on Affordable Housing', report by re:gender, January 2016, available at https://www.icrw.org/wp-content/uploads/2016/11/gender_lens_on_affordable_housing_by_regender_final-1.pdf, accessed 7 September 2018.

research'.[9] Alongside academic sexism, the reason why both historians and political scientists have largely assumed that women did not own property results from two specific aspects of early modern law as it relates to women: firstly, inheritance practices, specifically primogeniture; and secondly, the doctrine of coverture.

Primogeniture was the feudal arrangement by which titles and real property descended to the eldest son. It strictly applied only to intestates, but had been widely adopted – particularly by elite families – by the later medieval period, so that eldest sons inherited in preference to younger sons and daughters. In the absence of sons, daughters inherited equally as co-heirs and in preference over collateral male relatives, but by the early modern period landowners were using various legal devices to privilege nephews and brothers over daughters. Famously, Sir George Clifford shifted succession to his brother, Francis Clifford, who became 4th earl of Cumberland, leading to years of litigation by his widow, Lady Margaret Clifford, on behalf of her daughter, Lady Anne Clifford. By the late seventeenth century, many landowners used so-called strict settlements to exclude female heirs from successions. These agreements were drawn up between parties to a marriage and specified both the succession of the estate – typically restricting it to male heirs – and portions for younger sons and daughters. The precise impact of the emergence and growing popularity of strict settlements has been much debated by historians, with Eileen Spring arguing that these settlements effectively disinherited female heirs resulting in a long-term decline in women's property and rights which reached their lowest ebb in the eighteenth century.[10] Barbara English and John Saville noted that the reliance on providing for daughters through cash portions often meant smaller portions and their survey of the prevalence of strict settlements demonstrated a very clear shift from the later sixteenth

9 Nancy E. Wright and Margaret W. Ferguson, 'Introduction', *Women, Property, and the Letters of the Law in Early Modern England*, eds Nancy E. Wright, Margaret W. Ferguson and A. R. Buck (Toronto, 2004), p. 18.

10 Barbara English and John Saville, *Strict Settlement: A Guide for Historians* (Hull, 1983); Eileen Spring, *Law, Land and Family: Aristocratic Inheritance in England, 1300–1800* (Chapel Hill, NC, and London, 1993); Elieen Spring, 'A Comment on Payling's "Economics of Marriage"', *Economic History Review* 56:2 (2003), 347; Sara Mendelson and Patricia Crawford, *Women in Early Modern England* (Oxford, 1998), pp. 434–5; Pamela Sharpe, 'Dealing with Love: The Ambiguous Independence of the Single Woman in Early Modern England', *Gender & History* 11:2 (1999), 209–32; Mary Murray, 'Primogeniture, Patrilineage and the Displacement of Women', *Women, Property, and the Letters of the Law in Early Modern England*, eds Nancy E. Wright, Margaret W. Ferguson and A. R. Buck (Toronto, 2004), pp. 121–36. By contrast, Lloyd Bonfield, in *Marriage Settlements 1601–1740: The Adoption of Strict Settlement* (Cambridge, 1983), suggests that strict settlements improved women's access to property by protecting daughters' portions and wives' pin money.

century – and in greater numbers from the mid-seventeenth century onwards – from life estate entails to the use of strict settlements.[11]

The second key legal doctrine affecting married women's relationships with property in the period before the late nineteenth century was that of coverture. Coverture was the doctrine by which married women's legal identities were subsumed within those of their husbands during marriage.[12] A woman's rights at law depended entirely on whether she was an independent actor-at-law (*feme sole*) or *uxor*/wife and litigating under coverture (*feme covert*). Thus while single and widowed women had most of the same legal rights as men, the situation was very different for married women. As a *feme covert*, a married woman could not own land, enter a contract, make a will or sue independently of her husband.[13] Men assumed control of any property brought into marriage by their wives or inherited by them during the marriage. The profits of freehold and copyhold land were his, and while he could not dispose of the property without his wife's consent, he might – as contemporaries noted – 'kick or kiss' it out of her.[14] Leases were treated similarly under the law, but cash and movable goods were his alone.

Yet while primogeniture and coverture persisted under the 'letter of the law' – thus creating significant legal disadvantages for women throughout the early modern centuries – the situation on the ground was actually much more complicated. The possibilities for women to modify, evade or otherwise manipulate the common law doctrine of coverture have been charted in a wide variety of contexts, from access to the law courts to consumption, business dealings and transmission of property.[15] Access to equity and other courts – Chancery, the Court of Requests, Star Chamber and Exchequer – made coverture 'porous' in Natasha Korda's words, as did the fact that even the common law recognised exceptions to coverture by way of wives'

11 Barbara English, *The Great Landowners of East Yorkshire 1530–1910* (Hull, 1990), 90–2.

12 Tim Stretton and Krista J. Kesselring, *Married Women and the Law: Coverture in England and the Common Law World* (Montréal, 2013).

13 Briony McDonagh, *Elite Women and the Agricultural Landscape, 1700–1830* (Abingdon, 2017), p. 16.

14 C. S. Kenny, *The History of the Law in England as to the Effects of Marriage on Property and on the Wife's Legal Capacity* (London, 1879).

15 Joanne Begiato, 'Favoured or Oppressed? Married Women, Property and "Coverture" in England, 1660–1800', *Continuity and Change* 17:3 (2002), 351–72; Amy Erickson, 'Possession – and the other One-tenth of the Law: Assessing Women's Ownership and Economic Roles in Early Modern England', *Women's History Review* 16:3 (2007), 369–85; Anne Laurence, 'Women, Banks and the Securities Market in Eighteenth-Century England', *Women and their Money, 1700–1950: Essays on Women and Finance* (London, 2009), pp. 46–58; S. M. Okin, 'Patriarchy and Married Women's Property in England: Questions On Some Current Views', *Eighteenth-Century Studies* 17:2 (1983–84), 121–38; Margot C. Finn, 'Women, Consumption and Coverture in England, c.1760–1860', *Historical Journal* 39 (1996), 703–22; Cordelia Beattie and Matthew Frank Stevens, *Married Women and the Law in Premodern North-West Europe* (Woodbridge, 2013).

paraphernalia.[16] Coverture was after all transient for many women: it existed only *during* their marriage. This doubtless affected perceptions of property ownership. Korda makes this point, asking 'Did wives simply stop thinking of their property as their own during marriage?', while, as Garthine Walker notes in her study of women and stolen goods, 'popular perceptions of ownership did not strictly adhere to legal definitions'.[17] Similarly, coverture was also adopted by husbands and wives as a way to protect their business enterprises, with the wives acquiring credit and trading alongside their husbands when they needed credit and then pleading coverture when things went wrong.[18] Even after the Married Women's Property Acts of 1870, 1882 and 1893 were passed, married women were still unable to be sued for bankruptcy, meaning that – under bankruptcy law at least – they were viewed as legal equals to children and lunatics.[19] Indeed, men took out advertisements in the social register, *The Times*, to disavow their wives' debts, such a public statement being the only way a married man could escape liability for his wife's debts. The plurality of legal jurisdictions in early modern England also provided opportunities for married women's litigation, as Christine Churches demonstrates for early modern Whitehaven. She reminds us too that 'most women lived and worked as part of a family unit and did not perceive themselves as autonomous individuals'.[20] Indeed, while marriage deprived women of many of their property rights, it also provided women with opportunities to learn about estate management: as Harris points out of late medieval English aristocratic women, their 'careers' as wives did much to prepare women to manage property successfully as widows.[21]

16 Natasha Korda, 'Coverture and its Discontents: Legal Fictions On and Off the Early Modern English Stage', *Married Women and the Law: Coverture in England and the Common Law World*, eds Tim Stretton and Krista J. Kesselring (Montréal, 2013), p. 52.

17 Korda, 'Coverture and its Discontents', p. 46; Garthine Walker, 'Women, Theft and the World of Stolen Goods', *Women, Crime and the Courts in Early Modern England*, eds Jennifer Kermode and Gathine Walker (Chapel Hill, NC, 1994), p. 83.

18 Hannah Barker, *The Business of Women: Female Enterprise and Urban Development in Northern England, 1760–1830* (Oxford, 2006), p. 127; Nicola Jane Phillips, *Women in Business, 1700–1850* (Woodbridge, 2006), p. 86; Jennifer Aston and Paolo di Martino, 'Risk, Success, and Failure: Female Entrepreneurship in Late Victorian and Edwardian England', *Economic History Society* 70:3 (August 2017), 837–58, especially 855.

19 Aston and Martino, 'Risk, Success, and Failure', 844. See also Korda, 'Coverture and its Discontents', p. 50, who argues that coverture 'conferred privileges as well as constraints upon wives'.

20 Christine Churches, 'Putting Women in their Place: Female Litigants at Whitehaven, 1660–1760', *Women, Property, and the Letters of the Law in Early Modern England*, eds Nancy E. Wright, Margaret W. Ferguson and A. R. Buck (Toronto, 2004), p. 51.

21 Harris, *English Aristocratic Women*; Churches, 'Putting Women in their Place', p. 58 makes much the same point about more middling women in early modern Whitehaven; see too McDonagh, *Elite Women*, pp. 53–62 for examples of eighteenth-century women who managed their husbands' and sons' estates. See too Hannah Worthen, Briony McDonagh and Amanda

The extent to which a woman actually exercised control over her inherited property depended entirely on the legal entitlement of the woman in each individual case (which was itself dependent on her marital status and relationship with her spouse). Married women could not bring legal cases at common law without their husbands, and even at equity most did not. Separate estate under a trust may have been independently owned, but married women still needed to buck custom and take a social risk against the norms of patriarchal authority when they pursued their property rights.[22] Recent work on the Court of Chancery by Charlotte Garside has indicated that, although married women could theoretically bring cases to the court, they almost always appeared as *uxor* with their husbands, even whilst the internal evidence of the case papers sometimes reveals that the married woman was the driving force behind the litigation.[23] Similarly, Judith Spicksley has found that single women – even though they played a vital role in the credit market – were often reluctant to sue people for bad debts.[24] Nevertheless, times of crisis could create circumstances that compelled women to act independently and fight to retain inherited property. Hannah Worthen has shown, for example, that during the Civil Wars in England Royalist widows petitioned and used the Court of Chancery to recover property that had been confiscated by parliament because of the actions of their husbands.[25] Women could and did fight hard to protect property on behalves of themselves and their heirs.

Despite the biased patriarchal legal framework of primogeniture and coverture, women owned a significant – if minority – proportion of property in early modern and modern England. This was in part because – as Amy Erickson's hugely influential *Women and Property in Early Modern England* established – 'primogeniture did not dominate the distribution of property as a whole at an ordinary social level'. She also showed that it had less impact in the north of England, where 48 per cent of testators made equal

Capern, 'Gender, Property and Succession in the Early Modern English Aristocracy: the Case of Martha Janes and her Illegitimate Children', *Women's History Review* (forthcoming).

22 See also Susan Staves, *Married Women's Separate Property in England, 1660–1833* (Cambridge, 1990).

23 Charlotte Garside, 'Women in Chancery: An Analysis of Chancery as a Women's Court of Redress' (PhD diss., University of Hull, 2018). The authors would like to thank Charlotte for sharing this research finding ahead of her viva. See too Tim Stretton, *Women Waging Law in Elizabethan England* (Cambridge, 1998), who demonstrates that many married women 'waged law' with the support of husbands and other male relatives; Maria Cioni, *Women and Law in Elizabeth England with Particular Reference to the Court of Chancery* (New York, 1985).

24 Judith Spicksley, 'Women, "Usury", and Credit in Early Modern England: The Case of the Maiden Investor', *Gender and History* 39:2 (2015), 247–75.

25 Hannah Worthen, 'Supplicants and Guardians: The Petitions of Royalist Widows during the Civil Wars and Interregnum, 1642–1660', *Women's History Review* 26:4 (2017), 528–40; Hannah Worthen, 'The Experience of War Widows in Mid-Seventeenth Century England' (PhD diss., University of Leicester, 2017).

provision for all of their children because of customary partible inheritance practices.[26] Spicksley's work on men's wills has also shown that smallholdings may have been more equally distributed between sons and daughters than previously thought.[27] At the same time, demographic factors meant that not all marriages produced adult sons to inherit property: Richard Smith suggests that perhaps 20 per cent of marriages produced only daughters and a further 20 per cent no children at all.[28] Even in elite families – where the growing popularity of strict settlement meant that collateral males increasingly inherited in preference to daughters – demographic factors and personal preferences meant daughters did inherit, as Briony McDonagh's *Elite Women and the Agricultural Landscape, 1700–1830* powerfully shows. Importantly, these findings compellingly suggest that there were both regional differences – as yet relatively unexplored in research terms – and class differences in the gender ratio of landownership and lease-holding.

Women inheriting land and other property from family members might inherit either as *feme sole* or as *feme covert*, where their inheritance was protected as 'separate estate'. Prenuptial agreements formed a type of contract law which modified the strictures of coverture and allowed property to be set aside as a separate estate under the law of trusts. Women's control over land in trust was sometimes considerable and sometimes negligible, with estates left almost entirely to trustees to manage.[29] Some women also inherited as their deceased husband's heir, although the more usual practice was to provide for widows by means of either a dower or a jointure. Medieval widows were mostly provided for by means of a dower: that is, a right to one-third of the real property their husband had held at any time during the marriage. This was specific to the common law, but manorial and borough law made similar provision known as free bench. Yet the increasing difficulties of administering these legal rights meant that jointure had largely replaced

26 Amy Erickson, *Women and Property in England* (London, 1995), pp. 68, 71.

27 Judith Spicksley, 'Usury Legislation, Cash and Credit: The Development of the Female Investor in the Late Tudor and Stuart Periods', *Economic History Review* 61:2 (2008), 277–301.

28 Richard Smith, 'Some Issues Concerning Families and their Property in Rural England 1250–1800', *Land, Kinship and Life-Cycle*, ed. Richard Smith (Cambridge, 1984), pp. 40–6.

29 Erickson, *Women and Property*, pp. 102–13; McDonagh, *Elite Women*, pp. 21–3; Allison Tait, 'The Beginning of the End of Coverture: A Reappraisal of the Married Woman's Separate Estate', *Yale Journal of Law & Feminism* 26:2 (2014), 1–53; Amy Erickson, 'Common Law Versus Common Practice: The Use of Marriage Settlement in Early Modern England', *Economic History Review* 43:1 (1990), 21–39. Note that legal arrangements might not strictly match lived experiences and women could sometimes struggle to access property – or its profits – held as separate estate (McDonagh, *Elite Women*, pp. 22–3, 54). See too Korda, 'Coverture and its Discontents', p. 48, noting that the growth of married women's separate estate was potentially a source of 'considerable strife' in early modern society, in part because of fears that in keeping property as separate estate women would also assume the role of head of household – or even that economic agency might be associated with greater sexual freedom.

dower by the end of the seventeenth century. As originally conceived, jointure arrangements were essentially annuities secured on real property, often land bought by the husband using the cash portion his wife brought into marriage. Jointures could be serviced by financial instruments like bonds or by rent charges so that – unlike dower – they did not guarantee access to land itself. Scholars have debated the extent to which the shift from dower to jointure distanced women from real property, but in reality jointure arrangements – sometimes modified by family agreements made either before or after the death of the husband – brought many widows control of landed property, if only for life.[30] At the same time, a decline in remarriage amongst widows increased the rate at which widows enjoyed their estates.[31]

Finally, women might come to own or otherwise control property via a number of other means, including purchase and litigation, or as the guardians of young sons or daughters. Alimony arrangements might bring property to separated – or later divorced – women, while widows with even relatively modest incomes might choose to invest capital sums in land and other property and maintain mixed portfolios of investments.[32] Aristocratic widows also frequently controlled property on behalf of minor sons or those absent from the home estate at university or on the Grand Tour, as well as on behalf of absent or incapacitated husbands or fathers.[33] Here women effectively had *de facto* ownership even where they did not have *de jure* ownership. Further down the social scale the wives of merchants and mariners were often left with letters of attorneys in order to manage their absent husband's property and businesses.[34] Individual women might acquire property in multiple ways and at different points in their lives.[35] Just as importantly, emerging new research reminds us that property ownership potentially meant very different things to women at different stages in their life-courses.[36] Indeed – as the chapters in this book so powerfully attest – women were much more than the 'backwater', 'conduit' or 'temporary storage for wealth that would be transferred ultimately from one man to another'.[37]

30 McDonagh, *Elite Women*, pp. 18–21.

31 Barbara Todd, 'Demographic Determinism and Female Agency: The Remarrying Widow Reconsidered ... Again', *Continuity and Change* 9:3 (1994), 421–50.

32 Amy Froide, *Silent Partners: Women as Public Investors during Britain's Financial Revolution, 1690–1750* (Oxford, 2017).

33 McDonagh, *Elite Women*, pp. 15–25.

34 Churches, 'Putting Women in their Place', pp. 50–65.

35 McDonagh, *Elite Women*, pp. 23–4.

36 We are thinking here of ongoing work by PhD students in the Gender, Place and Memory cluster at the University of Hull, including that of Sarah Shields, 'Maid, Wife, Widow, Mother: Elite Women's Experiences of Landed Estate Management Across Their Life-Courses in Eighteenth-Century England' (PhD diss., University of Hull, 2019).

37 Amanda L. Capern, 'The Landed Woman in Early-Modern England', *Parergon* 19:1 (2002), 185–214; Christine Churches, 'Women and Property in Early Modern England: A Case Study',

Women, work and business

There has been a considerable amount of work in recent years on women's involvement with business and financial investments. Building on seminal work by Ivy Pinchbeck and Alice Clark, research by Bridget Hill, Judith Bennett, Margot Finn and others has shown that women were integral parts of the family economy in medieval, early modern and eighteenth-century England, whether that was through employment or engagement in the family business.[38] The blurred topographical lines between rural and urban space, which created overlapping spheres of finance, means that we can find women like Joyce Jeffreys operating in the nexus between the agricultural and financial business sectors to run quite complex businesses of their own.[39] Peter Earle's work indicates that women did not always contribute solely through supporting their husband's trade in London and it was very common for a wife to be engaged in a trade different from the one pursued by her husband.[40] New work on urban women of eighteenth- and nineteenth-century Britain by Nicola Phillips, Hannah Barker, Stana Nenadic and Jennifer Aston has extended this analysis. These new works argue that women were economically active throughout the eighteenth and nineteenth centuries, and although they were often involved in the family enterprise they were also able to be business owners on their own account, operating separately to the male figures in their lives.[41] Initially focusing on spinsters and widows, research has more recently

Social History 23:2 (1998), 165–80, 178 for the quote; A. R. Buck, 'Cordelia's Estate: Women and the Law of Property from Shakespeare to Nahum Tate', *Women, Property, and the Letters of the Law in Early Modern England*, eds Nancy E. Wright, Margaret W. Ferguson and A. R. Buck (Toronto, 2004), p. 183; Pamela S. Hammons, 'The Gendered Imagination of Property in Sixteenth- and Seventeenth-Century English Women's Verse', *Clio* 34:4 (2005), 396.

38 On women's labour history, see Nigel Goose (ed.), *Women's Work in Industrial England: Regional and Local Perspectives*, Local Population Studies (Hatfield, 2007); Jane Humphries, 'Enclosures, Common Rights and Women: The Proletarianization of Families in Late Eighteenth and early Nineteenth Century Britain', *Journal of Economic History* 50 (1993), 17–42; Bridget Hill, *Women, Work and Sexual Politics in Eighteenth-Century England* (Oxford, 1989); Ivy Pinchbeck, *Women Workers and The Industrial Revolution, 1750–1850* (London, 1930); Alice Clark, *Working Life of Women in the Seventeenth Century* (London, 1919); Michael Roberts, 'Sickles and Scythes: Women's Work and Men's Work at Harvest Time', *History Workshop Journal* 7 (1979), 3–28; Olwen Hufton, 'Women without Men: Widows and Spinsters in Britain and France in the Eighteenth Century', *Journal of Family History* 9:4 (1984), 355–76; Judith Bennett, *Women in the Medieval English Countryside: Gender and Household in Brigstock Before the Plague* (Oxford, 1987).

39 Judith Spicksley (ed.), *The Business and Household Accounts of Joyce Jeffreys, Spinster of Hereford, 1638–1648* (Oxford, 2012); Pamela Sharpe, 'A Woman's Worth: A Case Study of Capital Accumulation in Early Modern England', *Parergon* 19:1 (2002), 173–84.

40 Peter Earle, *A City Full of People: Men and Women of London, 1650–1750* (London, 1994).

41 Barker, *The Business of Women*; Phillips, *Women in Business*; Peter Collinge, 'A Genteel Hand in the Malt Business: Barbara Ford (1755–1840) of Ashbourne', *Midland History* 39:1

turned to the examination of married women and their contributions to both their husbands' businesses – for example as bookkeepers – and their own enterprises. The latter included businesses regarded as typically feminine with low entry skill and overhead thresholds, such as lodging houses, millinery and dressmaking, but also more major enterprises, such as shipbuilding, manufacturing and newspaper printing. The scale of female-owned enterprise can be difficult to quantify, however, with firms that might appear to be low-level extensions of domestic skills, such as sewing, actually being large-scale, professionally managed endeavours.[42] These findings have also been replicated across the globe, with a growing body of literature demonstrating that female entrepreneurs have played an important role in the economies of countries including Australia and New Zealand, Russia, Spain, Canada, the Caribbean, Japan, Turkey and the United States, again mostly in an urban context.[43] By contrast, rather less work has focused on rural businesses, even whilst women's contributions to farming economies as both paid labourers and as the providers of unpaid labour in the fields, dairy, poultry yard or house have long been recognised.[44] More recently, historians and historical geographers

(2014), 110–32; Jessica Collins, 'Jane Holt, Milliner, and Other Women in Business: Apprentices, Freewomen and Mistresses in The Clothworkers' Company, 1606–1800', *Textile History* 44:1 (2013), 72–94; Jennifer Aston, 'Female Business Ownership in Birmingham 1849–1901', *Midland History* 37:2 (2012), 187–206; Spicksley (ed.), *Joyce Jeffreys*; Patricia Crawford, 'A Decade in the Life of Elizabeth Harvey of Taunton 1696–1706', *Women's History Review* 19:2 (2010), 245–57; Helen Doe, *Enterprising Women and Shipping in the Nineteenth Century* (Woodbridge, 2009); Ria Snowden, 'Sarah Hodgson and the Business of Print, 1800–1822', *Periodicals and Publishers: The Newspaper and Journal Trade, 1750–1914*, eds John Hinks, Catherine Armstrong and Matthew Day (London, 2009), pp. 121–40; Christine Wiskin, 'Business Women and Financial Management: Three Eighteenth-Century Case Studies', *Accounting, Business and Financial History* 16:2 (2006), 143–61; Hannah Barker and Karen Harvey, 'Women Entrepreneurs and Urban Expansion: Manchester 1760–1820', *Women and Urban Life in Eighteenth-Century England: "on the town"*, eds Rosemary Sweet and Penelope Lane (Aldershot, 2003), pp. 111–30; Christine Wiskin, 'Urban Businesswomen in Eighteenth-Century England', *Women and Urban Life in Eighteenth-Century England: "on the town"*, eds Rosemary Sweet and Penelope Lane (Aldershot, 2003), pp. 87–110; Alison Kay, 'A Little Enterprise of her Own: Lodging-house Keeping and the Accommodation Business in Nineteenth-century London', *London Journal* 28.2 (2003), 41–53; Pamela Sharpe, 'Gender in the Economy: Female Merchants and Family Businesses in the British Isles, 1600–1850', *Historie Sociale* 34:68 (2001), 283–306.

42 Phillips, *Women in Business*, p. 254; Jennifer Aston, *Female Entrepreneurship in Nineteenth Century England: Engagement in the Urban Economy* (London, 2016), p. 128. It is important to recognise that, despite the popular image of Victorian factories, a nineteenth-century business employing twenty-plus people would have been considered a large firm.

43 Jennifer Aston and Catherine Bishop (eds), *Female Entrepreneurs in the Long Nineteenth Century: A Global Perspective* (forthcoming).

44 As well as early work on women's labour history see Jane Whittle and Mark Hailwood, 'The Gender Division of Labour in Early Modern England', *The Economic History Review* (2019, forthcoming) and Jane Whittle, 'A Critique of Approaches to 'Domestic Work': Women, Work and the Pre-Industrial Economy', *Past and Present* 243.1 (2019), pp. 35–70; Jane Whittle, 'Enterprising Widows and Active Wives: Women's Unpaid Work in the Household Economy of

have turned attention to women's contributions to running landed estates – undoubtedly one of the 'big businesses' of the rural landscape – with work by Briony McDonagh and others underlining the contributions of female landowners to early modern and eighteenth-century estate economies.[45] Such work has overturned previous assumptions that women who managed landed estates were 'exceptional' or a 'rarity'.[46]

There is also now a growing body of work on women's money and investments. This includes scholarship on credit provision via annuities, mortgages and other loans[47] and on wealthy women's investments in the stock market, particularly via government securities and shares in canal and railway companies.[48] The shift in attention of investors in the late eighteenth

Early Modern England', *History of the Family* 19:3 (2014), 283–300; Jane Whittle and Elizabeth Griffiths, *Consumption and Gender in the Early Seventeenth Century Household: The World of Alice Le Strange* (Oxford, 2012).

45 Briony McDonagh, 'Women, Enclosure and Estate Improvement in Eighteenth-Century Northamptonshire', *Rural History* 20:2 (2009), 143–62; Briony McDonagh, '"All Towards the Improvements of the Estate": Mrs Elizabeth Prowse at Wicken, 1764–1810', *Custom, Improvement and the Landscape in Early Modern Britain*, ed. R. W. Hoyle (Farnham, 2011), pp. 263–88; McDonagh, *Elite Women*, passim; Whittle and Griffiths, *Consumption and Gender*; Elizabeth Griffiths, *Family and Farming Records of Alice Le Strange, 1617–1656* (Norfolk, 2015). The following works also make brief reference to estate management undertaken by eighteenth- and nineteenth-century female landowners: Sandra Dunster, 'Women of the Nottinghamshire Elite, c.1720–1820' (PhD thesis, University of Nottingham, 2003); Ingrid Tague, *Women of Quality: Accepting and Contesting Ideals of Femininity in England, 1690–1760* (Woodbridge, 2002), pp. 123–26; Ivy Pinchbeck, *Women Workers in the Industrial Revolution 1750–1850* (Abingdon, 1930), pp. 29–33; Amanda Vickery, *The Gentleman's Daughter: Women's Lives in Georgian England* (New Haven, 1998), pp. 64, 152 and 157; Capern, 'The Landed Woman'. See too Harris, *English Aristocratic Women*, for medieval examples of women managing landed estates.

46 Anne Mitson, 'An Exchange of Letters: Estate Management and Lady Yarborough', *Women's History Review* 7 (1998), 547–66, who offers a useful analysis of a late nineteenth-century woman managing a landed estate (549 for the quote); John V. Beckett, 'Elizabeth Montagu: Bluestocking Turned Landlady', *Huntington Library Quarterly* 49:2 (1986), 149–64, 149 for the quote.

47 For women's involvement in lending in early modern England see B. A. Holderness, 'Widows in Pre-Industrial Society: An Essay upon their Economic Functions', *Land, Kinship and Life-Cycle*, ed. Richard Smith (Cambridge, 1984), pp. 423–42; Judith Spicksley, 'Usury Legislation, Cash and Credit: The Development of the Female Investor in the Late Tudor and Stuart Periods', *Economic History Review* 61:2 (2008), 277–301. For eighteenth-century examples, see B. A. Holderness, 'Elizabeth Parkin and her Investments, 1733–66: Aspects of the Sheffield Money Market in the Eighteenth Century', *Transactions of the Hunter Archaeological Society* 10 (1979), 81–7; Pamela Sharpe, 'Dealing with Love: The Ambiguous Independence of the Single Woman in Early Modern England', *Gender and History* 11 (1999), 209–32; Pamela Sharpe, 'A Woman's Worth: A Case Study of Capital Accumulation in Early Modern England', *Parergon* 19 (2002), 173–84.

48 David Green and Alistair Owens, 'Gentlewomanly Capitalism? Spinsters, Widows and Wealth Holding in England and Wales, c. 1800–1860', *Economic History Review* 56:3 (2003), 510–36; Janette Rutterford and Josephine Maltby, '"The widow, the clergyman and the reckless": Women Investors in England, 1830–1914', *Feminist Economics* 12:1–2 (2006), 111–38;

and nineteenth centuries to financial investments such as these is important because it reflects the growth of a middle class who had access to capital but not necessarily access to land. In an effort to placate this potentially influential social group – and to avoid the dismantling of their own large landed estates – the government supported this emerging commercial economy and encouraged financial investment in shares in both domestic and colonial markets.[49] As Amy Froide has shown, women investors were at the forefront of this financial revolution from its very beginnings in the late sixteenth century, and they not only followed but shaped investment behaviour both among their friends and family members, and more widely.[50]

When viewed as a whole, this literature on female economic endeavours demonstrates the many ways that women were able to cultivate their own relationships with property in all its various guises and, perhaps more importantly, that this was a story of continuity rather than change. The urbanised economy of the late eighteenth and nineteenth centuries does not appear to have dissuaded women from becoming financial investors, landowners or business owners: rather, it gave them greater opportunity to participate. Women seem to have acted in spite of the undoubtedly biased legal system. Moreover, as the work of Aston, McDonagh and Froide has shown, women also found ways to translate this economic activity into social power, whether through using their position to influence local politics, remodelling their homes and gardens in the most fashionable styles, or acting as sources of financial advice for family and friends.[51] There is also a story of continuity in

Ann Carlos, Karen Maguire and Larry Neal, 'Financial Acumen, Women Speculators, and the Royal African Company during the South Sea Bubble', *Accounting, Business and Financial History* 16:2 (2006), 219–43; Mark Freeman, Robin Pearson and James Taylor, '"A doe in the city": Women Shareholders in Eighteenth- and Early Nineteenth-Century Britain', *Accounting, Business and Financial History* 16:2 (2006), 265–91; Anne Laurence, 'Women Investors, "that nasty south sea affair" and the Rage to Speculate in Early Eighteenth-Century England', *Accounting, Business and Financial History* 16:2 (2006), 245–64; Anne Laurence, 'Lady Betty Hastings, Her Half-Sisters, and the South Sea Bubble: Family Fortunes and Strategies', *Women's History Review* 15:4 (2006), 533–40; Anne Laurence, 'Lady Betty Hastings (1682–1739): Godly Patron', *Women's History Review* 19:2 (2010), 201–13; Mark Freeman, Robin Pearson and James Taylor, 'Between Madam Bubble and Kitty Lorimer: Women Investors in British and Irish Stock Companies', *Women and their Money, 1700–1950: Essays on Women and Finance*, eds Anne Laurence, Josephine Maltby and Janette Rutterford (London, 2009), pp. 95–114; Lucy Newton and Philip Cottrell, 'Female Investors in the First English and Welsh Commercial Joint-Stock Banks', *Women and their Money, 1700–1950: Essays on Women and Finance*, eds. Anne Laurence, Josephine Maltby and Janette Rutterford (London, 2009), pp. 115–32; David Green, Alistair Owens, Judith Maltby and Janette Rutterford (eds), *Men, Women and Money: Perspectives on Gender, Wealth and Investment, 1850–1930* (Oxford, 2011).

49 David Green, Alistair Owens, Judith Maltby and Janette Rutterford, 'Men, Women and Money: An Introduction', *Men, Women, and Money*, p. 5.

50 Froide, *Silent Partners*.

51 Froide, *Silent Partners*; Aston, *Female Entrepreneurship*; McDonagh, *Elite Women*.

their use of the law courts to pursue property cases. The Court of Requests was very much a woman's court, as Tim Stretton has shown.[52] However, it was the other big equity court – Chancery – that witnessed the largest number of female litigants and its expansion in the early modern period was accompanied by further feminisation of its clientele.[53] Amy Erickson once calculated that 26 per cent of litigants in Chancery by 1714 were women.[54] Charlotte Garside's work on female litigation in Chancery 1670–1700 has confirmed the finding.[55] As the work of Amanda Capern, Steve Hindle, Tim Stretton, Krista Kesselring and others has shown, the social authority that women were able to exercise in the sphere of the law courts reflected the extent to which they could control (or not) family and neighbourhood affairs.[56] Furthermore, rights of guardianship gave women considerable power to manage (and receive profits from) land, sometimes over many years and decades.

At the same time, research has highlighted the involvement of upper- and middle-class women in a range of other spheres more traditionally seen as the preserve of men, including electioneering, politics and anti-slavery activism, a finding that has, for some time now, challenged the idea of separate, gendered spheres.[57] Much of the revisionist literature above offers a distinct challenge to Leonore Davidoff and Catherine Hall's hugely influential *Family Fortunes* (1987). They argued that the transition from the eighteenth to nineteenth century saw a growing pressure on middle-class women to withdraw from the public sphere – where they had previously been able to combine their

52 Stretton, *Women Waging Law*.

53 Amanda L. Capern, 'Maternity and Justice in the Early Modern English Court of Chancery', *Journal of British Studies* 58 (forthcoming, 2019).

54 Erickson, *Women and Property in Early Modern England*, 114–15.

55 Garside, 'Women in Chancery'; Churches, 'Putting Women in their Place'.

56 Amanda Capern, 'Rumour and Reputation in the Early Modern English Family', *Fama and Her Sisters: Gossip and Rumour in Early Modern Europe*, eds Heather Kerr and Claire Walker (Turnhout, 2015), pp. 85–113; Laura Gowing, *Domestic Dangers: Women, Words and Sex in Early Modern London* (Oxford, 1998); Bernard Capp, *When Gossips Meet: Women, Family and Neighbourhood in Early Modern England* (Oxford, 2003); Steve Hindle, 'The Shaming of Margaret Knowsley: Gossip, Gender and the Experience of Authority in Early Modern England', *Continuity and Change* 9 (1994), 391–419; Tim Stretton and Krista Kesselring (eds), *Married Women and the Law: Coverture in England and the Common Law World* (Montreal, 2014).

57 Kathryn Gleadle and Sarah Richardson (eds), *Women in British Politics, 1760–1860: The Power of the Petticoat* (Basingstoke, 2000); A. K. Mellor, *Mothers of the Nation: Women's Political Writing in England, 1780–1830* (Bloomington, IN, 2000); Helen Rogers, *Women and the People: Authority, Authorship and the Radical Tradition in Nineteenth-Century England* (Aldershot, 2000); Elaine Chalus, 'Kisses for Votes: The Kiss and Corruption in Eighteenth-Century English Elections', *The Kiss in History*, ed. Karen Harvey (Manchester, 2005), pp. 122–47; Elaine Chalus, '"That Epidemial Madness": Women and Electoral Politics in the Late Eighteenth Century', *Gender in Eighteenth-Century England: Roles, Representations and Responsibilities*, eds Hannah Barker and Elaine Chalus (London, 1997), pp. 151–78; Clare Midgley, *Feminism and Empire: Women Activists in Imperial Britain, 1790–1865* (London, 2007), pp. 41–86.

activities as wives and mothers with the day-to-day workings of the family business – to the private sphere where they became solely involved with domestic and philanthropic works. Yet despite the undoubted flaws of some of the key arguments in *Family Fortunes*, Davidoff and Hall skilfully describe the intricacies of a society where the newly formed middle classes deliberately cultivated different patterns of behaviour to the established aristocracy, rejecting primogeniture and instead establishing partible inheritance as the preferred mode of inheritance. They argue that the middle classes did still favour male children in the respect that the family business or property was more likely to be bequeathed to them directly: however, it was expected that daughters would inherit assets *to the same value*. Therefore, although male and female children inherited *differently*, there was the expectation that they would inherit *equally*.[58]

Yet, in light of our present day questions about gender, landownership, political power and authority, were these inheritances really equal? And did land and cash of equal financial value carry with them equal social value? We argue not. The fact that property and landownership were inextricably linked to political power has been discussed above, and this was especially true for aristocratic men and women who were able to use their vast estates to influence national affairs, including through networking at local elections. The 1832 Reform Act extended the franchise to those men who owned or rented property of a qualifying rate, increasing the electorate by some 300,000. Significantly for this study, however, the Reform Act – for the first time in parliamentary history – explicitly stated that the act did not extend to women. The champion for women's suffrage John Stuart Mill used his position as a member of parliament to call for the wording of the 1867 Second Reform Act to be changed to use the word 'person' rather than 'man'.[59] He worked in collaboration with his step-daughter Helen Taylor, who later unsuccessfully sought nomination as the parliamentary candidate for North Camberwell in London. Perhaps unsurprisingly, Mill's amendment was defeated and women remained largely disenfranchised, although legislative changes in the second half of the nineteenth century – namely the 1869 Municipal Franchise Act and the 1888 County Council Act – gave women the right to vote in local, council and borough elections, providing that they were rate-payers (although a court case in 1872 restricted this right to unmarried or widowed women). In other words, the significance of inheriting property rather than an equivalent sum or trust of a similar value was that property carried with it the security of home, the potential to generate further income through development of

58 Leonore Davidoff and Catherine Hall, *Family Fortunes: Men and Women of the English Middle Class, 1780–1850* (London, 1987).
59 Susan Groag Bell and Karen M. Offen (eds), *Women, the Family, and Freedom: The Debate in Documents, Volume One, 1750–1880* (Stanford, CA, 1983), p. 488.

land or property rental; but, most importantly of all, control or ownership of even modest land or property could convey political power.

Central to the story of inheritance, law, and property ownership in the later nineteenth century was the passing of the Married Women's Property Acts of 1870, 1882 and 1893. For the first time married women were able to retain independent ownership of property and earnings inherited, purchased or otherwise acquired during their marriage. They were also able to dispose of these goods by will. Prior to these acts, a married woman was able to write a last will and testament, but as she had no right to own any assets, she could only dispose of her personal belongings and any assets held under settlement (the reallocation of which would more than likely already have been accounted for under the terms of the settlement itself). Moreover, a married woman had to have her husband's permission to make a last will and testament and his permission could be withdrawn at any time before probate was granted, meaning that her wishes might never be carried out. It is important to note that the removal of married women's right to vote in municipal, county and borough elections came just two years after the Married Women's Property Act of 1870 gave them the right to retain and dispose of their own property, including personal belongings, real estate, land and earnings from business and trade. It seems that the (male) establishment was willing to give women the ability to maintain themselves independently but was decidedly less willing to share the political power that accompanied such investments. The intervening 130 years has seen a continuous negotiation of the relationship between women and property, and the next section turns to the question of women's property rights in the contemporary world.

Land, property and gender in the here-and-now

Women and the Land has not been written with the intention of offering the last word on women's property ownership: much still remains to be done to gain a fuller regional picture of women's engagement in rural and urban economies in early modern and modern England. Nor – as we hope the opening section of this introduction makes clear – is it intended solely to stand as a monument to research on the situation for women *vis-a-vis* property in the English past. Rather the intention is to generate much-needed debate about social and gender inequality in the present, not least on the issue of whether women's access to land and other property – be that as landowners or landholders – has actually improved since the early modern period. Indeed, we would argue that the long-term legacies of patriarchal property relations are still visible in modern society nearly one hundred and fifty years after coverture was effectively abolished. Ownership and control of real estate links very directly to overall wealth indicators, social status and power in any society. Research on gender and contemporary land rights clearly recognises that 'there is a direct relationship between women's right to land, economic empowerment, food security and poverty reduction'.[60] According to the Swedish International Cooperation Agency [SIDA], 'Women represent 43% of the agricultural labour force. Yet they rarely own the land they are working on, have tenure security or control over the land.'[61] SIDA estimates that 10–20 per cent of landholders in developing countries are women, a figure remarkably similar to those our contributors reveal for the seventeenth to the nineteenth centuries. The United Nations Entity for Gender Equality and the Empowerment of Women (or UN Women) regularly publishes on women's access to land, largely from the perspective of women's land *tenure* as a principle of the right to make a living. They, like SIDA and other similar organizations, are careful to use the terminology of 'landholders', in part because – as a recent project by the Food and Agricultural Organization of the United Nations (FAOUN) makes clear – data on women's *landownership* is unavailable for most countries.[62] The distinction made by modern non-governmental organisations between landowning and landholding is one that historians should make too. The UN holds rather more complete data on agricultural landholders, who are defined as 'the manager of the holding' and an individual with 'responsibilities in production'.[63] Women accounted for between c. 10 and 15 per cent of agricultural landholders in Britain, Ireland, the USA and much of Scandinavia, and between 20 and 30 per cent of landholders in France, Spain, Portugal and Canada. In only a very few countries – including Italy, Austria and the Baltic States – did women hold more than 30 per cent of agricultural property. Their data is by no mean complete, although they do note that 'landownership and management statistics are becoming increasingly available as multiple international efforts are underway with the aim to increase availability of, and access to, relevant data on gender and land'.[64]

Those efforts stretch back to at least 1975, when the first World Conference of Women was held in Mexico. Since then, the conference has brought women from every corner of the globe around the table every five to ten years to share experience and negotiate legal changes to the institutional cultures which

60 SIDA [Swedish International Development Cooperation Agency], 'Women and Land Rights', March, 2015, available at https://www.sida.se/contentassets/1cc2e9756fd04d80bba64d0d635fe158/women-and-land-rights.pdf, accessed 26 June 2019.

61 SIDA, 'Women and Land Rights'.

62 FAOUN (Food and Agricultural Organization of the United Nations), 'Gender and Land Rights Database', available at http://www.fao.org/gender-landrights-database/data-map/statistics/en/?sta_id=1162, accessed 26 June 2019.

63 FAOUN, 'Gender and Land Statistics: Recent developments in FAO's Gender and Land Rights Database', p. vi, available at http://www.fao.org/3/a-i4862e.pdf, accessed 26 June 2019.

64 FAOUN, 'Gender and Land Statistics', p. vi.

impede women's access to land and its profits. For example, in 2001 the UN Division for the Advancement of Women reported directly on the situation of rural women in the light of the challenges of globalization. It concluded that the United Nations Development Fund for Women (UNIFEM) needed to focus on women's responsibilities on the land in the face of male global 'economic migration' because of the strain imposed on women as they took on additional work in agriculture alongside domestic and familial labour. The 'Country Studies' report on Gender and Land Rights from FAOUN of 2005 aggregated the research results for Latin America, sub-Saharan Africa and Central Asia and found extraordinary levels of gender inequalities in landownership persisting in the twenty-first century because of a complex interplay of 'inheritance, purchase or state intervention'.[65] For example, the new market economy and privatization in Uzbekistan has led to a 'return to patriarchy'; customary systems of primogeniture have persisted under the new systems of Brazilian agribusiness; and in Muslim countries and ethnic groups, such as Senegal and in the Muslim Mossi community of Burkina Faso, Islamic law enshrines the inheritance rights of daughters, yet women still do not inherit. The overwhelming message of the report is that no matter what institutional structures are put in place, like the equality policies so clearly in evidence in post-Apartheid South Africa, it is 'the basic power relations that structure access to land' and 'the most persistent obstacles to improving gender equity in land rights have their roots in patriarchal values and practices'.[66] We can learn something important from this. In this sense, the findings of this report echo some of the historiography on women and the land in early modern England, *viz.* that law could twist and turn to sustain the privileges of men over the long-term. As in historical contexts, understanding the law as it applies to women and property is vital: as SIDA point out, in Africa the introduction of colonial systems of individual ownership eroded women's access to land.[67] Similarly, in early modern England changes to legal instruments of inheritance – in this case, the introduction of strict settlement – squeezed female inheritance of land over time.[68]

In the context of contemporary Britain we actually know very little about women's landownership. The most obvious contemporary source for landownership should be the Land Registry, a government department that was created in 1862 to register the ownership of property and land in

65 Susanna Lastarria-Cornhiel and Zoraida García-Frías, 'Gender and Land Rights: Findings and Lessons from Country Studies', FAOUN, Rome 2005, available at http://www.fao.org/docrep/008/a0297e/a0297e08.htm#bm8, accessed 26 June 2019.

66 Lastarria-Cornhiel and Garcia-Frias, 'Gender and Land Rights', pp. 6–7, 9, 11–13.

67 SIDA, 'Women and Land Rights'.

68 See, for example, Eileen Spring, 'The Heiress-at-Law: English Real Property Law from a New Point of View', *Law and History Review* 8:2 (1990), 273–96.

England and Wales.[69] Yet because the register is incomplete and the data difficult and expensive to access, national-level aggregate analysis of contemporary landownership by gender is impossible. This is despite the fact that an accessible and centralised registry has been the long-term demand of land reformers since at least the nineteenth century.[70] Women were the 'household reference person' – that is, the adult household member paying all or most of the housing costs – in 31 per cent of properties bought with a mortgage and 39 per cent of privately rented properties. According to data drawn from the 2011 Census, female HRPs were overrepresented amongst those living in one- and two-bedroom flats and terraced houses.[71] That is, the properties women lived in were on average smaller than those owned or rented by men. In this sense, women are considerably less likely to achieve one of the major social and cultural goals of their generation – to become homeowners – than their male peers. Moreover, while owner-occupation has undoubtedly increased significantly over recent decades, owner-occupiers still hold a very small proportion of land and other property, most of it focused in urban areas, themselves only making up 14 per cent of the UK area.[72] Outside of cities, most land remains in the hands of trusts, international corporations and other shadowy financial institutions – many of them registered overseas or even offshore – who invest in land as a commodity. Of course, like most big businesses, these are disproportionately controlled by men, with the notable exception of Crown land held by a female monarch. Indeed, as Kevin Cahill's work has shown, there is very little transparency on the issue of who owns Britain, though what little data that is available does not suggest a rosy picture in terms of gender equality.[73]

Our hope is that this book stimulates debate and further research on women's experiences not only in early modern and modern England but also in the contemporary world. Much research remains to be done, both in exploring the gendered dimensions of contemporary landownership and land tenure in the United Kingdom and elsewhere, and on the historical roots of this inequity. One of the main questions opened up by the book is why there has

69 Available at https://www.gov.uk/government/organisations/land-registry/about, accessed 26 June 2019.

70 In 2017 the Conservative Party manifesto promised 'an open database of land ownership, forming the largest repository of open land data in the world', but it is yet to appear (cited in Tichelar, *The Failure of Land Reform*, p. 202). The whoownsengland.org project continues to lobby the Land Registry for greater openness and access.

71 Housing and Gender: Briefing from the UK Women's Budget Group on the impact of changes in housing policy since 2010 on women, November 2017, available at https://wbg.org.uk/wp-content/uploads/2017/11/housing-pre-budget-nov-2017-final.pdf, accessed 7 September 2018.

72 Tichelar, *The Failure of Land Reform*, p. 185.

73 Kevin Cahill, *Who Owns Britain?* (Edinburgh, 2002). See too https://whoownsengland.org for an interactive GIS map which includes only a tiny proportion of British landowners.

not been more change over time in response to legal developments. The book stops in the late nineteenth century, yet we know that women's ownership of property and wealth remains at a much lower level than men's and that, notwithstanding the United Kingdom's 'Equality Act' of 2010, the customary gender gap in access to landed, domestic and commercial property persists. Therefore, it is not only change over time – or its absence – that demands further investigation. Rather, it is historical scrutiny of the cultural exchange between law and those embedded customs and patriarchal practices within the economy that will provide answers. The fact that women's experience of landed inequity is so much worse – statistically and in its social effects – in some countries than in others is also an important spur to historical enquiry across national and geographical boundaries.

The book

The book brings together historians, historical geographers and literary scholars in examining women's experiences of owning and holding land and other property across the long period between roughly 1500 and 1900. We deliberately focus on the period before the Representation of the People Acts of 1918 and 1928 extended the franchise to women. Land was the primary source of political and economic power, yet for much of this period married women were formally excluded from ownership (except by means of settlements and contract law). Here we ask important questions about women's involvement in landownership and the operation of economic, political and social power in this period. The chapters focus on women's experiences of property ownership in England and under the English common law. Thus, whilst we acknowledge that the English experience may have been distinct from that encountered elsewhere in Britain and early modern Europe, the chronological and regional scope gives breadth to the analysis. Taken together, the chapters in this book examine the experiences of women from very different backgrounds and from across the social hierarchy, from poor women and middling – and later middle-class – individuals to gentlewomen and aristocrats. They also consider the experiences of both *feme sole* (single women and widows) and *feme covert* (married women). Many of the chapters focus on ownership of land and residential property, but women as the owners of livestock, common rights and personal property also feature.

In what follows, we wish to flag up the two main contributions of the chapters in the book. Firstly, we will outline important new findings on the quantifying of female landownership. The contributors to this book have brought together data on women's property ownership in England across the early modern and modern periods, in both rural and urban settings, giving a picture both of continuity across the long period under discussion and of women adapting to changing economic circumstances and opportunities – brought about by enclosure, agricultural improvement, industrialisation and urbanisation, for example – ensuring their continued engagement in the property and land markets. Secondly, we will show how this book will significantly further our understanding of what owning property meant to women. Women's identities and lived experiences were shaped by the opportunities – and challenges – that their status as heiresses, owners and managers of property gave them. These identities varied across time and space, as they also did according to the women's social and marital circumstances and their individual aptitude and enthusiasm for property ownership and management. Thus, whilst the chapters of this book consider women from a wide variety of economic and social backgrounds, and adopt a range of methodologies in investigating them, taken together they show the complexity and the significance of women's relationship to the land.

Quantifying women's landownership

Women and the Land, 1500–1900 presents timely new data and perspectives on women's inheritance of real property, and their access to and management of land in England over an approximately four hundred year period. Several of the chapters in this book include significant quantifications of female landownership in periods from the sixteenth century to the nineteenth century. Judith Spicksley uses samples of wills dated 1545–1700 to demonstrate just how much land passed into the hands of women who were unmarried and were, therefore, legally autonomous as *feme sole* in common law. Using data from the eighteenth- and nineteenth-century Land Registers that exist for North Yorkshire, Joan Heggie reveals women's involvement in the transfers of urban as well as rural real estate. Janet Casson's work on the hungry acquisitions of land for railway building in the nineteenth century shows how female landowning represented the classic 'significant minority'.

In terms of quantifying female landownership, *Women and the Land, 1500–1900* thereby stands as a supplement to the work completed by Briony McDonagh on 250,000 acres of land enclosed under parliamentary act, which revealed that roughly 10 per cent of land was owned by female landowners, and to the earlier ground-breaking work of Amy Erickson's *Women and Property in Early Modern England*.[74] Smaller-scale studies have suggested similar figures for women's landholding in earlier and later periods: Sylvia Seeliger suggested that women may have held up to one-fifth of land in many

74 McDonagh, *Elite Women*.

Hampshire parishes between c. 1550 and c. 1850,[75] while Jane Whittle and others have that suggested female landowners may have made up somewhere between 10 and 20 per cent of tenants on medieval and early modern manors.[76] Research on the later seventeenth-century hearth taxes by Beatrice Moring and Richard Wall demonstrates that between 7.5 and 14.7 per cent of hearths assessed were in properties occupied by women (with one outlier of 25.2 per cent in Swansea).[77] Taken together with the chapters in this book, we can now suggest that women made up a significant minority of landowners/ landholders across the long period between the later Middle Ages and the second half of the nineteenth century.[78] There were regional variations – indeed, as Judith Spicksley points out in her chapter, regional variations in testamentary practice necessarily had knock-on effects on the geographies of women's landholding – and the percentages varied also according to type of land (whether freehold or copyhold). Yet it seems that for female landowners as a group there was broad continuity across time: from the beginning of the chronological framework of this book to its end, and perhaps beyond.

Landowning was business – sometimes big business – as the chapters in this book attest. Indeed, female landowning contributed to a concentration of land in the hands of the wealthy, reproducing the elite's social, economic and political power. Yet, for both rich and poor, holding land drove business expansion, for example into dairying, weaving and other small manufacture, as well as capital investments. The rural land market was as much about investment as inheritance, and it featured a high turnover, just as was the case for properties in the towns. More research could reveal interesting patterns over time about the gendering of land and property markets, for example in the expanding industrial towns of nineteenth century and the big landed estates at the same time. Early modern and modern England had

75 Sylvia Seeliger, 'Hampshire Women as Landholders: Common Law Mediated by Manorial Custom', *Rural History* 7 (1996), 1–14.

76 Jane Whittle, 'Inheritance, Marriage, Widowhood and Remarriage: A Comparative Perspective on Women and Landholding in North-east Norfolk, 1440–1580', *Continuity and Change* 13:1 (1998), 35; B. M. S. Campbell, 'Population Pressure, Inheritance and the Land Market in a Fourteenth-Century Peasant Community', *Land, Kinship and Life-Cycle*, ed. Richard Smith (Cambridge, 1984), pp. 87–134; Bennett, *Women in the Medieval English Countryside*, p. 33; Peter Franklin, 'Peasant Widows' "Liberation" and Remarriage before the Black Death', *Economic History Review* 39:2 (1986), 186–204; J. Cox Russell, *British Medieval Population* (Albuquerque, 1948), pp. 62–4; J. Z. Titow, *English Rural Society 1200–1350* (London, 1969), p. 87; all cited in Whittle, 'Inheritance, Marriage', 36–7. For new data on women's ownership of urban property, see Jennifer Aston, Amanda Capern and Briony McDonagh, 'More than Bricks and Mortar: Female Property Ownership as Economic Strategy in Mid-Nineteenth Century Urban England', *Urban History* 46.4 (forthcoming).

77 Beatrice Moring and Richard Wall, *Widows in European Economy and Society 1600–1920* (Woodbridge, 2017), pp. 81, 85.

78 McDonagh, *Elite Women*, pp. 24–32 and Appendix.

blurred topographical boundaries between agricultural space and industrial and commercial locations, and thus this book also shows the importance of looking at the nature of female landowning in both rural and urban spaces and economies. Jennifer Aston's work on female business owners uses a series of case studies from the mid-nineteenth-century Midlands, reminding us that female landownership was not just a rural phenomenon. Her chapter shows that there were integral connections between agricultural production and the rapidly growing towns that emerged for industrial and commercial purposes in the countryside. It also provides strong evidence for women relocating, rebuilding and expanding businesses they inherited from their dead husbands before handing them on to the next generation. As Aston puts it, these women were truly 'life partners' to their husbands: as such, they were categorically not simply acting as maintainers of the status quo until property made its way back to male hands. Briony McDonagh's chapter makes much the same point about the female landowners of large agricultural estates, arguing that a close analysis of previously under-utilised female-authored financial records reveals new evidence of propertied women's involvement in the financial and practical management and improvement of landed estates, while Amanda Capern's chapter indicates that, even when men tried to seize women's property through abduction and clandestine marriage, women who had inherited natal family property might refuse to relinquish their ownership.

This book, therefore, stands as a rebuttal to any implicit or explicit suggestion within the existing historiography that women were insignificant as landowners in early modern and modern history, thereby ensuring that future studies of land and property cannot ignore the contribution and role of women. Yet, its most important purpose is to serve as a starting point for research to go beyond the task of simply recovering women and quantifying their landownership as a group. The chapters within this book act as an important catalyst for that process, but there is still much to do. The overwhelming evidence from both the existing historiography and the chapters here shows broad continuity over time, despite changing economic and legal factors across the four centuries considered in the book. Yet it seems likely that different groups of women were affected in different ways by changing economic and legal circumstances. Further investigation is needed to pin down how marital status, wealth and a range of other factors intersected with gender in determining opportunities for property ownership in early modern and modern England. Moreover, comparing the data and broad findings on women and the land from this book with the growing literature on women's significant investment in the opportunities of 'the financial revolution' will yield significant and exciting new research results.[79] Female

79 Froide, *Silent Partners*; Judith Spicksley, 'Women, "Usury" and Credit', 263–92; Laurence, 'Women Investors', 245–64.

landowners frequently held mixed portfolios of land, stocks and shares, and analysis of the two synchronically represents an exciting way forward to gender our understanding of the English economy.

One of the other important things revealed – both during the conference that inspired the book and in many of the chapters here – is that a multi-source approach to quantifying women's landownership works extremely well to unveil the hidden history of women's share in landed wealth in the English past. This book brings together new data on female landownership in early modern and modern England, but it also demonstrates the multitude of methodologies that have to be employed in order to discover the full extent of women's complex engagement with property and land in this period. Our contributors make use of a range of source materials in uncovering women's experiences of the land – from landed family papers and tax records to estate accounts and court records, title deeds to correspondence and memoirs – to construct both quantitative and qualitative accounts of women's engagement with land and other property. Sometimes the sources have to be used laterally – as, for example, in Stephen Bending's chapter on the 'Brown' landscape created at Sandleford by Elizabeth Montagu – not least because scholars have to be creative in order to discover what are sometimes the faintest of footprints left by women in the archives. One of the arguments of Amanda Capern's chapter is that archives hold a key to unlocking women's autobiographical details, with the potential to enrich our knowledge of women's landowning, its legal premise and impact on family relations. Thus gendering the way we think about genre becomes vital to a better understanding of women and the land. It is often the case that female landowners were hidden in plain sight: that is, their ownership of and relationship to land and property was recognised by their contemporaries, and yet the difficulties of uncovering the evidence – along with the particular concerns of twentieth-century historians of property, the aristocracy and the agricultural revolution – has meant that until very recently the historiography has largely ignored women as a class of landowners.

Land, property and identity

Women and the Land, 1500–1900 is intended also to prompt broader thinking about what women's property ownership meant both to the women themselves and to others. We argue that land meant much more to women than just title: ownership provided an income stream (including when held in mixed portfolios with other financial investments), it proffered opportunities to build relationships with trustees, heirs and other family members, and it offered access to social and political capital at both the local and the national scale. Several of our contributors point too to the connections between land, property and the construction of feminine identities. Jessica Malay's work, both here and elsewhere, brings to life the extraordinary power conferred on Lady Anne Clifford through owning land, but also her conscious performance of what that actually meant as she progressed – as a prince would – through the landscape of her castles and estates.[80] For Clifford and other female landowners, building and landscaping works offered a means of asserting authority and articulating their social and political power to both their peers and those further down the social hierarchy. As cultural and historical geographers have long argued, this was a key means by which the elite bolstered their power, but for female landowners without the opportunity to serve as justices of the peace or MPs this was all the more crucial. In his chapter, Stephen Bending examines the bluestocking and landowner Elizabeth Montagu, who spent her widowhood remodelling her estates in her own image. He demonstrates the connectedness of her modelling of her London house with the rural idyll of her landed estate and shows that this blending of domiciliary architecture within the grounds of her countryside home gave Montagu an acute awareness of her power to control the lives of the rural workforce.

Briony McDonagh's chapter on women's estate accountancy demonstrates the embeddedness of women's economic identities and financial acumen as owners of landed businesses. For McDonagh's women, estate management was an intellectual exercise as well as a commitment to family and future heirs, including distant relatives who the current landowner may never have met. Her chapter demonstrates the aptitude of many of the women, their dedication and their considerable knowledge of land and property law. Yet female landownership was not a uniform phenomenon and several chapters also offer different perspectives on how female inheritance of land and real estate determined not only wealth and investment but also life experience. Amanda Capern's chapter on heiresses, for example, demonstrates the challenge that women's inheritance of land represented to men's expectations that they had right of ownership. Through the case study of one woman's experience, the chapter shows how sometimes land held little sentimental value to women and was, instead, symbolic of the tense gender conflict that could dominate women's lives. In other words, property might be a millstone as well as a form of capital that opened up opportunities for women.

Landed women of the elite were in a position not only to control and reap the profits from land but also to pass over it a proprietorial gaze, as Jon Stobart's study of Sophia Newdigate's travels across the countryside shows. As Stobart notes, Newdigate's journal was reflective of her 'interest in land and landscape, taste and connoisseurship, leisure and learning': it offers insights into her intellectual engagement with the landscape, both her

80 Malay (ed.), *Great Books of Record.*

own property and that of her landowning peers.[81] Yet, as this book makes clear, women's engagements with the land went far beyond ownership alone. Besides renting or leasing land, early modern women and men also engaged with the land in a range of other ways: as the holders of common rights, field labourers or rural artisans exploiting the economic potential of the countryside, or as those tourists taking pleasure visiting country houses, gardens and picturesque sites or otherwise walking or riding over the English countryside. As Amanda Flather points out in her chapter, landscape could play a role in identity formation even amongst poor and middling women who did not necessarily own – or even rent – land. At a very basic level, it provided a means to sustain themselves, leading – we might assume – to an emotional attachment to the land, although the precise nature of that attachment is typically hard to glean from surviving sources.

These chapters bring to light evidence of women's experience of the landscape that complicates previous understanding of women's lived 'spatial experiences' – to borrow a phrase from Flather – and shows that early modern women were never geographically restricted to a domestic, private sphere. Poor and middling women worked in the fields and tended animals on the commons as well engaged in 'housework', much of which took place outside the home, while wealthier landowning women regularly walked and rode over the landscape as part of their management practice. As Flather argues, access, control and use of the landscape was controlled by gender, age and social status, as well as local regional economies and season, though there were also always women that were prepared to buck gendered expectations about appropriate behaviour for young ladies (see, for example, McDonagh's discussion in *Elite Women* of Lady Amabel Hume-Campbell's barefoot walk across her property).[82] Thus, women's relationship with the land, and their identity as landowners, was profoundly shaped by their spatial experience of inhabiting, improving and managing that landscape as well as simply owning it. Interdisciplinary thinking is important here, not least because – as Flather points out – thinking about landscape as *space* allows us to move beyond the 'separate spheres' model. This in turn has the potential to upset metaphors of land and landscape as gendered female – and subject to a gaze that was typically gendered male – as, for example, in nineteenth-century land reformers' notions of the land as 'the womb of wealth'.[83]

There is much that remains to be done on the histories and geographies of women's property. Future research might usefully investigate non-elite

81 Stobart, this volume.

82 McDonagh, *Elite Women*, pp. 136–8.

83 See Malcolm Chase, *The People's Farm: English Radical Agrarianism, 1775–1840* (Oxford, 1988), p. 4 and 123 where he also gives an example of a speech by an unnamed woman at the Charlotte Street Institution on land as 'the garden of all production, the twin brother of labour'.

women's property, including the experience of female smallholders – who, as in the case of their male peers, probably made up the majority of female landowners[84] – and, just as importantly, female commoners. Commons were after all a very particular type of property and one crucial to the livelihoods of poor women and children.[85] Future research on female litigation patterns over time and between different jurisdictions has the potential to tell us a great deal about women's commitment to defending their access to property. There is also much scope for research that compares women's experience as landowners in different national (and legal) contexts. How did a woman's experience of owning and managing land in England under the common law compare to women's experience in the Americas or in other parts of the British Empire, for example? We might also usefully explore the many ways that gender shaped both women's and men's *experiences* of owning or renting property: as all the chapters here have shown, this went far beyond women's legal disabilities impacting on the *amount* of land they owned. Finally, joining up the research in this book with new research on the experience, and numbers, of female property owners today would demonstrate how the social and political power that comes with land has been wielded by women up to and including the present day. We hope that in writing this book, and fundamentally revising and reframing the history of land and property, we open up space for new gendered narratives, of both the historical past and the twenty-first-century present.

Acknowledgements

Our thanks go to the delegates and speakers at the *Women, Land and Landscape* conference held at the University of Hull in 2015 for their contributions to many fruitful discussions about gender, land and property in both historical and contemporary contexts. Thanks too to all those who have offered thoughts and comments at conferences and seminars and to all the PGRs, PDRAs and academic colleagues involved in the University of Hull's *Gender, Place and Memory Research Cluster*. Thanks especially to Joshua Rhodes and Hannah Worthen for their invaluable editorial assistance at various stages in bringing the book to press.

84 On this, see Casson, this volume, and McDonagh, *Elite Women*, p. 29.

85 Humphries, 'Enclosures, Common Rights and Women'.

1

Women, Work and Land: The Spatial Dynamics of Gender Relations in Early Modern England 1550–1750

AMANDA FLATHER

This chapter explores the neglected topic of the spatial experience of rural women in early modern England. Much has been written about the history of the work of men and women in the pre-modern past. It is now generally acknowledged that early modern ideological assumptions about a strict division of work and space between men and productive work outside the house on the one hand, and women and reproduction and consumption inside the house on the other, bore little relation to reality. Household work strategies, out of necessity, were very diverse. Women were employed in a wide range of productive occupations, if to a more limited degree, within and beyond the home and most men worked in, near or from the house, as people rarely had a separate workplace away from home. Boundaries were further complicated by the frequent employment of servants who lived and worked alongside families on close and fairly intimate terms.[1] What this spatial complexity meant for ordinary women and men on a day-to-day basis and its consequences for gender relationships is less clear and has received relatively little historical attention. In particular, and of relevance to this essay, while a significant historiography exists on female agricultural labour, few historians have examined how ordinary women used space in a rural context or how, during a period in which agrarian capitalism was undergoing significant transformation, women's experience of the landscape was changing. Indeed, at least implicitly, the landscape in early modern England has been presented in largely male terms, stressing the activities of male workers and marginalising

1 Keith Wrightson, *English Society: 1580–1680* (London, 1982); Joanne Bailey, *Unquiet Lives: Marriage and Marriage Breakdown in England, 1660–1800* (Cambridge, 2003); Robert B. Shoemaker, *Gender in English Society 1650–1850: The Emergence of Separate Spheres?* (London, 1998).

women's presence. This is in part perhaps because it has been assumed that the English legal system generally discouraged female property ownership and so there has been only limited research on women's management and control of land.[2] A focus on women's paid labour in the literature alongside a tendency to include women's unpaid occupations under the general label of domestic has also tended to suppress awareness of and interest in the variety of female spatial experiences in the sixteenth and seventeenth centuries.

This essay attempts to redress the balance and to add to our knowledge through a case study of the way that women used and experienced rural space for work in the county of Essex during the 'long seventeenth century'. The aim is to show that experience of the land was shaped by gender but also varied according to the age and rank of the individual, the nature of the regional economy, the size of the farm and the season of the year. The impact of the interplay of these variables – local social and economic structure, seasonality, gender roles, age and status – in the everyday determining of access, control and use of the landscape will be addressed in the course of the following discussion.

A broader concern of the study is also to show the tremendous potential that a focus on the concept of space has to comment on aspects of the often opaque constructions and workings of gender in early modern England. Over the past thirty years research in a wide variety of fields has demonstrated the close interrelation of gender, space and identity. The great strength of this scholarship lies in its understanding of space in social and performative terms. Hannah Moore has delineated that a space is more than, and different from, a physical location or place. A place is transformed into a space by the social actors who constitute it through everyday use: 'meanings are not inherent in the organisation of ... space, but must be invoked through the activities of social actors'.[3] Space is not simply the product of social relations, but also a ground of social construction and so space lies at the heart of our concerns.[4] As Doreen Massey has argued, space 'both reflects and has effects back on the ways in which gender is constructed and understood in the societies in which we live'.[5]

Recognition of the role of the subjects who give meaning to space through everyday use counters the charge that the study of space is 'unhistorical' in

2 Amanda L. Capern, 'The Landed Woman in Early-Modern England', *Parergon* 19:1 (2002), 185–214; Briony McDonagh, *Elite Women & the Agricultural Landscape, 1700–1830* (Abingdon, 2017).

3 Hannah Moore, *Space, Text and Gender: An Anthropological Study of the Marakwet of Kenya* (Cambridge, 1986), p. 8.

4 Joan Wallach Scott, 'Gender: A Useful Category for Historical Analysis', *American Historical Review* 91:5 (1986), 1053–76; Judith Butler, *Gender Trouble: Feminism and the Subversion of Identity* (London, 1991), pp. 139–41.

5 Doreen Massey, *Space, Place and Gender* (Cambridge, 1994), p. 186.

the sense that it studies static structures at the expense of change over time. Space conceptualised in terms of social relations is 'inherently dynamic', since social actors attribute different meanings to space at different times.[6] These insights also mean that historians can move beyond debates about an apparent opposition between structure and agency to explore the relationship between them. Various theorists have argued that subjects are simultaneously subject and active in what Anthony Giddens has termed the process of 'structuration' of institutions that characterise society.[7] Structures, in our case spaces, set boundaries, to both the conceptual and the practical options available to a person, but they do not wholly determine them.[8]

Thus a focus on space encourages attention to concepts of agency. One of the key points to emerge in spatial study has been the multiple and dynamic ways in which spaces can be conceived, used, experienced and understood by different users at different times. Such analysis brings important insights to bear on gendered use of space because it exposes ways in which context and the intersection of gender with other social factors such as age, social and marital status complicate social and spatial codes.[9]

The link between mental and physical space is important here. Writers in a variety of fields have shown ways in which spaces can be gendered, even when they are shared by men or women, through perception, experience and use. Individual sense of space, and behaviour within it, is influenced by a host of cultural clues that enable people to create 'mental maps' to help them to use spaces and to let them know when spaces might be difficult or dangerous to enter. These different perceptions and experiences are determined in large measure by the different degrees of power wielded by individuals or groups over how the space is accessed, used and given social and cultural meanings.[10]

Recognition of the influence of time, context, status and age on experience, imagination and control of space encourages a more sophisticated and nuanced analysis of gendered power relations within spaces that until recently have simply been classified as 'mixed'. It also enables research on gender relations to move away from arid arguments about 'prescription versus practice' or 'representational versus real' to attend to the complex relationship

6 Massey, *Space, Place and Gender*, pp. 2–3.

7 Anthony Giddens, *Central Problems in Social Theory* (London, 1979); Anthony Giddens, *The Constitution of Society* (Cambridge, 1984); Peter Burke, *History and Social Theory* (Cambridge, 1992), pp. 113, 161.

8 Pierre Bourdieu, *Outline of a Theory of Practice* (Cambridge, 1977), pp. 78–87; Pierre Bourdieu, 'Social Space and the Genesis of Classes', *Language and Symbolic Power*, ed. John B. Thompson (Cambridge, 1991), p. 230; Burke, *History and Social Theory*, pp. 110–14, 118–26.

9 Massey, *Space, Place and Gender*, p. 3; Moore, *Space, Text and Gender*, p. 7; Susan Kent, *Domestic Architecture and the Use of Space. An Inter-Disciplinary Cross-Cultural Study* (Cambridge, 1990), p. 3.

10 Peter Gould and Rodney White, *Mental Maps* (London, 1986), p. 108; Massey, *Space, Place and Gender*, pp. 185–6; Moore, *Space, Text and Gender*, p. 8.

between them. Some of the most exciting recent work on early modern gender has pointed out, for example, that the content of conduct literature was a product of the interests and concerns of its readership, just as 'real' lives were shaped by the texts that formed part of the culture. People might revise or reject normative notions, but the two are not wholly separable. Ideology shaped individual perception and experience of space in early modern society, even if the links between them were far from straightforward.[11]

Spatial analysis is therefore very useful for gender history because it is highly contextual. It requires consideration of links between people and spaces as well as between different types of space and so allows for extremely nuanced and dynamic analyses of gender and power. Early modern historical scholarship has moved a long way from the assumption that all men were autonomous patriarchs and all women simply victims and has begun to explore arenas for female agency created by the complex, varied, uneven and changing articulation of patriarchal authority and the distinct positions of different men and women within the early modern social system.[12] It has been emphasised that this agency can best be seen in the continual negotiation of everyday interactions rather than occasional acts of resistance. Michael Braddick and John Walter have recently called for a search for 'sources and spaces' in which the historian can see these informal, often opaque and complex aspects of the everyday politics of gender in process.[13] In similar vein, Alexandra Shepard has argued forcefully that 'to understand the social practice of patriarchy in early modern England, we need to be far more aware of precisely *which* men stood to gain, *which* women stood to lose, and in *which* contexts'.[14]

Yet, while we have large numbers of *thematic* studies of male and female labour in print, remarkably little work has been done on the *contexts* in which work was negotiated.[15] In particular, given the acknowledged significance of the links between space, work and the dynamics of power between the sexes, we need to know a good deal more about the organisation of the spaces of male and female work and the degree to which the sexes were integrated or

11 Alexandra Shepard, *Meanings of Manhood in Early Modern England* (Oxford, 2003); Laura Gowing, *Domestic Dangers: Women, Words and Sex in Early Modern London* (Oxford, 1996).

12 Bernard Capp, *When Gossips Meet: Women, Family, and Neighbourhood in Early Modern England* (Oxford, 2003); Laura Gowing, *Common Bodies: Women, Touch and Power in Seventeenth-Century England* (Yale, CT, 2003); Shepard, *Meanings of Manhood*.

13 Michael J. Braddick and John Walter, 'Grids of Power: Order, Hierarchy and Subordination in Early Modern Society', *Negotiating Power in Early Modern Society: Order, Hierarchy and Subordination in Britain and Ireland*, eds Michael J. Braddick and John Walter (Cambridge, 2001), p. 39.

14 Shepard, *Meanings of Manhood*, p. 4.

15 Miranda Chaytor, 'Household and Kinship: Ryton in the Late Sixteenth and Early Seventeenth Centuries', *History Workshop Journal* 10:1 (1980), 25–60.

separated during the working day. The following analysis therefore moves away from the concept of spheres and the models of economic change to which it relates to focus on the landscape as space, drawing on local and micro-historical methods in order to place evidence within an appropriate regional context.[16] The advantage of the approach is that it allows me to explore the impact on the spatial and sexual division of labour of the interaction between local economic and geographical conditions, ideological and cultural factors, local customs and patriarchal family arrangements in relation to one another. Several features of the county of Essex lend themselves to this study. The region had a strong and varied economy in the early modern period, with multiple proto-industrial activities in addition to agriculture. The growth of the cloth trade and proximity to London markets meant that it was a precociously market-orientated region, allowing an analysis of different aspects of the gendering of space that is especially sensitive to the influence of continuity and change.[17] The surviving source material is also rich and extensive. Instead of using institutional and tax records in which female work often went unrecorded, the research draws on descriptions of work found in the depositions of the church and secular courts, which offer a dynamic and detailed picture of what work women and men actually did, rather than what they were meant to do, and, more importantly for this study, where they did it.[18] For the purposes of clarity the analysis is divided into three main sections. It looks first at women's use of space outside the home for tasks included within the very broad early modern definition of housework; then it looks at agricultural work; and finally at craft-based and service activities. The purpose of the essay is two-fold: the first is to reconstruct the type of work that women performed and where they did it; the second is to explore the significance of the sexual and spatial division of labour for our understanding of gender relationships within households and communities in a landscape.

Housewifery

Women in early modern households spent a good deal of time cooking, cleaning, washing and looking after young children. But several routine aspects of housework were performed outside, complicating the assumption

16 Amanda Vickery, 'Golden Age to Separate Spheres? A Review of the Categories and Chronology of English Women's History', *Historical Journal* 36:2 (1993), 413–14.

17 For the classic account of these changes, see Wrightson, *English Society*.

18 For a similar approach, see Sheilagh Ogilvie, *A Bitter Living: Women, Markets, and Social Capital in Early-Modern Germany* (Oxford, 2002); Maria Ågren (ed.), *Making a Living, Making a Difference: Gender and Work in Early Modern European Society* (Oxford, 2017); Maria Ågren, *The State as Master: Gender, State Formation and Commercialisation in Urban Sweden, 1650–1780* (Manchester, 2017).

that women's domestic work was located in or near the house. Admittedly, the preparation of the simplest of meals tied middling sort women to the house for specific periods of the day. It is interesting to note in the conduct literature of the period the ways in which changes in the rural economy and the drive towards efficiency may have led the middling sort to regulate the timing of mealtimes much more closely to instil discipline and social distance. Thomas Tusser advised the good housewife that by noon she should have dinner 'readie and neate' but that she should 'let meat tarrie servant, not servant his meate. Plough cattle a baiting, call servant to dinner, the thicker together, the charges the thinner'.[19] On farms with several servants we find farmers' wives and their female servants presiding over breakfast early in the morning and dinner around midday. For example, when William Stapleton called at the house of William Woods, a husbandman of Dedham, to ask goodwife Woods to accompany him to a neighbour's house to discuss sale of some household goods, she explained that she 'was not at liberty to go along to Ellivett's howse', because she was busy serving her husband's 'folks [who] were at breakfast'.[20] The gendered character of cooking is also vividly, if unintentionally demonstrated by William Ffuller, late of Alford, who, in 1634, confessed to the theft of his master's hens. He explained that he took them to 'Mumfords howse at which the said Mumford promised him a feast *when his wife cam home*'.[21]

But labouring women who worked out of the house for wages most of the time did not enjoy the benefits of an oven or even a secure supply of grain, and so probably did not necessarily spend much time at home preparing family meals themselves.[22] Even in the small cloth towns of north and central Essex early modern 'fast food' was available, cooked and sold by women and men, and many labouring women in the countryside bought bread and beer to feed their families after they had finished their paid work for the day from local victualling houses.[23] Court cases offer glimpses of the reality of housewifery for women such as Elizabeth Page, the wife of a husbandman of Henham,

19 Thomas Tusser, *Five Hundred Points of Good Husbandry* (London, 1580), p. 174.

20 Essex Record Office (hereafter ERO), D/B5 S/b2/7 fol. 253.

21 ERO, Q/SBa 2/19 (my emphasis). See also ERO, D/ACA 37 fol. 134. Thomas Doyle of Goldhangar was presented to the church courts in 1630 for 'drinking at the widow Harrison's'. At the archdeacon's court he argued that his visit was entirely justified, 'because he had nobodie at home to dresse his dyett and therefore he was driven to take his dyett there'. See also Grove c. Spencer and Spencer (1618) London Metropolitan Archives (hereafter LMA), DL/C/225 fol. 175. Anthonie Cramphorne, singleman, who had his 'dyett dressed' by his mother or female neighbours.

22 Jane Whittle, 'Housewives and Servants in Rural England, 1440–1650: Evidence of Women's Work from Probate Documents', *Royal Historical Society Transactions* 15:1 (2005), 65–6.

23 Christopher Johnson, 'A proto-industrial community study: Coggeshall in Essex c. 1500–1750' (PhD diss., University of Essex, 1990), 46–8; ERO, Q/SBa 2/58.

whose regular practice was to visit Thomas Mead's alehouse in the village to buy bread 'of Meads wife', and Alice Woodhams of Wix, who was assaulted by two men in William Turnedge's alehouse 'as shee came from gleaning … to buy some bread and drink for their owne spending in their own howse as att other tymes shee had used to do'.[24] It is noteworthy that in 1600 the parish of Finchingfield petitioned to be allowed to license another victualling house; the town's one victualler could no longer supply the more than eighty households that had to buy their food. In the next few years, similar petitions came from Langham, Great Oakley, Halstead and High Easter.[25]

Women also spent a great deal of time outside trading for food to feed their families. Of course, shopping could take different forms in different places and wealth, geography and occupation determined that some women spent more time out of the house shopping than others. Rural women of the middling sort spent a good deal of time at home working on production of food for their families, cultivating the kitchen garden, making bread, beer and clothes. Nevertheless, very few households were self-sufficient by the seventeenth century. Jane Whittle has shown that different households produced different commodities in different regions and it is clear that middling-rank countrywomen shopped for some food and consumer goods.[26] Most middling countrywomen walked to the mill for flour or sent one of their servants to do so.[27] They also travelled to market every week to buy a variety of goods. 'Private' trading between individuals, outside of official control, was also rapidly increasing in the region during this period, and there are scattered glimpses in the records of women making private purchases of meat and grain from neighbouring farmers who sold produce door to door; books, ribbons, tobacco and cloth were purchased at home from itinerant traders who travelled around country districts; other necessities were bought on weekly visits to the nearest market.[28]

Poorer women in rural villages, who were occupied full-time working for wages, bought most of their food, mainly bread and beer, from local victualling houses, as we have seen; itinerant sellers of foodstuffs also visited villages that lay at some distance from a local town, so that working women

24 ERO, Q/SBa 2/70; ERO, Q/SBa 2/58; see also ERO, Q/SBa 2/70.

25 ERO, Q/SR 151/99; ERO, 155/31. It has been suggested that by the eighteenth century the poor purchased almost all their food: Sara Mendelson and Patricia Crawford, *Women in Early Modern England* (Oxford, 1998), p. 269.

26 Whittle, 'Housewives and Servants in Rural England', pp. 51–74; Jane Whittle, 'Enterprising Widows and Active Wives: Women's Unpaid Work in the Household Economy of Early Modern England', *Journal of the History of The Family* 19:3 (2014), 283–300.

27 Gutteridge c. Brett (1680) LMA, DL/C/240 fol. 170v; Mircocke c. Plummer (1635) ERO, D/AED 8 fol. 95; Greene c. Burrowes (1632) LMA, DL/C/232 fol. 82v.

28 For examples of women of a variety of social types doing shopping see, Warwick c. Marshall (1742) ERO, D/AXD 2 fol. 144.; Rule c. Rule (1675) LMA, DL/C/237 fol. 334; ERO, Q/SR 332/106.

did not have to lose valuable time walking long distances to market to buy their food.[29] Poverty also made the gathering of food and fuel out in the fields an essential part of labouring women's work, varying according to the season. In summer women picked fruit and greens such as 'wild sallet' and in winter wives of small farmers, poor women and female servants ventured out when necessity demanded for wood for the fire. As Fox has argued, from such bounty the poor were said to make shift even in periods of great scarcity or famine.[30]

Laundry was another activity that took women out of the house to the nearest source of water. In the countryside labouring women and female servants had to carry washing relatively long distances to the nearest stream or river. In a case from Sussex a coroner's report recorded that Joan Hassilden of Henfield, aged fourteen, 'finished washing linen in the accustomed washing-place in the stream near the mill at Henfield' but slipped when going to fill one last pail of water.[31] By the seventeenth century water supplies to middling and elite private houses had improved, and sources more often describe women, particularly maidservants, washing at home, either in the kitchen or outside in the yard. Nonetheless, because the job was so hard and tiring, work was still shared and so at least it remained a sociable activity.[32] In 1586, for example, Margery Oliver took her family's laundry, with her parents' permission, to Agnes Bolter's house so that they could talk while Margery dried and smoothed clothes.[33]

Childcare was also a predominantly female responsibility. But too often historians have assumed that in order to look after babies and young children women worked in locations close to the house. In reality the practical impact of childcare on the spatial arrangements of women's working lives was far more complex and depended on a variety of factors, including age, status, wealth and region. The idea of marriage as an economic partnership remains central to our understanding of the early modern economy. Recent and important work on pre-industrial Sweden by Maria Ågren has shown that the marriage unit was the most important labour unit in Swedish society, lending social authority to the married couple, with single people and children dependent on that.[34] Evidence from this study also shows that

29 ERO, Q/SBa 2/58; ERO, Q/SBa 2/70; ERO, Q/SR 157/30; ERO, Q/SR 151/99; ERO, Q/SR 155/31; ERO, Q/SBa 2/30.

30 Adam Fox, 'Food, Drink and Social Distinction', *Remaking English Society: Social Relations and Social Change in Early Modern England*, eds Steve Hindle, Alex Shepard and John Walter (Woodbridge, 2013), p. 179.

31 R. F. Hunnisett, *Sussex Coroners' Inquests 1558–1603* (Kew, 1996), p. 256.

32 Matthew Johnson, *An Archaeology of Capitalism* (Oxford, 1996), p. 176.

33 Oliver c. Stephens (1586) ERO, D/AED 3 fols 3v–4v.

34 For the classic account of marriage as an economic partnership, see Wrightson, *English Society*, pp. 93–4. For important comparative evidence on Sweden, see Ågren, *Making a Living*,

married women had to manage multiple tasks and balance the costs of caring for their children against the needs of the household economy, which meant that, depending on the size and wealth of the household, childcare was often delegated or shared with servants, spouses or neighbours to free up time for other types of work.[35] Female servants were routinely employed in most families of middling sort and often left to supervise small children. In smaller and poorer households in villages and small towns the local community was an indispensable aid in bringing up children.[36] Working women sometimes paid other women to nurse their babies while they worked out in the fields, for example, and defamation cases describe arguments that erupted within networks of female neighbours who nursed children while mothers lay sick.[37] The physical proximity of houses in close-knit village communities meant that casual surveillance of one another's children was also possible while they played together out in the street. Of course, this more extensive system of child-care was less feasible for women who lived in scattered rural settlements or on isolated farms. Women such as Elizabeth Broughton of Chishill, who was presented to the ecclesiastical court 'for seldom coming to church', did not have the support of other women living close by. Her explanation to the court, 'that by reason of the sickness of her child she cold not [repair] to the church', hints at the isolation of some countrywomen at home with small children. It is significant that the court accepted her explanation; she was simply admonished for her neglect and sent on her way.[38] Accidents that claimed the lives of young children at home provide further insights into the pressures that mothers could face in rural areas. Children came to harm while women took food out to their husbands at work in the fields, or died in cradle fires because nobody was around to watch over them.[39]

This is not to suggest that men were not involved with childcare at all. Seventeenth-century households were busy places and in such a setting all sorts of people could be left in charge of small children if necessity or emergency dictated. Male servants were sometimes left to look after children and fathers also helped out. A good example is the oatmeal man of Stanstead, who washed the wool bedding on which his children lay sick when they had

pp. 80–102.

35 On the relationship between the work of married women and servants see Whittle, 'Enterprising Widows and Active Wives'.

36 ERO, Q/SBa 2/12; Mott c. Mitchell (1638), D/ACD 5, fol. 127v; Morris c. Bustard (1630), D/AED 8, fol. 62v; D/B5 Sb2/ 9, fol. 229v.

37 Trewell c. Collins (1631), ERO, D/AED 8, fols 79v–80; ERO, D/B5 Sb2/2, not foliated; D/B5 Sb2/9 fol. 184v.

38 ERO, D/ACA 23, fol. 123v.

39 Elizabeth Towner and John Towner, 'The Hazards of Daily Life: An Historical Perspective On Adult Unintentional Injuries', *Journal of Epidemiology and Community Health* 62:11 (2008), 103.

smallpox during the autumn of 1636.[40] Moreover, as children left infancy behind, the behaviour of boys and girls began to diverge, and sons spent more time out and about with their fathers, while daughters stayed closer to home. Very early it seems that little girls parted company with little boys.[41]

The extent and nature of women's physical and social responsibility for the household undoubtedly shaped their use and experience of landscape in ways that were different from men. One historian has estimated that women spent six or seven hours a day doing housework, varying of course with wealth, geography and occupation.[42] But because much of the work was outside and because the nature and location of other female occupations were so diverse the impact on spatial experience was very varied.

Where men worked in agriculture, the largest male employment sector in early modern Essex, the coexistence of mixed systems of agriculture with the cloth trade in the county meant that husbands and wives worked in separate places for much of the time.[34] We find that men and women did different types of agricultural work in early modern Essex, as in most parts of early modern England. Women were involved in agricultural work but in fewer numbers and in different occupations at different times of the year. The Essex depositions contain no references to women ploughing. Obviously patterns varied to some extent, according to the size of the farm and the nature of the local economy. There are isolated examples from other regions of married women and female servants involved in ploughing work on small family farms, where labour was in short supply.[43] Patterns were never fixed. But a degree of flexibility that suggests interesting ways in which status and age blurred conventional gender boundaries does not undermine the conclusion that in general heavy winter fieldwork was left to men. This labour kept men out in the fields from September until the end of November, when they retreated to the house out of the cold and wet weather for a few weeks to mend tools and perhaps to weave some cloth. Ploughing and harrowing began again in January and February. Finally, in spring, the fields were ploughed and harrowed again.[44]

40 ERO, Q/SBa 2/27. There are examples of this for Sweden. See Dag Lindstrom, Rosemarie Fiebranz, Jonas Lindstrom, Jan Mispelaere and Goran Ryden, 'Working together', *Making a Living*, ed. Ågren, pp. 66, 135–39.

41 Towner and Towner, 'The Hazards of Daily Life', p. 104; Barbara Hanawalt, *The Ties that Bound: Peasant Families in Medieval England* (New York and Oxford, 1986), pp. 175–6; 185–6.

42 Lorna Weatherill, *Consumer Behaviour and Material Culture 1660-1715* (London, 1988), p. 143.

43 Sofia Ling, Karin Hassan Jansson, Marie Lenners, Christopher Pihl and Maria Ågren, 'Marriage and Work: Intertwined Sources of Agency and Authority', *Making a Living*, ed. Ågren, pp. 82–3.

44 Pamela Sharpe, *Adapting to Capitalism: Working Women in the English Economy, 1700–1850* (Basingstoke, 1996), p. 78; Whittle 'Housewives and Servants in Rural England', pp. 51–74; Shoemaker, *Gender in English Society*, p. 152. For evidence of flexibility see Alice Clark, *Working Lives of Women in the Seventeenth Century* (London, 1919, 3rd edn, 1992), p. 62;

Gendered patterns of prosecution in the church courts, upholding the ban on manual labour on saints' days and the Sabbath, provide some interesting insights into popular attitudes and practices. A comprehensive examination of the Act Books of the archdeaconries of Essex, Colchester, Middlesex and the bishop of London's commissary in Essex and Hertfordshire from 1630 to 1640, whose jurisdictions extended over different regional economies within the county, provides no examples of female presentments for ploughing, harrowing, carting, hedging or ditching. Married women and female servants were prosecuted in the main for performing 'domestic' tasks, such as baking, brewing or grinding of corn on the Sabbath. For example, in 1630, according to a neighbour, Bridget Scott,

> Cicily Lorde hath and doth profane saboth dayes by churninge and making of butter and by killing of pigges, geese, hennes, duckes at the time of divine service, ready for the market ... and this deponent saw him the said [John] Lord digge a ditche and hedge aboute service tyme.[45]

Sites of neighbourly disputes also reflect this physical separation of men and women during the working day. Details from defamation cases often describe conflicts between men out in the fields in winter in front of all-male groups of neighbours. Disputes between women more commonly occurred in or near the house in colder months.[46] Cases of theft also corroborate evidence of the spatial separation of husbands and wives during the winter working day. Wives were often the first to discover cases of theft because they were working in or around the house, or because they were the first to return home to prepare the meal.[47] It was only at midday that farmhouses saw the temporary return of the male population, when they came home to have their dinner.[48] During the winter months, at least, arable fields were predominantly male spaces and women spent most of their time working in and around the house and yard, cooking, cleaning, and caring for children. They also tended animals, including poultry, pigs, cattle, and sheep, that they kept on common land. Between times they carded and spun yarn for the clothiers, as they did in the rest of the year.

But gendered patterns of use, organisation and meaning of space were flexible and constantly shifting. This was in part because of the nature of the rural environment itself, which changed considerably with the seasons,

Keith Snell, *Annals of the Labouring Poor: Social Change and Agrarian England 1600–1900* (Cambridge, 1985), p. 52, and Michael Roberts, 'Sickles and Scythes: Women's Work and Men's Work at Harvest Time', *History Workshop Journal* 7:1 (1979), 9–10.

45 Hyde c. Rooke (1630) LMA, DL/C/232 fol. 84.

46 Hyde c. Rooke (1630) LMA, DL/C/232 fol. 200v; Sutton c. Rochell (1638) ERO, D/ABD 8 fol. 51; Greene c. Browne (1638) ERO, D/ABD 8 fol. 58.

47 ERO, Q/SR 425/104. See also Q/SR 138/20, 20a.

48 ERO, Q/SBa 2/73; Q/SBa 2/7; Boucer c. Irnard (1710), LMA, DL/C/252, fol. 26v.

creating contexts for female agency. In the spring labouring women worked in arable fields quite frequently, planting and weeding, sometimes working alongside their husbands.[49] Most significantly, during haymaking in June and when harvesting began in July whole households worked together out in the fields, reaping, gathering and binding to bring the crop back into the barns. Incidental detail in the depositions of the many defamation cases that were staged out in harvest fields in summer confirms ways in which the need for collaborative work at harvest time eroded social distinctions and spatial boundaries and drew husbands and wives, old and young, rich and poor, indeed entire neighbourhoods together to help to gather in the grain as best they could. We find, for example, that when some riotous and aggressive visitors caused a disturbance outside the large house of Elizabeth Archer, wealthy widow of John Archer, gentleman of Witham, in July 1611, she was caught unawares out in the fields with 'her reapers'.[50] Depositional evidence from tithe disputes reveals women's detailed knowledge of land management and its resources.[51] The knowledge of widows is striking in this respect. Giving evidence in a tithe dispute in 1628 Mary Strange, widow of Purleigh, recalled that 'aboute 13 yrs ago said piece of ground was sowen with wheat which being by her or her assignes reaped and carried to her barne'.[52] Interestingly, too, and by way of comparison, William Stout, who grew up on a small estate in the north west of England, recalls that his industrious mother was 'not only fully imployed in housewifery but in dressing their corn for the market, and also in the fields in hay and corn harvests, along with our father and our servants'. She added to the estate through land investment while her husband was alive and after his death took over management of the farm.[53]

At the end of harvest conventional notions of gender and space were turned upside down and arable fields became female arenas, as women and children were allowed to glean the remnants of the harvest to help feed their families over the winter. Gleaning, as Peter King has observed, was 'one of the few customary activities controlled exclusively by women'.[54] Gleaning

49 Sharpe, *Adapting to Capitalism*, pp. 78–9.

50 The National Archives (hereafter TNA), STAC 8/152/4. On Elizabeth Archer, see Janet Guyford, *Public Spirit: Dissent in Witham and Essex 1500–1700* (Witham, 1999), pp. 72, 75, 78.

51 For excellent studies of women, custom and memory see Andy Wood, *The Memory of the People: Custom, and Popular Senses of the Past in Early Modern England* (Cambridge, 2013), pp. 297–315; Nicola Whyte, 'Custodians of Memory: Women and Custom in Rural England c.1550–1700', *Cultural and Social History* 2:8 (2011), 153–73.

52 ERO, D/ABD4. fol. 61.

53 J. D. Marshall (ed.), *The Autobiography of William Stout of Lancaster* (Manchester, 1967), p. 68.

54 Peter King, 'Customary Rights and Women's Earnings: The Importance of Gleaning to the Rural Labouring Poor', *Economic History Review* 44:3 (1991), 462; Sharpe, *Adapting to Capitalism*, p. 83; Andy Wood, 'The Place of Custom in Plebeian Political Culture: England, 1550–1800', *Social History* 22: 1 (1997), 56.

fields figure prominently in the documents as sites of female sociability and dispute.[55] According to Margery Nottage of Great Dunmow, in 1637, 'in the latter end of harvest last past then in one John Vintner's field gleaning of barley and one Anne Reynolds was with them gleaning they fell to speeches about Joan Malt in the hearing of Elizabeth Branch'.[56] Similarly, in 1625, the daughter of George Stone of Totham was with Julianne Osborne, 'then gleaning in the same field', when she heard news of notice given by Osborne's father about 'the tithe of all corne and haye within the parish'.[57]

Elite women did not glean. Conventional boundaries of gendered labour were also blurred by age. Young boys as well as young girls are recorded performing this task.[58] But evidence from the depositions confirms what King has found for the eighteenth century, namely that gleaning was predominantly a female activity, performed by widows, working married women, children and female servants, but never by adult men.[59] It was a strictly regulated task and its organisation reinforced a temporary spatial, as well as sexual, division of labour out in harvest fields. Gleaning began once harvesters had carted the grain out of the field and in most villages was begun and ended by the ringing of a bell.[60]

Recognition of these shifting spatial patterns helps account for the timing of courtship, marriage and the birth and death of children. The pleasures as well as the risks to women of the social and sexual possibilities of working with men in the fields at harvest time were romanticised in seventeenth-century broadside ballads such as *The Countrey Peoples Felicitey*, which describes '*Meg, Nell and Nan*' in romantic assignations after harvest work. The reality is also reflected in a variety of documentary evidence. There was, for example, a surge of weddings after harvest was over, around Michaelmas (29 September) in East Anglia, when families felt prosperous and there was some respite from their working regime.[61] Baptism registers tended to single out the summer months when conception – both legitimate and illegitimate – was likely to occur.[62] Seasonal spatial factors also helped determine the

55 ERO, D/B5 Sb2/(not. fol); ERO, Q/SBa 2/31; ERO, Q/SBa 2/58; ERO, Q/SBa 2/25.
56 Malt c. Reynolds (1637) ERO, D/ABD 8 fol. 2.
57 Munt c. Sutton (1625) ERO, D/ACD 3 fol. 29v.
58 For a reference to a 'boy' gleaning, see ERO, Q/SBa 2/17.
59 Peter King has shown that the ancient association between women and gleaning had biblical and symbolic significance as well as practical importance for the farmer as a cleaning operation. It was also, as we have said, of vital importance to the family budget of labouring families: King, 'Customary Rights and Women's Earnings', pp. 461–76; Sharpe, *Adapting to Capitalism*, pp. 80–5.
60 Wood, 'The Place of Custom', 56.
61 David Cressy, *Birth, Marriage and Death, Ritual, Religion, and the Lifecycle in Tudor and Stuart England* (Oxford, 1997), p. 298.
62 E. Anthony Wrigley and Roger S. Schofield, *The Population History of England and Wales, 1541–187: A Reconstruction* (Cambridge, MA, 1981), pp. 286–90.

particular nature of the maternal role in early modern England. Close care of infants had to be balanced by economic reality. Infant mortality rates were higher in summer, and cases of childhood fatal accidents occurred most often between March and August, when mothers were more likely to be out in the fields and had less time to supervise their children.[63]

A key question in all of this is why women's working lives differed from men's in a particular time and place. It appears that in Essex decisions were framed less by cultural and legal restrictions than by regional economic conditions. Women as well as men in the county could make choices, if limited ones, about work because of the presence of the textile industry. It was economically advantageous for women to work at home most of the time because they could maximise their income through the opportunities that they had for spinning work in Essex. The cloth trade was the most important economic sector in the county after agriculture and operated under the putting-out system. Male clothiers controlled the organisation of the trade, and purchased and distributed wool to women at home, who carded the wool and spun it into yarn. A petition of Suffolk clothiers in 1575 regarding problems over control of the quality of their yarn explained that 'the custom of our country is to carry our wool out to carding and spinning and put it to divers and sundry spinners, who have in their house divers and sundry children and servants that do card and spin the same wool'. Detailed local research by Arthur Brown has shown that many more women were employed in cloth manufacture than men. Around 1700, there were close to four thousand weavers, wool combers and other male cloth workers in Essex villages and towns, as against twenty-five thousand female spinners. Wives of yeomen as well as labouring women were involved in this type of work. Indeed, in 1622, a warrant was sent to parish officials in certain villages just over the county border in Suffolk complaining that 'yeomens' and farmers' wives of good ability' were procuring for themselves and their children and servants the greater part of the spinning work from the packhouses, 'whereby the poor are being deprived of it'.[64] Spinning was not only more pleasant than agricultural work for labouring women; it was also more remunerative and provided an essential cushion against fluctuations in male employment, helping to pay for rent, food and fuel. In 1636 the wages of women in spinning in Essex were 8d a day, whereas the normal rate for female agricultural labour was only 6d a day. It is likely that these practical considerations, more than patriarchal precepts, shaped the decisions made by women about work. Since male wages

63 Towner and Towner, 'The Hazards of Daily Life', p. 106.

64 Arthur Brown, *Essex At Work, 1700–1815* (Chelmsford, 1969), p. 3; Sharpe, *Adapting to Capitalism*, p. 30; George Unwin, 'The History of the Cloth Industry in Suffolk', *Studies in Economic History: The Collected Papers of George Unwin*, ed. R. H. Tawney (London, 1927), p. 271; ERO, D/B5 Sb2/9, fol. 240v.

for agricultural work were always higher, the best 'survival strategy' in Essex was for women to remain responsible for child care and housework and to take on spinning and carding work based at home.

The social setting of male and female work is also an important consideration if we are to understand the wider significance of the spatial and sexual division of labour for individuals, households and communities. Although female occupations were essentially home-based, they were rarely solitary and women were not confined within the walls of the house.[65] Spinners worked outside when the weather was fine, frequently in groups.[66] There is visual evidence of women working together out in the fields and corroborative evidence of these communal patterns of work can be found in incidental detail in the depositions. We find, for example, that witnesses in an enclosure dispute in Nazeing, brought before Star Chamber in 1623, remarked that the wives of local farmers and craftsmen met on Nazeing common to do their 'knitting'.[48] Another common practice was to sit in the doorway of the house, to take advantage of the light, and from this vantage point women were able to chat with passers by and observe the goings on in the neighbourhood while they worked.[67] Thomas Baskerville, who travelled round England in the 1660s, observed the communal character of female patterns of work when he noted that the women of Suffolk:

> go spinning up and down the way … with a rock and a distaff in their hands, so that if a comparison were to be made between the ploughman and the good wives of these parts, their lives were more pleasant, for they can go with their work to good company, and the poor ploughman must do his work alone.[68]

The gentlewoman English traveller Celia Fiennes famously described observing the women of East Anglia, who 'knit much and spin, some with their rock and fusoe as the French does, others at their wheeles out in the streetes and lanes as one passes'.[69] In winter, women enjoyed friends' company working together in one another's houses.[70] Clothiers' correspondence sometimes mentioned 'spinning houses' in rural areas, which might offer an approximate English equivalent to the continental 'spinning

65 Bernard Capp, *When Gossips Meet*, pp. 42–55.

66 Norris c. Butler (1613) ERO, D/AED 5, fol. 200v; Matthewes c. Bennet (1627), D/AED 8, fol. 23v; Dod c. Mann (1627), D/AED 8, fol. 19v.

67 Norris c. Butler (1613), ERO, D/AED 5, fol. 199v.

68 "Thomas Baskerville's Journeys in England, Temp. Car 11", HMC, *Portland* XI (1893), p. 266.

69 *The Illustrated Journeys of Celia Fiennes*, ed. Christopher Morris (London: Macdonald, 1982), p. 136; TNA, STAC 8/125/16; Pettit c. Mosse (1633), ERO, D/ABD 7, fol. 127v.

70 ERO, Q/SBa 2/46; Moore c. Clark (1631), LMA, DL/C/232, fol. 194v.

bee'.[71] These references hint at a social setting in which farmers spent much of their time working out in the fields away from their village or small town alone or with other men, while female occupations kept them in close contact with their neighbours, although not necessarily inside the house. It seems that the respective roles and occupations of men and women in agricultural households provided husbands and wives with a high degree of day-to-day independence, distinctive networks of acquaintance and different forms of engagement with the landscape.

Obviously rural women who lived outside larger nucleated villages, in areas of Essex with settlement patterns of small hamlets and scattered farms (traditionally associated with areas colonised from woodland) lived a more solitary life. However, even they were not entirely isolated. Women's occupations required that they move around a great deal and this meant that they came into contact with individuals outside the household unit and beyond their immediate locality on a fairly frequent basis.[72] Most middling rural women rode to the local market town at least once a week to buy and to sell commodities. Age, geography and status determined that some countrywomen had a closer and more regular connection with the market than others. The wives of well-to-do yeomen travelled for purposes of trade, but the wives or widows of more humble farmers or craftsmen did so more often. Women from the dairying district around Epping or the marshlands on the coast had more involvement in the market than their counterparts in corn-growing areas further north around the Rodings. According to the depositions, men and women generally travelled no more than ten miles to market, but women from these dairying districts in the south and east of the county rode fifteen miles to London to sell their dairy produce every week during the summer because of the lucrative profits to be obtained from the city's markets.[73]

Women's engagement with their environment in terms of what they saw, what they heard and how they made their marks on the landscape also altered with economic change. The commercialisation of the regional economy, stimulated by the proximity of the growing London market as well as the expanding army of industrial workers employed in the cloth industry, generated possibilities as well as problems for women. A significant proportion of the growing number of professional provisions dealers who travelled along the roads of rural Essex, variously listed as 'badgers, higglers, kidders, laders and carriers' of corn and other foodstuffs, supposed to be

71 Brown, *Essex at Work*, p. 10.

72 Robert B. Shoemaker, 'Gendered Spaces: Patterns of Mobility and Perception of London's Geography, 1660–1750', *Imagining Early Modern London: Perceptions and Portrayals of the City from Stow to Strype, 1598–1720*, ed. Julia Merrit (Cambridge, 2001), pp. 144–65.

73 Cited in Sharpe, *Adapting to Capitalism*, p. 94; Rogers c. Lake (1619), LMA, DL/C/226, fol. 26v.

licensed by the county bench, were female.[74] Symptomatic of the growth of private marketing, these traders purchased produce principally at markets, as well as farms and estates, and took it back to their villages, where they set up 'shop' informally in an open space. They are well described by David Rollinson as the early modern equivalent of mobile shopkeepers. Of the individuals involved in this type of dealing in corn, butter cheese and eggs brought to the attention of the courts during the period, often for operating illegally, 22 per cent were women. The marital status of 36 per cent of the women is unknown; 37 per cent were described as widows and 27 per cent were married. Interestingly, however, 10 per cent were single, providing evidence of opportunities offered by the trade for female independence.[75]

Women traders therefore frequently formed contacts between the countryside and the town. The proximity of the London market encouraged women from the suburbs nearest to the capital to travel quite long distances along country roads in Essex to buy up produce to take back to London. Women from Plaistow, West Ham, Barking and Walthamstow were regularly brought before the courts with their male trading counterparts for engrossing Essex markets by the buying up of poultry, butter, cheese and eggs.[76] Trade was often on a relatively large scale. Judith Townsende, for example, widow of West Ham, was indicted in 1599 for engrossing 20,000 lbs of butter worth £300 at Brentwood market (some 17.5 miles), with intent to 're-sell the same', presumably in London.[77] In 1647 the inhabitants of Chelmsford and Moulsham complained that characters such as Goodwife Fisher and Goodwife Canan of West Ham were prepared to travel over twenty miles to buy 'a horseload of butter, corn and eggs every market day' to carry away to London to resell.[78] In 1590 John Webster's wife of Romford was indicted for forestalling at Chelmsford market, 'in buying of wheat in great somes of mault'.[79] The Websters were professional, and sometimes illegal, grain dealers. That same year John Webster bought 320 bushels of malt and wheat in the markets of Brentwood and Ingatestone for a total price of £47, later bringing the same back into the markets of Romford, Chelmsford and Brentwood for

74 According to Everitt, badgers, laders, kidders and carriers only developed slowly over the century into separate commercial species: Alan Everitt, 'The Marketing of Agricultural Produce', *The Agrarian History of England and Wales. Volume IV. 1500–1640*, ed. Joan Thirsk (Cambridge, 1967), p. 553.

75 ERO, Q/SR 5–560; Q/SBa 2.

76 For examples, see ERO, Q/SBa 2/28; ERO, Q/SR 118/74; ERO, Q/SR 131/88; ERO, Q/SR 132/46; ERO, Q/SR 135/62.

77 ERO, Q/SR 146/45.

78 ERO, Q/SR 332/106, 39/9, 493/65, 449/45, 132/46.

79 ERO, Q/SR 114/66. The term forestaller was applied to people who attempted to purchase foodstuffs privately, before the market bell had been rung, usually for the purpose of resale elsewhere, particularly in London.

sale at a higher price.[80] Later, in 1696, Margaret Thorpe of Prittlewell and Sarah Dowsell of Braintree were brought to the attention of the authorities because, 'between the 17 September and ... 6 October [they] bought and engrossed in Braintree market, divers quarters of wheat'.[81] Both women were also indicted for keeping false weights in their premises at the market.[82] One 'Mrs. Day of Altoupe Rouding' proved an even more persistent offender. She was indicted for attempting to bypass Chipping Ongar market altogether 'for refusing to get her malt in the market place of Ongar and carrying it to an inn yard and [for having] sold it before the bell did ring'. On two further occasions she was prosecuted for selling wheat 'to the value of 5 seames' and a six further 'seames' of malt 'violently in an inn yard'.[83]

Women's home-based labour in the cloth trade also took them out of the house on a regular basis to collect and to deliver spinning work. Usually women collected wool from a village shop or alehouse that had been dropped off by a clothiers' servant, spun it at home and handed it back as yarn when they obtained their next supply of wool. Depositions record women delivering 'dutche worke' to clothiers' houses, as well as to shops and to inns some distance from their homes. One Saturday in 1600, for example, Bridget Barber, wife of John Barber, a husbandman of the village of Nayland, 'brought her dutchworke' to Colchester, a distance of some ten miles.[84] Women's relative freedom had disadvantages. Roads were dangerous and so whenever possible women rode or walked together in groups, transforming routine journeys into companionable social occasions. So it was that in 1619 Jane Casse, wife of a husbandman of Stapleford Tawney, 'upon a markett daye rydinge from her owne house to London to sell herr commodities was overtaken by the way by Elizabeth Lake ... and this deponent glad of her companie rode together'.[85] The mobility of women must have made them important in the exchange of information between villages and urban centres, helping us understand their role in informal local politics as carriers of news and rumour.

All sorts of work took women out of the house on a regular basis. They sold surplus produce from their gardens or their dairy to other women door-to-door.[86] Historians have also underestimated how much both agricultural and craft-based households relied on the exploitation of common rights in the

80 ERO, Q/SR 114/65. For biographical details of John Webster see Margery McIntosh, *A Community Transformed: The Manor and Liberty of Havering, 1500–1620* (Cambridge, 1991), p. 149.

81 Engrossing involved buying up wholesale corn in order to retail it or to hoard it for resale at a higher price.

82 ERO, Q/SR 491/79; ERO, Q/SR 488/35b.

83 ERO, Q/SR 349/20; ERO, Q/SR 332/106.

84 ERO, D/B5 Sb2/6, fols 9v–10; ERO, Q/SR 400/131.

85 Luke c. Rogers (1619), LMA, DL/C/226, fol. 26v.

86 Marshall c. Waylett (1631), ERO, D/AED 8, fols 49v–50.

past, and the extent to which women were responsible for this kind of work. There is abundant evidence that labouring women and the wives of small farmers spent a significant proportion of their time outside working in the fields gathering food and fuel. They also cared for pigs, cattle and sheep that they kept on common land.[87] It is also striking in the records that married women often described livestock as their own. When Jane Wennington, Alice Pulley, Martha White and Dorothy Ashely, all wives of local husbandmen and artisans, were questioned about their involvement in a dispute about enclosure of common land in Childerditch in 1603, for example, they explained that their purpose, 'was to secure *their* poore right & *ther* cattell of *there* lawfull food ... '. Bennett Turner, wife of Phillip Turner, husbandman, further demanded 'if *her* sheep were spoiled who would maintaine her children', and that '*her* sheepe were the greatest part of their maintenance'.[88]

More generally, historians have often overlooked the fact that women of a variety of social types cared for livestock out in the fields. Witnesses often mentioned maidservants and married women gossiping together while milking their cows or caring for livestock out in the fields in summer. Elizabeth Sayer, wife of Thomas Sayer of Tollesbury, remarked that she heard words of defamation spoken, 'in an evening [when she] came from milking accompanied with Margaret Gormley who helped this deponent then to mylk'.[89] Joane Browne, wife of Richard Browne of Orsett, heard Hester Ayre defame Mr Godwin's servant William Deane as she was 'walking into the feildes unto her cattle'.[90] The well-known recollection of Dorothy Osborne, describing her day to her lover, gives only a somewhat idealised view of this form of social interaction: 'I walk out into a common that lies hard by the house, where a great many young wenches keep sheep and cows, and sit in the shade singing of ballads.'[91] When questioned by authority about location, women of all social types often referred to field-names, indicating a conventional presence and familiarity with the landscape created by regular use.

Such evidence should not be misinterpreted or mistaken for an easy matter-of-fact openness. Fields could be hazardous environments for women,

87 ERO, Q/SBa 2/19; Q/SBa 2/28, 30; ERO, Q/SBa 2/58. J. M. Neeson, *Commoners, Common Right, Enclosure and Social Change in England, 1700–1820* (Cambridge, 1990); Jane Humphries, 'Enclosures, Common Rights and Women: the Proletarianisation of Families in the Late Eighteenth and Early Nineteenth Centuries', *Journal of Economic History* 50:1 (1990), 17–42; Sharpe, *Adapting to Capitalism*, pp. 11–18, 71–94; Mendelson and Crawford, *Women in Early Modern England*, pp. 256–75; Olwen Hufton, 'Women and the Family Economy in Eighteenth-century France', *French Historical Studies* 9 (1975), 1–22.

88 TNA, STAC 8/259/28.

89 German c. Dikes (1587) LMA, DL/C/213 fols 253–7.

90 Goodwin c. Deane (1628) LMA, DL/C/231 fol. 129. See also ERO, Q/SBa 2/17; ERO, Q/SBa 2/19; ERO, Q/SBa 2/31; ERO, Q/SBa 2/58; ERO, D/B5 Sb2/9 fol. 33.

91 Cited in Clark, *Working Lives of Women*, p. 57.

who had to be careful about how they used these spaces in ways that men did not.[92] Defamation evidence, for example, regularly exploited a widely held association between fields and illicit sex, as when Joane Derrick of Colchester called Sarah Chissell a whore and that 'she was in Mr. Lucas fields with half a score of men'.[93] If women mentioned fields in court testimony they had to be careful to explain why they were there and where they were going.[94] Rape was also a real risk. When, in 1649, Susan Smith, a Colchester mariner's wife, went into 'Mr John Aylett's field to gather wormes and to get some cones to make medicine for her children', she was propositioned by George Barrell and then taken to the authorities when she resisted him.[95] Similarly, it was when Elizabeth Byford was 'going into Berechurch wood to fetch a bundle of wood' that Henry Green 'cam into the wood ... pulled the bundle of her head' and sexually assaulted her.[96] Around Christmas time in 1590 a maidservant of Downham was raped by one Rice Evans, 'beinge in a ploghe felde, serving of her dames cattel'.[97] Age and status was important in this respect. Wives of well to do yeomen had more options about where they went and with whom. Young and poor women often had no choice but to go out in the fields alone early or late when it was dark to complete necessary tasks and were vulnerable to violence.

Access for poor women was further complicated by economic and social change in England in the sixteenth and seventeenth centuries as landlords vigorously defended private property and seized exclusive control of common lands. What were previously regarded as common rights to gather and to pasture began to be redefined as crimes. Women's role in protest over enclosure is well documented in the literature. Less often recognised is that their role in the economics of custom meant that they were the ones more often than not who had to face the hostility of farmers and their servants out in the fields day to day as customary access came under attack from landlords who sought to harness rents to inflation and seize exclusive control of lands. Prosecutions of women and children for petty theft of grain provide

92 Laura Gowing, '"The Freedom of the Streets": Women and Social Space, 1560–1640', *Londinopolis. Essays in the Cultural and Social History of Early Modern London*, ed. P. Griffiths and M. S. R. Jenner (Manchester, 2000), p. 19; Mendelson and Crawford, *Women in Early Modern England*, p. 211.

93 Chissell c. Derrick (1620) ERO, D/ABD 1 fol. 120.

94 For examples of illicit sex in the fields, see ERO, Q/SBa 2/59; ERO, D/B5 Sb2/9 fol. 19. For examples of insults that referred to illicit sex in the fields, see ERO, D/ACA 31fol. 85; Shuttleworth c. Cass (1698) LMA, DL/C/245 fol. 194.

95 ERO, D/B5 Sb2/9 fol. 66.

96 ERO, D/B5 Sb2/7 fol. 183.

97 W. H. Hale, *A Series of Precedents and Proceedings in Criminal Causes, Extending From the Years 1475 to 1640: Extracted From the Act Books Of The Diocese Of London*, Edinburgh 1847: intro. R. W. Dunning (Edinburgh, 1973), p. 200. For further examples of rape in winter fields, see ERO, Q/SBa 2/60; ERO, D/B5 Sb2/7 fol. 134; ERO, D/B5 Sb2/9 fol. 96v; ERO, Q/SBa 2/56.

possible evidence of struggles over entitlements to glean.[98] In August 1661, for example, Joseph Lee Webster informed the justices that:

> Being in Nettleswell Common Field where Sam. Harrison of Harlow, father in law to this informant, hath several pieces of ground, he there saw 'Liddie' Oldham on one of the said pieces which had this year wheat growing on it, which was all cut and some bound up in sheave, and some lay in 'gavels', and that he saw her take from some of the 'gavells' as they lay unbound several parcels of wheat, which he 'see' [sic] her carry unto the next piece, and then made them into 'gleans', which shee saw this informant coming towards her she conveyed into a piece of standing barley, where this informant presently found them.[99]

A Witham woman complained to the Essex justices that she was beaten by the owner of a field where she had been gleaning 'according to the custom in harvest tyme'.[100] Women were also attacked and beaten by farmers or their servants for gathering wood. Margaret Moore of Southminster died from the blows inflicted on her by a landowner who found her gathering wood.[101] In February 1636, while John Norton was 'att plough for Mr Henry Fades his master the wife of Richard Godfrey of Sawbridgeworth did meet his said master in the next field to him she having a bundle of hedgewood'. John Waylett, husbandman, 'did see Mr Fades throw some stickes of the said wood away'. Fades was brought before the justices for assault, but was found not guilty.[102] The prosecution of poor women for milking 'other men's' cows on common pasture may also have been symptomatic of struggles for customary access, generated by a growing intolerance of acts of petty pilfering during a period of transition from a moral to a market economy.[103]

In conclusion, it is clear that economic change carried disadvantages for some women that in the eighteenth century were reflected in spatial, social and economic segregation. But it is a mistake to assume that women were absent from the early modern English countryside or that women's use of the land was a static, unchanging element in an immobile, marginalised group. For many women the landscape functioned as a central category in the creation of their identity. Moreover, gendered patterns of access to and use of the land were highly variable, dynamic and evolved with as well having

98 Peter King, 'Gleaners, Farmers and the Failure of Legal Sanctions in England, 1750–1850', *Past and Present* 125:1 (1989), 116–50; James Sharpe, *Crime in Seventeenth Century England: A County Study* (Cambridge, 1983, new edn 1985), pp. 98, 99, 169–70.

99 ERO, Q/SR 390/31. See also ERO, Q/SR 417/23, 24; ERO, Q/SBa2/25.

100 ERO, Q/SBa 2/81.

101 ERO, Q/SR 395/37, 71; ERO, Q/SR 396/29, 30; ERO, Calendar Assize File ASSI 35/103/9/22; 35/105/2/15.

102 ERO, Q/SBa 2/27; ERO, Q/SR 296/17, 99.

103 ERO, Q/SBa 2/74; ERO, D/B5 Sb2/9 fol. 133.

a part to play in long-term processes of change. Rigid and static gendered spatial patterns were not mapped on to spaces. Experience was constantly shifting and was shaped by a complex combination of factors – gender, age, status, 'place', occupation, time of day, season of the year and context. Where men and women worked in early modern England was more varied than either broad theories or local studies have sometimes suggested. The range of economic circumstances of individual families, together with the pressures and opportunities generated by the changing regional economy in which they were located, meant that working arrangements could not be, and were not, organised in a single, predictable pattern. As a consequence, the organisation and use of the landscape for work was the basis for social and gender relations that were continually, contested, negotiated and reconstructed. A deeper understanding of the role of landscape in identity formation for women, and of women's contributions to the landscape, demands more research into the local contexts in which the gendered division and meaning of work was negotiated.[104]

104 Important new publications on gender and work are forthcoming from Charmian Mansell, Jane Whittle and Mark Hailwood based on their research for the Leverhulme Funded Project at the University of Exeter: *Adopting a New Methodological Approach to Early Modern Women's Work*, led by Jane Whittle. For preliminary discussions of their fascinating findings see the project website at https://earlymodernwomenswork.wordpress.com/.

2

Spinsters with Land in Early Modern England: Inheritance, Possession and Use

JUDITH SPICKSLEY

This chapter offers an analysis of the land that was held by spinsters in England from the mid-sixteenth to the end of the seventeenth century. Although our knowledge of landholding by women is increasing, there is little published work on the amount of land held by those who did not marry, even though their number, as a proportion of the population, was expanding for much of the early modern period.[1] At the same time, and because the bulk of women (at least 75 per cent) still did marry, this analysis aims to shed new light on the relationship between women and land during that period. Research so far suggests that patterns of change varied between areas and according to social and marital status. Barbara Harris claimed that even though legal devices had been developed to circumvent primogeniture and the restrictions of male tail in the late medieval period, between 1450 and 1550 'much less than 20 per cent of the land that belonged to the aristocracy descended to female heirs'.[2] Eileen Spring's provocative study of the downward slide of the heiress-at-law between 1300 and 1800 was also largely built upon evidence from aristocratic and gentry families, although she argued that her findings applied more broadly.[3]

For 'ordinary' English families the picture appears to have been only slightly better. In the village of Brigstock in Northamptonshire in the early fourteenth century, Judith Bennett found that for every four sons who conveyed or

1 E. A. Wrigley and R. S. Schofield, *The Population History of England 1541–1871: A Reconstruction* (London, 1981; Cambridge University Press paperback edition, 1993), p. 260.

2 Barbara J. Harris, *English Aristocratic Women, 1450–1550: Marriage and Family, Property and Careers* (Oxford, 2002), p. 22.

3 Eileen Spring, *Law, Land and Family: Aristocratic Inheritance in England, 1300–1800* (Chapel Hill, NC, 1993), pp. 18, 180. See also Richard Grassby, *The Business Community of Seventeenth-Century England* (Cambridge, 1995), pp. 368–70, for a discussion of merchants increasingly attempting to consolidate lands in the hands of one heir.

received lands, only one daughter did so.[4] That few single women had large amounts of land can be explained by reference to the fact that daughters tended to inherit only in default of surviving sons, and then property was generally shared between all surviving daughters; inter-vivos transfers also favoured sons.[5] At Orwell in the sixteenth and seventeenth centuries, Spufford too noted that it was uncommon for women to inherit, although possibilities did exist: they could do so in the absence of a son, or 'at the whim of an eccentric father, or even grandmother'.[6] What Spufford's work does suggest, however, is that women's ability to access land had increased in some areas by the end of the early modern period. In Willingham and Chippenham very few women's names appear as possessors of land in the sixteenth and early seventeenth centuries.[7] Though little changed in Chippenham, by the 1720s, in Willingham at least, just over a quarter of those holding between two acres and a half yardland were women.[8] This was part of a general expansion in the number of tenants who held less than half a yardland in that village in the seventeenth century, as holdings fragmented and more landholders had by-employments.[9] In fenland areas such as Willingham the possibilities offered by dairying and stock-farming meant that smaller pieces of land remained viable options, and women appear to have been among those able to take advantage of this, whether through inheritance, gift or purchase.[10]

Amy Erickson's groundbreaking 1993 work, *Women & Property in Early Modern England*, revealed a fractured geographical picture that is also reflected in the experience of spinsters, but one in which primogeniture 'did not dominate the distribution of property as a whole at an ordinary social level'.[11] There were early modern communities in which daughters received land only in the absence of sons, but testamentary practice varied across the country. Fathers from Lincolnshire and Sussex, for example, were unlikely

4 The proportion of daughters with land was very similar to the 21 per cent level of participation in the land market in Brigstock by women overall; Judith Bennett, *Women in the Medieval English Countryside: Gender and Household in Brigstock before the Plague* (Oxford, 1987), p. 81.

5 Bennett, *Women in the Medieval English Countryside*, pp. 15, 33.

6 Margaret Spufford, *Contrasting Communities: English Villagers in the Sixteenth and Seventeenth Centuries* (Stroud, 2000), p. 111.

7 Spufford, *Contrasting Communities*, pp. 67–9, 135–6. Manorial lists of landholders can be misleading, as land in many cases was sublet.

8 Spufford, *Contrasting Communities*, pp. 145–7. The women in question, of whom two were described as widows, held between four and twelve acres of mixed copy, free and (less commonly) leasehold land.

9 In Chippenham there was a move in the opposite direction in which the disappearance of the small farmer was notable. Spufford, *Contrasting Communities*, pp. 90, 148, 157.

10 For similar medieval practice see Bennett, *Women*, p. 33.

11 Amy Louise Erickson, *Women and Property in Early Modern England* (London, 1993; reprint 1997), p. 71.

to bequeath land to their daughters if they had sons, but this was not the case in Yorkshire, where partible inheritance remained the norm for much of the early modern period. Elsewhere in the Northern Province it was in many places customary to follow principles of partible inheritance, providing each child with a 'reasonable part' of their family estate.[12] In addition, most fathers appear to have adhered to principles laid down in common law, in which land descended to lineal females rather than collateral males: daughters were preferred over brothers, nephews, or grandsons.[13] This differential practice had a significant impact, carrying over into women's adult lives: Yorkshire women's wills contain far more bequests of land than those of women in more southern counties.[14]

The idea of regional and local variation in the disposition of land received further support in the work of Christine Peters and Christine Churches. There were still gender biases: Peters' work, for example, revealed that even where it was customary for daughters to inherit together as co-heirs little land appears to have been transferred to them.[15] In Christine Churches' study of the manor court books of Whitehaven in the century after 1650, it was clear that men still preferred to bequeath land to their sons. But lineal females were chosen over collateral males and, where men died intestate, the custom of the manor was that the daughter would automatically inherit.[16] There were also some notable exceptions. In Ombersley between 1485 and 1500 over half the recipients of land were female, and nearly 10 per cent of them were unmarried.[17] Churches also noticed that during the period 1660–1750 'only half of the customary tenancies were in the hands of men as sole tenants; the rest were either joint between man and wife, usually with remainders, or held by women as heirs, or as survivors of joint tenancies, or even as purchasers'.[18] The picture is thus one of gains and losses. Though post-mortem inheritance by daughters did

12 Erickson, *Women*, pp. 68–72. See also George Meriton, *The Touchstone of Wills* (1668), pp. 105–13, for the custom in the province of York. Under gavelkind in Kent, if a man died intestate his estate had to be shared between all his sons; under the custom known as ultimogeniture, or Borough English, the youngest son was endowed rather than the eldest, though he did not have to be the sole heir. Grassby, *Business Community*, pp. 109–10. See also Jeff and Nancy Cox, 'Probate 1500–1800: A System in Transition', *When Death Do Us Part: Understanding and Interpreting the Probate Records of Early Modern England*, eds Tom Arkell, Nesta Evans and Nigel Goose (Oxford, 2000), pp. 19–25.

13 Erickson, *Women and Property in Early Modern England*, p. 63.

14 Erickson, *Women and Property in Early Modern England*, pp. 61–2.

15 In the north Worcestershire manor of Halesowen between 1485 and 1560 62.5 per cent of post-mortem transfers went to sons, but only 4.2 per cent of the remaining 37.5 per cent went to daughters. Christine Peters, 'Single Women in Early Modern England: Attitudes and Expectations', *Continuity and Change* 12:3 (1997), 336.

16 Christine Churches, 'Women and Property in Early Modern England: A Case-Study', *Social History* 23:2 (1998), 173.

17 Peters, 'Single Women', 339.

18 Churches, 'Women and Property in Early Modern England', 170.

vary, and the practice was more common in some manors than others, even within manors there were significant chronological shifts in levels of female access to land.[19] Moreover, while testamentary practice continued to favour sons, daughters were, it seems, able to gain control of land.

A final important strand of research has been to examine the impact of marriage on women's property holding, since, technically, under the rules of coverture, a woman could not hold property in her own right during her marriage.[20] This strand too has kicked against the effectiveness of legal prescriptions, as work by Amy Erickson and Susan Staves, for example, has revealed the impact of marriage settlements and separate estate in undermining the *de jure* restrictions of coverture in the seventeenth century. In Erickson's probate sample at least 10 per cent of the wives of husbandman, yeomen, labourers and craftsmen sought to protect their right to property with a marriage settlement.[21] Yet the longer-term impact of separate estate remains unclear. Staves saw some women making gains in the early modern period as a result of developments in equity, and the shift in marriage agreements towards the area of contracts, but argued that such gains were transient.[22] The families of McDonagh's genteel and elite women also turned to separate estate in the eighteenth century to protect their property while married, but the fact of its existence did not always ensure that a woman had complete control over her property during her marriage.[23]

What is then clear from the historiography of women's landholding in the early modern period is the difficulty of trying to establish a singular framework for change. Women in higher wealth and status groups may well have seen their rights to land, as well as their access to it, reduced by the later seventeenth century. Lower down the social scale, there is some evidence to suggest that more women were landholders by the end of the century, although the question of their rights remains unclear. But it was not just a question of socio-economic status. Amanda Capern has argued that the shift away from common law towards the increased use of equity in the later seventeenth century had 'uneven consequences for different legal categories of women'.[24] While 'the widow's right of dower was seriously undercut . . . the use of private conveyance, especially wills, could and often did work in favour

19 Peters, 'Single Women', 337–8.

20 Amanda L. Capern, *The Historical Study of Women: England 1500–1700* (Basingstoke, 2008; paperback edn, 2010), pp. 92–4. Women retained rights to freehold land. See Amy L. Erickson, 'Coverture and Capitalism', *History Workshop Journal* 59 (Spring 2005), 3.

21 Erickson, *Women and Property in Early Modern England*, p. 150.

22 Susan Staves, *Married Women's Separate Property in England, 1660–1833* (Cambridge, MA, 1990), Conclusion (pp. 197–230).

23 Briony McDonagh, *Elite Women and the Agricultural Landscape, 1700–1830* (Abingdon, 2017), p. 22.

24 Capern, 'The Landed Woman in Early Modern England', *Parergon* 19:1 (2002), 187.

Table 1. Distribution and coverage of the documents in the spinster will sample, 1545–1700

Ecclesiastical jurisdiction	Number of spinster wills	Period covered	Number with inventories
Chester	420	1595–1700	320 [76%]
Durham	238	1611–1600	153 [64%]
Lincoln	320	1545–1700	184 [58%]
Norfolk	189	1605–1686	66 [35%]
Total	1,167		723 [62%]

of single women though in practice strict settlement was a reactionary legal tool designed to prevent female inheritance.'[25]

This chapter looks at changes in landholding by spinsters during the late sixteenth and seventeenth centuries from three different perspectives – inheritance, possession and use – in order to consider not just how many spinsters were holding land but how they came to hold, or have access, to it. It draws on two significant collections of probate documents: the wills of 1024 fathers in the Lincoln Consistory Court between 1559 and 1693; and the wills (and in some cases probate inventories) of 1167 never-married women across the four ecclesiastical jurisdictions of Chester, Durham, Lincoln and Norfolk between 1545 and 1700. The distribution and coverage of these documents is outlined in Table 1. Some additional insights are then provided by reference to the account book of Joyce Jeffreys of Hereford, a wealthy money-lending spinster. The term 'spinster' is used throughout the chapter as a synonym for a never-married woman, because it is the term that appears most frequently in the probate material; other designations include 'single woman', 'maid' and 'maiden', and 'virgin'. We cannot be absolutely sure that these women had never been married, but the absence of references to partners or children in their wills suggests this is most likely to have been the case.[26] The term 'spinster' can prove trickier when there is no surviving will, however. Emerging first as an occupational definition for women and men, by the seventeenth century the term 'spinster' had come to signal a never-married woman by dint of the availability of other appropriate terms for those who were, or had been, married: 'wife'; and 'widow'. But the term was sometimes appended to probate documents of women who appear to all intents and purposes to have been either married or widowed, and without clear evidence

25 Capern, 'Landed Women', 191.

26 Cordelia Beattie, *Medieval Single Women: The Politics of Social Classification in Late Medieval England* (Oxford, 2007), pp. 141–3.

that an occupational meaning was intended. There is evidence of its use as a legal fiction in the criminal courts, and this may also have been a feature of the probate process.[27] Cross referencing titles on wills and inventories in the Lincoln material, for example, where the two types of documents are separately indexed and filed, suggests that up to 5 per cent of those designated as 'spinsters' on their probate inventories may in fact have been women with some form of marital relationship.

If it is sometimes difficult to be categorical about the marital status of women from their probate documents, recovering the full extent of their landholding through those documents is almost impossible, since post-mortem bequests constitute only one of the ways in which land could be transferred. Deeds, another form of private instrument developed during the early modern period, were not infrequently used to transfer land, and manorial land, which had to descend according to the custom of the manor, often received no mention at all in wills.[28] Since leases were considered to be personalty in law, and were to be recorded on the probate inventory, without access to both this and the will some leased land can be missed.[29] Information on inter-vivos transfers too is limited. Occasionally these are hinted at in wills, but again they are largely unknown without access to additional records.[30] The number of transfers varied across time and place, but they could be substantial. Lloyd Bonfield suggested some time ago that nearly half of all copyholders in Preston used inter-vivos settlements to transfer land, while in Juliet Gayton's more recent work on nine Hampshire manors post-mortem transfers of land amounted to around a third of all transfers, affecting 38 per cent of land.[31]

Several other factors are relevant here. About 13 per cent of the wills that make up the spinster sample are nuncupative testaments, with the proportion varying considerably across the areas of study.[32] Because such testaments

27 I am currently working on a paper entitled 'Spinster Mothers in the Church Courts' that examines these issues. For criminal cases see Carol Z. Wiener, 'Is a Spinster an Unmarried Woman?', *American Journal of Legal History* 20 (1976), 27–31, and Valerie C. Edwards, 'The Case of the Married Spinster: An Alternative Explanation', *American Journal of Legal History* 21 (1977), 260–5.

28 Churches, 'Women and Property in Early Modern England', 168.

29 Leases for lives in the early modern period were regarded as a form of real estate, but those for years as a part of personal estate; these were then recorded on the inventory. Jeff and Nancy Cox, 'Probate 1500–1800', 32.

30 Erickson, *Women and Property in Early Modern England*, p. 67.

31 Cited in Richard Adair, *Courtship, Illegitimacy and Marriage in Early Modern England* (Manchester, 1996), p. 116; Juliet Gayton, 'Tenants, Tenures and Transfers: The Landholding Experiences of Rural Customary Tenants in some Hampshire Downland Manors, 1645–1705' (PhD diss., University of Exeter, 2013), p. 101.

32 The highest proportion was in the Lincoln group, where 16 per cent of the wills were nuncupative. The figures for Chester and Durham were 8 and 15 per cent respectively. No

were not supposed to be used to transfer land, even though these transfers are occasionally found there, a greater proportion of nuncupative documents in one area will affect the usefulness of the comparison.[33] Wills rarely give evidence of age, but this too affects the value of any analysis of landholding. Although lands were bequeathed to children under twenty-one, they were often entrusted to adults while the children were minors, and lands could not be devised by anyone under that age.[34] Thomas Segrave of Helpringham noted on his will, for example, that he was renting both land and money from his late wife's daughter Rebecca Bell, who was at that point still in her minority.[35] There is also the question of reversion. If a spinster had been granted land only while she was living, she may have felt no need to mention the disposal of the land in her will.[36] For all these reasons, landholding, as evidenced in the wills and testaments of this study, is likely to represent the bare minimum of that which existed in actuality.

Nor is this analysis likely to be directly comparable with others undertaken so far. Studies of landholding tend to assume the reader knows what is meant by 'land', and give no description of what their particular definition entails. Here the broadest possible definition of 'land' has been adopted, from both a tenurial and agricultural perspective. This extends to the usual mentions of leased, freehold and copyhold land, and the more unusual charterhold and tenant right, as well as arable, pasture and meadow. Although there were examples of bequests of corn or hay or ploughing gear – which imply access to arable or meadow land – the women in question have not been included as landholders unless there was in addition a specific reference to land. But the definition does cover what may not normally be accounted; references to orchards, gardens, a close, a garth, a croft and commons, along with any other small parcels of land, made it into the analysis. Putting an accurate numerical value on the amount of land an individual testator held is not always possible, however: bequests of unspecified 'land' or 'lands' without accompanying quantification are not unusual in the documents.

nuncupative documents were recorded for Norfolk.

33 At least two examples are included in the Lincoln sample: Lincoln Archives (hereafter LA), Stow Wills 1664–5/10 Ann Parkinson, Burringham, 1664 [cottage and croft]; and LA, DC Wills 16/71 Ann Brown, the Castle, Lincoln, 1689 [lands in Pinchbeck].

34 William West, *Symbolaeography: which may be termed the art, description or image of instruments* (London, 1592), sect. 676.

35 He owed her £24 in cash, in addition to a further £18 12s, part of which was 'Statute rent & parte for land I hier of her'; his executor was to repay her in full when she reached twenty-one, 'with the use thereof'. LA, LCC Wills 1631/346 Thomas Segrave, yeoman, Helpringham, 1631.

36 See, for example, Durham University Library (hereafter DUL), DPRI/1/1638/M4 Elizabeth Marshall, Haydon, Northumberland, 1638.

Inheritance

Patterns in the inheritance of land appear to have been laid down in the medieval period, shortly after the Norman Conquest. Through primogeniture, developed in the eleventh and twelfth centuries, the bulk of any transferrable land was devolved to the eldest son.[37] This was not just an English phenomenon. According to Merry Wiesner, 'most areas of Europe passed laws which either established primogeniture ... or favoured sons over daughters' from the thirteenth century onwards, although the motives for this were not the same everywhere.[38] But while the English common law gave preference to eldest males, this preference was limited: in the absence of sons land was to descend to the eldest daughter, and not any collateral males.[39] From the 1130s parents without sons began to move away from the idea of primogeniture for the eldest daughter, and divided their lands between surviving daughters, possibly as a result of a royal decision referenced in a charter of 1145. This practice continued for the remainder of the Middle Ages.[40]

By the beginning of the early modern period, when most individuals died without making a will, primogeniture, according to common, but not all customary, law, was the default position. Increasingly, however, private conveyancing – through a variety of legal contracts, including wills – could override the common law. The transfer of manorial land according to the customs of the manor was incorporated into common law in the later seventeenth century.[41] This tempering of common law by private law and customary practice may not always have been beneficial for daughters as a group. Recognised by the early modern period as normal practice, co-parceny may have operated to distribute land to a greater number of daughters, but at the same time depressed the amount of family land any one daughter could inherit.[42] This must have undermined the utility of the land as a productive investment, especially in arable areas. In addition, strict settlement, developed through wills and marriage arrangements and recognised in common law by the end of the seventeenth century, saw daughters bypassed in favour of nephews and male kin, as well as brothers.[43]

37 Spring, *Law*, p. 9; Erickson, *Women and Property in Early Modern England*, pp. 26–7.

38 Merry E. Wiesner, *Women and Gender in Early Modern Europe* (Cambridge, 1993), p. 108.

39 Spring, *Law*, pp. 9–10; Erickson, *Women and Property in Early Modern England*, pp. 26–7.

40 Jennifer Ward (tr. and ed.), *Women of the English Nobility and Gentry 1066–1500* (Manchester, 1995), pp. 87–8.

41 Capern, *Historical*, pp. 121–3; Churches, 'Women and Property in Early Modern England', 167.

42 John Page, *Jus Fratrum, The Law of Brethren* (1657), p. 67.

43 Spring, *Law, Land and Family*, chapter 5. Families of lesser gentry status adopted strict settlement from the 1660s, and by the 1680s it was the choice for over 60 per cent of such families in Kent and Northamptonshire. The 'mechanics of the strict settlement' were incorporated into common law in 1697. Lloyd Bonfield, *Marriage Settlements, 1601–1740: The Adoption of the*

The number of daughters who received land from their fathers in the Lincoln diocese between 1559 and 1693 was not large.[44] It was most common for legacies to girls to take the form of household goods, livestock or cash, with cash growing in popularity and livestock and household goods declining from the late sixteenth to the late seventeenth centuries.[45] Where sons were present, fathers often appear to have balanced land with moveables and shared out their estates as equitably as possible given the difficulties involved.[46] Daughters tended to be granted portions that were to be paid out of the family lands, often within a stipulated period; occasionally they received annuities.[47] That sons did not necessarily do better is confirmed by an analysis of the relative value of livestock, chattels and real estate: the cash value of land and goods remained in close parallel until the mid-eighteenth century.[48] Nevertheless, the symbolic significance of land remained high throughout the early modern period, and it constituted a valuable investment tool.

If we look first at eldest daughters, there are seventy-seven cases (8 per cent) in which fathers left their daughters some amount of land. In at least twenty-four of those cases sons were also in evidence, and also in receipt of land, in some cases of the bulk of it.[49] William Bunworthe, a gentleman from Barkston, allowed his daughter the benefit and profit of two gorse closes for four years as her portion, and his wife the same for a further three years,

Strict Settlement (Cambridge, 1983), pp. 84, 90–92. Where daughters did get land there was a further trend in inheritance practices that assisted them in gaining access to it as spinsters. This involved the shift away from the use of singular to bilateral marital restrictions in which fathers allowed daughters to access their portions at a given age or marriage rather than marriage alone. See Judith Spicksley, 'Usury Legislation, Cash and Credit: The Development of the Female Investor in the late Tudor and Stuart Periods', *Economic History Review* 61:2 (2008), 291–4.

44 Fathers may have attempted to secure access to land for their daughters through marriage. Thomas Blakye had an agreement with his future son in law that the latter would renew the lease of his farm in Blakye's daughter's name on receipt of her portion, if she were to survive him. See DUL, DPRI/1/1630/B3 Thomas Blakye, yeoman, Kelloe, County Durham, 1630.

45 See Spicksley, 'Usury Legislation', for an analysis of this change.

46 Erickson, *Women and Property in Early Modern England*, pp. 68–78; Spicksley, 'Usury Legislation', 298.

47 See, for example, LA, LCC Wills 1601/ii/98 Thomas Staplo, yeoman, Tempsford, Bedford, 1597, whose daughter Elizabeth was to receive an annuity of 40s when her brother came into his lands, in addition to her £20 portion; and LA, LCC Wills 1601/i/84 John Larkes, yeoman, Leake, whose arrangements for his wife's possible pregnancy included an annuity of £10 per year for the child if male and £6 if female during his wife's life once either had reached fourteen.

48 Erickson, *Women and Property in Early Modern England*, pp. 64–6.

49 Wrigley suggested that in a stable population there was a 20 per cent chance that a family would have no male heir, a 20 per cent chance that a family would have a female heir or heirs, and a 60 per cent chance that the family would have at least one male heir. In a population growing at a rate of around 1 per cent, comparable with England in the Elizabethan period and in the eighteenth century, 32 per cent of families would have no sons surviving. Wrigley, 'Fertility Strategy for the Individual and the Group', *Historical Studies of Changing Fertility*, ed. Charles Tilly (Princeton, NJ, 1978), pp. 137–9, 150–1.

plus a third of his lands, but his son Thomas was to have the reversion and the remainder 'according as the Lawes of our Land doth cast them upon him'.[50] There were occasional cases in which lower-status fathers mimicked the behaviour of those higher up the social order, as they sought to preserve their patrimony. Edmund, son and heir of Edmund Robertson, a husbandman from Kimbolton in Huntingdon, received all his father's lands and tenements at the expense of his four sisters.[51] Gender biases are sometimes clearest in relation to children in waiting. Richard Allen of Benington left his unborn child – if male – four oxgangs of copyhold 'from my owne Auncestors to me desendinge'.[52] George Emerson, a butcher from Brigg, was quite insistent that his lands were to descend only to his sons, and in the event none survived, 'unto the next heires male of my kin lawfully begotten'.[53] Keeping land in the family name could be important. Thomas Mawmill, a husbandman from Fotherby, made the following plea in his will: 'that the lease of my farme shall not goe oute of the name of Mawmills during the yeares of the whole lease'.[54] Occasionally girls were preferred over boys. Sometimes this was the result of manorial rules: John Robertson alias Robinson the younger, a husbandman from Newton in Kimbolton, left his copyhold land to his wife during Agnes, his daughter's, minority, but instructed that at twenty-one it transfer to her as the custom of the manor dictated.[55] In other instances particular family circumstances must have driven a father's priorities. Martin Cooke of Trusthorpe left his daughter Alice the lease of his farm for the years yet to come; only if she died in her minority were her brothers to inherit.[56] It was also possible that daughters would have gained access to land as a result of a contingent remainder, added by a parent to a will to ensure payment of the girls' portions. These were rare in the Lincoln will sample, probably because – at least in part – they ran counter to cultural views on women and landholding. But when Henry Dance made his will in 1601 he clearly felt such a step was necessary. He left his son Nicholas the right of his lease, a significant amount of livestock, ploughing gear, some grains and beans and a bed; the remainder went to Nicolas' three sisters as joint executors. Henry instructed that they were to provide Nicolas with what he might need for his

50 LA, LCC Wills 1631/96 William Bunworthe, gentleman, Barkston, 1631.

51 LA, LCC Wills 1571/218v Edmund Robertson, husbandman, Kimbolton in Huntingdon, 1571/2.

52 LA, LCC Wills 1604/i/15 Richard Allen, yeoman, Benington, 1604[?].

53 LA, LCC Wills 1601/i/23v George Emerson, butcher, Brigg, 1601.

54 LA, LCC Wills 1601/i/103v Thomas Mawmill, husbandman, Fotherby, 1600.

55 LA, LCC Wills 1571/10v John Robertson alias Robinson, husbandman, Newton in Kimbolton, Huntingdon, 1571.

56 LA, LCC Wills 1570/42v Martine Cooke, Trusthorpe, 1569/70.

meat and drink, but he was to allow them to enter and take their corn; if he failed to do so the will became void, and everything went to his sisters.[57]

Co-parceny, if applied occasionally amongst sons, was a much more recognised if not overriding influence amongst daughters, especially where no son was present (although, given the laconic nature of much of the detail about land, this is difficult to evidence).[58] John Knight, a yeoman from Swineshead, left his lands and tenements to his wife until his only daughter Elizabeth was eighteen, but he added the following contingent remainder: if his wife was with child, and the child was male, then he was to inherit alone; if female, the daughters were to share the land.[59] Of those men who left land to their eldest daughter, only twenty-six (34 per cent) referenced a second daughter, and in seventeen (65 per cent) of those cases she also received some amount of land; as to the remainder, two received property, six cash and one shared the household goods with her mother. That there are examples in which preference was given to the eldest daughter indicates that, for some parents, ideas about birth order were important in driving inheritance practices for daughters as well as sons.[60] But other fathers, such as the yeoman John Larkes of Leake, managed to divide their lands almost exactly: Mary the eldest, got twenty-five acres; and Susan her younger sister just short of twenty-four.[61] Robert Wyntor of Grimoldby, who had three daughters, gave each of them half an acre of wheat and up to an acre of beans (although the bequests of land to his three sons appear to have been determined by their birth positions, with the eldest gaining the most).[62] Nevertheless, that the overall picture is one in which co-parceny dominates is clear from Figure 1 below. If in 8 per cent of cases eldest daughters were in receipt of land, for second daughters the figure is only slightly lower, at 6 per cent.

Second daughters may not have been in receipt of exactly the same amount as their elder siblings, but they certainly did not appear to get a raw deal. Splitting the analysis into two periods – the first up to and including 1640 and the second after 1640 – provides additional insights. Second daughters may have been passed over by fathers more often before 1640 in relation to land transfer, but by the later seventeenth century this imbalance has disappeared. In addition, and though there was no dramatic fall, bequests of land to daughters were diminishing somewhat after 1640.

57 LA, LCC Wills 1601/ii/24v Henry Dance, Stainton near Langworth, 1601.

58 Sometimes this might involve the sale of the land so that it could be shared out. LA, LCC Wills 1569/i/10 Robarte Buttrie, Cawthorpe, 1569; and LA, LCC Wills 1571/i/8v John Jogin, Needingworth, Holywell, 1570.

59 LA, LCC Wills 1604/i/97v John Knight, yeoman, Swineshead, 1603.

60 For birth order and sons see Susan E. James, *Women's Voices in Tudor Wills, 1485–1603* (Farnham, 2015), pp. 165–6.

61 LA, LCC Wills 1601/i/84 John Larkes, yeoman, Leake, 1600.

62 LA, LCC Wills 1601/i/85 Robert Wyntor, yeoman, Grimoldby, 1597/8.

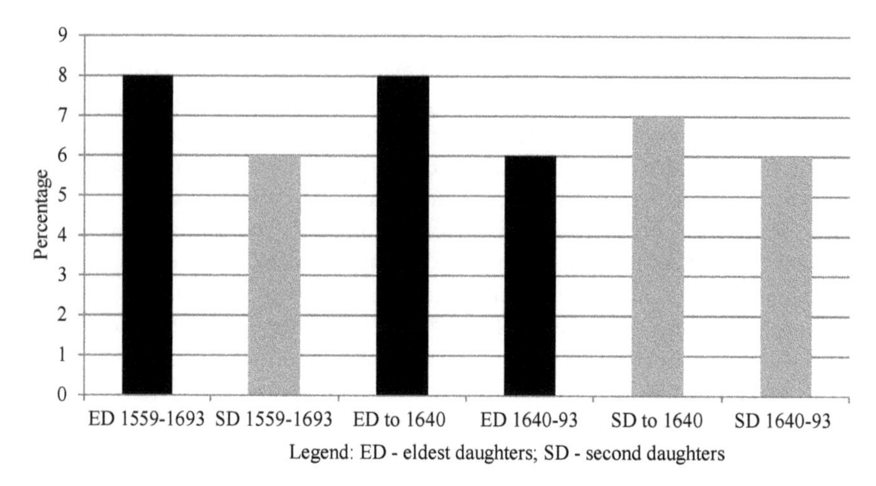

Figure 1. Bequests of land to daughters by Lincoln fathers, 1559–1693

Possession

The second part of this chapter looks at the possession of land by spinsters. The amount of land held by testators was not always clearly outlined in their documents. Bequests of small amounts of land – usually around five acres or less, and often with a cottage or dwelling – were commonly enumerated, but descriptions of larger holdings, frequently attached to messuages, tenements or farms, give little idea of overall acreage. Yet a number of spinsters, such as Frances Buckley of Cheadle in Cheshire, do appear to have held considerable amounts of land: her will recorded her possession of three manors in 1688.[63] At least twenty-two spinsters across the whole sample referred to messuages with lands, including Mary Foster of Bayfield and Wiveton in Norfolk, whose portfolio of lands in mixed tenure – free, copy and charterhold – is suggestive of a substantial holding.[64] Others, like Dorothy Edmonds of Saxthorpe in Norfolk in 1644, and Margaret Marshland of Bosden in Cheshire in 1610, held farms, with Mary Dowdswell of East Randall in Lincolnshire mentioning two, named in her will as Wiltons farm and Dannetts farm.[65]

In terms of *how many* spinsters were in possession of land, rather than *how much* land they held, the answer is relatively few. Figure 2 displays the levels of landholding by spinsters across the four ecclesiastical jurisdictions in

63 Chester Record Office (hereafter CRO), EDA2/3 Francis Buckley, Cheadle, 1688.

64 Norfolk Record Office (hereafter NRO), Tennant 28 Mary Foster, Bayfield and Wiveton, Norfolk, 1660.

65 NRO, Amy 127 Dorothy Edmonds, Saxthorpe, 1644; CRO, WS 1610 Margaret Marshland, Bosden, 1610; LA, LCC Wills 1683/ii/144 Mary Dowdswell, East Randall, 1683.

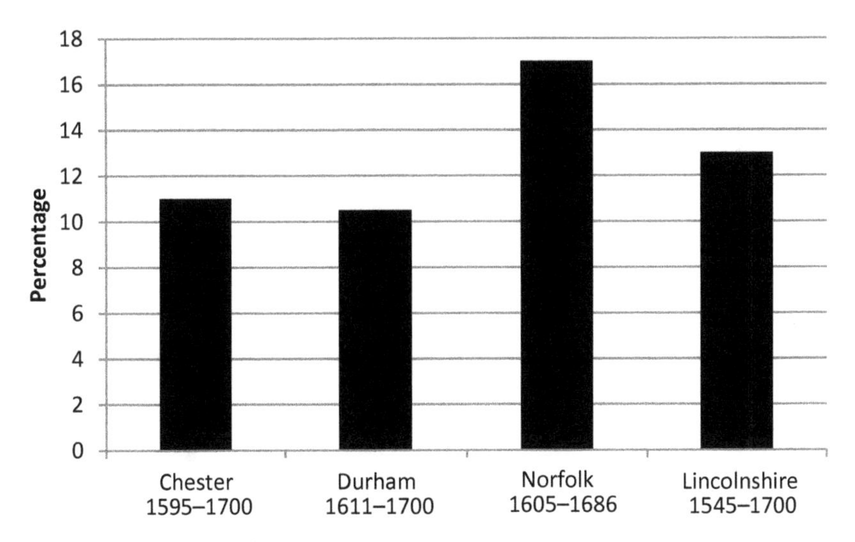

Figure 2. Landholding by spinsters, 1545–1700

question for the period from 1545 to 1700.[66] Overall, wills from Norfolk and Lincoln, with important arable interests, showed the highest levels, at 17 and 13 per cent respectively, while the more pastoral economies of Chester and Durham saw lower levels of around 11 per cent.[67] But this pattern of higher levels of landholding in Norfolk and Lincoln were to a considerable extent the result of gains made in the later seventeenth century, when both arable and pastoral farming was undergoing consolidation.[68]

Prior to 1640, levels of landholding were highest in the Chester sample, at 11 per cent, followed by Norfolk and Lincoln at 9 per cent and Durham at 7 per cent. After 1640 levels in Chester remained at 11 per cent, while in Durham landholders now constituted 12 per cent of the probate sample and in Norfolk and Lincoln 24 and 21 per cent respectively. Because the number of landholders is small the significance of the findings is limited. Nevertheless, it is useful to consider what might have been driving differential changes in

66 It was not possible to achieve exact chronological comparison across all jurisdictions because of different survival rates and indexing tools; coverage is indicated in Figure 2.
67 Probate records for bachelors in three of the jurisdictions indicate their relatively higher levels of access: Chester 17 per cent; Norfolk 27 per cent; Lincoln 23 per cent (this sample relies on inventories only). For the character of farming regions see Joan Thirsk (ed.), *The Agrarian History of England and Wales Volume IV 1500–1640* (Cambridge, 1967), pp. 16–49, 80–9.
68 Capern found a rise in the proportion of women holding leases on the Jervaux estate in North Yorkshire after 1700. See Amanda L. Capern, 'Women, Land and Family in Early-Modern North Yorkshire', Economic History Society Conference Paper, available at www.ehs.org.uk/dotAsset/404abd64-cbb1–459c-a2ff-7d7806f9681f.doc, accessed 5 June 2018.

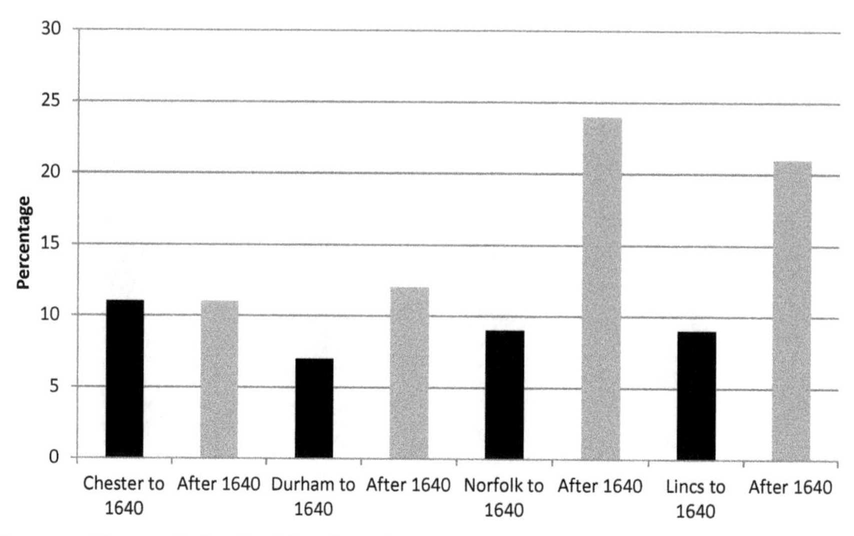

Figure 3. Changes in landholding by spinsters, 1545–1700

the levels of landholding after 1640. We know in the case of Lincoln, at least, that it was not the result of testamentary practice; nor can it be explained by reference to the untimely demise of male siblings, although this would always have been a factor in facilitating daughters' access to land.[69] What, then, do spinsters' own probate records tell us about their opportunities to gain land through the remaining two categories of non-parental gift and purchase?

If we begin with the will of Joyce Jeffreys, her large landholding legacy looks somewhat remarkable given that none of it appears to have come from her parents. This extended to 'messuages, burgages, cottages, gardens, orchards, lands, tenements, rents, revercions and hereditaments whatsoever, scituate, lyeing and being in Hereford, Holmer, Withington, Sutton, Marden als Mawarden, Bodenham, Warton, Newton, Brierley, Broadward and Leominster in the county of Hereford or elsewhere with and singular their and every of their appurtenances'.[70] The earliest of her properties that we are aware of are those she acquired from her step-brother, Humphrey Coningsby, in the 1610s; he left her his interest 'in leases of houses, stables, Gardaines and other commodities whatsoever in or within Five miles of London'.[71]

69 See, for example, LA, LCC Wills 1601/i/18 John Torey, labourer, Panton, 1601[?], whose closes and lands were to go to his daughter Agnes if his son William died; LA, LCC Wills 1601/ii/123 John Tinckler, husbandman, Saleby, 1601, whose daughters were to share his property and lands in the event of his son's death; and LA, LCC Wills 1604/i/72 William Elsye, yeoman, Kirton in Holland, whose daughter was only to get any land if her brothers died, 1604[?].

70 The National Archives (hereafter TNA) PROB 11/24, will of Joyce Jeffreys [Jefferies].

71 TNA, PROB 11/129/796, will of Humphrey Coningsby.

She also held the title to a farm or capital messuage called Fernolls, which, according to his will, Sir Thomas Coningsby had purchased from her some time before September 1617.[72] Other spinsters' documents tell similar stories. Like Joyce, Mary Riley of Welbourn, Lincolnshire, benefited from the actions of her wider kin network; according to her will of 1675 she had received a gift of five acres of land and pasture from her grandmother; Elizabeth Nicholl of Great Yarmouth in Norfolk had inherited land from her grandfather; and Mary Foster, in the same county, mentioned above, had received land from her uncle.[73] Others were endowed by friends or neighbours, some of whom may have been lovers. The will of Frances Salmon of Carlton Scroop in Lincolnshire in 1678 referred to the twenty acres of land that she had lately inherited from Anthony Barker, deceased.[74]

Spinster wills also provide examples of gifts of land to other women. Mary Crickmer of Hoxne in Suffolk left her sister all but four acres of her land, for example, with the remaining part going to her kinswoman Elizabeth Chapman at twenty-one.[75] Isabell Wright of Norton, County Durham, left her lands in Stockton in 1670 to Elizabeth Winch, daughter of Robert, when she reached the age of twenty-one, and in 1693 Rachel Ellenworth of Wootton left her three acres of arable land in Barton upon Humber to her mother Rachel in perpetuity.[76] Even servants were occasional beneficiaries: Ann Maland of Durham city left her servant Margaret Arrowsmith all her real property in 1693, including her gardens in Elvet, her shop on Elvet Bridge and a range of houses and tenements.[77] Yet spinsters could not entirely escape the weight of custom and law that gendered the transfer of land. Jane Done of Utkinton in Cheshire, for example, left instructions that £200 was to be laid out in land to provide cash sums for the eldest sons or if none, the eldest daughters, of 'the poorer sort of Inhabitants of Utkington'.[78] And even when land was devised to women it was not infrequently gifted on a temporary basis, reverting back to male beneficiaries in the longer term.[79] There were exceptions. Ann Dinnin left her close to her brother John Person in 1697, for example, with instructions that it revert to Elizabeth Person, the daughter of

72 TNA, PROB 11/148/530, will of Thomas Coningsby.

73 LA, LCC Wills 1675/120 Mary Riley, Welbourn, 1675; NRO, Smythe 65 Elizabeth Nicholl, Great Yarmouth 1638; NRO, Ten 28 Mary Foster, Bayfield and Wiveton, 1660.

74 LA, LCC Wills 1678/380 Frances Salmon, Carlton Scroop 1678[?].

75 NRO, Amy 81 Mary Crickmer, Hoxne, Suffolk, 1643.

76 DUL, DPRI/1/1675/W53 Isabell Wright, Norton, County Durham, 1670; LA, LCC Wills 1695–6/ii/457 Rachel Ellenworth, Wootton, 1670.

77 DUL, DPRI/1/1693/M2 Ann Maland, Old Elvet, Durham City, 1693.

78 CRO, EDA2/3 Jane Done, Utkinton, 1662.

79 Bequests of land to men who do not appear to have been kin may have been intended spouses. See, for example, NRO, Ald 139, Luce Mancer, King's Lynn, 1670, who left her three acres of land and the remainder of her estate to Francis Sporne, single man.

Charles, after his death.[80] But if the practices surrounding the bequeathing of land often appear to reflect received notions of gender propriety, without additional information it is difficult to extrapolate such ideas from the role of personal relationships. Joyce Jeffreys was a wealthy elderly spinster and money-lender who had accumulated a substantial amount of land and property by the end of her life; she chose to bequeath it to her 'beloved and well deserveing nephew' William Jeffreys in 1648.[81] The picture is complicated by regional variations. Of the beneficiaries given in the Durham and Chester samples, land appears to have been divided pretty evenly between male and female recipients in the seventeenth century; in the Lincoln and Norfolk samples, however, only around a third of those receiving land were female. Indeed, brothers and nephews were the most common recipients of land overall. Sisters, mothers and nieces also appear regularly as recipients of land, along with aunts and other kinswomen, if not always as heirs in perpetuity.[82]

Evidence of spinsters involved in the purchase, lease or rent of land is also a feature of the surviving documents, although comments like those of Joane Browne, in which she refers to the 'one acre of free and coppiehold land' that she had 'lately purchased' remain rare.[83] A further option was to lease or rent land. Twenty-four spinsters mentioned leases in their wills, including Jane Pacye of Thurlby, in Lincolnshire, who held four acres of meadow from John Cooke and bequeathed 'two yeares profit & Comoditie' from the land to her niece Anne in 1600.[84] Although details about the length and value of leases were usually minimal, those held in Durham provide an informative exception. Dorothy Gray of Berwick upon Tweed held the lease of a manor and demesne valued at £300 in 1631, while in 1635 Anne Vepond of Alston in Cumberland held a third part of a lease for three years after the death of Margaret Vepond, valued at £15; in Elwick in 1673 Katherine Hudlestone's lease – valued at £400 – had another forty years to run; finally Mary Lax of Barnard Castle left her sisters Jane Lax and Margaret Newby the fifth part of one fourth part of the lands belonging to the hospital of St John the Baptist there, the lease having a ninety-year term worth £7.[85] However, only Gray

80 DUL, DPRI/1/1687/D9 Ann Dinnin, Bowes, Yorkshire and South Shields, County Durham, 1697.

81 TNA, PROB 11/24, will of Joyce Jeffreys [Jefferies].

82 Under canon law, the estates of spinsters dying intestate were distributed equally between their siblings. Jeff and Nancy Cox, 'Probate 1500–1800', p. 20.

83 LA, LCC Wills 1681/ii/582 Joane Browne, Hanthorpe in Morton, 1681[?]. See also NRO, Spend 233 Bettrise Palling, Rollesby, who noted in 1636 that she had bought copyhold land from her brother Simon. Joyce Jeffreys bought fifteen acres of grange land near Leominster from William Wanklin sometime before 1638. Judith Spicksley (ed.), *The Business and Household Accounts of Joyce Jeffreys, Spinster of Hereford, 1638–1648* (Oxford, 2012), p. 158.

84 LA, DC Wills 4/27 Jane Pacye, Thurlby 1600.

85 DUL, DPRI/1/1631/G2 Dorothy Gray, Berwick on Tweed, 1631; DPRI/1/1635/V2 Anne Vepond, Alston, Cumberland 1635; DUL, DPRI/1/1673/H25 Katherine Hudlestone, Elwick,

and Vepond listed livestock in their wills, suggesting that landholding by the later seventeenth century may have been more clearly orientated towards rental income than access to pasture. The proportion of pasture land held by spinsters relative to other types of land is difficult to establish from the will references, but it was clearly in evidence. Although the counties with the highest number of leases recorded were the pastoral areas of Chester and Durham, this is likely to be a function of the documents rather than a real correlation. Leases, as forms of personal property, had to be listed on inventories, and a higher percentage of the wills in these samples has accompanying inventories; in addition, no more than half of the leaseholders in either county recorded any form of livestock.[86] Joyce Jeffreys' accounts, too, reveal that she held pastures in Ewe Withington in the 1630s and 1640s, rented for £14 per year. But, like other spinsters, Joyce did not work all her pasture land herself: she was subletting one of the two Ewe Withington pastures to a local widow, Widow Smith, for the sum of £6 a year.[87] Similar examples in the spinster sample include Mary Riley of Welbourn in Lincolnshire, whose five acres of land and pasture, bequeathed to her brother Anthony in 1678, were at the time of her death in the tenure of Robert Clarke; and Alyse Sherife of Coleby, who left the one half oxgang of land that was in the possession of William Tindall to her nephew, Anthonie Winckle.[88] Gardens could also bring in income. In 1699 Isabel Bulman of Newcastle left her brother Thomas the two-thirds part of her garden that was currently in the occupation of Nicholas Ridley.[89]

The probate collection reveals a further way in which spinsters had access to land: through their moneylending activities. The expansion of interest-bearing lending during the seventeenth century, and more especially after mid-century, provided an unexpected route to landholding for some women, either temporarily as a form of security or permanently as a result of default.[90] In English common law the pledging of land for a debt had originally allowed the pledgee possession of the land until the debt had been repaid. In practice, by the seventeenth century, the pledger or mortgagor appears increasingly to have been able to retain possession, assisted by the

1666 (inventory, 1673); DUL, DPRI/1/1684/L2 Mary Lax, Barnard Castle, 1682/3.

86 For the proportions of testators with inventories in each diocese see Table 1. In the Chester sample fifteen spinsters made a reference to a lease but only six to livestock.

87 Spicksley (ed.), *Business*, p. 18.

88 LA, LCC Wills 1675/120 Mary Riley, Welbourn, 1675; LA, LCC Wills1675/97 Alyse Sherife, Coleby, 1674.

89 DUL, DPRI/1/1699/B11 Isabel Bulman, Newcastle, 1699.

90 Spicksley, '"Fly with a duck in thy mouth": Single Women as Sources of Credit in Seventeenth Century England', *Social History* 32:2 (May 2007), 191–3.

growth of equitable remedies.[91] Most spinsters were lending relatively small amounts of capital and, without the resources to work and maintain land, may well have avoided this particular form of security; certainly, bills and bonds were the most common instruments in evidence.[92] Nevertheless, some did hold mortgages, and more especially in the later seventeenth century. Joyce's accounts, for example, reveal that she held several mortgages through the 1630s and 1640s, and that some of the land she held was directly related to her credit activities. In 1638, when her accounts open, she was in possession of three farms on the periphery of Hereford: Broadward and Wharton to the north; and the Free Town estate, to the east. Only the Free Town farm seems to have been unrelated to her lending. Joyce also held pasture land at Brookend in Oxfordshire by way of security for a loan of £200 owed by her cousin Edmund Ansley, and added around another thirty acres to her portfolio during the period of the accounts. The first and largest part of this, twenty-four acres of mortgaged land in Sutton that James Dudson had forfeited to her, she began paying rent for at Michaelmas in 1640. Then in March 1647 Philip Wallis, having defaulted on his mortgage, surrendered five acres of tilled land in Holmer to her.[93]

Amongst the spinster collection several women were in possession of a mortgage, all in the latter part of the seventeenth century. Not all were clearly charged on land. In the Durham sample, the wills of Mary Freville and Alice Wilkinson in the final decade of the century simply referred to a mortgage, while in the Isle of Axholme Ann Woode's will of 1658 included a house that she held on a ten-year mortgage, three years of which remained outstanding.[94] Alice Dale of Fallibroome in Cheshire appears to have had a charge on part or all of a building, since she referred in 1677 to an interest 'by Specialties in and unto, a Certaine tenement or parte thereof' that was to go to her niece.[95] Of those who did hold a mortgage on land, Joane Browne of Hanthorpe in Morton, minor gentry like Joyce, was in possession of a close and two acres

91 Harold J. Berman, *Law and Revolution, II: The Impact of the Protestant Reformations on the Western Legal Tradition* (Cambridge, MA, 2003), pp. 336–7. The trend towards equity of redemption assisted families wishing to retain possession of key family estates, and may in part have emerged from it. For a discussion of the equity of redemption see David Sugarman and Ronnie Warrington, 'Land Law, Citizenship, and the Invention of "Englishness": The Strange World of the Equity of Redemption', *Early Modern Conceptions of Property*, eds John Brewer and Susan Staves (London, 1995), pp. 113–19; H. L. E. Verhagen, 'Ius Honorarium, Equity and Real Security: Parallel Lines of Legal Development', *Law & Equity: Approaches in Roman Law and Common Law*, eds E. Koops and W. J. Zwalve (Leiden, 2014), p. 151.

92 Spicksley, '"Fly with a duck"', 195–6.

93 Spicksley (ed.), *Business and Household Accounts of Joyce Jeffreys*, pp. 17–18 and fn 78.

94 DUL, DPRI/1/1700/F7 Mary Freville, South Biddick, County Durham, 1690/1; DUL, DPRI/1/1692/W17 Alice Wilkinson, Old Elvet, Durham City, 1691; LA, Stow Wills 1660–3/46 Anne Woode, Graiselound in Haxey, 1658.

95 CRO, WS 1677 Alice Dale, Fallibroome, 1677.

in 1681 by virtue of a £60 mortgage held of her brother William Browne, on which she noted that no interest had ever been paid.[96] Elizabeth Caton of Syleham in Suffolk held lands mortgaged to her brother, James, in 1675, while Elizabeth Cokler of Norwich held 'bills, bonds, and Mortgadges' to the value of £420, according to her inventory, in 1670.[97] If the holding of a mortgage on land appears unusual amongst spinsters in the jurisdictions here, in other areas this was not always the case: in the five Hampshire manors studied by Juliet Gayton between 1644 and 1705 twenty out of 190, or 11 per cent of lenders, were spinsters.[98] The use of statute staple to secure debt, employed on at least one occasion by Joyce, also gave spinsters the right to enter as a tenant on lands until overdue debts were repaid.[99]

Use

A final and more puzzling aspect of spinsters' access to land relates to their livestock holdings. The probate documents in the four jurisdictions reveal that references to livestock in every area except Norfolk far exceeded possession of land. Since the Norfolk sample contained the lowest proportion of probate inventories it is possible that this was adversely affecting the results. But a further analysis that used only the cases where both a will and inventory were available, though it raised the levels of livestock holding, did not significantly alter the pattern.

This poses an interesting conundrum for our discussion of spinsters and land, for some had a significant amount of livestock. Take Katherine Gilding of Osbornby, for example, who in 1609 bequeathed a total of thirty-six sheep in her will; or Margaret Wright of Walworth, Heighington, who was in possession of eighty-one sheep, nine horses, thirty-three cattle and ten oxen in 1696.[100] How, then, were spinsters pasturing their livestock? At least four possibilities present themselves. First, where there was a relatively large amount of livestock, it seems most likely that testators were in fact holding land but for some reason had not alluded to it in their wills. Second, it appears that a number of spinsters were involved in what might be termed micro-rentals, their livestock being pastured with employers, relatives or friends, presumably for some agreed compensation; what the cost of this arrangement had been, however, is rarely apparent. Sometimes this pasturing

96 LA, LCC Wills 1681/ii/582 Joane Browne, Hanthorpe in Morton, 1681[?].

97 NRO, WISE 156 Elizabeth Caton, Syleham, Suffolk, 1675; NRO, INV 56/78 Mary Cokler, Norwich, 1670.

98 See Gayton, 'Tenants', pp. 235–6.

99 John Baker, *The Oxford History of the Laws of England Volume VI 1483–1558* (Oxford, 2003), p. 707; Spicksley (ed.), *Business*, pp. 28–9.

100 LA, LCC Wills 1609/i/432 Katherine Gilding, Osbornby, 1609; DUL, DPRI/1/1696/W25 Margaret Wright, Walworth, Heighington, County Durham, 1696.

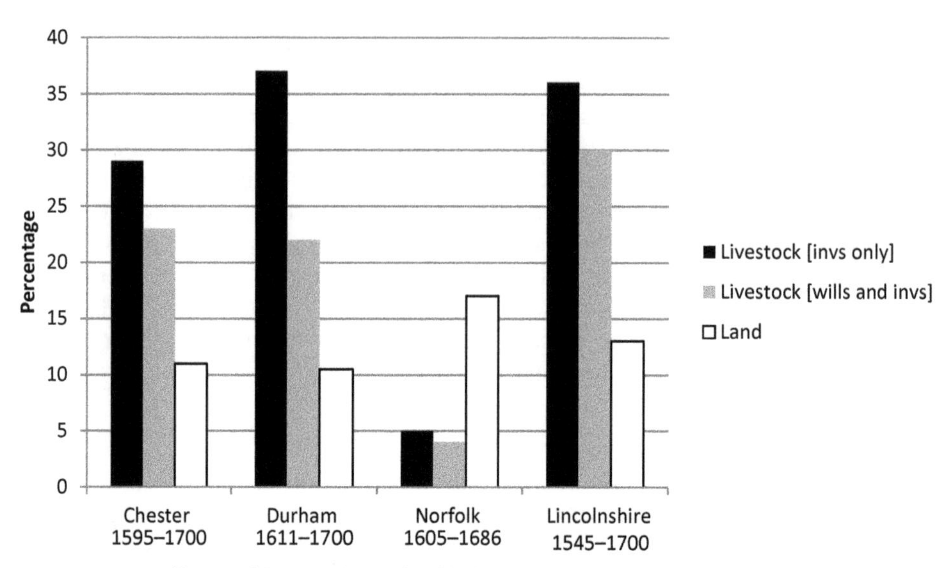

Figure 4. Differential livestock and landholding by spinsters in Chester, Durham, Norfolk and Lincolnshire, 1545–1700

could involve quite large numbers and more than one location. In 1696 in Utkinton, Cheshire, for example, Mary Meakin's sixteen cows, two horses and eighty-two sheep were split between two addresses: the cows and horses were listed as being at Little Budworth and the sheep at Eddisbury in the hands of Thomas Meakin. But the outsourcing of livestock was commonly undertaken on a much smaller scale. Anne Woode of Graizelound in the Isle of Axeholme, who made her will in 1658, had an unspecified number of bee hives at John Kelsye's house, a 'toppe swarme' at the house of her brother James Woode and three geese at Edward Halifax's house.[101] Margaret Forte of Haxey, also in the Isle of Axholme, left a single cow to Nicholas Forte (her brother?) in 1576, which, as she noted in her will, was already in his hands.[102] Servants with livestock may have been especially reliant on the use of other people's pasture land. Isabell James, for example, in service in Great Grimsby, had a tupp at John Crowston's house in 1612, while in 1614 Cicilie Archer of Caistor, probably in the employ of Mr George Spensley, the local vicar, had a ewe and a hogg that were in the custody of Robert Kirmonde.[103] Ann Rawson

101 LA, Stow Wills 1660–3/46 Anne Woode, Graiselound, Isle of Axholme, 1658.

102 Spinsters were not the only group involved in micro-rentals. Labourer John Geele of Quarrington, who was also without land, had ten ewes with William Groobie, another ten with John Hole, twelve with Thomas Gurrill and two cows with men in neighbouring villages. LA, LCC Wills 1601/i/6 John Geele, labourer of Quarrington, 1601.

103 LA, LCC Wills 1612/558, Isabell James, Great Grimsby, 1611; LA, DC Wills 5/107v Cicilie Archer, Caistor, 1614.

of Edlington had two ewes pastured with her master, and such practices were not unusual.[104] Henry Best, the Yorkshire farmer, noted that some servants 'will condition to have soe many sheepe wintered and sommered with theire Maisters' as part of their agreement; he charged 18d per sheep.[105] In Lincolnshire this practice appears to have been quite commonplace. Many of the hiring agreements recorded for Ingoldmells in Lincolnshire in the late sixteenth-century petty sessions refer to the keeping of sheep by servants, although the bulk are male.[106] It may also have been normal elsewhere. In 1643 Joyce Jeffreys was holding twenty sheep that belonged to her servant and agent, Matthias Rufford.[107] She made good her costs by sharing in his profit.

Third, spinsters could have been in possession of grazing rights in their local commons. In addition to the two ewes pastured with her master above, Ann Rawson had two ewes 'in the marsh' in 1672, for example, while Cicilie Benniworth, living at Bishop Norton in 1606, had a cow in the keeping of Brian the neatherd (cowherd), so presumably on some form of community land.[108] Though sheep were often bequeathed, cows were the next most common form of livestock to appear in the wills. Helene Shepard, single woman of Sutterton, had as many as three milk cows in 1570, all of which were pastured in different places. This is hardly surprising. The supplementary income that could be earned from the produce of a cow remained significant throughout the early modern period, and they were prized both for their milk and their offspring.[109] Moreover, the poverty of those without one was well known. Richard Walles, a husbandman of South Ormsby, left 6d to everyone 'that hathe not a Cowe' on the day of his burial.[110] But a cow was also an investment good that, like land and capital, could be let out for profit: Ann Lemon of Quadring, who owned three cows in 1615, had two of them out for rent.[111] The profit from such rents were not infrequently bequeathed independently of the asset itself. In 1569, for example, Helene Shepard left instructions that the 3s 4d rent of the cow that she left to Humfrey Tonnerd was to be shared between five children.[112] In 1629 Ann Man

104 LA, LCC Wills 1672/ii/450 Ann Rawson, Edlington, 1672.

105 D. Woodward (ed.), *The Farming and Memorandum Books of Henry Best of Elmswell, 1642* (Oxford, 1984), p. 140.

106 Anne Kussmaul, *Servants in Husbandry in Early Modern England* (Cambridge, 1981), p. 39.

107 Spicksley (ed.), *Business*, p. 123.

108 LA, LCC Wills 1672/ii/450 Ann Rawson, Edlington, 1672; LA, DC 4/157 Cicilie Benniworth, Atterby in Norton, 1606.

109 Jane Humphries, 'Enclosures, Common Rights, and Women: The Proletarianization of Families in the Late Eighteenth and Early Nineteenth Centuries', *Journal of Economic History* 50:1 (1990), 24–31.

110 LA, LCC Wills 1601/i/67v Richard Walles, husbandman, South Ormsby, 1601.

111 LA, LCC 1615/74 Anne Lemon, Quadring, 1615.

112 LA, LCC Wills 1570/37 Helene Shepard, Sutterton, 1569.

or Mam of Wigtoft left £4 plus a cow to her sister, which she was to receive at twenty-one; she also bequeathed her the rent of that cow at 6s 8d until she was twenty-one.[113] Here, then, we have the fourth and final possibility: that spinsters were letting out their livestock as a source of cash income, thereby embedding the cost of pasturing within a rental agreement and avoiding any immediate requirement for land.

Adding the number of those having livestock but not referencing land to existing landholders raises the overall proportion of those who had access to land significantly.[114] In Norfolk, most of the landholders did not list livestock, but there were fourteen women with livestock who did not list land – the proportion of women with access to land then rises to 20 per cent. In Cheshire the figure rises to 28 per cent, in Durham to 29 per cent and in Lincolnshire to 31 per cent. This does not explain the rise in landholding in the later seventeenth century, however, as the possession of livestock, as Figure 5 reveals, was falling everywhere by that period.[115]

Increasing levels of proletarianisation are well documented in the literature, and rising urbanisation would also have contributed to an overall decline in livestock holdings.[116] A further reason for the decline, however, relates to a switch in investment practice. In the sixteenth and early seventeenth centuries livestock appears as the investment good of first choice for young children. This is evidenced not only in the number of documents that bequeath gifts of livestock to children but also in the instructions for their use. Peter Trotte of Gedney Fen left his daughter Elizabeth a cow in 1601, instructing that it be put forth for her profit until she reached twenty-one, and a cow and a heifer to his niece Anne, who was also to receive them at twenty-one 'with yearelie encrease for the same'; Humfrey Stife of Wyberton left his daughter Alice five ewes 'to be put out for her when she cometh to the age of ten yeares'.[117] Sheep do not appear to have been as common as rental objects, but at least one spinster, Johan Smyth, bequeathed a ewe with its rent and profit to her brother Thomas in the same year.[118] Though livestock remained popular as a form of bequest for much of the period, its value as a form of investment was increasingly undermined by the rise of the cash gift. As changes in usury

113 LA, MISC Wills E/16 Anne Man, Wigtoft, 1629.

114 Here the figures for livestock have been derived from the combined will/inventory analysis.

115 Norfolk is excluded from the inventory-only analysis because a mere three inventories listed livestock.

116 Christopher Clay (ed.), *Rural Society: Landowners, Peasants and Labourers 1500–1750, Chapters from the Agrarian History of England and Wales*, Volume 2 (Cambridge, 1990), pp. 165–7; E. A. Wrigley, 'Urban Growth in Early Modern England: Food, Fuel and Transport', *Past and Present* 225:1 (2014), 79–112.

117 LA, LCC Wills 1601/i/122 Peter Trotte, yeoman, Gedney Fen, 1600/1; LA, LCC Wills 1601/i/80 Humfrey Stife, mason, Wyberton, 1600/1.

118 LA, LCC Wills 1570/25 Johan Smyth [no location], 1569.

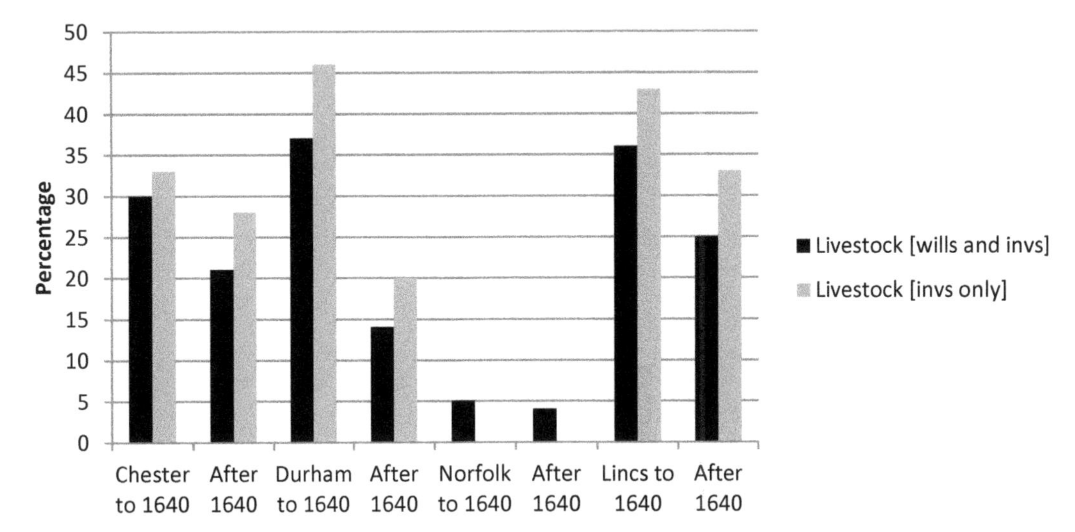

Figure 5. Changes in livestock holding in four jurisdictions over the seventeenth century

legislation allowed cash to be 'put forth' or rented for profit for the benefit of children, fathers increasingly turned to monetary investments to provide for their children.[119]

Since we know interest-bearing lending became the preferred choice of investment for fathers and that formal lending – lending secured on legitimate credit instruments – expanded along with landholding in the spinster documents of the later seventeenth century, could there have been a relationship between the two?

Figure 6 reveals the changing levels of landholding amongst spinsters who were also involved in interest-bearing lending up to and after 1640. Interestingly, it is only in Chester – where there was no growth in landholding after 1640 – that the proportion of formal lenders with land decreases after 1640. In each of the other jurisdictions, where there was a rise in the amount of land held by spinsters, there was also a rise in the proportion of formal lenders in possession of land, and more especially in Norfolk and Lincoln, in which all of the growth was post-1640. Changes in land tenure, evident from the early seventeenth century at least, saw the shortening of leases and the steady demise of copyhold, although the pace of change was regional

119 Moneylending was conceptualised as a form of investment comparable to the renting of livestock or real estate: William Osburne of Braceborough bequeathed his daughter £45 in 1630 at her marriage or 28, 'and in the meane tyme to have rent paide by mine Executor unto her according to the Statute'. LA, LCC Wills 1630–31/267 William Osburne, gentleman, Braceborough, 1630.

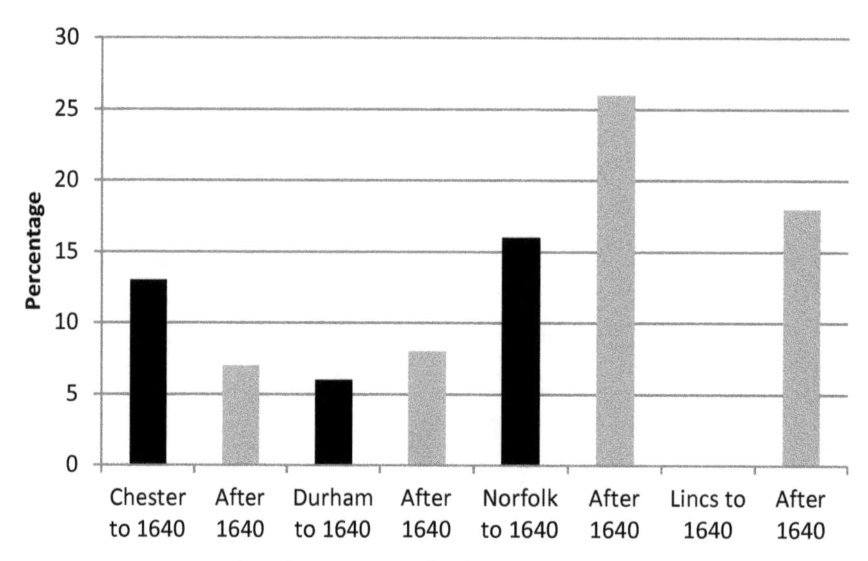

Figure 6. Proportion of single women involved in formal lending with land, 1545–1700

and uneven.[120] Did the expansion of commercial rents offer spinsters more opportunities to hold land through their credit activities? While references to mortgages were few, and absent before the mid-seventeenth century, the securitising of land may well have been more common. Elizabeth Tipping's inventory in 1627, for example, listed a tack of ground belonging to Raphe Barlow that was worth 20s; the inventory also noted that Barlow owed her the sum of £10.[121] This analysis rests on a relatively small number of cases, but it seems possible that some spinsters at least were gaining access to land through their formal credit activities. This is strengthened by the fact that spinsters themselves were less likely to devolve land to women in the two areas where landholding was rising fastest, Norfolk and Lincoln.

Conclusion

In her study of high-status women between 1450 and 1550 Barbara Harris indicated that 'there is not a single example of a never-married aristocratic woman who accumulated large amounts of property, real or movable, or who occupied a central position in her immediate or extended kin network'.[122]

120 Thirsk (ed.), *The Agrarian History of England and Wales*, p. 74.

121 CRO, WI 1627 Elizabeth Tipping, Hale, 1627.

122 Harris collected information on 1,200 aristocratic couples and their children. Harris, *English Aristocratic Women*, pp. 88, 16.

Rowena Archer's study of aristocratic women as landholders and administrators tends to bear out Harris' argument, although she gives no examples of spinsters, only wives and widows.[123] By the early modern period, if Eileen Spring is correct, the position for the higher-status groups was little different. There were, nevertheless, a number of spinsters of the lesser gentry, such as Joyce Jeffreys, who managed to buck the trend and carve out a fair amount of landholding for themselves, through a combination of inheritance, gift or purchase, or even through the process of default. For spinsters lower down the social scale, again, landholding was relatively rare, but does appear to have risen during the later seventeenth century in all but one of the ecclesiastical jurisdictions under investigation. In the Lincoln diocese at least, it was not a change in inheritance practice by fathers that resulted in higher levels of possession. Even though many fathers operated close to a system of co-parceny, few daughters were bequeathed land in Lincolnshire between the 1560s and the 1690s, and that proportion fell after 1640. Spinsters too appear to have felt the weight of custom and law, and were not likely to bequeath land in their possession to female heirs. Yet, despite this, levels of landholding by spinsters were rising, indicating that other mechanisms were having a more positive outcome for women.

We find that spinsters were buying land and leasing or renting land, often in conjunction with ownership of livestock. The fact that there were those who held livestock without referencing land suggests the number with access to land was higher. Adding in those spinsters without any stated connection to land, who pastured their animals through micro-rentals or hired out their cows and sheep for profit, raises the average level of landholding by spinsters from 13 to 27 per cent between 1545 and 1700. But livestock ownership was not driving the accumulation of landholding after 1640. It seems that the switch to a different form of investment may well have been responsible. The proportion of landholders who were also formal lenders rises in each of the three jurisdictions in which landholding levels increased.

Where does this leave us in terms of the debate on female landholding? As a group, spinster landholders were not numerous, but throughout the late sixteenth and seventeenth centuries, and despite the fact that custom and law seem to have favoured men as custodians of land, they were able to access land through failure in the male line, gifts from relatives and friends, the purchase, rental and shared use of land and, more latterly, the pledging of land as formal security for credit. Women could also benefit from land through their ownership of livestock. Although the falling levels of livestock

123 Rowena E. Archer, '"How ladies ... who live on their manors ought to manage their households and estates": Women as Landholders and Administrators in the Later Middle Ages', *Woman is a Worthy Wight: Women in English Society c. 1200–1500*, ed. P. J. P. Goldberg (Stroud, 1992), pp. 149–81.

ownership through the seventeenth century would have reduced the ability of spinsters to benefit in this way, spinsters in some areas appear to have been able to expand their levels of landholding in the later seventeenth century by virtue of their money-lending. This usually involved relatively small parcels of land as security for a loan. Capern has argued that legal changes affecting women's rights to land did not affect women's access to land equally. Spinster landholders reflect the general attitudes of contemporaries to the transmission of land. But with legalisation of interest-bearing lending from the later sixteenth century, some were able to access land that had been used as formal security for credit. Indeed, in the later seventeenth century it may be that interest-bearing lending provided increased opportunities for a number of spinsters to circumvent the male-centric custodial cycle of land, at least where economic conditions were favourable for them to do so.

3

Becoming Anne Clifford

JESSICA L. MALAY

Lady Anne Clifford (1590–1676) is best known for her decades-long battles to inherit the huge northern estates of her father, George Clifford, 3rd earl of Cumberland. In 1643 she finally outlived all those who stood between her and her inheritance. *Her Great Books of Record* and her *Great Picture*[1] both celebrated what she saw as the providential justification of her resistance to the authorities, including a king, archbishops, great lords, a husband and father, who had continually demanded she relinquish her claims. In 1643 she triumphed over these men, but could do little to insist upon what she believed to be her divinely ordered destiny, to embody her lordship over these lands in Westmorland and north-west Yorkshire. Yet, through her work on the *Great Books of Record*, with its six hundred year history of the Cliffords in the region, Anne Clifford derived a firm sense of her rights and a clear understanding of the challenges facing her. Her experience of regal courts, especially that of Elizabeth I, reminded her of the necessity of display and reciprocity. Watching Charles I's will flouted and the country devolve into civil war taught her the dangers of losing authority. These, along with her wide reading in history, theology, philosophy and literature, contributed to the strategies she developed for exercising her own authority in what she always termed 'the lands of mine inheritance'. When she arrived in the north in 1649 she faced a number of challenges but was determined to undermine those individuals who claimed a separate authority in the region. In the following years, often facing down great difficulties, she established a network made up of people and places, movement and action, which allowed her authority to circulate in the north and to radiate southward, including to London, and even in the halls of Charles II's government.

1 All three extant sets of the Great Books are housed with the Cumbria Archive Service (hereafter CAS), Kendal. The Great Picture is also in Kendal, at Abbot Hall Gallery.

Anne Clifford's twentieth-century biographer, Richard T. Spence, remarked that Anne Clifford enacted the role of 'surrogate northern royalty' in Westmorland. In this he was acknowledging a tradition that had survived for over four centuries.[2] In 1691 Anthony Wood reminded his readers that 'it must be noted that this Anne Countess of Pembroke was the same person who lived like a Princess'.[3] Later writers reveal that this reputation did not diminish. In 1833 Hartley Coleridge described her regime in Westmorland as 'little less than regal', and John Craik in 1855 commented that she was regarded as the 'Queen of the North'.[4] Even during her life there was the sense that in Westmorland her authority was analogous to that of a monarch. In his 1663 discussion of the customary duties of subjects to the king, Fabian Philips used Anne Clifford as the only example:

> It cannot be thought to be correspondent to the greatness and Majesty of a King or the duty of his subjects that he should want those ordinary and not very chargeable respects [such as] the privilege to have his goods in progress or upon removals carryed for him at easie rates by his subjects ... and [they] should not at all grumble or grudge to perform those duties and remunerations to their King whose honor and jurisdictions they are sworn to defend and maintain, when they do it willingly ... [for] the Lady Anne Clifford Countess of Pembroke, Dorset and Mountgomery, doth at this day of her oblidged Tenants in the North whose Carts are not to be denyed at any removal from her Castle of Skipton in Craven in Yorkshire, by certain proportioned journeys to her Castle at Appleby in Westmerland.[5]

Here Philips uses the example of Anne Clifford in arguing that customary rights should not be denied the king. In doing so he also infers that Anne Clifford was operating, as Spence suggests, as a type of surrogate royalty in Westmorland by the 1660s.

These comments from the seventeenth to the twentieth centuries are retrospective and do not accurately represent what Anne Clifford found when she inherited Westmorland, but what she built. Upon her inheriting of Westmorland in 1643 there had been no resident Clifford lord there since the death of her mother Margaret Russell in 1616. Anne Clifford visited her mother in 1616, and her impression of the allegiance of the population and the disposition of the tenants was based on this experience. She wrote in her diary in May 1617:

2 Richard T. Spence, *The Lady Anne Clifford* (Sutton, 1997), p. 204.

3 Anthony Wood, *Athenæ Oxonienses* (London, 1691), p. 380.

4 Hartley Coleridge, *Biographia Borealis: Lives of Distinguished Northerns* (London, 1833), p. 243; George Lillie Craik, *The Romance of the Peerage: or Curiosities of Family History*, vol. 4 (London, 1850), p. 128.

5 Fabian Philipps, *The Antiquity, Legality, Reason, Duty and Necessity of Præ-emption and Prourveyance, for the King* (London, 1663), p. 417.

> The 31st Mr Hodgson told me how my cousin Clifford [Henry] went in at Brougham Castle and saw the house but did not lie there and that all the tenants were very well effected towards me and very ill towards them.[6]

This positive feeling towards Anne in 1617 was related to the stewardship her mother Margaret Russell had nourished during her control of the Clifford lands in Westmorland after the death of her husband George Clifford in 1606.[7] Spence describes how after the death of her husband Margaret Russell set up a commission made up of eleven men drawn from both Westmorland and higher-status gentlemen to ensure her wishes were carried out. She rigorously pursued and protected her rights and, as Spence puts it, these were 'settled by local argument, legal action and the due enforcement of law'.[8] After Anne Clifford's marriage, Margaret Russell travelled to Westmorland, where she lived out the rest of her life, ensuring during her lifetime that her daughter's rights were pursued and protected. Part of her strategy was not only to establish a clear legal relationship with her tenants but also to develop personal relationships in the area that would incline the tenants towards herself and her daughter. She accomplished this through acts of charity to the poor, generosity to the local tradespeople, farmers and labourers, and patronage to the gentry (drawing upon her still robust network of elite contacts).[9] She was resident in Westmorland for close to seven years and did much to increase the income from that estate, achieving revenues that in 1611 totalled £1,070, a much greater income than George Clifford had been able to achieve.[10] She used this money to fund the legal battles over the Clifford hereditary lands, hoping to win them for her daughter, as she notes in an annotation to a letter to Anne written 30 October 1615: 'written pleasantly from Brougham, your castle hereafter'.[11] Margaret Russell's control of Westmorland was essential to Anne Clifford's battle to inherit her father's lands. Not only did Margaret Russell lead in developing their legal strategy; her control of Westmorland also allowed her to influence those with local power. As the lawsuit dragged on, Anne Clifford's husband Richard Sackville,

6 Jessica L. Malay (ed.), *Anne Clifford's Autobiographical Writing: 1590–1676* (Manchester, 2018), p. 62.

7 These were Margaret Russell's jointure lands, confirmed to her by an act of parliament. See Jessica L. Malay (ed.), *Anne Clifford's Great Books of Record* (Manchester, 2015), pp. 656–7.

8 Spence, *Anne Clifford*, p. 26.

9 For a discussion of Margaret Russell's strategy in Westmorland see Spence, *Anne Clifford*, pp. 23–39.

10 Spence, *Anne Clifford*, pp. 34–5.

11 CAS, WD HOTH 44, Kendal. Anne Clifford read this statement as prophetic, as she believed her mother was at times able to prophesy. After she inherited the Clifford hereditary lands, Anne wrote on the back of this letter 'which shows that Brougham Castle should be mine hereafter'. Spelling in manuscript sources has been updated to modern spelling conventions throughout this chapter.

who had received no money upon his marriage to Anne, was increasingly willing to trade Westmorland (and the Yorkshire estates) for a financial settlement. In order to forestall this it appears that in May 1616 Margaret was considering signing over her jointure income to Sackville.[12] Margaret and Anne also showed a willingness to give up all claims to Skipton and the Yorkshire estates in exchange for Westmorland. Anne Clifford's attachment to Westmorland was so strong that she records telling James I, in a meeting with him on 18 January 1617: 'I would never part with Westmorland while I lived upon any condition whatsoever.'[13]

One might wonder why Anne was so determined to inherit Westmorland, a region which in the first decades of the seventeenth century was impoverished, vulnerable to Scottish raids, and with few natural resources. A Lieutenant Hammond, travelling past Brougham Castle in Westmorland in 1634, describes the country as 'a solitary wilderness' with 'hideous hanging hills, and great pooles'. He describes the roadways as stony, and complains that they travelled through such ways as 'we hope wee never shall againe, being no other but climing, and stony, nothing but Bogs, and Myres, or that tops of those high Hills, so as we were enforce'd to keepe these narrow, loose, story, base wayes ... so troublesome and dangerous'. He was no more taken with the people, remarking that they were 'rude, rusticall, and ill-bred People, with their gainging and yating, have not will, nor will enough to put us in; we could not understand them, neither would they understand us'. He concludes his description of the region with a glimpse of Brougham Castle:

> We pass'd by another bridge, another river, neere to the brinke whereof stands Broom Castle; few other seats in this dayes tiresome march did appear, unlesse some small Clusters of poore Cottages in those deep valleys by. I thinke the Sun had never shone upon them, yet by these bare-legg'd Rusticks yeleped villages, sick they were, as we never saw before, nor likely ever shall see againe.[14]

Why, given this description, would a woman raised in the south of England, often in London near the court, be at all interested in defying father, husband, archbishop, lords and king to become the lord of this unattractive region? The answer to this is complex, but lies in Anne Clifford's sense of heritage, which appears to have become, in early youth, a part of her identity.

Westmorland had for centuries been the Clifford dower lands, passing from one remarkable Clifford wife to another. Anne Clifford's *Great Books of Record*, especially the biographical summaries she wrote, make clear that

12 Malay, *Autobiographical Writing*, p. 32.

13 Malay, *Autobiographical Writing*, p. 48.

14 Hammond, *A Relation of A Short Survey of 26 Counties ... 1634*, ed. L. G. Wickham Legg (London, 1904), pp. 41–3.

Anne Clifford admired these women. More importantly, Westmorland came to the Cliffords through two women, Idonea and Isabella de Veteripont. Anne Clifford identified closely with both women, but especially Isabella de Veteripont, from whom the Clifford lords descended. Anne proudly states in her biography of Isabella that:

> The office of Sheriffwick of Westmorland was allotted to Isabella ... which office and the execution thereof rested in her ... She had the honour to execute the same office in her own person and sat herself upon the bench as hereditary Sheriffess of Westmorland upon trials of life and death.

Here she also notes that Isabella 'ought be bee remembered of her posterity with honour and reverence in that she brought so fair and noble an inheritance unto them'.[15] The importance of this narrative for Anne's actions during the inheritance battle can be seen in a letter written by Margaret Russell to Edward Bruce, Lord Kinloss. Russell proclaims that the Clifford hereditary lands, especially Westmorland, came 'from women heretofore and [would now be] going to women again'.[16] It is clear that Margaret Russell from the mid-1590s knew that George Clifford intended to leave his lands to his brother Francis, and from that time developed strategies that would ensure Anne was heir to the Clifford hereditary lands. The Westmorland Anne Clifford grew up with was a place of romance and history, and, most importantly, she believed belonged unequivocally to her. She told King James she would not part with it – meaning not only that she would not part with the actual place, Westmorland, but also she would not part with her sense of belonging to that place.

Unfortunately, upon Margaret Russell's death Anne was given little choice. Francis Clifford, 4th earl of Cumberland, inherited the Clifford estates in Westmorland in accordance with the terms of George Clifford's will, though lawsuits continued to challenge this will and thus the legality of Francis Clifford's possession of the estates continued to be actively challenged in the courts.[17] On 14 March 1617 the king brokered an agreement between the Cliffords and Anne's husband Richard Sackville that was for the most part in line with George Clifford's will. The King's Award placed Anne as heir of the Clifford hereditary lands of Westmorland and Yorkshire after the male heirs of Francis and his son Henry.[18] And, while Henry had no living sons at

15 Malay, *Great Books*, p. 153.

16 Longleat House Archives, Letter 11 December 1608, Portland Papers PO/VOL. 23, p. 52, Warminster.

17 For a discussion of this lawsuit see Malay, 'Introduction', *Great Books*, pp. 6–8; Spence, *Anne Clifford*, pp. 40–8.

18 Malay, *Great Books*, pp. 772–5.

that time, there was still the real possibility he would father a son and put Westmorland out of Anne's reach altogether.[19]

The financial stipulations of the King's Award were an advance on the £15,000 settled on Anne in her father's will. Instead, a sum of £20,000 was to be paid to Richard Sackville in instalments, and this had repercussions for the Clifford tenants of Westmorland. Despite the fact that Anne and the tenants of Westmorland never acquiesced to this agreement, their situations were tied to it. Francis Clifford raised £5,000 from sales of lands, including Clifford's Inn, in London. The rest of the money, £15,000, was raised from the tenants of Westmorland. Chancery depositions from 1650–51 reveal the ruthless manner in which Francis and his son Henry raised the money in Westmorland. A tenant from Stainmore, Thomas Johnson, complained in his deposition that the tenants of Francis and Henry were forced to pay as a result of the King's Award 'very excessive and unreasonable fines for their several estates so that many tenants were greatly impoverished and utterly ruined and undone and were constrained to sell their estates for raising and payments of the same'. [20] At least twenty tenants were forced into extreme poverty, many were imprisoned and two died there. Nicholas Fothergill describes how his mother, he himself and all his siblings were driven off their farm by Francis Clifford for seven years, and that twelve of fifty-two tenants suffered the same fate. Francis and Henry Clifford raised not just the additional £15,000 they needed to pay to Richard Sackville from the Westmorland tenants but also a further £11,000 which they folded into their estate. The tenants complained to James I of hard usage during this period, but his reply was unsympathetic and he ordered them to pay the large fines he had allowed in the King's Award.[21] The financial hardship of the Westmorland tenants was exacerbated by bad harvests and disease in the mid-1620s. The payment of £17,000 to Richard Sackville was witnessed by at least two of the tenants, Christopher Pettie of Sowerby and John Atkinson of Mallerstang, who described the sight of 'thirteen porters and their carriages carry it away'.[22] And while Anne Clifford was not the direct beneficiary of all their suffering, and did not herself sign the King's Award, this difficult chapter in Clifford–tenant relations did not

19 Henry Clifford, 5th earl of Cumberland, had two son after 1617: Francis in 1619 and Henry in 1622. Both died in infancy, leaving his eldest daughter, Elizabeth, later countess of Cork, as his heir.

20 John Breay, *Light in the Dales: Studies of Religious Dissent and Land Tenure* (Norwich and Canterbury, 1996), p. 122–3. See also The National Archives (hereafter TNA), SP/C.21/P.25.1 Anne Countess of Pembroke v. Robert Atkinson & others.

21 For a thorough discussion of the King's Award and its impact see Breay, *Light in the Dales*, pp. 117–31. The King's Award allowed Francis Clifford to exceed customary demands for fines and rent. See also Spence, *Anne Clifford*, pp. 40–58 for a less nuanced view of the King's Award and its impact on the Westmorland tenants.

22 Breay, *Light in the Dales*, p. 124.

endear her to the tenants and explains some of the bitterness that met her new demands on them when she inherited the Clifford lands in Westmorland in 1643. Unfortunately, the work Margaret Russell had invested in developing good tenant relations was forgotten in the following decades as a result of ruthless enforcement of financial burdens by Francis and Henry Clifford.

This ill will was exacerbated because, unlike Margaret Russell, Francis and Henry Clifford also chose to reside on their Yorkshire estates, thus depriving the tenants, labourers, business people and gentry of their custom, charity and patronage, which had the effect of distancing the area even further from Clifford authority. This was the situation on the ground at the outbreak of the Civil Wars of the 1640s. Many of the more important tenants secured for themselves authority in the area through their parliamentarian commissions. Robert Atkinson, who would be one of Anne Clifford's primary opponents, became the governor of Anne's castle of Appleby, and Captain Lancelot Skaife had administrative control of some of her estates. His brother was in charge of levying assessments for support of the army from these estates. Others were part of the parliamentary contingent that participated in the siege of her Yorkshire castle of Skipton.[23] These men looked to parliament for authority and disregarded the aging countess. Many of her tenants also saw these men as holding the main authority in the region and used this as an opportunity to thwart Anne Clifford's agents when they attempted to collect the rents, and later resisted her attempts to revise the terms of their leases. And, while the war furthered the careers of some Westmorland men, the area was also devastated by heavy taxes and the disruptions of the war, including the billeting of Scottish soldiers in the region. Thus poverty also played a role in the inability of many tenants to pay their rents. However, Anne Clifford, sitting out the war in Baynard's Castle, London, was not as naive about the situation as her twentieth-century biographer Richard Spence suggests.[24] Her letters to her cousin Sir John Lowther, who was acting as her overseer in Westmorland, show that she understood the difficulties of the situation in the North. On 14 October 1646 she wrote to Lowther:

> Concerning the tenants that are so unwilling to pay me, that which is my right: [those in] Brougham, them about Stainsmore and Kirkby Stephen, they will live to see that their scruples and doubts are in vain ... I hope the example of the good tenants will draw out the rest to follow. If not I will send down writs and other processes in Law as I shall be advised by my friends and counsel here, though if I can avoid it, by gentle and fair means I will not begin to use rough courses towards my tenants there for you know how much I love that country; and am sorry for the case it is now in. But all

23 Spence, *Anne Clifford*, pp. 136–7. See also Richard Spence, *Skipton Castle in the Great Civil War 1642–1645* (Skipton, 1991).
24 Spence, *Anne Clifford*, p. 136.

> places where armies are in, must of necessity have a share of these distresses be their armies never so well governed.[25]

This letter makes clear that Anne Clifford had some degree of sympathy for her tenants but was determined to enforce her rights. There is a mixture of sentiment here – her declared love of the country, which included both the geographical space and the inhabitants – with a pragmatic and even dismissive attitude towards the suffering of the region in relation. Underpinning this attitude was a certainty that her re-establishment of her rights in the region was for the benefit of all, and that those tenants who exhibited right behaviour would help re-establish stability and prosperity in the region for all. Anne Clifford believed that good governance could not necessarily protect the people from suffering in times of war, but was essential ultimately to relieve that suffering.[26]

The tensions between Anne Clifford and her tenants meant that Anne Clifford's arrival at Appleby Castle in August of 1649 and her subsequent trips later in the month to visit the ruins of Brough and Pendragon castles, and the partially restored Brougham Castle, were not occasions of celebration for her tenants, and others in the region, including the gentry, who were either too occupied by military service or harried by the ongoing military threats, shifting loyalties, shortages and other issues to concern themselves with the countess. Anne Clifford herself notes in a letter to the dowager countess of Kent written in January 1650 from Appleby Castle: 'I pray your Lady vouchsafe to remember my love and service to worthy Mr. Selden; and tell him; if I had not excellent Chaucer's book here to comfort me; I were in a pitiful case having so many troubles as I have here.'[27] A biblical reference in her own hand after an entry in her autobiography made in 1651 gives insight into both the difficulties Anne was experiencing and her sense of prophetic purpose and destiny:

> Ezekiel 36.33,36: Thus saith the Lord God; In the day that I shall have cleansed you from all your iniquities I will also cause you to dwell in the cities, and the wastes shall be builded; Then the heathen that are left round about you shall know that I the Lord build the ruined places, and planted which was desolate: I the Lord have spoken it, and I will do it.[28]

25 CAS, DLons/L1/I/28/4, Carlisle.

26 It should be noted that John Lowther had acted as her agent in Westmorland since she inherited her estates, and that the comment about good governance was also probably meant to avoid any insinuation that the suffering of the region was a result of his poor governance.

27 British Library (hereafter BL), Harley 7001 fol. 212, London.

28 Malay, *Autobiographical Writing*, p. 122; *Great Books*, p. 817. Biblical quotation taken from the King James Version. Anne Clifford was familiar with the Geneva Bible, but also appears to have used the KJV.

She annotates a number of passages in her autobiography with this biblical reference until 1659, after which she does not use it again. The heathens here are clearly meant to refer to her recalcitrant tenants. Anne Clifford's confidence in the righteousness of her actions can also be heard here. In 1654 her legal strategies began to bear fruit and she commented 'I had a reasonable good success having obtained a special verdict against them, though my tenants still persisted in their wilful refractoriness and obstinacy against me.'[29] She added a biblical reference at the end of this passage in her own hand making clear her assessment of the tenants that opposed her, which also alludes to her belief that in opposing her they were also harming the poor and vulnerable of the region:

> Job 5.12–15: He disappointeth the devices of the crafty, so that their hands cannot perform their enterprise. He taketh the wise in their own craftiness: and the counsel of the froward is carried headlong. They meet with darkness in the day time, and grope in the noonday as in the night. But he saveth the poor from the sword, from their mouth, and from the hand of the mighty.[30]

A survey of the biblical references in her autobiographical portion of the *Great Books of Record* make clear that Anne Clifford saw herself as the handmaiden of God, and that Westmorland was her particular mission field. Her most often repeated biblical reference, which she inserts in her autobiography of 1650–75 ten times and engraved on all her castles and several of the churches she repaired, comes from Isaiah 58.12: 'And they that shall be of thee shall build the old waste places: thou shalt raise up the foundations of many generations; and thou shalt be called, The repairer of the breach, The restorer of paths to dwell in'. Thus when she makes an entry in her autobiography such as that for April 1651 concerning the repairing of Caesar's tower she was not passing on a bit of personal trivia but was evidencing her role as God's appointed repairer of the breach and restoring not only the physical but also the social fabric of the region:

> And in this year the one and twentieth of April, I helped to lay the foundation stone of the middle wall in the great tower of Appleby Castle in Westmorland, called Caesar's Tower to the end it may be repaired again and made habitable if it pleases God, Isaiah 58.12; Ezekiel 36.33,36 after it had stood without a roof or covering or one chamber habitable in it ever since about one thousand five hundred sixty-nine, a little before the death of my grandfather of Cumberland, when the roof of it was pulled down in the great rebellion time in the North in 1569.[31]

29 Malay, *Autobiographical Writing*, p. 134; *Great Books*, p. 827.

30 Ibid.

31 Malay, *Autobiographical Writing*, p. 122; *Great Books*, p. 817. The Rising of the North of 1569 (also called Revolt of the Northern Earls or Northern Rebellion) occurred when Catholic

Anne Clifford had hoped that she could avoid open conflict with her tenants, believing that her modernisation of rents and terms would be to the benefit of all. Upon inheriting Westmorland in 1643 she wrote to her tenants stating her desire to be a 'good landlord to them after the commendable custom of my noble ancestors the Veteriponts and Cliffords who have been lord and barons of Westmorland from the 5th year of King John's time until now; and most of them good to their tenants'. However, she reminded them: 'It is absolutely in my power to give and dispose of my lands in the Country of Westmorland how I please.'[32] Unfortunately, in 1650 she realised that her claims of good intentions, her hereditary rights and her assertion of authority were not going to be enough to subdue the tenants, hardened as they were by years of suffering and with a leadership embolden by new-found authority in their parliamentarian positions. She quickly filed lawsuits in the courts, but it fell to her to establish and enforce her authority in this region made nearly ungovernable through the disruptions of the Civil Wars.[33] It is not surprising, then, that Anne Clifford looked not only to legal mechanisms which were of limited use on the ground but also to regal models in those dark and no doubt cold and wet days in the northern winter.

Anne Clifford spent decades observing the way royal courts performed their authority, transforming space into places which enhanced and radiated that authority. In her youth she records sleeping on a pallet in the court lodgings of her aunt, Anne Russell, countess of Warwick. Anne Russell was one of the longest serving of Elizabeth's Ladies of the Privy Chamber, and Anne Clifford felt confident that, had Elizabeth lived longer, she too would have served the queen. While it is unclear how much direct contact the young Anne had with the queen, she certainly witnessed the activities of the court close up.[34] In the court of James I she did not serve the queen, Anna of Denmark, but she was often at court, performed in masques with the queen, and often followed the court as it moved from place to place. She was familiar with the workings and movements of the court of Charles I, especially after her marriage (1630) to Philip Herbert, earl of Pembroke, the Lord Chamberlain to Charles I. She was also in London in the fraught political climate at the outbreak of the Civil Wars, not leaving for the north until the summer of 1649.

Anne Clifford's experiences of monarchs and their courts informed her own understanding of how authority was established and maintained, and also the way authority could be diluted, diminished or wrested away. She recognised that, as Norman Jones puts it, 'English governance ... was a

nobles in the north attempted to remove Queen Elizabeth and place Mary, Queen of Scots on the throne. Henry Clifford, 2nd earl of Cumberland, refused to join the rebellion.

32 CAS, Letter to Tenants c. 1643 (autograph draft), WD HOTH 44, Kendal.

33 See Breay, *Light in the Dales*, pp. 151–7; Spence, *Anne Clifford*, pp. 136–45.

34 See Malay, *Autobiographical Writing*, p. 15.

process in which subjects were intimately involved', which was carried out 'through overlapping formal and informal grids of power'.[35] In approaching the situation with her tenants and the wider population in Westmorland her chosen model remained Queen Elizabeth – especially Elizabeth's strategy of engaging in a type of controlled reciprocity in her personal relationship with her subjects. This strategy had worked well for Anne's mother thirty years before in Westmorland. But circumstances were much more fraught in the 1650s and on the ground Anne realised that she needed a more dramatic strategy that drew not only upon Elizabeth's model of reciprocity but also looked back to Henry VIII's great building campaigns and the circulation of his bodily presence between his great houses and castles.

Henry VIII, while inheriting a much less disrupted estate than Anne Clifford, was still only a couple of decades from the devastations of the medieval civil wars and from a dynasty that was only recently established. His ambitious building projects can be seen in the light of his desire to emplace his authority in the landscape. Peter Sillitoe has observed that a moveable and less spatially confined court enhanced the authorising presence of the monarch.[36] Anne Clifford's rebuilding of her four Westmorland castles can be seen in this light. With tenants refusing to pay their rents, men with parliamentary commissions usurping her rights, including her hereditary right as Sheriff of Westmorland, and with the threat (and at times the reality) of military presence on her estates, Anne Clifford rightly understood that her 'authorising presence' was needed throughout the region. Scholars have in the past expressed surprise that a woman who danced in masques designed by Inigo Jones, and who lived in and also visited a number of notable renaissance houses, including Wilton and Hardwick New Hall, would choose to rebuild her ancient castles on a relatively anachronistic model. John Goodall gives perhaps the most comprehensive response to this. He points out that many of the most important seats of the ancient nobility, including of the monarch, were, in the 1650s, castles. By rebuilding her castles she was, as Goodall puts it, 'articulating her lordship over the lands attached to them', an essential step to re-establishing her authorising presence.[37] That this rebuilding was disturbing to those who resented Anne Clifford's attempts to restore her authority in the region can be seen in the reaction to the first castle she rebuilt, in Skipton in North Yorkshire. The ancient fortified section of Skipton Castle had been destroyed by parliamentary forces after a long siege. She rebuilt this part of

35 Norman Jones, 'Governing Elizabethan England', *The Elizabethan World*, ed. Susan Doran and Norman Jones (New York, 2011), p. 19.

36 Peter Sillitoe, '"Where the Prince Lieth": Courtly Space and the Elizabethan Progresses', *Tudor Court Culture*, ed. Thomas Betteridge and Anna Riehl (Selinsgrove, GA, 2010), p. 92.

37 John A. A. Goodall, 'Lady Anne Clifford and the Architectural Pursuit of Nobility', *Lady Anne Clifford: Culture, Patronage and Gender in 17th Century Britain*, ed. Karen Hearn and Lynn Hulse, Yorkshire Archaeological Society, Occasional Paper, No. 7 (2009), p. 74.

the castle, with its architectural affinities to Windsor Castle, but her building campaign quickly raised the ire of those resisting Anne's reorganisation of tenancies and her imposition into the power structure of the area. In response Anne petitioned Adam Baynes, a parliamentarian officer and 'key satellite' of Cromwell's Major-General John Lambert.[38] On 10 September 1659 Anne Clifford wrote to Baynes concerning a threatened second slighting of Skipton Castle:

> I have been informed as well by your kinsman Master Richard Clapham, as by other hands, how much I have been obliged to you for your readiness to afford me all friendly offices and respects in any of my businesses, wherein I have had justice and right on my side; which I shall ever thankfully acknowledge to you. It is the vindication of my just rights, that hath created me (unjustly) some enemies in these parts who not being able to compass their ends in a legal manner, seek to do it by way of revenge, in endeavouring to have my castle of Skipton pulled down and demolished and to that end I am informed, have been procuring hands to a petition against it.[39]

This and other letters to Baynes insist that those opposing her rebuilding were acting out of reasons of local politics and not military concerns.[40] Her request for a military expert to assess the building suggests she had no intention of making Skipton defensible, but her rebuilding of the ancient portion of the castle (there was a very suitable Tudor section for her to live in) was clearly meant to re-establish her authority with a grand visual gesture in the area. In this way she sought to reinvigorate in cultural memory the centuries-long relationship between the Clifford dynasty and the inhabitants of Skipton. The ancestral identities of many of the families who lived in the area stretched back to 1310.[41] These families were intricately interlinked with the Cliffords, as can be seen in the documents found in the *Great Books of Record*. Interestingly, not long after her building works at the castle were completed the Skipton tenants came to an agreement with Anne.

In Westmorland Anne had begun repairing Brougham Castle even before she was able to travel north. In October 1646 she writes to John Lowther: 'It joys me much that Brougham Castle is in repairing.'[42] This is the same

38 David Farr, *John Lambert, Parliamentary Soldier and Cromwellian Major-general, 1619–1684* (Woodbridge, 2003), p. 94. Lambert was from a Skipton family. Baynes was also a kinsman of Richard Clapham (a client of Anne Clifford) and in 1649 Baynes was appointed as a member of parliament for Appleby by Richard Cromwell – a borough that was increasingly under the political control of Anne Clifford.

39 BL, Letter, September 1659, Add. MS 2145 fol. 127, London.

40 BL, Add MS. 21425 fols 18, 148, London.

41 For example, the Fannell family of Skipton first appear as tenants in the Clifford records in 1312 (Malay, *Great Books*, p. 264).

42 CAS, DLons/L1/I/28/4, Carlisle.

letter in which she expresses her concerns about her tenants' recalcitrance, inferring a possible connection with the re-establishment of her presence through the proxy of the repaired Brougham Castle. Her most important Westmorland castle was Appleby. With this castle firmly in parliamentarian control, Anne Clifford's repairs to it, including the rebuilding of the ancient Caesar's tower, a Norman tower reminiscent of the Tower of London, must again be seen as an exercise in visual display that emphasised her lordship in the region. She also rebuilt Brough Castle in 1660, recording: 'This Brough Castle and the Roman Tower in it was so well repaired by me that on the 16 of September in the next year I lay there for three nights together which none of my ancestors had done in 140 years before till now.' The last castle she rebuilt was Pendragon Castle, to which Anne had an emotional and romantic attachment. It featured in a poem her father wrote to Queen Elizabeth, but perhaps more importantly it was the main castle of Idonea de Veteripont, as Anne notes: 'it was the chief and beloved habitation of Idonea the younger daughter and coheir of Robert de Veteripont, my ancestor'.[43] In 1660 Anne Clifford writes that Pendragon 'was lately repaired and made habitable by me, to my great costs and charges, after it had lain desolate ever since about the 15th year of Edward the third in 1341 which is 320 years ago'.[44] And, while this was after her suits with her tenants were mainly settled and her authority was established, it served as a reminder of lordship in the local community in Mallerstang, the area of Westmorland where she met the greatest resistance to her authority. The rebuilt Pendragon Castle also provided the opportunity to invest in the community, as she bought supplies for her frequent visits to Pendragon and employed local people in the castle, in both its rebuilding and its maintenance. Anne Clifford would go on to establish a chapel and school near this castle as well.[45] Thus charity, reciprocity, legal actions and visual presence convinced the people of Mallerstang to accept Anne's authority. The rebuilding of these two ancient castles that had lain in ruins for centuries was not necessary for any purpose beyond the expression of Anne Clifford's authority and rights. After her death, long after her rights were indelibly etched in the landscape and the hearts of the people of Westmorland, Brough, Brougham and Pendragon castles were allowed to fall again into ruins, with only Appleby maintained by her descendants. Anne Clifford's castles were the most obvious manifestation of her authorising presence. She also built

43 CAS, WD HOTH 1/6, Kendal, Malay, *Autobiographical Writing*, p. 160; Malay, *Great Books*, p. 851.

44 Malay, *Autobiographical Writing*, p. 160; Malay, *Great Books*, p. 851.

45 In 1664 Anne Clifford records: 'And before I came away from Pendragon Castle did I, upon the 12 day of this Januarie, purchase of … landes to the value of 11 pounds per annum for which I payd two hundred and twentie pounds. Which landes I gave for the maintenance of a person qualified to read prayers and homilies of the church of England, and to teach the children of the Dale to write and reade English in Mallerstange Chappel forever'. Malay, *Great Books*, p. 861.

monuments in the landscape, such as the Countess Pillar for her mother. She placed monuments or markers at Hugh's Seat, high up on the fell above Mallerstang, along with pillars at either end of Appleby reminiscent of the Countess Pillar. She also repaired and rebuilt a number of churches in the region, along with bridges, mills, farmhouses and an almshouse. These visible markers of Anne Clifford's authority were also visible markers of her charity and reciprocity, for which she was famed. They communicated a confident prosperity in which the population had a share. The population increasingly conflated Anne Clifford's authority with their own prosperity. The built environment began to function as both a celebration of this prosperity and a visible link to the source of the prosperity, Anne Clifford, thus enhancing and securing her authority.

The complexity of social, spatial and cultural dynamics in Westmorland through which Anne Clifford's power and authority was established and circulated can be usefully explored through Bruno Latour's concept of networks of associations made up of both human and non-human 'actors'. These actors, as Latour puts it, 'zigzag from one to the other', becoming 'mediators or intermediaries' and creating interlocking networks through which social forces flow.[46] They become visible in moments of crises or when new associations are being made, as in the case of Anne Clifford's arrival in Westmorland. Her building projects, her social interactions, the resultant behaviours of her expanding client group, her legal actions and the unsuccessful reactions of those who opposed her all contributed to the construction of this network of associations in Westmorland. As her authority became less and less contested, the functioning of this network and its 'actors', described above, began to operate, helping to infuse the region with Anne Clifford's authorising presence. Anne Clifford's performances in space both contributed to and maintained this burgeoning network, creating a robust conduit – or series of intermediary associations – which would eventually operate as Latour suggests, creating unseen an understanding of the social realities of Westmorland that was undifferentiated from Anne Clifford's authorising desires.

With her castles rising across the skyline of Westmorland, and her many other works literally transforming the countryside, the stage was set, and Anne Clifford began what would be a twenty-five-year performance that would infuse Westmorland even further with her authorising presence – her progresses from castle to castle. In her first ten years in the North during the 1650s, Anne Clifford moved between her castles twenty-eight times, staying from a few days to several months at one castle before moving on to the next. In the 1660s she moved between castles thirty-five times. And, in her last five years – remembering that at this point she was in her eighties – she moved

46 Bruno Latour, *Reassembling the Social: An Introduction to Actor–Network Theory* (Oxford, 2005), p. 75.

twelve times. The first move she describes in some detail in her autobiography is her move from Brougham Castle to Appleby in 1669:

> The 26th day of June in this year, after I had lain in Brougham Castle in Westmorland in the chamber wherein my noble father was born and my blessed mother died ever since the 18th of October last, being eight months and some eight days over, did I remove from thence in my horse litter, (my women riding in my coach drawn with six horses and my menservants on horseback) through Whinfell park and by the Hart's Horn Tree, and by the house called Julian Bower in my said park to see it (though I did not alight to go into it) and so from thence through Temple Sowerby, Kirkbythure, and Crackenthorp, and over Appleby Bridge into my castle of Appleby in the same county, where I now began to lie in the same chamber wherein I formerly used to lie and now lay in it till the [19th of October 1669].[47]

In this entry she provides a textual map of her journey but does not give any sense of the performance or reception of this act. However, later entries include details of who attended her. In August 1671 she writes of her move from Appleby to Brougham, with 'my women attending me in my coach drawn with six horses, and my men servants on horseback, and a great many of the chief gentry of this county, and of my neighbours, and tenants accompanying me in this my removal'.[48] Her account books give even greater details about these progresses and confirm that they were celebrations in which Anne Clifford performed her authorising presence amidst a backdrop of gentry and tenants who waited upon her; for example, she records:

> Paid the 12th day what was given and disbursed at my removal yesterday from Brough Castle to this Appleby: to the poor at Brough 6s, to the ringers there 5s, to the poor by the way 3s and 10p. and to the ringers by the way 2s, 6p, to the poor at Appleby 5s, to the ringers 5s. To the piper 2s, 6p, and to the prisoners there 2s, 6p, in all one pound twelve shillings and four pence.[49]

Anne Clifford's charitable giving provided a potent message of her understanding of the correct exercise of authority. Her account books thus functioned not only as a financial management practice but as an accounting of right and just behaviour through which she understood her moral and spiritual obligations to the region flowed. They also illustrate the synergies inherent in Anne Clifford's practices, which were firmly grounded in her material performances of the Lady of the North, most obviously exemplified in her progresses between castles.

47 Malay, *Autobiographical Writing*, p. 190; Malay, *Great Books*, p. 876.

48 Malay, *Autobiographical Writing*, p. 209; Malay, *Great Books*, p. 892.

49 CAS, Kendal, Clifford Accounts 1669–1675, JAC 495, 496 (microfilm).

These progresses were carefully orchestrated and were recorded in her memoirs, giving them both immediacy in the act and informing the future through her text. She records these progresses numerous times and they all conform to a pattern that is essentially ritualistic. In the castle courtyard Anne Clifford would ascend into a horse litter, in which she could both travel with greater ease and also see and be seen by those along the way. Her servants would mount their horses or enter the coach. The gentry, along with her chief tenants, would also gather there in preparation for the progress. The entire party would then leave the castle, the riders before and after Anne's horse litter, with the coach following behind. As they entered each town the church bells rang out and the local pipers and waits, or village musicians, would play her through the streets lined with townspeople. The town dignitaries would also be out in force as she progressed through the town. Rather than taking the main road, she would cut her way through the land, emphasising her right to traverse all land over which she was lord. But she would temper this assertion of her physical rights by paying the tenants for making the way clear for her and as a gift as she passed through the land. Throughout the journey she would disburse money to the poor. By showing herself, she continually reinvigorated those networks through which her authorising presence flowed. Through her dispersal of money and gifts she potently represented her greater largesse in the region. Her entourage, made up of local gentlemen, tenants and dignitaries, created a tableau that placed her as the pinnacle of regional authority through which all prosperity flowed.

Anne Clifford's life of lordly itinerancy certainly drew upon the courts she had seen on the move in her youth, especially those of Elizabeth and James, but also tapped into a much older, feudal practice. Anne Clifford's research in early medieval monarchy gave her numerous examples of the way in which the monarch used his or her physical movement to maintain authority.[50] John M. Steane explains that, as far back as Charlemagne, kings utilised this strategy of itinerancy to prove that they 'had the ability to undertake a journey without hindrance throughout the realm ... gifts and honours were conferred, charters issued, justice pronounced and rebels punished'.[51] This sounds surprisingly close to Anne Clifford's activity throughout her twenty-six-year residence in Westmorland. As the hereditary Sheriff of Westmorland, as well as her close association with the assize judges that visited each year and received her hospitality at Appleby, justice in Westmorland was increasingly synonymous with Anne Clifford's will. Her reputation for charity was

50 Anne Clifford's *Great Books of Record* not only chart the progress of the Veteripont and Clifford families but also include much material on their relationship with medieval kings, and much of the material provides examples of this itinerancy of kings as they maintained their authority through their regal presence.

51 John M. Steane, *The Archaeology of Power* (Stroud, 2001), p. 26.

held up as a model throughout not only Westmorland but the entire country. The antiquarian William Dugdale, in a letter to an Isaac Basier, describes Anne in 1669 as 'the most noble Countess of Pembroke, who exceeds all in her memorable works of piety and charity'.[52] Her account books prove the extensive nature of her charitable giving across all social boundaries.

From these accounts, as well as her *Great Books of Record*, autobiographies, the letters and autobiographies of others and, finally, her funeral oration by Edward Rainbow, the bishop of Carlisle,[53] it is possible to trace Anne Clifford's extensive client network and the way in which she utilised patronage to construct a social reality in Westmorland that was dependent upon her and which sustained, deepened and protected her social and political values there, but also radiated throughout England. There is a tendency to forget that Anne Clifford had extensive holdings in the south of England through her jointure lands from her two marriages. Her agents acted in accordance with her will in these areas and, while she had much less power here, she continued to exert influence in the region through her financial interests, which gave her some authority over succeeding earls of Dorset and Pembroke and their families. In 1564 Frances Cranfield, countess of Dorset, pleads for Anne Clifford's help with matters concerning Anne's jointure lands. The countess pleads that issues regarding these are so problematic that, without resolution, they 'will hinder the settling of our family and be the utter ruin of it'. She goes on to plead, 'I beseech your Ladyship to make the case your own, and I am sure you, that have the fame of doing good to all the world, will not be the occasion of our ruin, for I am sure none hath more honour and respect.'[54] This letter, while probably employing some hyperbole, illustrates the real power Anne Clifford's jointure lands in the south afforded her.

Anne Clifford was also the matriarch of a large and powerful family. Anne's daughter Margaret Sackville married John Tufton, 2nd earl of Thanet, and raised eleven children to adulthood. Anne's grandson Nicholas Tufton became the 3rd earl of Thanet with large estates in Kent and interests in colonial America. He married his cousin Elizabeth Boyle, daughter of Richard Boyle, 2nd earl of Cork and Elizabeth Clifford, daughter of Henry Clifford, 5th earl of Cumberland, thus going some way to repair the breach between these two branches of the family. Anne Clifford's fourth grandson, Thomas Tufton, later 6th earl of Tufton, served as a groom of the bedchamber to James II when James was the duke of York, and was also chosen by Anne Clifford as

52 Durham University Archives, Cosin Letter-Books, 1B, 176, Durham, UK.

53 See the manuscript diary of George Sedgewick, CAS, DLons/L 12/2/16, Carlisle, and the manuscripts of Thomas Machell CAS, DCHA/11/4/1–4, Carlisle. Bishop Rainbow's funeral sermon was published in 1677: 'A sermon preached at the funeral of the Right Honorable Anne, Countess of Pembroke, Dorset, and Montgomery' (London, 1677).

54 Letter to Anne Clifford from Frances Cranfield, Countess of Dorset, 1 August 1664, CAS, WD HOTH 44, Kendal.

a member of parliament for Appleby. He married into the Cavendish family. The Tufton daughters married into the Hatton, Coventry and other gentry families. Anne's daughter Isabella Sackville married James Compton, 3rd earl of Northampton. He served as Lord Lieutenant of Warwickshire and Constable of the Tower of London. Even after the death of her daughter, Isabella, Anne Clifford and James Compton corresponded regularly, and often weekly until Anne Clifford's death.[55] Through these connections Anne Clifford was able to extend and maintain influence and authority throughout the country, which further enhanced her authority in Westmorland, as she was able to promote the position and prospects of local gentry.

By the 1660s Anne Clifford's authority was so pervasive in Westmorland and important in the rest of the country that even the most powerful politicians in England were unable to prevail against her wishes. The best example of this was the Appleby by-election of 1668. It was held to fill a vacant place in Charles II's 'Cavalier Parliament'. Given the longevity of this parliament (1661–69) there was little prospect for individuals to begin a parliamentary career. The vacancy of the Appleby seat after the death of John Lowther provided a rare opportunity for an individual seeking to build his career. It was also an opportunity for politicians at a national level to make inroads in an area that Anne Clifford had worked to make resistant to national control. In Westmorland she was the political power and all subsidiary power flowed from her (thus her posthumous reputation as a queen or princess of the region).

After years of Anne Clifford's investment and careful management Westmorland, while not prosperous, was increasingly economically stable and thus was seen as worth some national attention. It is probably this reason, rather than simply an interest to further the career of a client, that led Henry Bennet, 1st earl of Arlington, to propose his own candidate, Joseph Williamson, for the vacancy. Arlington was Secretary of State, a member of the Privy Council of Charles II and a significant voice in setting policy in Charles's reign. He enlisted the support of Arthur Annesley, 1st earl of Anglesey, also of the Privy Council, to take up the matter. The concerted pressure of two prominent men in government was expected to secure Williamson's appointment. However, Anne Clifford had little interest in allowing an outside political force into Westmorland. At the death of her cousin, John Lowther, she informed the mayor and aldermen of Appleby that they were not to support any candidate until she sent further instructions.

At seventy-eight, Anne Clifford was looking past her own lifetime into the future. She intended to retain political as well as social and financial control of Westmorland through her daughter and then her grandsons, expecting that

55 Malay, *Autobiographical Writing*, pp. 229–35.

they would follow her example and continue her stewardship of the region.[56] When a letter from Joseph Williamson arrived on 16 January 1668 asking for her support she responded courteously and firmly that she was pre-engaged to support the candidacy of one of her Tufton grandsons.[57] This set off a flurry of correspondence, with pressure applied first to Anne Clifford and then, when this proved ineffective, to her daughter Margaret Sackville. Anne wrote to her daughter to help Margaret's resolve, insisting that 'I intend not to recede from my first resolves.'[58] Williamson's supporters also attempted to enlist the aid of a number of Cumberland and Westmorland gentlemen. Some of these agreed to send letters to Anne, others simply expressed their regret that they did not believe success could be gained for Williamson against the will of Anne Clifford. Anne herself made this clear to Lord Arlington in a letter dated 6 February 1668. Here she insists that it was she, not her daughter or grandsons, who was responsible for her decision to 'attempt the making of one of her [Margaret's] younger sons a Burgess for Appleby'. In this way she sought to minimise any political damage to her daughter and grandsons by focusing Arlington's irritation on her only. She further explains that 'I think I am bound in honour and conscience to strive to maintain my own, as far as it lies in my power.' She acknowledges, perhaps slightly disingenuously, Arlington's power, and then turns this back upon him, alluding to his greater duty beyond that to his current favourite:

> I know very well how powerful a man a Secretary of State is throughout all our Kings dominions; so as I am confident your Lordship, by your favour and recommendations might quickly help this Mr Joseph Williamson to a burgesship, without doing wrong or discourtesy to a widow that was but two of fourscore years old; and to her grandchildren, whose father and mother suffered as much in their worldly fortunes for the King as most of his Majesties subjects did.[59]

56 Anne Clifford intended her second grandson John Tufton to inherit the Westmorland Clifford estates, but her elder grandson Nicholas Tufton was successful in thwarting this, though he died a little over two years after Anne's death, and John Tufton inherited in any case. John also held the land in Westmorland for a short time, with his brother Richard inheriting upon his death a year later; and, finally, Anne's fourth grandson, Thomas Tufton, inherited. He held the inheritance in Westmorland for forty-five years and was known as 'Good Lord Thomas' (Robert Pocock, *Memorials of the Family of Tufton* (London, 1800), p. 125). His additions and annotations in two sets of the *Great Books of Record* provide evidence of the influence of Anne Clifford's political and social philosophy on Thomas, as do records related to his management of both the Clifford estates in Westmorland and the Tufton estates in Kent.

57 TNA, Letter from Anne Clifford to Joseph Williamson, 16 January 1668. SP 29/232, fol. 191.

58 TNA, Letter from Anne Clifford to Margaret Sackville, 17 January 1668. SP 29/232, fol. 203. This letter is in some ways reminiscent of Margaret Russell's many letters to Anne in the early seventeenth century encouraging Anne to resist the pressure to give up her rights to Westmorland.

59 TNA, Letter from Anne Clifford to Lord Arlington, 6 February 1668. SP 29/234 fol. 161.

Shortly after this letter the Williamson candidacy was given up. For, as Dr Thomas Smith, brother to the mayor of Appleby, explained to Williamson, 'they of Appleby, having so absolute a dependence upon her [Anne Clifford] (as indeed they have) it would be vain to strive against that stream'.[60]

At seventy-eight Anne Clifford was so confident of her position and authority, both in Westmorland and in the halls of national government, that she felt no need to accommodate these powerful men. The Appleby by-election of 1668 proved Anne Clifford's unassailable political power in the region and illustrates the success of her practices in Westmorland and her national status. She had come a long way from her return to the region in 1649, when her castle of Appleby was governed by one of her tenants, most of her tenants refused to pay their rents, soldiers were billeted in her castles and parliamentarian authority threatened with sequestration for her use of the *Book of Common Prayer* and the Anglican rites in her private worship. Anne Clifford, by legal means, regal reciprocity, her patronage, her charity and her continued visual presence in the region instituted a network through which her authority flowed unquestionably throughout the lands of her inheritance and beyond by the 1660s.

Her political strategy, implemented relentlessly over thirty-three years, shows in her actions a consistency of purpose. Throughout these decades she worked to protect the region from the vagaries of national politics. She transferred vast resources from her southern jointure lands to the North. She invested a great deal of energy in rebuilding the infrastructure of the region that had been destroyed or damaged by the financial devastation wrought by Francis and Henry Clifford's exacting financial policy, the billeting of Scottish soldiers during the Civil Wars and the costs levied for the support of the parliamentarian army. She supported education, social services and religious stability in the region.[61] She built up networks of cooperation between business people and the gentry. Through her patronage she influenced her national network of aristocratic connections in what she believed to be appropriate gentry or elite behaviour – i.e. supporting the local community, charitable behaviour to alleviate poverty and suffering, upholding the Church of England and providing mutual support within the elite (which also ensured the Westmorland elite had the ability to resist destabilising national interference).

Richard Spence disdainfully comments that Anne created an independent fiefdom in the north, and he is correct. This was the model she believed

60 TNA, Letter from Dr Thomas Smith to Joseph Williamson, 18 January 1668, SP 29/232 fol. 238.

61 While Anne Clifford was a staunch supporter of the Church of England, appointing (and, where it was not in her gift to appoint, approving) solid Church of England clergy, her autobiographies, letters and accounts show her private religious tolerance and charity towards dissenters and Catholics.

was most effective in accomplishing her purpose, which was to protect Westmorland and to be, as she put it, a 'good landlady'. Perhaps most revealing of her political philosophy is a passage she underlined in John Barclay's *Argenis*, which she read in 1625 and again in 1651:[62] 'Many of us are sicke of Kings diseases in our private fortune: Wee are Kings to our Suppliants and again he is king to us who has that in his power for which we beg.'[63] She adds in her own hand the annotation 'Most True'.[64] Anne Clifford had watched the effects of 'King's diseases' on her own fortunes and those of others, including her Westmorland tenants. Her research on the Clifford dynasty, which reached back to just after the Conquest, convinced her that the remedy was to establish regional political autonomy that could insulate familial and regional interests from the changing fortunes of the monarchy. Her model was Queen Elizabeth and the political practices she witnessed at close hand in her youth. Anne Clifford's reflective Christianity and theological study, along with her extensive historical research, also provided justification, exempla and cautionary tales that she made good use of in developing her political strategy. Her *Great Books of Record* communicate this philosophy, with its suspicion of male lords and their involvements in 'King's diseases' – that is, king's wars that often caused great hardships within the Veteripont and Clifford lands, and at times devastated both dynasties. The women of the *Great Books*, by contrast, protected the lands, communities and families through wise governance and charity, ameliorating the effects of national crises in the region. Anne Clifford saw herself as their rightful heir in virtue and responsibility as well as in material possession of the lands. She expended tremendous sums of money to reshape the landscape and its socio-political structures to reflect her political ideal of a benevolent feudal state. The 1668 by-election was evidence that she had succeeded.

One might consider that, by the time she had reached her eighties, with her authority secured, Anne Clifford would choose to simply rest in one of her grand castles. She did not. Her movements between castles, with all the accompanying pomp, clearly held great significance for her. She graphically describes the immense physical discomfort she was willing to endure to make these moves in 1673:

> And now as I came from Appleby Castle I went through the withdrawing chamber and Great Chamber into the chapel for a while, where being taken with a swooning fit, I was carried into the Green Chamber and after I was

62 Julia A. Eckerle, *Romancing the Self in Early Modern Englishwomen's Life Writing* (New York, 2013), p. 49.

63 John Barclay, *His Argenis* (London, 1625), p. 197. See Anne Clifford's copy of this text, Huntington Library, CSmH RB 97024, San Marino, California.

64 For further discussion of Clifford's use of this book, see Heidi Brayman Hackel, *Reading Material in Early Modern England: Print, Gender, and Literacy* (Cambridge, 2009), p. 238.

> by God's blessing recovered of it, I came from thence again down the stairs through the hall into the court, from whence being a taken by another fit of swooning, I was carried up for a while into the Baron's Chamber, but having also by God's blessing got well past it, I went down again into the court where I took my horse litter, in which I rid through Appleby town.[65]

She was to progress between her castles five more times before her death at Brougham Castle in March 1676. She travelled to Appleby in July 1673, Pendragon in March 1674 and Brough in September 1674, returning to Appleby in May 1675 and travelling on to Brougham on her last progress in October 1675; this was, for the most part, the same schedule she kept in the 1650s.

Here again her experiences and observations of royal courts may have been the motivation for her continued insistence on progressing through the countryside and inhabiting her castles. Her reading during this time reinforced her understanding of the importance of providing a robust visual presence in her lands. In the 1670s she had read over to her, from her copy of a *Mirror for Magistrates* (1610), Thomas Heywood's 'England's Eliza', which she annotated in her own hand and also instructed her secretary Edward Hasell to annotate. The first reading during this period began on 21 March 1670 on a nearly daily basis for three months. A second occurred in April 1671 and a third in September 1673.[66] In this poem is a description of the queen on progress:

> In stately portance like Joves braine-borne dame,
> To wit, that virgin Queene, the faire Elize,
> That whilom was our Englands richest prize;
> In princelie station with great Junoes grace
> (Mee seem'd) she came in her majesticke pace,
> Grac'd with the lookes of daunting majestie,
> Mixt with the meekeness of milde clemencie;
> Such have I seene her, when in Princely State
> She goddess-like in chariot high hath sate,
> When troops of people with loud shouts and cries,
> Have sounded out the Avies in the skies;
> And rid each other in the present place
> With great desire to see her heav'nly face.[67]

Anne Clifford's own descriptions of her progresses, while not reaching quite this level of praise, include key elements, especially the troop of followers. Her continual reading and interest in this queen in the last years

65 Malay, *Autobiographical Writing*, p. 215; Malay, *Great Books*, p. 898.

66 Stephen Orgel, *The Reader in the Book: A Study of Spaces and Traces* (Oxford, 2015), pp. 140–5.

67 John Higgins, 'England's Eliza', *A Mirrour for Magistrates* (London, 1610), pp. 780–1.

of her life may have convinced Anne that, despite her growing ill health and real physical pain, it was essential to continue reinvigorating her authorising presence in Westmorland through these progresses.[68] She had watched three monarchs reach the end of their reigns and understood clearly the way in which authority could seep away; how those moments of crises Bruno Latour describes could not only make the actors of a network visible but often did so through the dismantling of the very network of associations which once functioned so well and so invisibly, leaving the monarch vulnerable. It may have surprised Anne Clifford to know that the network she instigated to distribute her authorising presence through Westmorland would remain incredibly robust for centuries.

Today two of her castles, Skipton and Appleby, remain in private hands and in good repair, while the ruins of Brough and Brougham and the Countess Pillar are well maintained by English Heritage.[69] All emphasise Anne Clifford's connection to them as one of the most important aspects of these sites, and her presence remains closely associated with the landscape, with byways in the area such as the Anne Clifford Way. Her contributions to the churches she repaired and built are still celebrated by local dignitaries, and her almshouse in Appleby continues to provide charitable housing, with one of her descendants sitting on the board of trustees for this institution. Her *Great Picture* and a number of her other portraits are displayed at Abbot Hall Gallery in Kendal. Interest in Anne Clifford supports the local tourist economy in an area that continues to struggle economically and is now heavily dependent on tourism. Anne Clifford's arrival in Westmorland in 1649 was met with suspicion and hostility, but in the intervening years she employed her own social, material and political strategies to transform this suspicion and hostility into trust, obedience and even gratitude. Her presence in the former county of Westmorland, now part of Cumbria, remains palpable in the landscape and also in the imaginations of the people of the area, who continue to speak with reverence of 'The Lady Anne'.

68 In her daybook of 1676 she recalls the Elizabeth I and her swift punishment of the earl of Essex: Malay, *Autobiographical Writing*, p. 244.

69 Pendragon is a ruin and is less well preserved. It sits on private land.

4

The Heiress Reconsidered: Contexts for Understanding the Abduction of Arabella Alleyn

AMANDA L. CAPERN

In early modern English law the legal heirs/heiresses were the beneficiaries of a person's estate either by common-law provision or by device of a will. Through the doctrine of primogeniture the common law defined the heir of the whole estate as the eldest surviving son or a sole surviving daughter. Estates were split between co-heiresses in the case of more than one daughter. This division of landed estate between surviving daughters reinforced cultural association of land with male landownership. The very term 'heiress' acquired complex cultural meanings in social commentary and in the rhetorical print world of pamphlets, ballads and plays, which could have negative connotations. This chapter explores those cultural meanings and asks questions about how common it was for heiresses to be abducted by men for their wealth. The bigger question addressed, though, is about how much coercion and violence a woman might consider to be 'normal' when gender conflict erupted over inherited property. To throw light on this, the chapter uses a manuscript containing the autobiographical account of Arabella Alleyn (1655–1746).[1] A key argument of the chapter will be that, while it is rare to have a female account of abduction and forced marriage, the abduction itself was not out of the ordinary.

The Alleyn Manuscript and Contexts for Understanding Abduction

Arabella Alleyn's manuscript is virtually unknown. It is not, for example, on the *Perdita* database of early modern women's manuscript writing.[2] It survives in the papers of the Thompson family, which are embedded within those of

1 Hull History Centre (hereafter HHC), U DDHO/12/8, entitled 'Ms Account' ('drawn up by my mother' – Arabella [Alleyn] Thompson'). Foliation has been created for the purposes of this chapter.

2 *Perdita Manuscripts: Women Writers 1500–1700*: available at http://www.perditamanuscripts.amdigital.co.uk/default.aspx [sign-in required].

the Hotham family of Scorborough and South Dalton in East Yorkshire. Early modern women's autobiography is a rare find and accounts written by abducted heiresses are rarer still. The material form of the manuscript is that of a stitched book. It is roughly quarto-sized, with red, blue, green and yellow marbled covers.[3] If it were a woman's recipe book it would be beautiful. However, the story Alleyn tells is of male predation, abduction of a child, intimidation, psychological manipulation, forced marriage (possibly rape), violence within marriage and familial abuse. Inside the flyleaf Alleyn's son – William Thompson – has written: 'those Great troubles did very much indanger her life'.[4] William Thompson knew all about his mother's unhappiness – he was the product of her forced marriage and was named after his grandfather, who had abducted her. He recorded that his mother had drawn up the manuscript 'with Design to lay it before the Parliam[en]t and by that means force my Grandfather and Father [Francis Thompson] into a better allowance after separation [from his father]'.[5]

I have written about Arabella Alleyn twice before, once to reveal the extent of women's land ownership and then to show how past record-creation has obscured female voices in the archives.[6] The intention in this chapter is to listen to the 'voice' of Alleyn herself and consider feminine subjective identity after abduction. The date of the Alleyn manuscript is uncertain, but the evidence suggests it was written in the 1680s, after Alleyn finally fled her husband following the birth of her son. Her son later wrote that the manuscript was written by his mother to threaten his father and 'Compell him to reasonable Terms, rather than let these Practises be layd open so publickly'.[7]

There is a research imperative for paying close attention to any manuscripts that contain snippets and snatches of women's lives told in what is essentially legal testimony. Such testimony can all too easily be overlooked as autobiographical writing or as a female voice in the archives. Yet, hidden away in court records and family papers, these accounts of women's lives are arguably one of the richest sources surviving for women's history. My recent analysis of women's writing from the period 1640–80 shows that before 1675 almost *everything* in print falls into the genre of spiritual, theological or devotional text.[8] Therefore, gendering the genre of 'I-writing' to include these other

3 The manuscript is just less than twelve inches in height, approximating to a quarto.

4 HHC, U DDHO/12/8, 'Ms Account', [fol. 8^{v}].

5 HHC, U DDHO12/8, 'Ms Account', [fol. 1].

6 Amanda L. Capern, 'Early Modern Women Lost and Found: Case Studies in the Selection and Cataloguing of Historical Sources and the (In)visibility of Women', *Women's History Notebooks* 5:2 (1998), 15–22 and 'The Landed Woman in Early Modern England', *Parergon* 19:1 (2002), 185–214.

7 HHC, U DDHO/12/8, 'Ms Account', [fol. 1].

8 Amanda L. Capern, 'Visions of Monarchy and Magistracy in Women's Political Writing, 1640–80', *From Republic to Restoration: Legacies and Departures*, ed. Janet Clare (Manchester,

secular sources historicises women's life experiences further. It frees women from their spiritual reflections, allows us to get closer to their daily practice of household and land management and takes us with them into the sphere of lawyers' offices, court rooms and other public spaces.

Alleyn's threat to publish her story for legal reasons needs to be set in the context of three things. The first context is just the very long history of the abduction of heiresses that spanned the period before Alleyn was snatched in 1657 and went on long after her ordeal. Alleyn's abduction was not an uncommon event and abduction itself was embedded in the British cultural psyche. One historian who has quantified male predation and forced marriage is Caroline Dunn, who used trespass cases in the criminal courts and royal writs of Chancery under the formula of *rapuit et abduxit* or 'ravishment' to uncover 1,198 instances of abductions between 1100 and 1500. Ravishment de gard could relate to a wife or a ward, both types of case assuming trespass on the property of a man embodied in the person abducted. Dunn found that 'most women targeted for capture' were wealthy widows.[9] James Kelly's work on Ireland has also found that '[f]emale abduction took place, at least intermittently between the fifth and the nineteenth centuries', sometimes resulting in women's loss of life from stray bullets.[10] During the research for this chapter dozens more cases were found just by trawling the *Oxford Dictionary of National Biography* and *Old Bailey Online*. Importantly, when found, women's stories were embedded in the biographies of men, reflecting the largely male perspective that has existed on the topic.[11] This makes the Alleyn manuscript compelling evidence for the other side of the story.

Focusing on law and cultural representation in abduction histories reveals an entrenched sexual double standard and high levels of violence against women. Early statutes dealing with abduction and capture (*abductis & detentis*/abduction and detention) focused entirely on boys, especially royal wards. The 1382 Statute of Rapes defined rape as a crime against the will of

2018), pp. 102–23.

9 Caroline Dunn, *Stolen Women in Medieval England: Rape, Abduction, and Adultery, 1100–1500* (Cambridge, 2013), pp. 6–8, 86–8.

10 James Kelly, 'The Abduction of Women of Fortune in Eighteenth-Century Ireland', *Eighteenth-Century Ireland* 9 (1994), 7–9.

11 See, just by way of example, for the period before the Alleyn abduction, George W. Bernard, 'Grey, Richard, third earl of Kent (*b.* in or before 1478, *d.* 1524)', Joseph A. Nigota, 'Vernon Family (*per.* 1411–1515)', Eric Ives, 'Egerton, Sir Ralph (*b.* before 1476, *d.* 1528)', Andrew McKillop, Jean Munro and R. W. Munro, 'Campbell Family of Cawdor', Richard W. Hoyle, 'Percy, Henry Algernon, fifth earl of Northumberland (1478–1527)', Christine Anne McGladdery, 'Seton Family (*per. c.* 1300–*c.* 1510)', *Oxford Dictionary of National Biography* (2004): doi:10.1093/ref:odnb/58355 (2008) & 52800 (2008) & 70787 (2007) & 70941 (2011) & 21936 (2004) & 54318 (2004). *The Proceedings of the Old Bailey Online*, 1 September 1697, Trial of Andrew Palmer (Ref: t16970901–9).

a woman's husband or male guardian.[12] In both cases the law was interested in the property as embodied in the abductee rather than the physical body of the person 'carried away' or 'seized'. The end of the Wars of the Roses was marked by the passing of the 'Acte against taking awaye Women against their Willes', yet violent abductions of women remained a feature of the sixteenth century.[13] The punishment meted out to offenders, though, was often dependent on their status. For example, Thomas, second Baron Dacre, was transformed 'from impoverished border baron to regional magnate' while only paying a fine to Henry VII for abducting Elizabeth Greystoke in 1471; by contrast, John Copynger was hauled before Star Chamber and fined 500 marks for the abduction of the heiress Elizabeth Sotehill in 1517.[14]

An Elizabethan statute against abduction tackled the issue again, extending the original crime of *abductis & detentis* to female heirs and shifting attention to *raptis & abductis* (seize/rape and abduction). The term *rapere*, itself, just meant 'seize', and it was some centuries before it acquired a different meaning, including rape in the modern sense. The Elizabethan statute gained cultural currency as 'the heiress protection statute' and was embedded, for example, in the 1642 edition of Edward Coke's *Institutes of the Lawes of England*.[15] Yet the changes of the sixteenth century had little effect on the rate of abductions and there was only sporadic punishment of men for the crime.

After a perfect storm of abductions from 1690 to about 1710 there were some high-profile executions. John Johnson and Hagon Swanson were hanged for their violent abductions of Mary Wharton and Pleasant Rawlings respectively. A ballad version of Johnson's last speech on the gibbet blamed Wharton's 'cruel Heart more hard than Stone' and laws 'most severe', and

12 Dunn, *Stolen Women in Medieval England*, pp. 11–12, citing Emma Hawkes, '"She was ravished against her will, what so ever she say": Female Consent in Rape and Ravishment in Late Medieval England', *Limina* 1 (1995), 47–54 and idem, 'Preliminary Notes on Consent in the 1382 Rape and Ravishment Laws of Richard II', *Legal History* 11 (2007), 129–32.

13 See, for example, George W. Bernard, 'Grey, Richard, third earl of Kent (*b*. in or before 1478, *d*. 1524)', Joseph A. Nigota, 'Vernon Family (*per*. 1411–1515)' and Eric Ives, 'Egerton, Sir Ralph (*b*. before 1476, *d*. 1528)', *Oxford Dictionary of National Biography* (2004): doi:10.1093/ref:odnb/58355 (2008) & 52800 (2008) & 70787 (2007). Andrew McKillop, Jean Munro and R. W. Munro, 'Campbell Family of Cawdor' and Richard W. Hoyle, 'Percy, Henry Algernon, fifth earl of Northumberland (1478–1527)', *Oxford Dictionary of National Biography* (2004): doi:10.1093/ref:odnb/70941 (2011) & 21936 (2004). Christine Anne McGladdery, 'Seton Family (*per*. *c*. 1300–*c*. 1510)', *Oxford Dictionary of National Biography* (2004): doi:10.1093/ref:odnb/54318.

14 Steven G. Ellis, 'Dacre, Thomas, second Baron Dacre of Gilsland', *Oxford Dictionary of National Biography* (2004): doi:10.1093/ref:odnb/50220 (2008); *State Papers Online*, Hen. VIII.3752 p. 1180, 17 October 1517.

15 Charles Stanley Ross, 'Avoiding the Issue of Fraud: 4 and 5 Philip and Mary c. 8 (the heiress protection statute)', Portia and Desdemona, *The Law in Shakespeare*, eds Constance Jordan and Karen Cunningham (Basingstoke, 2007).

Swanson's execution was similarly popularised in the press.[16] Yet the trial judge had heard that Johnson 'Forcibly, Violently and Felloniously [took Wharton] Away, and against her Consent' she was married to a younger son of Archibald, ninth earl of Argyll, when 'a Virgin under the Age of 14 Years'.[17] In Ireland 'half-hung McNaughton', who abducted Mary Ann Knox in 1761 and forced her into marriage, became written into folklore because the rope snapped during his execution.[18] In all such celebrations of the anti-hero the experiences of women have been lost to proper historical scrutiny. The abduction of Frances Montagu, countess of Mar, in 1728 lay at the extreme end of the consequences of abduction for women. She was the sister of Lady Mary Wortley Montagu, who wanted to take her into legal custody through the court of Chancery as a 'lunatic', but Mar was violently snatched back by her husband so that he could retain control of her jointure lands.[19] Women whose mental health led to their legal definition as 'lunatic' were generally in danger of abduction to seize property. Dame Mary Ashe, a 'lunatic', was 'seized by 30–40 men ... in a most outrageous manner' in 1702.[20]

However, not only did the abductions continue into the eighteenth century, but a comic genre developed to replace medieval chivalric tales of male derring-do. Female authors – Susannah Centlivre, for example – began to contribute to a form of literature and cultural representation of 'the heiress' that has served a male historical narrative and come largely out of the male imaginary.[21] Art ended up mimicking life in a kind of inversion of Aristotelian mimesis. Actresses who played heiresses themselves at times became the victims of abduction in real life. Anne Bracegirdle was seized in a mock-heroic display in London in 1692 and poor Susannah Cibber in 1738 was violently

16 Anon., *Capt. Johnsons last farewell* (London, 1690). The ballad went into multiple reprints.

17 Stuart Handley, 'Johnston, Sir John, third baronet (1647/8–1690)', *Oxford Dictionary of National Biography* (2004), doi:10.1093/ref:odnb/14945 (2004); *The Proceedings of the Old Bailey Online*, December 1690, Trial of John Johnston, William Clewer, Grace Wiggan (Ref: t16901210–56); Anon., *The Full Tryalls and Conviction of Hagon Swanson and Sarah Benton* (London, 1702); Anon., *The Condemn'd Bridegroom, or the Sorrowful Lamentation of Mr. Hogan Swanson* (London, 1702); Anon., *The Last Dying Words and Confession of Haagen Swendsen* (London, 1702).

18 Kelly, 'The Abduction of Women', 17–18, 26, 37.

19 Richard Scott, 'James Erskine, Lord Grange (*bap.* 1679, *d.* 1754)', *Oxford Dictionary of National Biography* (2004), doi:10.1093/ref:odnb/8861 (2004).

20 British Library (hereafter BL), 816.m.5, Anon., *Case of Anne, the Daughter of Dame Mary Ashe* (date unknown).

21 For eighteenth-century abductions see Katherine Turner, 'Thicknesse, Philip (1719–1792)', Michael Bevan, 'Foot, Jesse (1744–1826)', Rosalind K. Marshall, 'Bowes, Mary Eleanor, countess of Strathmore and Kinghorne (1749–1800)', *Oxford Dictionary of National Biography* (2004), doi:10.1093/ref:odnb/7052 (2004) & 28318 (2014) & 58796 (2004) & 27181 (2008) & 9803 (2004) & 3056 (2012). Wendy Moore, *Wedlock: The True Story of the Disastrous Marriage and Remarkable Divorce of Mary Eleanor Bowes, Countess of Strathmore* (London, 2010). See Susannah Centlivre, *The Stolen Heiress of the Salamanca Doctor Outplotted* (London, 1703).

abducted at the hands of her deeply unpleasant husband when she tried to escape him.[22] The ribald political membership of the Scriblerian Club had at its heart Alexander Pope, who wrote tales of romantic trysts while pursuing Martha and Teresa Blount from 1707.[23] Henry Fielding attempted to abduct his fifteen-year-old heiress-cousin before going on to write sharp satires on coffee-house politicians and the highly controversial lampoon of elite male life in *The Grub Street Opera* of 1731.[24] The one powerful female voice in the eighteenth century, though, was the Scottish balladeer Anna Gordon, whose songs about abductions and rape were framed 'from an explicitly female, indeed even feminist, perspective', revealing the 'dark underside of male-female relations' in early modern society.[25]

The historiography of the long history of abductions has also reflected the original legal definitions of 'ravishment', which implied female complicity in the event. Caroline Dunn found that 11 per cent of her sample of abducted women may have involved some female complicity.[26] However, Dunn is perhaps too quick to adopt the language of medieval law in relation to 'consensual elopement'. One purpose of this chapter is to use the voice of Arabella Alleyn to challenge what is meant by female complicity in abduction. Dunn's observation that there has been a swing in the historiography against feminist interpretations of women being viewed by men as property should alert us to one question.[27] Why has there been a backtracking on feminist thinking about male perceptions of women as property?[28] Despite several laws against the abduction of heiresses, forced marriage was rarely prosecuted as rape. 'Ravishment' was, as has been noted, a crime that conceptualised the body of the woman as the locus for the man's ownership of the stolen land itself. Dunn's research uncovered only three convictions for rape 'and two of those convicted did not receive the full extent of the punishment available'.[29]

22 Olive Baldwin and Thelma Wilson, 'Bancroft, John (1655–1696)', Lesley Wade Soule, 'Cibber [*née* Arne], Susannah Maria (1714–1766), *Oxford Dictionary of National Biography* (2004), doi:10.1093/ref:odnb/1271 (2006) & 5417 (2004).

23 Valerie Rumbold, 'Martha Blount (1690–1763)', *Oxford Dictionary of National Biography* (2004), doi:10.1093/ref:odnb/2691 (2004).

24 Martin C. Battestin, 'Fielding, Henry (1707–1754)', *Oxford Dictionary of National Biography* (2004), doi:10.1093/ref:odnb/9400 (2004).

25 William Donaldson, 'Gordon, Anna (1747–1810)', *Oxford Dictionary of National Biography* (2004), doi:10.1093/ref:odnb/55496 (2004).

26 Dunn, *Stolen Women in Medieval England*, p. 9.

27 Dunn, *Stolen Women in Medieval England*, pp. 17, 82–3.

28 There have been multiple feminist arguments about the male view of women as property: see Patricia Crawford, 'Women and Property: Women as Property', *Parergon* 19:1 (2002), 151–71.

29 Dunn, *Stolen Women in Medieval England*, pp. 11–12, 73. Dunn cites Hawkes, '"She was ravished against her will, what so ever she say"and idem, 'Preliminary Notes on Consent in the 1382 Rape and Ravishment Laws of Richard II'.

The second context for understanding Arabella Alleyn's abduction is that it took place just after a period of civil war, when there were intensified levels of competition over land and when male death rates had heightened men's anxieties about not having male heirs. Alleyn was abducted in 1657, when London was filled with religious radical sectarians, maimed soldiers and desperate widows, all milling about petitioning Cromwell's government for financial relief and freedom of worship.[30] She had also been born into an anxious royalist kin network, some of whom were Catholics. Stephen Thompson, the elderly patriarch, was a Catholic royalist, while his children occasionally used the camouflage of conformity to Anglicanism.[31] Royalists were 'twist[ing] like eels in largely successful ploys to avoid sequestration and confiscation' by the Committee for Compounding.[32] In the Thompsons' county of East Yorkshire, one in five of the gentry made opportunistic changes of side during the war. Sir John Hotham and his son – with whom the Thompsons were neighbours and related by marriage – were spectacularly executed in 1645 for being turncoats.[33] Childlessness in the nobility peaked at almost a quarter in the decades after war and the percentage of men who died with no son to succeed them rose from about a quarter before the civil war to 43 per cent.[34] East Riding figures of childlessness and failures of the male line were actually worse than in other parts of the country. Fifty per cent of the thirty-seven landed families in the county experienced failures of the male line between 1650 and 1750 (rising to 66 per cent amongst the richest families).[35]

30 Andrew Hopper, David Appleby, Lloyd Bowen, Mark Stoyle, AHRC Project: Welfare, Conflict and Memory during and after the English Civil Wars, 1642–1700, available at https://www.nottingham.ac.uk/humanities/departments/history/research/research-projects/current-projects/welfare-conflict-memory.aspx, accessed 27 June 2019, and AHRC Project: Civil War Petitions, available at https://www.civilwarpetitions.ac.uk/about-the-project/, accessed 27 June 2019. See also Hannah Worthen, 'The Experience of War Widows in Mid Seventeenth-Century England, with special reference to Kent and Sussex' (PhD diss., University of Leicester, 2017) and 'Supplicants and Guardians: The Petitions of Royalist Widows during the Civil wars and Interregnum, 1642–1660', *Women's History Review* 26:4 (2017), 528–40.

31 The National Archives (hereafter TNA), C10/78/4, Answer of Stephen Thompson, 25 August 1664. Stephen Thompson's oath 'sacraments corporale' in this Chancery case reveals that he was a Catholic.

32 Barbara English, *The Great Landowners of East Yorkshire 1530–1910* (Hull, 1990), pp. 83, 130–9.

33 See Andrew Hopper, *Turncoats and Renegadoes: Changing Sides during the English Civil Wars* (Oxford, 2012) and idem, *The Papers of the Hothams during the Civil War*, Camden Fifth Series (Cambridge, 2011).

34 E. A. Wrigley et al., *English Population History from Family Reconstitution, 1580–1837* (Cambridge, 1997), p. 295; T. Hollingsworth, 'The Demography of the British Peerage', *Population Studies* 18 (Supplement to 1964), 56–7, 62–3; Lawrence Stone and Jeanne Fawtier Stone, *An Open Elite? England, 1540–1880* (Oxford, abridged edn, 1986), pp. 61–3.

35 Case study based on the landed family papers of the Hull History Centre.

The multiple transfers of land to other men in the extended kin networks is testament to men's desire to keep land in male hands.[36] It is no accident that after the war marital fertility became wrapped in the language of political loyalty. The Restoration world became awash with jokes about male impotence – in bed, in coffee houses and in the state.[37] Aphra Behn's jaunty *The City Heiress* of 1682 reflected cultural obsession with Tories and 'commonwealth-men' and the broad concerns left by civil war about rebellion, allegiance and anxieties over land and succession. Indeed, such comic representation quickly replaced the Senecan tragedian form seen in John Webster's *The Duchess of Malfi* of 1612. Heiresses even crept into the newly fashionable minor operatic works, such as Thomas D'Urfey's comedy *The Richmond Heiress* of 1690, composed by Henry Purcell. The 'mad dialogue', featuring a small soprano section between two recitatives, was a fairly recent dramatic innovation. Female singers – in this case Mrs Lynley – were, thus, drafted in to become complicit in constructing the life of an heiress as something that was only ever great fun.[38]

The third context for understanding the Alleyn story and the manuscript is the involvement of women in increasing levels of litigation through direct petitioning and as complainants and defendants in Exchequer, the court of Common Pleas, the court of Requests and Chancery. As Tim Stretton, Christine Churches and others have shown, equity, in particular, opened a space for female legal agency.[39] Frances Dolan has recently argued that a woman's subjectivity can push through a legal text, even when written with the guidance of a lawyer and using legal jargon.[40] The Alleyn manuscript

36 See English, *The Great Landowners of East Yorkshire.*

37 These two sections on demography and reproductive concerns is informed by research done jointly with Dr Judith Spicksley for 'Body Explanations and Impotence in Early Modern England', forthcoming in *Castration, Impotence, and Emasculation in the Long Eighteenth Century*, ed. Anne Greenfield (New York, 2019/20). I am grateful to Judith Spicksley for allowing me to use some of our research for this chapter.

38 Thomas D'Urfey, *Maiden Fresh as a Rose sung by Mr Pack acting a Quaker in the Richmond Heiress* (London, 1693); idem, *The Richmond Heiress, Or a Woman Once in the Right* (London, 1693); [Henry Purcell], *The Mad Dialogue* [fragment of musical score] [London, 1693?]. With thanks to Professor Christopher Wilson for playing and singing this fragment for me

39 Tim Stretton, *Women Waging Law in Elizabethan England* (New York, 1998); Worthen, 'Supplicants and Guardians'; Charlotte Garside, 'Women in Chancery: An Analysis of Chancery as a Court of Redress for Women in Late Seventeenth-Century England' (PhD diss., University of Hull/The National Archives, submitted 2018); Christine Churches, 'Putting Women in their Place: Female Litigants at Whitehaven, 1660–1760', *Women, Property and the Letters of the Law in Early Modern England*, eds Nancy E. Wright, Margaret Ferguson and A. R. Buck (Toronto, 2004).

40 For the debate about when the 'voice' of the narrator can be heard over that of a lawyer or scribe (or not) see Joanne Bailey (Begiato), 'Voices in Court: Lawyers or Litigants?' *Historical Research* 74:186 (2001), 392–408; Frances Dolan, *True Relations: Reading, Literature, and Evidence in Seventeenth-Century England* (Philadelphia, PA, 2013), p. 117.

features scribal use of the third person pronoun. There is also very standard repetitious use of the concept of 'kindness/unkindness' in rhetorical form, just as in most bills of complaint in Chancery. However, like so much legal testimony, despite the narration being one step removed from the textual subject, the content of the Alleyn manuscript represents 'I-writing' and is, in this sense, an ego-document.

The manuscript was retained by Alleyn (and her son) and later brought to public attention in *The Case of Arabella Lady Howard on Behalf of her Protestant Relations*.[41] In printed form Alleyn's autobiography later came to serve several legal uses to protect her title to land. Once was in the 1690s, after her first husband died, and then again around 1705 to 1707 when her second marriage disintegrated.[42] The context for this is discussed in more detail below. However, suffice it to say here that Alleyn's abduction shifted her from a Protestant to a Catholic household and her later printed versions of the abduction story tried to prove that 'instruct[ion] in the Religion she now professes' had led to her involuntary conversion.[43] Later in life Alleyn hid her Catholicism strategically, including practising occasional conformity to Anglican worship. She even wrote to a Church of England clergyman to seek reassurance about swapping the Catholic Mass for Anglican Communion and was advised that it would not affect her soul if she attended to daily confession as a substitute for penance and participation in liturgical transubstantiation.[44] The final printing of *The Case of Arabella Lady Howard* came in 1716 in response to bills in parliament that were designed to remove powers of testation from landholding Catholics.[45] She appended to the original story a rhetorical question, *viz.* was it really fair that the Thompsons, who have 'already received out of her Family above Thirty thousand Pounds', 'should now, by a new Law, prevent her from the Disposal of her own Inheritance'?[46] In the end, though, as for so many Catholic heirs of land, Alleyn resorted to trusts, as will be seen.

41 BL, 816.m.5 (148 & 84), *The Case of Mrs A Thompson, widow [of F. Thompson] in relation to the bill for preventing Papists from disinheriting their Protestant heirs* (London, 1693).

42 Lincoln's Inn Library, *The Case of Arrabella Lady Howard On the Behalf of Her Protestant Relations* (London, 1705?) [accessed *Early English Books Online* 19 July 2018].

43 *The Case of Arrabella Lady Howard On the Behalf of Her Protestant Relations*. n.p.

44 Anon., *A Lady's Religion in a Letter To the Honourable My Lady Howard* (London, 1697), pp. 60–71.

45 *The Case of Lady Arabella Howard on the behalf of her Protestant Relations [in respect to a bill for enquiring into the estates of Traitors and Popish Recusants]* (London, c. 1716). Both were printed by her to control transmission of her property to her son and, later, to members of the Alleyn family. A fragment of *The Case of Lady Arabella Howard* is also at HHC, U DDHO/12/7.

46 BL, 816.m.5 (148 & 84), *The Case of Mrs A Thompson*, and *The Case of Lady Arabella Howard on the behalf of her Protestant Relations*.

The Abduction

The main commentator on heiresses has been Eileen Spring, who has argued that male English landowners moved systematically against women who were heiresses-at-law to bring about constant shifting from lineal to patrilineal principle and practice and female disenfranchisement from land.[47] The argument raises questions about whether contingent events, such as war, might affect the intensity and success of the process. If strict settlements with male entail were the main legal instrument of this process – as Spring suggested they were – could it be that abduction of heiresses was just one extreme tactic used by landed men to reassert their claim to land? Alleyn's abduction occurred only ten years after the Long Parliament passed an ordinance against 'all such persons as shall steale, sell, buy, inveigle, purloyne, convey, or receive little children'.[48] The ordinance implies there was a problem. Alleyn was not the only infant to be abducted during civil war disruption. The adult daughter of the earl of Newport, Anne Blount, was snatched in 1655 by Thomas Porter, the son of the dispossessed royalist Endymion Porter. One biography notes that after the event '[t]he parties were reconciled, a marriage took place'.[49] It is this reporting of *post facto* agreement that this chapter challenges using the Alleyn manuscript.

The disruption of civil war and religious affiliation is the key to understanding what happened through Arabella Alleyn's life. Alleyn was born on 5 November 1655 during the Cromwellian republic. Her extended kin network contained a large number of royalists, some of whom were Catholic. Alleyn married twice, first to Francis Thompson, a member of East Yorkshire's lesser gentry, and then to George Howard, a younger son of the duke of Norfolk. Her recollections from infancy are refracted through the accounts of aggrieved kin members; the emotional retelling of events later in childhood is from her memory. Alleyn was orphaned after her mother, Frances Alleyn, died in early 1658. The death followed that of her father, Edmund Alleyn, in early 1658.[50] The landed estate she was left – mostly in

47 Eileen Spring, 'The Heiress-at-Law: English Real Property Law from a New Point of View', *Law and History Review* 8:2 (1990), 273–96.

48 *An Ordinance of the Lords and Commons assembled in Parliament, for the apprehending and bringing to condigne punishment, all such lewd persons as shall steale, sell, buy, inveigle, purloyne, convey or receive little children* (London, 1645).

49 Jean Pierre Vander Motten, 'Porter, Thomas (1636–1680)', *Oxford Dictionary of National Biography* (2004), doi:10.1093/ref:odnb/22579 (2004).

50 Edmund Alleyn (father) died 2 November 1656. Frances Alleyn (mother) died probably 15 January 1658 or soon after (probate copy 1 February 1658 at TNA, PROB 11/272/542), TNA, Chancery Pleadings, C6/41/7, Arabella Alleyn, by William Thompson and Richard Thompson [guardians] *v.* John Robinson, John Tunstall and others, 1659). H. Kent Staple Causton, *The Howard Papers with a Biographical Pedigree and a Criticism* (London, 1862), p. 350.

Essex – was substantial. Alleyn tells us herself that her father left estate in Hatfield Peverell all worth about £1,000 per annum in rentals. Her mother's death added jointure lands to bring the total to a yearly fortune of £1,400, in addition to the landed asset itself.[51] The modern equivalent is close to £150,000 of tax-free income every year.

A family copy of Alleyn's mother's will survives. According to some sources, at least, it is dated the very day that she died. The paternal family later claimed undue coercion as she lay dying, followed by subversion of some of the will's contents. Alleyn certainly came to believe this as an adult. She recorded in her autobiographical account that one female kin member said that when she was 'permitted to see the sick lady' it was her judgement that Frances Alleyn 'was not then Capable or in a condition to make a will'.[52] The copy of the will clearly states that Alleyn was to be placed in the physical care of two female cousins – Julyann Thompson and Susannah Metcalf – who were to be given £200 and an annuity of £50 (in the case of the former) and £50 plus an annuity of £20 (for the latter) out of the estate. The arrangement was for them to have 'oversight' of her education and provide her with 'advice' and 'direc[t]ion' until she was fourteen.[53] The women of Alleyn's family later told her their stories of disempowerment, as male relatives took charge. One kinswomen said she had been barred from entering the death chamber and 'it is most likely ye poore Lady did not knowe what was in ye will there being none [of] that family named for trustees'.[54]

The trusteeship was certainly complicated. After bequests of between £20 and £50 to servants, and similar amounts left to Sir William Jones (husband of Edmund Alleyn's sister) and other kin, Frances Alleyn gave £200 each to William Thompson of East Yorkshire and Richard Thompson, a London cloth merchant, who were kin on her side of the family.[55] She named them as trustees of charitable bequests as well as co-executors of her will with her 'deare Childe Arabella Alleyn' because 'she is an Infant and not as yett capable to take ye same upon her'.[56] However, the copy of the will records them as named guardians of the child's estate, that it 'may be secured from wast & spoile'.[57] The latter was a standard formula under the laws of guardianship, and was designed to take children through to the age of fourteen, when the appointed trustees became accountable to them for all expenditure

51 HHC, U DDHO/12/8, 'Ms Account', [fol. 2].
52 HHC, U DDHO/12/8, 'Ms Account', [fol. 2].
53 HHC, U DDHO/12/5, 'A Copie Dame Fran.[nces] Aleyns Will', 15 January 1657[8].
54 HHC, U DDHO/12/8, 'MS Account', [fol. 2].
55 HHC, U DDHO/12/5, 'A Copie Dame Fran.[nces] Aleyns Will', 15 January 1657[8].
56 HHC, U DDHO/12/5, 'A Copie of Dame Fran.[nces] Alleyns Will', 15 January 1657[8].
57 HHC, U DDHO/12/5, 'A Copie of Dame Fran.[nces] Alleyns Will', 15 January 1657[8].

past and proposed.[58] Accountability was later to become a serious issue for Arabella Alleyn. She asked William Thompson to 'account for her personall Estate which must needs have been very considerable', but found that she could never believe what he told her and much of what was said was 'no more than a cheate'.[59] The fact that Alleyn's mother appointed members of her family – the Thompsons – rather than paternal Alleyn kin as the guardians, with all of the capacity to raise 'reasonable expenses' for guardianship under statutory law, helps to explain what happened next.

Edmund Alleyn had followed the trend noted by the writer of *The Lawes Resolutions of Womens Rights* that fathers (the author did not mention mothers) preferred daughters of 'right line, right blood' to men in a 'transversall line'.[60] Alleyn had been too young when her father died for him already to be looking around with an acquisitive eye at other men's sons to marry his daughter and take his name. Alleyn later recalled the memories of relatives that when her mother died she was 'with a Beloved who finding there was a great dispute whether the father or Mothers family should have the Goverment [sic] of A and her Estate resolved to keepe her till ye thing was desided [sic]'.[61] However, while the female relative was caring for her, a male relative bribed a servant and she was 'stol[e]n'.[62] The theft of the infant was something that the Thompsons never once seem to have thought of as against the law or even immoral.

A case in the court of Chancery in 1659 helps to throw further light on the abduction of Alleyn as a toddler. It also demonstrates how guardianship rivalries could lead to counter-accusations of theft of a child. William Thompson and Richard Thompson sued several tenant farmers on the Alleyn estate in Hatfield Peverel for the arrears of rent that the tenants had been paying to Sir Nicholas Miller. One tenant, John Tunstall, deposed that he had been paying out to Miller because the latter insisted that he was the rightful guardian of Arabella Alleyn. Miller's claim was based on his assertion that he and his wife had been granted the physical care of the baby. He admitted that he had himself 'endeavoured to force the bodie of the sayd Arabella' two years earlier, but that the Thompsons prevented his intended abduction of her through their 'secrett keeping and close conveying' of her as a baby in the city of London.[63] In other words, by Sir Nicholas Miller's

58 *Lord Nottingham's Chancery Cases*, vol ii, Selden Society, ed. D. E. C. Yale (London, 1961), pp. 53, 204, 477.

59 HHC, U DDHO/12/8, 'Ms Account', [fols 3^{v}, 5].

60 Anon., *The Lawes Resolutions of Womens Rights* (London, 1632), pp. 6–24.

61 HHC, U DDHO/12/8, 'Ms Account', [fol. 2].

62 HHC, U DDHO/12/8, 'Ms Account', [fol. 2].

63 TNA, C6/41/7, Arabella Alleyn, by William and Richard Thompson *v.* John Robinson, John Tunstall and others, Answer of John Tunstall, 20 October 1659.

account, he began thinking of abducting the infant heiress too, but the Thompsons beat him to it.

John Tunstall's deposition in Chancery in 1659 – that Sir Nicholas Miller had said he wanted the rents-in-hand because the Thompsons were guilty of *rapuit et abduxit* – represented a serious charge. The Cromwellian government of the 1650s adapted and adopted the ancient statutory framework of guardianship by chivalry.[64] The consequence was that the Thompsons could not afford to be accused of the abduction and theft of a child who might be made a state ward. Given that the extended Alleyn family still all lived in Little Leighs Hall and in the timber-framed buildings of the old Hatfield Priory, Miller's actions were designed to provoke widespread neighbourhood and family rumours and discord in Essex.[65] Miller later told tenants on the Alleyn estate that he could not 'find certainly against whom to bring his writ of ravishment de gard'.[66] Ravishment de gard was the legal term for abduction of a ward and, as with most Chancery cases, Miller was trying to force the Thompsons to produce evidence of their rights. He asked the court to subpoena them over Frances Alleyn's will and demonstrate that the child was living. Ravishment under the law of guardianship by socage ultimately had this double meaning: rights of socage over the landed estate, which were themselves actually embodied in the life of a child. A guardian in socage could place two writs for damages which had to be delivered to the actual location of the child: one was for 'ravishment of ward' and the other for *de ejectione* from the land.[67] Ravishment, therefore, was about colonisation or taking possession of the land – as title and legal concept – via the body of a person whose status at-law was 'infant'.

Alleyn recorded that her father's family attempted to bring the Thompsons to court over the abduction 'upon which Mr T[hompson] mareyed her to his sonne when she was about 7 years old'. She was 'concealed one yeare in England in the house of Mrs C a Roman Catholick Lady then conveyed … into ffrance and fflanders and in ffrance placed … sometime in a Nunnery'.[68] The preamble of her mother's will indicates that Frances Alleyn was Protestant, yet her daughter was brought up Catholic. In law, religious

64 English, *The Great Landowners of East Yorkshire*, pp. 82–3, 86. Guardianship by Chivalry was not abolished finally until 1661.

65 *Historic England*: https://historicengland.org.uk/listing/the-list/list-entry/1000206.

66 TNA, C6/41/7, Arabella Alleyn, by William and Richard Thompson *v.* John Robinson, John Tunstall and others, Answer of John Tunstall, 20 October 1659.

67 Edward Coke, *The Second Part of the Institutes of the Laws of England* (London, 1797), pp. 439–40.

68 HHC, U DDHO/12/8, 'Ms Account', [fol. 2]. 'Mrs C' may have been a member of another Catholic family in the East Riding, the Constables of either Everingham or another line at Burton Constable.

abduction of a ward was also classified as 'ravishment'.[69] Alleyn's internalisation of being 'the wife' of William Thompson's son, thus, began at the age of seven, while she was under the tutelage of the extended Thompson family. The age at which the forced marriage took place is significant. Children of both sexes became subject to adults deciding their futures at seven: apprenticeship agreements and future marriage deals were struck and it was the age at which parochial care in the custodial birth-place was validated.[70]

According to Alleyn's account, John Alleyn, from the paternal side of the kin network, 'had an order of Counsell to take her from them [the Thompsons]'.[71] Thus Nicholas Miller was not the only other man in pursuit of the child. On 24 October 1663 a bill was lodged with the court of Chancery from joint complainants Arabella Thompson and Sir William and Elizabeth Jones against the Thompsons.[72] The Joneses claimed that *they* were Alleyn's guardians (and, therefore, could co-litigate) and that, indeed, Elizabeth 'was nearer of kinne'.[73] As was standard in equity cases, they wanted production of 'the evidences', in this case the Alleyn wills and deeds and title documents. Their bill of complaint did result in Richard Thompson admitting that the family documents were in his custody (presumably in London) and Stephen Thompson, the elderly father of William Thompson (nearly 'fourscore years'), defending his guardianship rights with the claim that he had closer kinship to Alleyn as uncle of Frances Alleyn. He admitted he did have 'the custody of the Body of the said Arabella' which, he said, 'belongs to him as he is Guardian in Soccage [sic]'.[74] The legal embodiment of the land in the child was equated with the perpetuity of title transmitted through Arabella Alleyn's life.

Alleyn's recollection of a *de praesenti* marriage was that when she was aged twelve the Thompson family all arrived at the cottage in the Yorkshire countryside where she was being kept and she was forced to share a bedroom with William Thompson's son Francis. She was told that there was not enough room in the house for the young boy to sleep anywhere except with her. This, she recalled, 'was cun[n]ingly designed to confirm the Marriage'.[75] She remembered that a church minister was bribed and 'they made a formall

69 Edward Coke, *The Second Part of the Institutes of the Laws of Religion* (London, 1797), p. 440.

70 Louis Knafla, *Kent at Law 1602. The County Jurisdiction: Assizes and Sessions of the Peace* (London, 1994).

71 HHC, U DDHO/12/8, 'Ms Account', [fol. 2].

72 TNA, C10/78/4, Arabella Alleyn and Sir William Jones and Elizabeth Jones *v.* Stephen Thompson, William Thompson and Richard Thompson, 24 October 1663, Bill.

73 TNA, C10/78/4, Arabella Alleyn and Sir William Jones and Elizabeth Jones v. Stephen Thompson, William Thompson and Richard Thompson, 24 October 1663, Bill.

74 TNA, C10/78/4, Answer of Richard Thompson, 27 April 1664 and Answer of Stephen Thompson, 25 August 1664.

75 HHC, U DDHO/12/8, 'Ms Account', [fol. 2^v].

Marriage'.[76] This was easy to do and was little different from the clandestine marriages conducted at the Fleet Prison.[77] Alleyn's account was that she complied because she was 'in great feare of those who imposed this husband upon her, and seeing none whose interest it was to incourage her to oppose'.[78] There were no adults there to support her resistance to the marriage. She complied with the marriage because, in her own words, it was 'no longer in her power to refuse him'.[79] As one historian has noted in the 1655 case of Anne Blount: '[t]he parties were reconciled, a marriage took place'.[80] Is this *really* consensual? This is a question that would strike a chord with modern #MeToo campaigners.

The Alleyn manuscript, therefore, demands our reconsideration of what contemporaries meant when they claimed the collusion of heiresses in their own abduction. There is also the need to revisit the question about why agreements were struck by families after a forced marriage took place. Only *before* the marriage was the situation reversible. The witnessed 'consummation' – sharing the bedroom – marked the point of no return for women. Only annulment could follow. Relatives were later pressured into encouraging Alleyn to tell everyone that, in Alleyn's words, it was 'her free choice and she will never marry another'. Everybody complied *after* it had 'no longer [been] in her power to refuse him'.[81] This one line in the manuscript is the closest Alleyn comes to saying she was raped. But, as is known from the language used in early modern rape trials, women gave accounts that distanced them from the act and even took them out of their own bodies – 'then he occupied me' was a common phrase. Powerlessness and the objectification of the abducted heiress, then, is the key to understanding abduction as a subjective experience for women and the consequences for their lives.

Though only twelve at the time of the actual marriage ceremony, Alleyn knew that through the marriage her 'Husband and his Father gained above Twenty Thousand Pounds personal Estate, besides Seven Thousand Pounds worth of Wood'. The latter, she said, was 'cut off from her Inheritance, which by such Wasts and other Neglects was reduced from Fourteen Hundred to One Thousand Pounds per annum'.[82] Alleyn described the Thompsons as having 'a designe to get her Estate from her' using devious means to get her

76 HHC, U DDHO/12/8/, 'Ms Account', [fol. 2^{v}].

77 Lawrence Stone, *Uncertain Unions: Marriage in England, 1660–1753* (Oxford, 1992); John Southerden Burn, *The Fleet Registers Comprising the History of Fleet Marriages* (London, 1833).

78 HHC, U DDHO/12/8, 'Ms Account', [fol. 2^{v}].

79 HHC, U DDHO/12/8, 'Ms Account', [fol. 2^{v}].

80 Vander Motten, 'Porter, Thomas (1636–1680)'.

81 HHC, U DDHO/12/8, 'Ms Account', [fol. 2^{v}].

82 HHC, U DDHO/12/8, 'Ms Account', [fol. 2].

to 'giv[e] all her estate to them'.[83] However, by the 'doctrine of a wife's equity to a settlement' they could not simply take the estate without a settlement on her jointure for life use, something she seems to have understood.[84] She recalled making it 'more difficult then they Imagined to gett her Estate from her and make a small Jointure as they did designe'.[85]

One of the most valuable and interesting things about the Alleyn manuscript is that it was written by a woman who had an extremely clear sense – from a very young age – of her financial value as an heiress to the men who abducted her. Ironically, this was probably acquired by her from the Thompsons themselves. Eileen Spring has pointed out that the economic value of heiresses dropped from twenty times more valuable than a portioned daughter in the sixteenth century to only ten times more valuable by the eighteenth century. However, territorial endowments of an heiress remained larger than a marriage-portion.[86] Spring's view is that what male landowners wanted – and used the law to achieve – was 'to cut heiresses down'.[87] The counter-argument has been put by Payling, *viz.* that male landowners tended to seek heiresses for their younger sons to defray costs against their main estate.[88] Payling cites Thomas, Lord Dacre, as saying that heiresses were 'ryght costly'. [89] Having abducted one himself, perhaps he was in a position to know. However, the abduction of Alleyn calls into question Payling's argument that 'there was a strong disincentive against heiress hunting'.[90] Men did not just hunt, they abducted and surprisingly often.

Of course, as more men left large cash portions for daughters, the premium on finding an heiress who actually had some land grew. Indeed, men cast around for heiresses with sufficient lands to bring in enough rental profit to pay off the family portions. This was a factor in the Alleyn abduction. Stephen Thompson's eldest son William Thompson was desperate to pay the portions not only of his sisters and brothers but also of his own younger children. He wanted to keep intact what he liked to call the 'Cheife Seate' of Humbleton.[91] The Alleyn manuscript tells us that 'Arabella told him it was not reasonable he should provide for his children out of her Estate'.[92] He countered that he could have found 'any other woman for his sonne', but

83 HHC, U DDHO/12/8, 'Ms Account', [fol. 2ᵛ].
84 George Williams Keeton, *An Introduction to Equity*, 4th edn (London, 1956), p. 150.
85 HHC, U DDHO/12/8, 'Ms Account', [fol. 3ᵛ].
86 See J. C. Holt, 'Feudal Society and the Family in Early Medieval England: IV. The Heiress and the Alien', *Transactions of the Royal Historical Society* 35 (1984), 1.
87 Spring, 'The Heiress-at-Law', 349.
88 S. J. Payling, 'The Economics of Marriage in Late Medieval England: The Marriage of Heiresses', *Economic History Review* 54:3 (2001), 413–29.
89 Payling, 'The Economics of Marriage', p. 419.
90 Payling, 'The Economics of Marriage', p. 427.
91 HHC, U DDHO/12/8, 'MS Account', [fol. 4].
92 HHC, U DDHO/12/8, 'Ms Account', [fol. 4].

Alleyn knew this was not so and apparently pointed out that 'she brought them a fortune in moneyes as well as Estates in Lands'.[93]

Alleyn calculated that as a minor she 'could not doe herself any Injury'.[94] Under equity, a wife could claim separate estate after a voluntary marriage, but only 'through the medium of trustees'.[95] However, Alleyn was dependent on her guardian, William Thompson, to set up separate estate for her private use, something he was unlikely ever to do. William Thompson began seriously to pressure her to settle her estates, which she says she 'refused' to do. They entered years of stalemate and conflict over settlement of the Humbleton estate in exchange for jointure. She was in the difficult position of having to negotiate with her own guardian her marriage settlement. In her manuscript account she claimed that when her young husband fell ill with a bout of smallpox his parents tried to get him to write a sick-bed will leaving Alleyn's estate to them and asking her to sign things 'of dangerous consequence'.[96] She continued to refuse to do this and expressed repugnance at the use of their son's illness to invoke her guilt and sympathy.

Even though still very young, Alleyn's later recollection was that she told the Thompsons it was not just or fair that they should give her estate to her husband. Indeed, the manuscript indicates that Alleyn was acutely aware of her inherited wealth and her financial value to them as an heiress. She told her father-in-law that he 'had a very Considerable personall Estate of hers, soe had reason to make some returne for that'. Furthermore, she complained that they robbed her of independence, despite her social status, giving her nothing 'more than twenty shillings at a tyme till she was 17'.[97] She recorded that she had told them they had a very great obligation of 'kindness' to her (and her natal family) for the acquired wealth.[98] Kindness was, as Linda Pollock has pointed out, the commonly used term for the expected *quid pro quo* of kinship.[99] Alleyn knew she had no direct control over her own wealth, but she also worked out that she could prevent absolute ownership by others. She bargained for a house as settlement because she wanted to be maintained, she said, in a house that was not 'tumble down' and be able to socialise with

93 HHC, U DDHO/12/8, 'Ms Account', [fol. 4^{v}].
94 HHC, U DDHO/12/8, 'Ms Account', [fol. 3].
95 Henry Ballow, *A Treatise of Equity* (1793), ed. John Fontanblanque (New York & London, 1979), p. 94.
96 HHC, U DDHO/12/8, 'Ms Account', [fol. 2^{v}].
97 HHC, U DDHO/12/8, 'Ms Account', [fols 2^{v}–3^{v}].
98 HHC, U DDHO/12/8, 'Ms Account', [fol. 3].
99 Linda Pollock, 'Honor, Gender, and Reconciliation in Elite Culture, 1570–1700', *Journal of British Studies* 46 (2007), 3–29.

family in London – mostly Sir William Jones and his wife – and travel to spas for her health.[100]

Arabella Alleyn's place of safety became London. However, such was the power of a marriage – even forced marriage – in early modern society that once the Thompson family appeared conciliatory she was persuaded to return with them again to Yorkshire. Thirty miles outside London they stopped over night at a house where 'her husband whome they governed as they pleased treated her with all the unkind agravating [sic] threats he could think of' and 'this gave her a very great Melancholy which made her very ill'.[101] Conflict in the family followed, and an aunt (Elizabeth Hotham) stayed with her because Alleyn 'was resolved not to stay any longer there'.[102] After the elderly Stephen Thompson, who had acted as something of a brake on his son's behaviour, died in 1677, William Thompson told her he would build her 'a pretty little house', but she believed he was lying and when her husband brought her a document offering £300 a year she thought it 'a p^r[e]tended settlement'.[103] The issue of the house to live in became central to Alleyn's discussions with the Thompsons and the content of the manuscript 'Account' makes clear that she could not abide living with them.

Throughout these negotiations over finance Alleyn lived with a female relative. She called it 'a tedious year' of 'burying my selfe alive'.[104] She kept pressing her father-in-law about his promise in London to settle estate on herself and her unwanted husband, but revealed in a letter to him that she was 'so familiarized with unkindnesses by long being used to them that I am not surprized att any thing'.[105] William Thompson's answer was that it was Alleyn's 'Imperiousness' that prevented settlement and he termed himself someone whose position 'any reasonable man' would understand.[106] Thus the Alleyn manuscript is very instructive about the sort of slow process of being drawn into a marital family that an abducted heiress experienced, whether she wanted it or not. It is arguably the nature of that process that leads to a form of historiographical forgetting, when family histories relate events as either an agreement eventually reached or even female complicity in a forced marriage.

100 HHC, U DDHO/12/8, 'Ms Account', [fols 4, 9^v–10^v]. For the fashion for spas, see: Amanda Herbert, 'Gender and the Spa: Space, Sociability and Self at British Health Spas, 1640–1714', *Journal of Social History* 43:2 (2009), 361–83.
101 HHC, U DDHO/12/8, 'Ms Account', [fols 4–4^v].
102 HHC, U DDHO/12/8, 'Ms Account', [fol. 4^v].
103 HHC, U DDHO/12/8, 'Ms Account', [fols 4^v–5].
104 HHC, U DDHO/12/8, 'Ms Account', [fols 5^v–6].
105 HHC, U DDHO/12/8, 'Ms Account', [fol. 6].
106 HHC, U DDHO/12/8, 'Ms Account', [fol. 6^v].

Marriage and Violence

Although Alleyn had 'married' Francis Thompson at twelve, she did not become pregnant until she was twenty-two. The conception occurred while she was staying at a house leased for her in York. Alleyn never speaks in the manuscript of sex and never uses the term 'rape' or even any euphemism such as 'forced union' to describe what happened to lead to the conception. Once over the age of twenty-one years and under coverture it became impossible for her to prevent the Thompsons from accessing full control over her inherited property and the attitude of her father-in-law completely changed – he refused to negotiate with her further. 'I have done what I can doe to oblige you', he told her, further saying that if she would not settle her estates on the expected heir (and further children), then she and her husband/his son would never have any life interest in the Thompson lands.[107] This could be interpreted as a veiled threat that he would redirect the patriline to another son. The behaviour of Francis Thompson changed too and he became abusive.

Alleyn's mother-in-law and other female kin were complicit in the verbal violence and abusive behaviour. According to Alleyn, her mother-in-law, Frances Thompson, was manipulative, describing Alleyn as having 'no kindness' because she would not settle her estates on the son.[108] Frances Thompson would say 'such foolish things to worke her son into an ill opinion of his wife', leading Alleyn to attribute her new husband's 'great unkindness' to his mother's attitude.[109] Domestic violence followed, happening under the noses of father-in-law, mother-in-law and the extended Thompson–Hotham family network. Alleyn recalled being made to travel to the family house at Humbleton 'when very neare her time & have liked to have dyed on the way'.[110] Her husband became belligerent and aggressive and 'if his nearest Relacons were kind to her he hated them and would not suffer them to come in his house'.[111]

The specifics of the abuse are identical to that seen in other domestic violence cases at the time and, indeed, today. Alleyn's husband became controlling in his behaviour, restricting her access to food, servants, other people and rooms in the house.[112] The manuscript records that 'His Aunt who

107 HHC, U DDHO/12/8, 'Ms Account', [fols 7–8].
108 HHC, U DDHO/12/8, 'Ms Account', [fols 2^{v}–3].
109 HHC, U DDHO/12/8, 'Ms Account', [fol. 2^{v}].
110 HHC, U DDHO/12/8, 'Ms Account', [fol. 8].
111 HHC, U DDHO/12/8, 'Ms Account', [fol. 8].
112 See Jennine Hurl-Eamon, 'Domestic Violence Prosecuted: Women binding over their Husbands for Assault at Westminster Quarter Sessions, 1685–1720', *Journal of Family History* 26:4 (2001), 435–54; Joanne Bailey (Begiato), '"All He Wanted Was To Kill Her That He Might Marry The Girl": Broken Marriages and Cohabitation in the Long Eighteenth Century',

came from London to assist the tyme of her lying in, was forced to leave the house and take a Chamber in the Towne.'[113] Alleyn was told that if she chose her own midwife 'she must goe out of his house for noe other should come there'.[114] Her husband intercepted letters to the midwife she wanted. When servants were sent by her with a letter to her chosen midwife he sent them the wrong way and she waited three weeks for medical aid before the birth. He controlled all access to food and help in the house: 'if her servants did obey her or show a respect for her which was noe more than she might reasonably expect from them there was noe staying further for them in his house'.[115] His language was constantly 'unkind' and he made it clear that the child would not be named after her father 'whose Estate it was likely to enjoy'.[116]

Alleyn stayed in 'her sick bed' for many weeks, kept there as much by her condition as by the threat issued by her husband that if she left – as she said she wanted to do – 'she should be damned before he would give her a Groate'.[117] Some relief came when her husband went to London for a while. Her attempt to be civil to him when he returned worked until he had spent some time with his mother and father. The next morning he was 'in the same humour ... beating the servants till the one had her arm tyed up the other her face bruised and the boy forced to hide himselfe in the Hay'.[118] He tried to break open her trunk to seize any money she had, said that he would bring someone into the house to ensure that she did not even get six pence and told 'her it was more for shame then any other Consideracon which kept him from beating out her Braines'.[119] She recalled that this was without him even having had anything alcoholic to drink, 'for when he had been in Company she never did dare to come in his sight'.[120] Alleyn went to York briefly to a relation and when she returned she hid away closed off in one section of the house. She said he 'could soe little Comand [sic] his passions when sober she had great reason to feare he might one tyme or other kill her if he mett with her when he was in drink which was very often'.[121]

Ultimately Alleyn escaped from the marital home after one final violent incident. The aunt who had been forced out sent her daughter to sleep with Alleyn in the quarantined section of the house. The two women were woken

Cohabitation and Non-Marital Births in England and Wales, 1600–2012, ed. Rebecca Probert (Basingstoke, 2014), pp. 51–64.

113 HHC, U DDHO/12/8, 'Ms Account', [fol. 8].
114 HHC, U DDHO/12/8, 'Ms Account', [fol. 8].
115 HHC, U DDHO/12/8, 'Ms Account', [fol. 8].
116 HHC, U DDHO/12/8, 'Ms Account', [fol. 8].
117 HHC, U DDHO/12/8, 'Ms Account', [fol. 8^{v}].
118 HHC, U DDHO/12/8, 'Ms Account', [fol. 8^{v}].
119 HHC, U DDHO/12/8, 'Ms Account', [fol. 8^{v}].
120 HHC, U DDHO/12/8, 'Ms Account', [fol. 8^{v}].
121 HHC, U DDHO/12/8, 'Ms Account', [fol. 8^{v}].

from their beds by a terrified maid calling up the stairs to them in 'a frighted tone'.[122] She had been sent to tell them by Alleyn's husband that if he found his cousin in the bed chamber he would 'be her death', whereupon the cousin fled to some neighbours in her night shift. Alleyn herself was too scared to move and tied the door handles with 'all the Ribbons and strings she could find' so that when the neighbours came to get her out of the house – as they bravely did – they were forced to put a pair of 'sizzers under the door that she might Chipp her way out'.[123] A few days later Alleyn returned on the urging of a church minister, but the marriage had become so toxic that another male relative was brought in to mediate.

Later she recalled that she was pleased because it had become 'her greatest Concerne' to remove the child from the Thompson family and her husband.[124] She paid the husband of her wet-nurse 'to lett his wife goe with the child', but as soon as her husband found out she had gone he chased her by coach, 'overtook them on the road to London before she could reach the city' and, drawing up to Alleyn's coach, said to the child 'young man your Journy [sic] is at the furthest'.[125] The incident was remembered by her as leaving her 'halfe dead to see him'. He said he had come to retrieve the child – which he did – 'but would not have come half so farre for you'.[126] At no stage in the manuscript does Alleyn talk about her emotions at the abduction of her child from the coach. Nor does she speak of the arrangements for her to see the child (if any were made), but female Thompson kin did later write to update her on his welfare and education.

Once in London, Lady Elizabeth Jones sent a coach to fetch her niece and Alleyn never again returned to the marital home. Sir William Jones began correspondence and negotiations with William Thompson and in the end the two men arrived at a contractual arrangement for 'pin money' of £200 per annum to be sent for Alleyn to live on. Alleyn later recounted that she walked in the garden with her father-in-law, who tried to persuade her to return to Yorkshire. She simply told him 'that she had undergone much affliction' and if she resumed relations with her husband it would end with her 'acting the same Melancholy part over againe'.[127] For the whole day her husband failed to speak to her at all. It was the last time she saw him.

The origins of the composition of the manuscript account of Arabella Alleyn's early life lie here in the 1680s. Sir William Jones died in 1682, after which Alleyn consulted another lawyer because it was hard to get the agreed allowance regularly out of the Thompsons. The lawyer advised her 'to sue her

122 HHC, U DDHO/12/8, 'Ms Account', [fol. 9].
123 HHC, U DDHO/12/8, 'Ms Account', [fol. 9].
124 HHC, U DDHO/12/8, 'Ms Account', [fol. 9^{v}].
125 HHC, U DDHO/12/8, 'Ms Account', [fol. 9^{v}].
126 HHC, U DDHO/12/8, 'Ms Account', [fol. 9^{v}].
127 HHC, U DDHO/12/8, 'Ms Account', [fol. 10].

husband for Aleymoney'. The threat of public exposure was enough and a deed was drawn up for £350 per annum plus payment of her rent.[128] Alimony could follow in separation cases and even be granted outside ecclesiastical jurisdiction by the court of Chancery.[129] The problem for Alleyn was that only an exceedingly small number of married women sued their husbands through Chancery, even when co-litigating with supporting adults.[130] So she looked to publication of her story as a shaming device. The threat hanging over the Thompsons was that it might be taken one step further and be lodged in parliament, as was already going on in the infamous marriage-separation case of the earl of Rutland. Meanwhile, Alleyn's husband just carried on business as normal, collecting rents from her estates and pursuing Chancery cases to declare *his* right – in joint names – to his wife's most profitable properties, especially Birdbrook manor in Essex.[131]

Alleyn lived in London for most of the remainder of her life. William Thompson the elder died in February 1691. His son, Francis Thompson, died in October 1693, after which Alleyn moved to 65 St Giles in the Fields, Lincoln's Inn. In 1717, her house was 21 Queen Anne's Gate.[132] Before Francis Thompson died Alleyn received several letters from her sister-in-law about family rows over money. The dowager widow would give no financial aid to her other children and Francis Thompson behaved in ways that were 'very unreasonable'.[133] The young William Thompson was only about thirteen years old when his father died and he was left sole executor of his father's estate with four uncles for his guardians. Alleyn was told they would be coming to London pretending 'to offer you such terms as you cannot refuse', but she sought legal advice about getting back the arrears of rental profits on her fee-simple land. In other words, she interpreted her husband's death as an opportunity to fight again for her landed inheritance. The legal answer she received was that she was probably 'cutt off' from this and her chattel by act of parliament.[134] However, as Alleyn had never reached a marriage settlement with the Thompsons the fate of the ownership of her land became ambiguous. Her sister-in-law let her know that 'the trustees have gott a steward ... to git up ye rents & bring y^m^ to any of ye trustees to pay of as ye think fitt', meaning that her son's guardians now managed the estate for her child.[135]

128 HHC, U DDHO/12/8, 'Ms Account', [fols 10–11].
129 Ballow, *A Treatise of Equity*, p. 96.
130 Garside, 'Women in Chancery'. I have found only four cases of women under coverture suing husband in Chancery alone.
131 TNA, C7/342/32, Francis Thompson and wife Arabella Thompson *v.* John Crouch and Elizabeth Crouch, 20 January 1681. Bill.
132 *Survey of London*, vol. 3, 'St Giles in the Fields, Pt. I: Lincoln's Inn Fields' (London, 1912).
133 HHC, U DDHO/12/1, Arabella Thompson (II) to Arabella Thompson (I), 8 July 1692.
134 HHC, U DDHO/12/2, Henry Constable to Arabella Thompson, 9 November 1693.
135 HHC, U DDHO/12/1, Arabella Thompson (II) to Arabella Thompson (I), 27 April 1694.

After the death of his father, the young William Thompson also found himself at odds with his aunts and uncles, who lodged a collective bill of complaint in Chancery over their unpaid portions. They deposed that his father had 'poss[ess]ed himself ... of ye [marriage] settlem[en]t' of his grandmother to deprive them of their portions, a claim backed by his grandmother.[136] The case went against him. In 1693 Alleyn had married George Howard, the third son of the duke of Norfolk, who had just succeeded to some family lands.[137] The young William Thompson's financial problems increased his mother's need to push George Howard 'to relinquish and resign all his Clame and Title' to her dower so that it could be diverted to her son.[138] The tiny request Alleyn wrote to the lawyer 'to favour me to come along with my son to morow' is the only document in the archive actually in her handwriting.[139] Ahead of the case, her son noted that 'it will be more safe that wee only insist on what advantages or profits Mr. Wm Thompson my Grandfather[e]r made of my Mothers Estate after her marriage with my father' – he noted that at the time of the marriage both his mother and his father 'were both but Children'.[140] He recalled that his grandfather had been so controlling that his father was never allowed to manage the estate.[141]

From 1706 George Howard revoked any claim he might have had on the Humbleton and Essex estates through a series of indentures and conveyances.[142] However, Alleyn's second marriage ended in separation on 23 January 1707, when 'the lord George Howard's lady swore the peace against him'.[143] Alleyn had drawn up a pre-nuptial agreement with her second husband that 'made her estate all in trust for her owne use'.[144] She had settled some estate on her second husband for his life use, but disputes over this led to him threatening to leave her by going overseas. On one occasion he argued with her so badly while she was pregnant that she 'came very ill and kept her bed' under threat of miscarrying the child.[145] It is possible she did miscarry, for there is no

136 TNA, C5/284/101, Mary, Susannah, Arabella, Isabella and Elizabeth [Thompson] *v.* William Thompson and others, 20 July 1700. Bill and Answer; HHC, U DDHO/12/1, John Robinson to William Thompson, 22 January 1700, Legal counsel to William Thompson, 13 July 1700 and 22 November 1700, Ben Hayward to William Thompson, 22 January 1703.

137 Staple Causton, *The Howard Papers*, p. 349.

138 HHC, U DDHO/12/10, 'Lady Howard's Case' [no date].

139 HHC, U DDHO/12/10, 'Lady Howard's Case' [no date].

140 HHC, U DDHO/12/11, 'Memo about the terms of agreement', William Thompson [no date].

141 HHC, U DDHO/12/11, 'Memo about the terms of agreement', William Thompson [no date].

142 HHC, U DDHO/36/60, Copy of a Fine, 18 January 1706.

143 Staple Causton, *The Howard Papers*, p. 353.

144 HHC, U DDHO/12/9, Articles of Agreement, Arabella Thompson and Lord George Howard [1693].

145 HHC, U DDHO/12/9, Draft of a Bill [no date].

record of a second living child in her papers. Howard constantly demanded money from her and during negotiations with him similar issues arose as in her first marriage. For example, he failed to deliver on his promise of a coach, so reducing her mobility. He 'sometimes treated her with threatening rough Language, at other times with Contempt and Neglect'.[146] In other words, in her second marriage Arabella Alleyn suffered further domestic abuse. Like her first husband, Howard was violent towards her. He 'swore God Damn her, and twisted her fingers that the veins did immediately swell and her hand was Black a long time after' and then he hit her around the face and head so hard that a neighbour had to call a surgeon while blood poured from her nose.[147]

Arabella Alleyn died on 9 July 1746. She outlived George Howard, who died in 1721. Her son predeceased her in 1744, leaving behind a monument in Humbleton Church to record his 'due Regard to the Memory of his [male] Ancestors', while nevertheless recording that he was the son of 'Arabella a sole dau and hier [sic] of Sr Edmund Alleyn'.[148] It is such traces of the past that masculinise the story of land, even when female ownership and transmission of their property may lie behind a patrilineal family tree. Ultimately, Alleyn was able to rescue her inheritance for her [Protestant] Alleyn relations. The very valuable manor and advowson of Birdbrook was listed on 8 October 1717 in the Register of Papist Estates as being 'all in her own occ[u]p[atio]n, commencing from her intermarriage with Lord George Howard for 500 y[ea]rs' and then it was enrolled in sale to Arthur Dabbs in trust ahead of testation.[149] It was settled with reversion largely on Edmund Alleyn of Little Leighs, with £2,000 left to his sister, who bore her given name.[150] In her will, Alleyn asked to be buried beside her mother and father – people she had never known – in the vault of the chancel of St Nicholas in Hatfield Peverel, leaving £200 for a monument 'in memory of me'.[151] She identified as 'the heiress' of her parents and went to lie beside them in Alleyn soil. Thus, while her son located his landed identity in the county of his father, Alleyn, who came to hate Yorkshire, was emotionally attached to the land of her natal county of Essex.

Conclusion

Two of the contexts for understanding Arabella Alleyn's abduction are just the long and unchanging history of women being kidnapped by men to gain their landed property and the acceleration of this activity at times of

146 HHC, U DDHO/12/9, Draft of a Bill [no date].
147 HHC, U DDHO/12/9, Draft of a Bill [no date].
148 Personal observation of Humbleton parish church, Holderness, East Riding of Yorkshire.
149 Essex Record Office, Q/RRp1/50, Register of Papist Estates, 8 October 1717.
150 BL, Add. MS. 36,191, Copy of will of Arabella Alleyn, 30 June 1746, fol. 293.
151 BL, Add. MS, 36,191, Copy of will of Arabella Alleyn, 30 June 1746, fol. 293.

intra-familial conflict and violence or breakdown of civil society. A third context is the genre and cultural meanings of abduction narratives. In literary form and litigation the abduction of heiresses was told mostly from the male perspective. Ravishment de gard was a legal formulation covering a minor under the age of twenty-one (or 'infant'). Statutory refinements did bring more nuance to this, but ravishment ultimately did not have exactly the same meaning as rape and it applied to land and religion as well as the actual abducted body of the child or woman. Forced marriage fell under the umbrella of *rapere*, which just meant 'to seize', so obscuring rape and leading to accounts of abductions that were regarded as consensual in nature. What the Alleyn manuscript tells us is that because women and land – as legal entities – were collapsed into something unitary at the moment of *de praesenti* marriage, the abducted woman could feel as if she was left with no choice but to 'consent' to the marriage *post facto*. Internalising the state of *being married* was not the same, however, as relinquishing legal rights to inherited landed property, as the case of Arabella Alleyn so clearly shows.

The Alleyn abduction was not unusual and it can be interpreted as merely an extreme tactic used by the Thompsons to steal her land. Just how much land they would get in exchange for jointure became central to the marriage settlement negotiations she had with her father-in-law after the event. Men were rarely punished for abducting heiresses and the activity even became sanitised as 'seduction' in literary genres and family histories alike in the eighteenth century. This should prompt some reconsideration of two historiographical paradigms – what do historians mean when they speak of a 'first sexual revolution' or of love being the 'prop of patriarchy'?[152] Perhaps abduction – like strict settlements – was just another way of drawing land back into the hands of elite men.[153] The fact that there was a fairly constant level of elite women's ownership of land is, after all, a puzzle. Given that male death rates were high mid-century and resulted in the collapse of patrilines, why was there not a spike in women's landholding?[154]

Furthermore, while narratives about abduction abound in everything from family histories and genealogies to ballads, songs and plays, they all emanated mostly from the male imaginary. Stories of abduction over time have been more about the chivalric or adventurous hero/anti-hero of tragedy or comedy than about female experience of events. This is what makes the Alleyn story so common, but hearing it in a woman's own voice so rare. Alleyn placed

152 Anthony Fletcher, *Gender, Sex and Subordination in England, 1500–1800* (New Haven, CT, 1994); Faramerz Dabhoiwala, *The Origins of Sex: A History of the First Sexual Revolution* (London, 2012).

153 *Cf.* Spring, 'The Heiress-at-Law', 278, 282, 292; idem, 'The Strict Settlement: Its Role in Family History', *Economic History Review* 41:3 (1988), 454–60.

154 Briony McDonagh, *Elite Women and the Agricultural Landscape, 1700–1830* (Abingdon, 2017).

herself at the centre of the narrative of the abduction and forced marriage. The literary (and legal) agency she created for herself partially mitigated the extreme loss of agency she suffered at the hands of some highly abusive men. Her authorial motivation was to tell her charged emotional tale for legal reasons and, because the story was given several lives in printed form, it became the 'twice-told tale' of litigious intentions. Unintentionally, Alleyn has left a much longer legacy – the manuscript is one of the only accounts we have of abduction that is actually written in the female voice.[155] However, what *is* common is the language of litigation. Alleyn's actions are further evidence of women's knowledge of their legal rights in relation to landed property and the increased level of female contact with the law, lawyers and law courts over the seventeenth century.

Alleyn's actions were in keeping with the early modern social expectation that women became involved in litigation over land. But this idea still seems to be so at odds with modern thinking about what early modern women could do that one family historian on the internet has described Alleyn as 'a woman of independent views and strong character', as if her actions should surprise.[156] Alleyn was, of course, exceptional, not least because she left behind a unique story – told from the woman's point of view – about what it was like to be abducted. However, her litigious voice was *not* exceptional for a woman and if historians want to hear more female voices that sound secular instead of spiritual they need to keep turning to the archives. In this way it is possible to gender the genre of autobiography itself, by using the legal ego-documents that can be found in court records and landed family papers.[157]

Eileen Spring once observed that '[t]he treatment of the heiress in works of history ... has been almost as unfortunate as her treatment at the hands

155 This consideration of literary understandings of the construction of narrative and the narrator's voice is informed by several readings on Nathaniel Hawthorne's *Twice-told Tales* of 1842, especially G. R. Thompson, 'Literary Politics and the "Legitimate Sphere": Poe, Hawthorne, and the "Tale Proper"', *Nineteenth-Century Literature* 49:2 (1994), 167–95, especially 191–2.

156 Nick Kingsley, 'Landed Families of Britain and Ireland', available at https://landedfamilies.blogspot.com/2014/01/105-alleyn-of-hatfield-peverel-and.html, accessed 27 June 2019. The assessment of Arabella Alleyn's character is repeated by Brad Verity, who recommends Kingsley's blog for male genealogies. Ironically, Verity's hyperlink for his source is to my original research on Alleyn in a special issue of *Parergon* (2002) devoted entirely to women's property.

157 I have not yet found a likeness of Arabella Alleyn. However, Henry Causton's 1862 edition of *The Howard Papers* noted that 'Henry Howard of Corby excites curiosity with the remark, that "the lady's portrait, with her history," is to be found at Mr. Galley Knight's, at Firbeck Hall"'. The 'history' could well be a copy of Alleyn's 'Ms Account'. The location of the painting is explained by Alleyn's will: the executors, who received all remaining property after bequests, were Philip Howard, Edward Webb and Ralph Knight. Ralph Knight's descendant, Elizabeth, inherited Firbeck Hall in 1768 and married Henry Gally. Their son was the author Henry Gally Knight. I am currently trying to trace the painting through the Friends of Firbeck Hall.

of history itself'.[158] This chapter offers broad agreement with her assessment of the plight of heiresses, who were always in some danger of abduction. The chapter also suggests that the way in which abduction was represented over time changed and took on new cultural forms that effectively diminished representation of the violence that can be seen in forced marriages. It is cultural acceptance of abduction, then, that has led to the chimera of female complicity in events that ended with an unwanted sexual union, as far as women were concerned anyway. Alleyn's voice from the archives tells us this. Alleyn did *not* have Stockholm Syndrome – this much is clear from her description of the many years of resistance she put up to her captivity against her captors. What is also clear is that when Alleyn articulated the emotions of her abduction, she did this using the voice of an heiress and landowner who was willing to litigate for her property rights.

158 Spring, 'The Heiress-at-Law', 285.

5

From Magnificent Houses to Disagreeable Country: Lady Sophia Newdigate's Tour of Southern England and Derbyshire, 1748

JON STOBART

As part of a two-month tour of the southern counties, undertaken during the summer of 1748, Lady Sophia Newdigate was travelling from Bristol, where she had stayed the night. She passed in sight of Badminton House, the seat of the duke of Beaufort, with its three-mile avenue of trees, which, she wrote, 'will make a great appearance'. She then moved on into a 'very disagreeable country, [with] scarce a tree to be seen and all the inclosures divided by stone walls'.[1] The journey itself, undertaken in company with her husband, sister and two family friends, and the fact that Sophia took the trouble to write about it in a journal that at least employs the conceit of being written for others to read, are both entirely typical of the eighteenth-century elite. Indeed, travel for pleasure was one of the chief ways in which the elite distinguished themselves from the lower orders.[2] It comprised two main elements, both of which were well-established practices by the mid-eighteenth century. The first was the tradition of country house visiting, which itself grew out of the imperative for hospitality placed on wealthy landowners. Tinniswood has traced the development of these practices as they spread beyond the welcoming of other members of landed society to incorporate a broader social mix and what might be better regarded as tourism. As the social profile changed, so too did the motivation of visitors, from curiosity through

1 Warwickshire Record Office (hereafter WRO), CR1841/7, Lady Newdigate's tour in the south of England (1748), fol. 52. I would like to thank Dale Townshend for his helpful comments on an earlier draft of this chapter.

2 Jane Whittle and Elizabeth Griffiths, *Consumption and Gender in the Early Seventeenth-Century Household. The World of Alice Le Strange* (Oxford, 2012), pp. 191–6.

critical appraisal to nostalgia and nationalism.[3] In the mid-eighteenth century, though, the typical visitor remained another member of the gentry or their companions. The second was the Grand Tour, a cultural practice that, despite much debate over its precise form and function (both of which shifted over the course of the eighteenth century), remained important in opening cultural and social horizons, especially for young men.[4] The letters and journals that formed an integral part of the Tourist's experience have been drawn on by historians to provide insights into their varied motivations, priorities, itineraries and practices, and as a lens through which to view the social and cultural mores of the day.

Alongside these historical analyses has grown a burgeoning literature on travel writing.[5] Drawing more on published journals, this literary analysis has highlighted several important themes in eighteenth- and early nineteenth-century travelogues, especially those written by women. Post-colonial perspectives have generated a particular focus on questions of empire, nation and national identity, with Pratt, Colley and others arguing that the 'other' encountered whilst travelling was important in shaping both metropolitan and British identities.[6] For some, like Mills, this had an important gendered dimension, imperialism being linked closely to the construction of a particular masculine identity.[7] At the same time, however, travel writing was critical in allowing women to construct their own identities, not least because it offered an escape from 'the interiority of the domestic sphere'.[8] Foster and Mills caution against easy assumptions that women naturally wrote differently

3 Adrian Tinniswood, *The Polite Tourist: Four Centuries of Country House Visiting* (New York, 1999). See also Carole Fabricant, 'The Literature of Domestic Tourism and the Public Consumption of Private Property', *The New Eighteenth Century*, eds Laura Brown and Felicity Nussbaum (London, 1987), pp. 254–75.

4 See, for example, Jeremy Black, *The British Abroad: The Grand Tour in the Eighteenth Century* (London, 1992); Henry French and Mark Rothery, *Man's Estate: Landed Gentry Masculinities, 1660–1900* (Oxford, 2012), pp. 137–84. Brian Dolan, *Ladies of the Grand Tour* (London, 2001) and Rosemary Sweet, *Cities and the Grand Tour. The British in Italy, c.1690–1820* (Cambridge, 2012) stress the growing number of women and families also undertaking tours of Europe.

5 See, for example, Elizabeth Bohls, *Women Travel Writers and the Language of Aesthetics, 1716–1818* (Cambridge, 1995); Katherine Turner, *British Travel Writers in Europe, 1750–1800* (Aldershot, 2001); Shirley Foster and Sara Mills (eds), *An Anthology of Women's Travel Writing* (Manchester, 2002); Casey Blanton, *Travel Writing: The Self and the World* (London, 2002); Nigel Leask, *Curiosity and the Aesthetics of Travel Writing* (Oxford, 2002); Clare Broome Saunders (ed.), *Women, Travel Writing and Truth* (London, 2014).

6 M. L. Pratt, *Imperial Eyes: Travel Writing and Transculturation* (London, 1992); Linda Colley, *Britons: Forging the Nation, 1707–1837* (New Haven, CT, 1992). See also Steve Clark (ed.), *Travel Writing and Empire* (London, 1999).

7 Sara Mills, *Discourses of Difference: An Analysis of Women's Travel Writing and Colonialism* (London, 1991).

8 Foster and Mills, *Women's Travel Writing*, p. 9.

from men; as with masculinity, there was a range of nuanced female identities constructed through travel and travel writing. Yet it is striking how arguments about the private sphere, womanhood and family permeate so much of the literature on women's writing – at least that which appeared in print.[9] Moreover, Bohls sees women writers as having a particular perspective on aesthetics in its various forms, arguing that they mounted a critique of several founding principles of Kantian aesthetics: the unity of the subject, the possibility of disinterested contemplation and the autonomy of aesthetics from other moral or practical concerns.[10]

These arguments are largely and sometimes necessarily based on the writing of men and women who travelled overseas. Much less attention has been given to the journeys and writings of those who chose to stay within Britain, at least before the surge in domestic tourism and travel writing that gathered pace from the 1760s onwards. This had two distinct strands: the growing number of middle-class travellers visiting country houses (touched on earlier) and the wider appreciation of the 'picturesque and historical credentials of the British landscape',[11] the latter being given real impetus by Gilpin's various *Observations* and Pennant's *Tours*.[12] These were not unrelated phenomena, of course, but neither were they new. In addition to those travelling the country with an eye to recording the 'state of the nation' – most famously Daniel Defoe, but also John Mackey and, a generation earlier, Celia Fiennes – there were scores of gentlemen and their families criss-crossing the country to view houses and historical monuments, visit towns (especially spas) and admire the natural beauties of the countryside. Publishing accounts of these travels became popular later in the century,[13] but unpublished journals and travellers' letters can be found amongst the private papers of many landed families. Journals such as that of Sophia Newdigate thus provide a window into a world of travel and pleasure, cultural and social critique and identity construction that has all too rarely been looked through.[14] In following Sophia on her journey I pick up in this chapter on

9 See Turner, *British Travel Writers*, pp. 128–50; Foster and Mills, *Women's Travel Writing*, pp. 10–11.

10 Bohls, *Women Travel Writers*, esp. pp. 7–8.

11 Turner, *British Travel Writers*, p. 31.

12 See Malcolm Andrews, *The Search for the Picturesque: Landscape Aesthetics and Tourism in Britain, 1760–1800* (Stanford, 1989), pp. 241–7; Turner, *British Travel Writers*, pp. 30–4; Emma McEvoy, 'Exploring Britain's Ruins', *Writing Britain's Ruins*, eds Michael Carter, Peter Lindfield and Dale Townshend (London, 2017), pp. 131–57.

13 See, for example, Arthur Young, *A Six Weeks Tour through the Southern Counties of England and Wales* (London, 1768); William Gilpin, *Observations, Relative Chiefly to Picturesque Beauty, Made in the Year 1772, on Several Part of England*, 2nd edn (London, 1788).

14 But see Rosie MacArthur, 'Gentlemen Tourists in the Early Eighteenth Century: The Travel Journals of William Hanbury and John Scattergood', Hanneke Ronnes and Renske Koster, 'A Foreign Appreciation of English Country Houses and Castles: Dutch Travel Accounts on

several of the themes highlighted in the literature and explore three broad issues: first, the geography and rationale of her itinerary, assessing the extent to which it conformed to a predictable circuit of famous houses and historic sites; second, the ways in which she wrote about the places she visited and how this linked to the expected conventions of travel journals and/or the commentary offered by topographical guides; third, and most particularly, the insights afforded into the character and identity of aristocratic women – were her reactions and reflections shaped more by her gender or her status?

Itineraries, Influences and Writing Styles

The Grand Tour, as has often been pointed out, was shaped by a set itinerary. The idea that tourists were herded around a series of set pieces is an exaggeration, but there were key destinations – Florence, Naples, Venice and especially Rome – and a list of sites to be seen in each place which structured itineraries and dominated many journals and letters home. Even the route to Italy was mapped out, with Paris the key place to stop at on the way out or back.[15] Tours of Britain, by contrast, were altogether less constrained by convention and were geographically more varied. The equivalent of the great Italian cities were British country houses, amongst which a select group loomed large: initially, these comprised the royal palaces and prodigy houses of the Home Counties, and later a range of ducal palaces including Blenheim, Chatsworth and Wilton. By the mid-eighteenth century there were established circuits in East Anglia, the south, the south-west and the Midlands. These aristocratic houses were crucial in cementing the credentials of the English landscape,[16] a process that was aided by the publication from 1715 onwards of Colin Campbell's *Vitruvius Britannica*, long before the writings of Gilpin and Pennant. Although by no means a guidebook in the modern sense of that term, Campbell's publication highlighted what he felt to be the most important houses architecturally and was compiled with the explicit intention of celebrating the greatness of British architecture, even in comparison with

Proto Museums Visited *En Route* (1683–1855)' and Kristof Fatsar, '"Enjoying country life to the full – only the English know how to do that!": Appreciation of the British Country House by Hungarian Aristocratic Travellers', all in *Travel and the Country House*, ed. Jon Stobart (Manchester, 2017).

15 See John Towner, *An Historical Geography of Recreation and Tourism in the Western World* (Chichester, 1996). For discussion of these sites and the different reactions prompted by four key cities, see Sweet, *Cities and the Grand Tour*.

16 See Fatsar, 'Enjoying Country Life to the Full'; Ronnes and Koster, 'Foreign Appreciation of the English Country House'.

the best to be found in Italy.[17] More specifically, topographical writing helped to shape not only what to see, but also how best to understand it. Here the work of William Camden was the most important, frequently acting as a point of reference (for example, by Daniel Defoe and Mrs Lybbe Powis) and sometimes even as a guide in the field (William Hanbury carried his copy with him on his tour in the 1720s, marking off the places he had visited).[18] However, even with these key points of geographical and chorographical reference, there was considerable scope for tourists of England to vary their route, as is apparent from the different places seen by Mrs Lybbe Powys, Lord Torrington, Arthur Young, and so on.[19] The lack of a fixed cultural and social agenda to these tours meant that they were much freer in their format, a feature that also makes them, in some ways, far more interesting: the route taken and sights seen can tell us much about the interests and priorities of the writer rather than the expected norms and conventions of the Grand Tour.

The basic geography of the tour traced by Sophia's journal is fairly straightforward: a two-month trip down to the Isle of Wight, out via Middlesex and Essex and back via the south-west, followed by a shorter trip into Derbyshire lasting about eight days. The journeys included the familiar and the unfamiliar, both in terms of places being known and being within the sphere of previous experience.

The early stages of the journey were dominated by visits to houses that would have formed a familiar part of her social and cultural milieu. Sophia (1718–74) was the daughter of the Essex landowner and one-time MP Edward Conyers; she married Sir Roger Newdigate in 1743, whilst he was MP for Middlesex. We know little about her early life, but she was well connected (her aunt was the countess of Pomfret, formerly one the ladies of the bedchamber for Queen Caroline) and was clearly well versed in country house visiting. The trip took in some of the established set pieces (Stowe, Windsor, Hampton Court, Wilton and Chatsworth), plus other places of renown, including Bulstrode, Cliveden, Monkey Island, Canons, Claremont and Badminton. Familiarity with many of these places was shared with her assumed readers, accounts of Stowe, Windsor and Hampton Court being very brief because, as she said of Windsor, it 'being so well known to all who will ever read this,

17 See Dana Arnold, *The Georgian Country House. Architecture, Landscape and Society* (Stroud, 1998), pp. 12–14.

18 William Camden, *Britannia* (London, 1607). His work was frequently excerpted and reprinted in smaller, portable and locally produced guidebooks, as was William Dugdale's *Monastocon Anglicanum*. For discussion of William Hanbury, see MacArthur, 'Gentlemen tourists'.

19 Emily Climenson (ed.), *Passages from the Diaries of Mrs Philip Lybbe Powys of Hardwick House Oxon. 1756–1808* (London, 1899); David Souden (ed.), *Byng's Tours. The Journals of the Hon. John Byng, 1781–1792* (London, 1991); Young, *A Six Weeks Tour through the Southern Counties.*

I shall say nothing of its Magnificence'.[20] These well-known places corresponded only broadly with the masterpieces identified by Campbell, Sophia's landmarks comprising royal and ducal palaces. Indeed, her itinerary is dominated by the residences of the aristocracy, which account for well over three-quarters of the houses visited. There are some surprising omissions (Blenheim and Woburn, for example), perhaps because the geography of the journey was in part structured around the Newdigate estate at Harefield in Middlesex (where they stayed for several nights during August, finally leaving on the 26th of the month) and the Conyers estate at Copped Hall in Essex (where they stayed on the night of 10 August). The marked clustering of visits around these places suggests that the party was moving within familiar country, even if its members were not always on personal terms with the owners of the houses.

Moving south of London, the route took in further landmark houses before arriving at Portsmouth, where Sophia describes the ships and the harbour. It then diverted from the beaten track with a trip to the Isle of Wight – still something of an adventure in the late 1740s, despite being only a short boat journey away.[21] On the island they went to a variety of houses (Carisbrooke Castle, Barton, Appuldurcombe), but it was the countryside that occupied more of their attention: from the cliffs at Underway (now Undercliffe) and the Needles to the fields and woods on the central uplands.[22] These were places that Sophia had clearly not seen before, and neither did she assume familiarity amongst her readers; the result is that we have detailed descriptions of many of the sites. Of Underway, for example, she wrote that:

> it lies under Immense Cliffs in ye most southerly part of ye Island, It has a most extraordinary effect to look down from ye top of these Cliffs and to see two or three little parishes beset thickly with cottages hanging almost into ye Sea for two miles together in a very rich soil and so warm a climate that Myrtles grew wild and very beautifully.[23]

Returning to the mainland, the emphasis switched again to historic towns (Winchester, Salisbury and Wells), ancient sites (Stonehenge, Avebury and Glastonbury) and natural wonders (Cheddar Gorge and Wookey Hole), destinations that suggest that the itinerary was also informed by antiquarianism

20 WRO, CR1841/7, Lady Newdigate's tour, fol. 7.

21 Celia Fiennes visited the island in the late seventeenth century, but Defoe does not seem to have crossed the Solent; Mrs Lybbe Powys viewed it as an easier alternative to the Lake District in 1792. See Celia Fiennes, *Through England on a Side Saddle* (London, 1888); Daniel Defoe, *Tour Through the Whole Island of Great Britain* (Penguin edition, London, 1972); Climenson, *Diaries of Mrs Lybbe Powys*, pp. 255–73.

22 WRO, CR1841/7, Lady Newdigate's tour, fols 31–3.

23 WRO, CR1841/7, Lady Newdigate's tour, fol. 33.

– perhaps unsurprising, given Sir Roger Newdigate's interests. Again, this took them out of the familiar realm of country houses and landed society, but Sophia's journey remained within a sphere of famous sites about which much had been written. The appearance and history of these places had been discussed at length by Camden and, more recently, William Stukeley, who pioneered the archaeological investigation of Stonehenge and Avebury.[24] Whilst not part of his antiquary circle, Sir Roger would have known about this scholarship and Sophia herself was clearly familiar with many of the theories and stories relating to these sites, although she rarely related them in her journal.

A similar mix of houses, antiquarian sites and natural wonders characterised the subsequent trip into Derbyshire: Chatsworth, Keddleston and Calke Abbey were all visited, along with Dovedale, Matlock and the river Derwent, and the caverns in the High Peak. This last group became popular destinations later in the century, as the taste for the picturesque became more widespread. However, the presence of other parties of tourists in the area and the willingness of locals to act as guides and facilitate access to the caverns make it clear that the visitors were already a familiar feature in the 1740s. Overall, then, this was essentially a rural tour to which towns, unless they offered something of historical interest and significance, were largely incidental. Many were simply places to stay (sometimes in rather unsatisfactory circumstances) – a marked contrast with the Grand Tour and a reflection of the under-developed state of British urbanism and tourist infrastructure at this time. It was also a mix of familiarity and novelty; yet even the unfamiliar had to be sufficiently known to make them suitable destinations. In the absence of published guides and tours, this suggests that correspondence and unpublished journals (such as that written by Sophia) were important in shaping itineraries and perhaps opinions.

Like many travel journals that were not intended for publication, Sophia's is essentially a day-by-day account of the places visited, with the amount written varying according to the interest of the day. The extant copy comprises two separate elements. The tour of the southern counties is recorded in a leather-bound volume containing fifty-six numbered pages of text and five hand-drawn pictures; key places are named in the generous margin and form a finding guide for the reader. The account of the trip to the Peak District is very different: twenty leaves of text loosely stitched together, where the writing all but fills the page. The circumstances and timing of the production of each element are more difficult to discern. The immediacy of

24 David Haycock, *William Stukeley: Science, Religion and Archaeology in Eighteenth-Century England* (London, 1985). See also Rosemary Sweet, 'Antiquaries and Ruins', *Writing Britain's Ruins*, eds Michael Carter, Peter Lindfield and Dale Townshend (London, 2017), pp. 43–71.

the text and the responses to places visited suggest that it was written on the road, but there is little crossing out and on one occasion she refers forward to a later section, indicating that it is more likely to be a fair copy produced after the event. This is an important consideration, as it moves the narrative away from initial reaction and towards considered reflection, and indicates the presence of a more self-conscious approach to the process of recording her impressions. We should be wary of drawing too fine a distinction between these two modes of writing, however; certainly there is no attempt to systematise the narrative or gloss over strong first impressions.

The style of writing is confidential and familiar, and the purpose appears to be to entertain and inform the reader, rather than explicitly communicate the erudition of the writer. In this, it contrasts with the impersonal and detached style favoured by antiquarians, and which formed the model for Grand Tourists at this time.[25] Sophia was certainly capable of writing in this more detached manner, as is seen in her responses to Stonehenge and Winchester. Here, her accounts go beyond the descriptive in order to incorporate historical accounts as a way of better understanding the places described. Unlike other travel writers, including Defoe, Hanbury and Lybbe Powys, she does not make direct reference to Camden and Stukeley, but she is clearly well informed.[26] For the most part, however, this is a personal account, littered with her opinions and preferences, although subjectivity is tempered by her habit of writing her judgements as bald statements. Thus, for example, she informs her reader that 'Axbridge is a long poor ugly Town at ye end of which stands Mr Brown's house where we dined; tis an old indifferent building wth a small garden prettily laid out.'[27] Moreover, she uses the first-person pronoun 'I' only sparingly, referring more generally to 'we'. This sharing of narrative position links her experiences to those of her party and broadens the authority of the knowledge communicated, but it also dilutes the strength of the narrative 'I', which Foster and Mills associate with the personal and the subjective.[28]

Sophia wrote about incidents that occurred along the way: her husband's dislocated shoulder; the problem of finding decent accommodation; the locals at Matlock providing music whilst they rowed on the Derwent. However, these neither dominate nor structure the journal; this is not an account of

25 See Elizabeth Bohls and Ian Duncan (eds), *Travel Writing, 1700–1830: An Anthology* (Oxford, 2005), p. xxiv; Turner, *British Travel Writing*, p. 13. Travel guidebooks from the late eighteenth and early nineteenth century dismissed antiquarian modes of writing as the style of 'pompous history', preferring a more entertaining and engaging tone of the kind adopted by Sophia – see McEvoy, 'Exploring Britain's Ruins', pp. 152–3.

26 WRO, CR1841/7, Lady Newdigate's tour, fols 35–8, 41–2; Defoe, *Tour*, p. 257; MacArthur, 'Gentlemen Tourists'; Climenson, *Diaries of Mrs Philip Lybbe Powys*, pp. 51–3.

27 WRO, CR1841/7, Lady Newdigate's tour, fol. 51.

28 Foster and Mills, *Women's Travel Writing*, pp. 9–10.

the hardships (real or imagined) of travelling nor of the process of being in transition.[29] Instead, it is an account of the state of the nation, a nation seen not through the commercial lens adopted by Defoe – who was preoccupied with signs of the country's trade, wealth and socio-economic progress – but rather through the eyes of the aristocratic elite and therefore reflective of their interests in land and landscape, taste and connoisseurship, leisure and learning. In this, it resembles the later accounts of leisure tourism written by Pennant, Gilpin and others.[30] This places Sophia's journal outside the conventions of travel writing and challenges established models and chronologies of the development of different genres. In part, this might reflect the fact that the journal, although apparently written to be enjoyed by others, was unpublished and probably never intended for publication. Focusing on published journals quite rightly draws attention to the intentionality of writing, but even then the audience of the book and their reading of the text is rarely considered in detail.[31] Moreover, we need to think about what becomes of this when there is no wider audience. Unfortunately, we know nothing about the subsequent use or even the location of the journal.[32] The style of writing makes it doubtful that Sophia was writing simply for herself – as an aide memoire or an expected literary discipline – so she clearly had some reader or readers in mind. Lybbe Powys states that she initially wrote her diaries for her father to read, and close friends and family are the most likely audience for Sophia's journal. With a close and private circulation, we should be wary of looking for conscious agendas of the type highlighted by Turner and others.[33] Indeed, I might go further and argue that this kind of unpublished account allows us to get closer to the underlying attitudes of travellers, and especially female travellers.

Reactions and Reflections

In her analysis of women's accounts of their visits to Italy, Sweet identifies several key themes: taste, virtue and erudition; sociability and social life; domesticity, and art and its appreciation.[34] Unsurprisingly, a similar range

29 See James Duncan and Derek Gregory (eds), *Writes of Passage: Reading Travel Writing* (London, 1999), p. 4.

30 On 'state of the nation' travelogues and the rise of leisure tourism writing, see Bohls and Duncan, *Travel Writing*, p. 96; Turner, *British Travel Writers*, p. 49.

31 For a useful example of where this is attempted see Jocelyn Anderson, 'Remaking the Country House: Country-House Guidebooks in the Late Eighteenth and Early Nineteenth Centuries' (PhD diss., Courtauld Institute of Art, 2013).

32 I have been unable to trace Sophia's journal in the library catalogues of either Sir Roger or his second wife, Hester Newdigate, or in the correspondence between Sophia and Sir Roger.

33 Turner, *British Travel Writers*, pp. 132–5.

34 Sweet, *Cities and the Grand Tour*, pp. 23–54.

of concerns run through Sophia's account of her English tour, but there were important differences in emphasis. For instance, she has remarkably little to say about domesticity, beyond passing notes on the dirt apparent in some towns (Waltham Abbey, for instance was one of the 'dirtiest towns in England') and the unsatisfactory arrangements in some of the inns where the party stayed. Her interest in the many houses that she visited never strayed into the domestic arrangements or the everyday life of their inhabitants, although she occasionally commented on the convenience with which rooms were arranged, as at Stowe, where the addition of a loggia to the dressing room made the apartment 'extremely agreeable'.[35] Of course, Sophia rarely encountered unfamiliar domestic environments, a topic that lent fascination to the published letters of Mary Wortley Montagu; nor did she have an agenda of marking the inferiority of foreign modes of living – a recurrent concern for many on the Grand Tour.[36] It might be that her silence here reflected a desire to distance herself from mundane domestic concerns and thus challenge implicit gender hierarchies, but she also has little to say about manners and customs or about social life beyond her immediate party. Although the names of house owners are carefully noted, there is no suggestion that she and her husband routinely had social contact with them; they are labels on the house rather than a record of who she met. Even when the Newdigates were guests at a house we hear nothing of domestic sociability. Sophia is peculiar in this: Mrs Lybbe Powys, for instance, was always careful to record the company present and to detail her engagement with their social activities, whilst the *Short Tour*, published anonymously by Elizabeth Percy, duchess of Northumberland, is 'essentially a name-dropping catalogue of social engagements at various Courts'.[37] In this way, at least, Sophia's journal bears a closer resemblance to those written by gentlemen such as William Hanbury and the Hungarian aristocrats studied by Fatsar, with their emphasis on taste and aesthetics.[38]

As Sweet observes, although taste was generally seen as a masculine domain, elite women were expected both to appreciate the antiquities of Rome and to deploy an appropriate language of taste and virtue.[39] As Sophia's journal makes clear, these attributes were also expressed in an appreciation of English architecture, gardens and collections. Of these, she had well-formed and strong opinions, both positive and negative. These were sometimes expressed in very brief or dismissive terms: Wooton Farm near Chertsey, for example, was 'a mere box built of bricks'; the house at

35 WRO, CR1841/7, Lady Newdigate's tour, fol. 4.
36 See Bohls, *Women Travel Writers*, pp. 23–45.
37 Climenson, *Diaries of Mrs Lybbe Powys*; Turner, *British Travel Writers*, p. 142.
38 MacArthur, 'Gentlemen Tourists'; Fatsar, 'Enjoying Country Life to the Full'.
39 Sweet, *Cities and the Grand Tour*, p. 27.

Waltham Abbey was 'dark damp and unpleasant', despite lavish spending by the last owner; Claremont, belonging to the duke of Newcastle, was 'ugly enough on the outside but convenient within', although its furniture was 'in general very indifferent, the Hangings chiefly paper & hardly any good pictures', and Barton, Goodwood and Farnborough, among several others, were simply 'indifferent'. On other occasions, the appraisal was fuller. Monkey Island, 'a small spot of ground in one of the least beautiful part of ye Thames' where the duke of Marlborough had built a small pair of buildings, is described in detail. In one building there was a 'parlour painted all over with Monkeys', whilst the second, an oblong wooden structure, was 'richly fitted up with Chocolate Colour & gold Ornaments in ye French tast [sic]'. Both seem to have fallen short of the expected norms of good taste, with Sophia lamenting that they 'gave us so little pleasure that we repented ... that we had spent so much in seeing it'.[40] Similarly, her appraisal of parks and gardens could be acerbic: at Goodwood, the fifty acres of gardens were 'laid out well', but the Stone Dell was filled up with a ruined church, hermit's cave, Chinese House, Lapland House and 'two or three other odd (& we thought tasteless) buildings'. Similarly, and with the exception of two great fountains, the waterworks at Chatsworth were condemned as 'quite Baubling' and 'Childish fancies'.[41]

It is easy to dismiss these opinions as superficial and uninformed by any rational system of taste, but in reality Sophia's critique, like that of many other elite women, was shaped and informed by contemporary understandings of architectural and stylistic genres. For example, in the grounds of Langley Park she noted a 'very elegant Temple [which] stands on eight arches, ye room above an octagon, ye dome & sides of which are very richly work'd in Stucco in very high taste'. Everything here was correct and in proportion. In contrast, at the duke of Queensbury's house at Amesbury the garden was 'in a stiff formal taste ... . They have lately built a Chinese house of flint, no very proper material for ye purpose.'[42] She clearly understood the principles of classical architecture and recognised both the changing taste in garden design and the crucial role of buildings within the emerging fashion for landscaped gardens. Her opinions and knowledge were, no doubt, shared with her husband – a renowned classical scholar – and may have been derived from him; but there is little evidence to suggest that Sophia fell into the category of 'second-class practitioners and passive consumers' into which,

40 WRO, CR1841/7, Lady Newdigate's tour, fols 15, 18, 21, 30, 1, 10–11.

41 WRO, CR1841/7, Lady Newdigate's tour, fol. 15, separate sheets on Peak District, fol. 14. Mrs Lybbe Powys shared this view of many of the waterworks at Chatsworth, the famous copper willow tree being 'beneath the dignity of the place' – Climenson, *Diaries of Mrs Lybbe Powys*, p. 29.

42 WRO, CR1841/7, Lady Newdigate's tour, fols 26, 34.

in Bohls's estimation, many women were placed.[43] On the contrary, she was active in the processes of shaping as well as applying informed appreciation of taste. Two further examples serve to illustrate this point. At Stowe she differentiated between the earlier and later buildings in the garden, picking out the recently completed gothic church for particular commendation, but suggesting that 'if they were much thinner sown would be more pleasing to ye eye'. Here, she was certainly in accord with others. Mrs Lybbe Powys, visiting a quarter of a century later, in 1775, observed that 'the buildings used, I know, to be thought too numerous', a fault she attributed to the immaturity of the planting that allowed several to be seen at once, which 'must have had very different and crowded effect'.[44] Sophia offered a similar critique of excess at Wilton, much visited and generally admired as a paragon of luxury and taste. She complained that 'the Coat of Arms, Crests & coronets painted & gilt & several bustos ye Colours refreshed lately & make a very tawdry appearance'. As with the later criticisms of Henrietta Cavendish's construction of 'pictorial family tree' at Welbeck Abbey, the affront to taste came through going too far with a motif – even one as central to elite identity as rank and pedigree.[45]

It is telling that these were not conventional readings of such places, but rather an expression of her (or perhaps their) interpretation of refined taste. In this way, Sophia demonstrates how women could participate in Kantian notions of taste, bringing to bear extrinsic parameters and disinterested analysis – both usually associated with men.[46] Of course, Sophia was not alone in participating in the definition, expression and application of systems of taste. Lybbe Powys was similarly engaged, and was both aware and proud of her abilities in this area. It is telling, therefore, that their opinions on places did not always match up, as we have already seen in terms of the buildings at Stowe. For both women this incorporation into discussions of taste was based in part on their social status, but it also relied on their specific knowledge. In this, they linked into rather than challenged established models of behaviour more generally seen as masculine.[47] We have already noted that Sophia demonstrated a good grasp of the principles of architecture and was particularly drawn to gothic structures, finding them in a remarkable number of places. This is especially noteworthy, as Gothicism was very much in its

43 Bohls, *Women Travel Writers*, p. 2.

44 WRO, CR1841/7, Lady Newdigate's tour, fol. 5; Climenson, *Dairies of Mrs Lybbe Powys*, pp. 154–5.

45 WRO, CR1841/7, Lady Newdigate's tour, fol. 42; Kate Retford, 'Patrilineal Portraiture? Gender and Genealogy in the Eighteenth-Century English Country House', *Gender, Taste and Material Culture in Britain and North America 1700–1830*, eds John Styles and Amanda Vickery (New Haven, CT, 2006), pp. 315–44.

46 See Bohls, *Women Travel Writers*, pp. 8–9.

47 Foster and Mills, *Women's Travel Writing*, pp. 89–90; Sweet, *Cities and the Grand Tour*, pp. 27–38.

infancy at this time; pioneers included her husband Sir Roger, who was just about to embark on the gothicisation of Arbury Hall.[48] It is possible that his enthusiasm was being expressed through Sophia's writings, although her descriptions and assessments reveal the writer's level of architectural knowledge and familiarity with technical terms, and they assume a corresponding degree of expertise in the reader. At one level, we get her familiar expression of strong opinion: Cowdrey Castle was 'a noble Gothick building' whereas the chapel at Wilton was condemned as 'small, ill proportioned, & lately fitted up in ye Gothick taste with such tawdry Angels & such variety of colours & gold that there is not the least appearance of solemnity'.[49] This hints at something deeper: an appreciation of what gothic interiors *should* look like that was fuelled by careful observation of genuine gothic architecture at Windsor Castle, Eton College and especially Winchester and Wells cathedrals.[50] At Winchester she links the 'beautiful Gothick work' with an account of the foundation and construction of the cathedral and of some of its key patrons – the one giving authenticity to the other and demonstrating her ability to deploy her learning in a palatable and digestible manner. Her journal is thus not simply about the touristic gaze but also about the recall and connection of past and place.

These accounts stopped well short of pedantic connoisseurship and 'pompous history', but they conformed with ideals often associated with polite masculinity and underline the ability of women to participate in these cultural and behavioural norms.[51] A similar balance is struck in Sophia's writing about the works of art that furnished many of the houses that the party visited. She mentions artists and specific pieces with which her readers are assumed to be familiar, combining appraisal with description in much the same way as travellers to Europe described key sights on the tour. At Wilton, for example, she pays particular attention to the dining room, 'richly furnished with pictures by Vandyke; at one end is that Capital piece of ye earl of Pembroke who was Treasurer to Charles ye 1st'.[52] Whilst she goes on to offer an annotated list of the people included in the painting, it is apparent that the reader is assumed to know exactly which painting she means by

48 For more discussion, see Peter Lindfield, *Georgian Gothic: Medievalist Architecture, Furniture and Interiors, 1730–1840* (Woodbridge, 2016).

49 WRO, CR1841/7, Lady Newdigate's tour, fols 24, 44.

50 The distinction between the tastelessness of what was referred to in the period as 'modern gothic' and the value of true and authentic gothic and medieval architecture is discussed by Lindfield, *Georgian Gothic*, esp. pp. 7–41.

51 Sweet, *Cities and the Grand Tour*, pp. 29–30; McEvoy, 'Exploring Britain's Ruins', p. 153. See also Brian Cowan, 'An Open Elite: The Peculiarities of Connoisseurship in Early Modern England', *Modern Intellectual History* 1:2 (2004), 151–83.

52 WRO, CR1841/7, Lady Newdigate's tour, fol. 43.

'that Capital piece'.[53] Much the same might be said of the lists of principal paintings included for Wilton, Windsor and Hampton Court. Perhaps naming these pieces allowed her to tick them off a mental list of things to be seen, but it could also have served to conjure mental images for her readers and herself when rereading the journal in later months or years. Whatever the precise motivation, it demonstrated an interest in the paintings hung on the walls of country houses that went well beyond their subject matter and value. In this sense, Sophia was demonstrating a more modern appreciation of art, where the identity of the painter and the quality of the work were the most important criteria in appreciating their worth. They also demonstrated a fuller commitment to art appreciation than was managed by many young men on the Grand Tour.[54]

Lists speak of a systematic approach: a way of thinking that sought to lay some kind of order on the world. The same mindset is apparent in Sophia's attempts to grasp and communicate something of her surroundings by recording their dimensions. The new ballroom at Stowe, for instance, was carefully described as being 70 feet long, 25 feet wide and 25 feet high; that at Claremont was 46 by 36 and 40 feet high, whilst the hall at Cowdrey Castle was 48 by 27 by 50 feet.[55] At one level, these might be dismissed as shorthand for the magnificence of the houses being described, but the need to underpin a textual account with the precision of measured numbers links Sophia into enlightenment notions that the world is best understood through empirical measurement.[56] A similar process is apparent in the way that the interior dimensions of buildings (especially assembly rooms) were a staple of town histories being produced in growing numbers during this period. Their authors were no doubt inspired by what we might now call civic boosterism, but there was also the practical concern to demonstrate in numbers that these rooms were fit for purpose and could accommodate several sets of dancers.[57] Sophia's own recording of measurements went further, and links to her knowledgeable interest in architecture. Thus, at Wooton Farm she noted a

53 WRO, CR1841/7, Lady Newdigate's tour, fols 43–4.

54 Sweet, *Cities and the Grand Tour*, p. 30. Sir Roger Newdigate drew up similar, but undated lists of paintings for Hampton Court, Windsor and Blenheim – see WRO, CR764/211, List of paintings. Such lists helped to reproduce the canon of key works and artists – see Jocelyn Anderson, '"Worth Viewing by Travellers": Arthur Young and Country House Picture Collections in the Late Eighteenth Century', *Travel and the Country House*, ed. Jon Stobart (Manchester, 2017), pp. 127–44.

55 WRO, CR1841/7, Lady Newdigate's tour, fols 4, 21, 24. The acreage of parks and gardens were also estimated in many instances and on one occasion the group measures the girth of a tree.

56 It also linked her into antiquarian practices and approaches. See Sweet, 'Antiquaries and Ruins', p. 48.

57 Jon Stobart, Andrew Hann and Victoria Morgan, *Spaces of Consumption: Leisure and Shopping in the English Town, c.1680–1830* (London, 2007), p. 119.

hexagonal structure in the garden, three sides of which were 'open Gothick Arches, about 8 f^{t} ½ diameter & 10 f^{t} high'.[58]

There is a danger here of over-interpreting a few numbers, which were perhaps little more than estimates provided by their guide. Even so, their inclusion is noteworthy because, as Turner argues, measuring the world in this way formed part of a 'quantifying discourse of British, anti-aristocratic manliness'.[59] If this is right, then nobody told Sophia or her husband. Sir Roger spent much of his time on his second Grand Tour sketching meticulous floor plans of ancient monuments and carefully noting their dimensions – a practice which was common to many aristocratic Tourists.[60] On a modest scale, Sophia did much the same in her journal, sketching some of the stones at Stonehenge, noting their height and breadth, and drawing a neat diagram of the arrangement of the inner and outer circles. She also drew Mr Pierce's hermitage at Lilliput near Bath, complete with a floor plan on which dimensions were again marked. Notwithstanding Turner's assertion, then, the aristocracy were clearly not averse to a bit of measuring, albeit of ancient monuments and country houses. Moreover, like many visitors to Stonehenge, Sophia also drew on the authority of others to speculate on the purpose of the monument and the methods used in its construction. William Hanbury, when he visited in the 1720s, travelled with his copy of Camden to hand and corresponded with Stukeley over the nature and purpose of the site, and Lybbe Powys referred specifically to Stukeley's ideas in her diary entry.[61] Although Sophia is less specific in her attributions, it is clear that she is familiar with both authors, and it is telling that her musings about the history of Stonehenge, Glastonbury and Winchester are the only places where she appears to detach herself from both the story and the place, adopting a version of chorography, with its scepticism about the historical myths attached to particular sites.

The involvement of women in this world of knowledge and discourse was subjected to considerable criticism and rebuke.[62] Smollett, for instance, parodied this in the tale of Mrs Baynard who, having travelled in Europe:

> affected to lead the fashion, not only in point of female dress, but on every article of taste and connoisseurship. She made a drawing of the new facade to the house in the country; she pulled up the tress, and pulled down the

58 WRO, CR1841/7, Lady Newdigate's tour, fol. 15.

59 Turner, *British Travel Writers*, p. 51.

60 See, for example, WRO, CR136/a/578, Notebook from the Grand Tour, c.1777, which contains floor plans and projections with dimensions for, *inter alia*: the pyramid of Cestius, the temple of Faune, the Diocletinus Therma, the Palatine hill and the temple of Minerva Medici.

61 MacArthur, 'Gentlemen Tourists'; Climenson, *Diaries of Lybbe Powys*, p. 52.

62 Turner, *British Travel Writers*, pp. 141–4.

> walls of the garden, so as to let in the early winds, which Mr Baynard's ancestors had been at great pains to exclude.[63]

These were precisely the areas of knowledge and expertise apparent in Sophia's journal, although they do not seem to have led to similar disasters or conflict at home. Her interest in the design and planting of the gardens visited on the tour was repeated at Arbury Hall, where she kept a journal of the plants and their flowering seasons during the early 1750s. And there is good evidence that she shared her husband's enthusiasm for the remodelling of Arbury Hall – her dressing room being the first place subjected to gothicisation – and she frequently corresponded with Sir Roger on the changes being made whilst he was away from Arbury.[64] More generally, this suggests that any critique of learned women was far from being universal. Indeed, Turner notes that reviews of published travelogues applauded 'masculine qualities of rationality and accuracy' in women's writing, especially when they were leavened with vivacity of composition.[65]

That such vivacity was neither a simple product of the predilections of publishers and reviewers nor a development of the late eighteenth-century boom in tourist guides is apparent from Sophia's reaction to her surroundings, especially the natural countryside. We have already seen her lively description of the cliffs at Underway; her reaction to the countryside on the eastern side of the Isle of Wight was similarly animated. Barton House 'stands high and all ye hills down to ye sea feathered beautifully wth woods wch wth ye view of ye opposite shore forms a very delightful scene'.[66] Here, she is drawing on a complex language of aesthetics. Bohls sees women travel writers as attacking the 'very foundations of modern aesthetics', but this goes well beyond how most women travellers drew on and fed into the broader language and discourse of aesthetics during this period. Both women and men adopted such an approach as a conscious alternative to the dullness and pedantry of the scientific and antiquarian discourse discussed above.[67] Sophia's journal reveals a lot about women's deployment of aesthetics at a time when it was still being theorised, and in particular their use of three key components: the picturesque, the sublime and the beautiful.

The picturesque, at least in its later Gilpinian manifestations, is often associated with a painterly view of the landscape and thus with the practical skills and practices of painting. It is an aesthetic that informs many travelogues, which tend to frame the landscape within the language of prospects

63 Tobias Smollett, *The Expedition of Humphrey Clinker* (1771; Oxford, 1966), p. 289.

64 WRO, CR136/A/248, Notebook of Sophia Newdigate, containing a list of trees and shrubs at Arbury, 1753; Geoffrey Tyack, *Warwickshire Country Houses* (Chichester, 1994), p. 12.

65 Turner, *British Travel Writers*, p. 129.

66 WRO, CR1841/7, Lady Newdigate's tour, fol. 30.

67 Bohls, *Women Travel Writers*, p. 10; Foster and Mills, *Women's Travel Writing*, p. 91.

and scenes, sometimes capturing this in accompanying sketches or watercolours.[68] We can see something of this painterly perspective in Sophia's descriptions of views, although she was writing more than forty years before Gilpin. At Barton, for instance, we have the feathering effect of the woods in the foreground and the opposite shore in the background; in the Mendips she admired 'a fine view of ye Severne [sic] & ye Holmes, two Islands in ye Severn wch greatly improve the landschape [sic]'; and at Cliveden House 'Nature has done so much that there is little left for art, ye winding & dividing ye river with ye rich & beautiful banks one each side form a most picturesque scene to which a bright moon light I thought made no small addition.'[69] As in a landscape painting, each scene is visually balanced, and light is important in creating atmosphere and generating a sense of the picturesque. Having already praised Dovedale as 'the most Romantick and Charming Place I ever beheld', Sophia waxed lyrical about 'a friendly Moon wch made ye prospect still more Agreeable'.[70]

Reference to the 'romantic', here, suggests a more personal and emotional response to her surroundings, something more regularly and closely associated with the aesthetic of the sublime. Typically, this is seen in reactions of fear and trepidation when faced with mountainous terrain, a response that, in the wake of the publication of Edmund Burke's influential *A Philosophical Enquiry into the Origin of Our Ideas of the Sublime and Beautiful* (1757), was often felt and recorded by visitors to the Lake District and North Wales. This, Bohls argues, was because the sublime, Burke's 'king of terrors' or death, was fuelled ultimately by notions of self-preservation.[71] But, of course, the category of the sublime predates Burke and may be traced at least as far back as Longinus.[72] As an emotional response it is apparent in Sophia's description of the landscape of the Peak District, although it is perhaps telling that she does not use the word itself. At Dovedale she traced the course of the river as it passes through 'a vale between Stupendous Rocks, whose forms alter every step you take, & make a more charming variety than I had ever seen before, we climbed up to a place wch makes me almost Giddy to relate'.[73] These dizzying heights were tempered by a desire to quantify and perhaps to control

68 See Andrews, *Search for the Picturesque*, pp. 24–38; Dale Townshend, 'Aesthetics of Ruins', *Writing Britain's Ruins*, eds Michael Carter, Peter Lindfield and Dale Townshend (London, 2017), pp. 97–9.

69 WRO, CR1841/7, Lady Newdigate's tour, fols 30, 51, 12. Rivers formed a key element of the picturesque – Andrews, *Search for the Picturesque*, pp. 85–108.

70 WRO, CR1841/7, Lady Newdigate's tour, separate sheets on Peak District, fol. 7.

71 Andrews, *Search for the Picturesque*, pp. 153–96; Bohls, *Women Travel Writers*, p. 15.

72 T. M. Costello, *The Sublime: From Antiquity to the Present* (Cambridge, 2012). For a discussion of sublime aesthetics in the eighteenth century, see Andrew Ashfield and Peter de Bolla (eds), *The Sublime: A Reader in British Eighteenth-century Aesthetic Theory* (Cambridge, 1996).

73 WRO, CR1841/7, Lady Newdigate's tour, separate sheets on Peak District, fol. 7.

the sublimity of natural phenomena, at least in mental terms. At Matlock, for example, she notes 'some rocks higher than any of ye rest, wch have been measured & are 147 y^{ds} high, many of these are almost perpendicular, some bow down over ye river wch winds among them in a stream above a hundred foot wide'.[74] These measurements, whether accurate or not, bring the terrors of the landscape into the realm of the estimable and knowable.

The sublime was also tamed with poetic descriptions and gentler emotions: expressions of awe and danger were less frequent than those of beauty and ease, the sublime's polar opposites. Again at Matlock, Sophia describes the 'beautiful hills amongst wch run natural Cascades, wch murmur amongst ye Rocks & make an agreeable and melancholy sound'. This takes Sophia's deployment of aesthetics further into the realm of the beautiful, with its channelling of 'social emotions'.[75] We see this in her delight in the romantic nature of scenery, but it is repeated over and again in her use of 'beautiful' to describe a wide range of landscapes and experiences. Thus, at Shanklin on the Isle of Wight there was a 'beautiful sandy shore'; on the boat ride from the island to Southampton there were 'beautiful prospects all ye way', and the caverns at Dovedale were 'extremely beautiful and Romantick'.[76] Sophia's precise understanding of beauty is difficult to gauge, but it appears to have encompassed a range of emotional responses as well as aesthetic evaluations of her surroundings. Certainly, it was more than simply a bland description of something that she found vaguely pleasing and was often deployed in a more analytical manner. When assessing and describing the church at Derby she wrote that it 'has a very high and Beautiful Gothick Tower, ye Body of ye Church is new Built from a design of Gibbs and is esteemed Good Architecture'.[77] Unlike the obscurity and irregularity of the sublime, beauty, as in the later work of Burke, seems to reside in a sense of rhythm and proportion. Her subjective response to the beauties of the tower forms an interesting contrast to the measured assessment of the church, and stands as evidence of her employing different aesthetic registers for the appreciation of different architectural features and styles.

In reality, these distinctions between the sublime, the romantic and the beautiful are somewhat false: they are the construct of linguistic and cultural analysis as much as an individual's responses to the world round them. Significantly, they were only fully theorised in the decades following Sophia's travels and her reaction to the landscape varied in relation to the nature of the scenery, blending the picturesque, sublime and beautiful.

74 WRO, CR1841/7, Lady Newdigate's tour, separate sheets on Peak District, fol. 16.

75 WRO, CR1841/7, Lady Newdigate's tour, separate sheets on Peak District, fol. 16; Bohls, *Women Travel Writers*, p. 15.

76 WRO, CR1841/7, Lady Newdigate's tour, fols 31, 34; separate sheets on Peak District, fol. 8.

77 WRO, CR1841/7, Lady Newdigate's tour, separate sheets on Peak District, fol. 3.

What is clear, however, is that, like other elite women, she was confident, mature and articulate in her reaction to and assessment of landscape. All this confirms that the male world of aesthetics was not exclusive, at least of elite women, whose status entitled them in ways that their gender perhaps did not. That said, there is little feel in Sophia's writing that she is seeking to colonise alien territory; like several of the female Grand Tourists studied by Sweet, she deploys the language and discourse of aesthetics in an unself-conscious manner.[78] Moreover, Sophia could also take a far more pragmatic and economic view of the landscape, one which again linked to her status as a member of the landowning classes. She read the productivity of the land she surveyed, often measuring this in trees: Bulstrode, for instance, was commended for its 'well wooded' park and Mrs Dillington's house on the Isle of Wight stood 'in ye middle of a very fine thick Wood'. These augmented the picturesque qualities of the landscape, but were also being appraised as an economic asset. Much the same was true of the countryside, with the absence of trees marking both desolation and a lack of productivity, the land around Buxton being the 'most uninhabited hilly Bleak Country' through which they travelled 'for many miles without ye sight of a Tree or even a Shrub'.[79]

Writers' reactions to their surroundings were not restricted to mental and philosophical categories, although these have dominated the literature, not least because they link travel and travel writing to broader cultural agendas. In practice, many travellers also had a visceral and sensory response to their surroundings, responses that were anchored in their physical presence in the landscape and an immediacy that produced different responses from those wrought by the impartial aesthetic gaze.[80] These were sometimes expressed through strong emotions and an early manifestation of the eighteenth-century cult of sensibility. Sophia took delight in the smell of flowers, for example, especially the tulip trees at Thorndon Hall, of which she wrote: 'its fragrancy I think exceeds any flower I ever smelt'. She also derived joy and pleasure from the scenery around Dovedale and from rowing on the river Derwent one moonlit evening. But there were also negative feelings linked to Sophia's experience of the Derbyshire countryside. Emerging from the caverns in the Peak, she noted that she was 'heartily glad to return to ye daylight wch appeared more beautiful than it ever did before'.[81] In part, this reflects the physical and perhaps social discomfort which entering the caves could create. Indeed, she refused to board the boat 'almost like a tray wch holds only two persons, who are obliged to lye down in it as flat as they can' that took some

78 Bohls, *Women Travel Writers*, p. 19; Sweet, *Cities and the Grand Tour*.

79 WRO, CR1841/7, Lady Newdigate's tour, fols 13, 31; separate sheets on Peak District, fol. 8.

80 See Duncan and Gregory, *Writes of Passage*, p. 5.

81 WRO, CR1841/7, Lady Newdigate's tour, fol. 20; separate sheets on Peak District, fols 16, 9.

of her companions deeper into the caves at Peak Hole.[82] These were, in a small way, adventures that made her travels more exciting. Foster and Mills argue that adventure and the overcoming of adversity were important aspects of the colonial project and of colonial writing, as well as projecting a particular type of heroic masculinity.[83] Sophia's adventures and dangers were of a different order, but they also carried a rather different message, communicating her sensibility rather than her heroism and fortitude. Such things were firmly the domain of her male companions, both the adventurers in the boat in Peak Hole and her husband, Sir Roger, who sustained a dislocated shoulder when the chair in which he was travelling overturned, but who, after resting for a day, quickly returned to their sight-seeing tour.[84]

Despite her apparent sensibility and her heightened receptiveness to the influx of empirical experience, Sophia matched her husband in the enjoyment of walking on the Isle of Wight and in the Peak. Both the activity itself and her writing about it heralded the later fashion for pedestrian tourism.[85] This is especially apparent in her account of the days spent in Dovedale and Matlock, where walking was an enjoyment in itself as well as a means to view the landscape. In the former, they walked two miles along the river Dove and then 'rambled with great pleasure' in the caves at the upper end of the valley. At the latter, 'the walks … are excessively delightful, after strolling about them till we were quite weary, we got into a boat & row'd up ye River'. They were later approached by a local who offered to 'take ye trouble off our hands wch ye Gentlemen refus'd telling him they thought it a pleasure'.[86] The physical exertion of walking and rowing, and of being physically immersed in the landscape, were both key to their enjoyment of these places – sentiments that surface in much of the later published works on the Lake District, north Wales and Scotland. It seems unlikely that Sophia and her party were really that much ahead of their time – indeed, they met other parties of genteel tourists at both of these places. It appears, then, that some practices that emerged only later in published travel writing were already commonplace, albeit revealed only through unpublished travelogues.

82 WRO, CR1841/7, Lady Newdigate's tour, fol. 20; separate sheets on Peak District, fols 7–8, 16, 10.

83 Foster and Mills, *Women's Travel Writing*, pp. 252–5.

84 WRO, CR1841/7, Lady Newdigate's tour, fol. 29.

85 See Robin Jarvis, *Romantic Writing and Pedestrian Travel* (Basingstoke, 1997).

86 WRO, CR1841/7, Lady Newdigate's tour, separate sheets on Peak District, fols 8, 16.

Conclusion

Country house visiting was not simply about name-dropping and admiring beautiful interiors or about grumbling about the lack of access or hospitality, as John Byng was wont to do.[87] As Tinniswood has argued, it also involved refining taste and passing judgement – activities in which women as well as men could engage (see McDonagh's chapter in this volume). Yet visiting was also set within the context of wider practices of domestic and overseas travel, and of travel writing. Linking the two, which inevitably means focusing on domestic tourism, is a useful corrective to (post-colonial) analysis of foreign travel. Being set within a familiar culture and environment, domestic travel writing offers different insights into the construction of self and of wider systems of taste and understanding. This is especially true of unpublished accounts that do not have the agendas which come with addressing a public and critical audience; they form a body of writing that is far more widespread than published journals and which often fail to conform to established genres.[88]

What, then, do Sophia Newdigate and her journal tell us about domestic travel and about the nature and construction of identity by elite women in the mid-eighteenth century? Underpinning everything was a wide-ranging interest in the places that she visited. Whilst country houses headed the list of sights, she also took in historic sites, a variety of countryside and a range of physical activities, from sailing to the Isle of Wight to walking in Dovedale. This engagement with the landscape took her well beyond the domestic concerns that are seen as characterising the published travelogues of women, especially those travelling abroad. She seems to be only passingly interested in such things: her accounts of houses dwell more on architecture, design and artwork than they do on domestic arrangements or social activities. We might take this further and suggest that neither is she concerned with constructing a (female) identity through her writing. This is not to say that her journal is merely a descriptive account devoid of any broader agenda, but neither does it appear to be trying to impress the reader with her social contacts, knowledge or superlative taste. These last qualities are worn lightly, perhaps because of the intimate and familiar tone struck in unpublished writing of this kind, but they are certainly present. Indeed, Sophia's assessment of the places that she visits reveal a well-articulated sense of good taste, a knowledge of architecture and art and a firm grasp on the language and discourse of aesthetics. None of these were debarred to women, as Sweet makes clear in the context of the Grand Tour, but all were seen as lying more firmly within the realm of polite and learned masculinity. In some ways, the privilege of her status

87 Souden, *Byng's Tours*.

88 See also Sweet, *Cities and the Grand Tour*; French and Rothery, *Man's Estate*, pp. 137–84.

allowed her to cross boundaries into what are often seen as more overtly male spheres; however, her experiences, reactions and writings also question gender divisions in aesthetics, taste and erudition. Of course, we must be cautious about reading too much into a single case study; yet Sophia shared in the culture of elite taste and drew on traditions of chorography in describing her surroundings whilst also anticipating the appreciation of the picturesque and sublime and the expression of sensibility. Moreover, it is apparent that she was not unusual in this. Reading her journal, this is not the voice of a woman seeking to carve out a distinct (female) identity, but rather one who is seeking to share her experiences and opinions with a set of equally learned friends, both male and female.

6

On Being 'fully and completely mistress of the whole business': Gender, Land and Estate Accounting in Georgian England

BRIONY MCDONAGH

> Permit one of your sex to give you, as far as her small knowledge will reach some hints to the right understanding of Accounts: an Art so useful for all sorts, sexes and degrees of persons especially for such as ever think to have to do in the world in any sort of Trade or Commerce …
>
> *Advice to the Maidens of London … By One of That Sex* (1678)

> Keep your accounts clear // Throughout the year // Let no mistake be made // Either in paying, or pay'd
>
> Account book of Elizabeth Hood (c. 1787–1808)

Penned roughly a century apart at either end of the long eighteenth century, the lines above signal something of the importance of accounting for women. As the anonymous author of *Advice to the Maidens of London* suggested, a working knowledge of accounting methods was a valuable skill for middle-class women to have. The full title made clear the author's thinking:

> Advice to the Women and Maidens of London: Shewing, that instead of their usual Pastime; and education in Needle-work, Lace, and Point-making, it were far more Necessary and Profitable to apply themselves to the right Understanding and Practice of the method of keeping books of account: whereby, either single, or married, they may know their Estates, carry on their Trades, and avoid the Danger of a helpless and forlorn Condition, incident to Widows … By one of that Sex.[1]

1 Anonymous, *Advice to the Maidens of London* (London, 1678). For a discussion of the author's gender, see John Richard Edwards, 'Accounting Education in Britain during the Early Modern Period', *Accounting History Review* 21:1 (2011), 36–67, especially 48–9.

Likewise stressing the importance of good accounting, the rhyming couplets were penned by a woman from a rather different social background than the supposed consumers of the advice book. Elizabeth Hood was a Somerset gentlewoman who spent more than sixty years managing a modest landed estate in Butleigh Wootton and the surrounding area, keeping the estate accounts not just as a widow but also before and during her marriage. She wrote the couplets in the inside cover of an account book used to record sales from the home farm, purchases of land and investments in drainage works, activities which while at least partially profit-driven certainly did not constitute an engagement in the kind of trade or commerce envisaged by the advice book's author. Yet as evidence of transactions and a record of her modifications to the local landscape, Hood's accounts were crucial to her management of the family's agricultural holdings, a business which expanded significantly – in terms of both acreage and turnover – under her stewardship.[2]

This chapter explores elite women's contribution to accounting practice specifically as it occurred in the context of their ownership, management and improvement of agricultural land and property. It does this with reference to the accounts and other records of fifteen women, all of whom owned or managed large agricultural properties, and thereby offers new insights into elite women's engagement with the land and landscape around them. As outlined in the introduction to this volume, there is almost no discussion in the existing literature of wealthy women's contribution to estate accounting, nor indeed of their management of landed estates more generally. As John Beckett put it almost thirty years ago, 'eighteenth-century landowning was a man's world' and aristocratic women who ran landed estates were a 'rarity'.[3] Seen to have been active in seventeenth-century estate management – and especially during the Civil Wars and Interregnum – the wives, widows and daughters of the elite are understood to have retired into domesticity in the eighteenth century.[4] Such an account is a result both of continuing academic interest in the idea of 'separate spheres' – specifically the ideology that, while eighteenth-century men occupied the public sphere, women were more closely confined to the domestic sphere, as outlined in Davidoff and Hall's *Family Fortunes* – and some reluctance on the part of agricultural and economic historians to address women's experiences as landowners and improvers.

2 Somerset Heritage Centre (hereafter SHC). Enquire with the repository for more information.

3 J. V. Beckett, 'Elizabeth Montagu: Bluestocking Turned Landlady', *Huntington Library Quarterly* 49:2 (1986), 149.

4 See Amanda Vickery, *The Gentleman's Daughter: Women's Lives in Georgian England* (New Haven, CT, 1998), pp. 1–6 for a brief review of the relevant literature. For examples of seventeenth-century women active in estate management see Amanda Capern, 'The Landed Woman in Early Modern England', *Parergon* 19.1 (2002) and Jane Whittle and Elizabeth Griffiths, *Consumption and Gender in the Early Seventeenth-Century Household: The World of Alice Le Strange* (Oxford, 2013).

That such an assessment of the balance of property and power in Georgian England has met with little in the way of challenge is all the more surprising in the light of recent research on early modern women's involvement in making investments and running business usually in an urban context, on their contributions in traditionally male spheres of activity such as electioneering and politics, and on gendered experiences of the law (on which see the introductory essay of the volume).

At the same time, accounting and business historians have addressed women's participation in the accounting profession in the late nineteenth and early twentieth century and their struggle to gain admittance to professional bodies,[5] as well as the feminisation of bookkeeping in the late nineteenth century, both as it took place in the home and beyond.[6] Exactly how far the existing corpus of research really adds up to a '*herstory* of accounting' is still open to debate, not least because so much of the work by accounting historians has focused on the nineteenth and twentieth centuries rather than the earlier period.[7] This is not to say that the accounting practices of early modern and eighteenth-century women have been entirely ignored. Work on women's business enterprises have necessarily relied on the evidence provided by business accounts and related documents – and, in doing so, reflected on the nature and construction of those sources – while both women's historians and literary scholars have shown an interest in female-authored accounts, particularly as they relate to wider histories of consumption.[8] Amanda

5 Cheryl R. Lehman, 'Herstory in Accounting: The First Eighty Years', *Accounting, Organizations and Society* 17:3/4 (1992), 261–85; Linda Kirkham and Anne Loft, 'Gender and the Construction of the Professional Accountant', *Accounting, Organizations and Society* 18:6 (1993), 507–58; idem, 'The Lady and the Accounts: Missing from Accounting History', *The Accounting Historians Journal* 28:1 (2001), 67–90.

6 S. Walker 'Identifying the Woman behind the "Railed-in Desk": The Proto-Feminisation of Bookkeeping in Britain', *Accounting, Auditing & Accountability Journal* 16:4 (2003), 606–39; C. Cooper and P. Taylor, 'From Taylorism to Ms Taylor: the Transformation of the Accounting Craft', *Accounting, Organizations and Society* 25 (2000), 555–78; C. W. Wootton and B. E. Kemmerer, 'The Changing Genderization of Bookkeeping in the United States, 1870–1930', *Business History Review* 70 (1996), 541–86. On women's bookkeeping for charitable institutions, see S. Walker, 'Philanthropic Women and Accounting: Octavia Hill and the Exercise of 'Quiet Power and Sympathy', *Accounting, Business & Financial History* 16:2 (2006), 163–94; A. M. Boylan 'Timid Girls, Venerable Widows and Dignified Matrons: Life Cycle Patterns among Organized Women in New York and Boston, 1797–1840', *American Quarterly* 38:5 (1986), 779–97.

7 S. Walker 'Accounting Histories of Women: Beyond Recovery?', *Accounting, Auditing & Accountability Journal* 21:4 (2008), 580–610. See also Kirkham and Loft, 'The Lady', 87, who assert that 'The invisibility of women as managers or accountants in accounting history in the 16th, 17th and 18th centuries is pervasive', a deficiency which has yet to be fully address by accounting historians.

8 Vickery, *Gentleman's Daughter*; idem, 'His and Hers: Gender, Consumption and Household Accounting in Eighteenth-Century England', *Past and Present* 1:suppl. 1 (2006); Whittle and Griffiths, *Consumption*; Helen Berry, 'Prudent Luxury: The Metropolitan Tastes of Judith Baker, Durham Gentlewoman', *Women and Urban Life*, eds Rosemary Sweet and Penelope Lane

Vickery's work is of particular note, but the whole body of material has done much to recover the home as an important site of accounting as well as to re-evaluate household accounting and provisioning as women's work – that is, as the business of the household and an 'exercise in power'.[9]

Yet for all the interest in middle-class women and urban businesses, far less has been written about upper-class women's involvement in either bookkeeping or business, particularly within rural settings. We know little about gentle and aristocratic women's role in keeping the accounts of landed estates, or about upper-class women's contributions to rural economies more generally or their attitudes to managing and improving landed property.[10] As Helen Berry notes in her discussion of the Durham gentlewoman Judith Baker, 'the engagement of eighteenth-century gentlewomen in meticulous daily management of the minutiae of account-keeping too often slips from view in the current historiography'.[11] Judith Baker, of course, kept not just the household accounts but also the estate and mining accounts for her Elmore property, six miles to the east of Durham. The mining enterprise in particular provided a significant income stream for the family and Baker maintained close oversight of all aspects of estate management throughout her life.[12] Women who controlled landed estates – whether as a result of inheritance, widowhood or other circumstances – had responsibility for what were fairly large family businesses. While there were important differences between landed estates and other more commercially orientated businesses – not least around issues of social capital and the reinvestment of profits into areas of the estate that were not profit-focused, including building works, landscape improvements and charity – large agrarian estates were nevertheless big enterprises that employed significant numbers of people and had an annual turnover far in excess of many of the small urban businesses on which much of the literature on women's accounting and business activities has so far

(Abingdon, 2003); Jennie Batchelor, 'Fashion and Frugality: Eighteenth-Century Pocket Books for Women', *Studies in Eighteenth-Century Culture* 32 (2003), 1–18; Rebecca Connor, *Women, Accounting and Narrative: Keeping Books in Eighteenth-Century England* (London, 2004).

9 Vickery, *Gentleman's Daughter*, p. 127; see too Alexandra Shepard, *Accounting for Oneself: Worth, Status, and the Social Order in Early Modern England* (Oxford, 2015).

10 Vickery, for example, says little about her subjects' involvement in estate management in *Gentleman's Daughter* (though see pp. 64, 152 and 157 for brief discussions). See too Elizabeth Griffiths, *Her Price is Above Pearls: Family and Farming Records of Alice Le Strange, 1617–1656* (Norfolk, 2015) for an example of seventeenth-century woman keeping estate accounts. For first-hand accounts of more middling women's involvement in farming, see Anne Hughes, *Her Boke: The Diary of a Farmer's Wife 1796–1797* (Preston, 2009); Ruth Facer, *Mary Bacon's World: A Farmer's Wife in Eighteenth-Century Hampshire* (Newbury, 2010). On women and dairying, see Deborah Valenze, 'The Art of Women and the Business of Men: Women's Work and the Dairy Industry c. 1740–1840', *Past and Present* 130 (1991).

11 Berry, 'Prudent Luxury', 150–1.

12 Ibid.

focused.[13] For that reason they – and the women that sometimes owned or otherwise managed them – deserve far closer attention.

This chapter offers just that, exploring elite women's contribution to estate accounting and assessing the extent to which elite women's involvement in practices of accounting reveals them to be 'the sole proprietors of their enterprises', as Christine Wiskin has argued was the case for middle-class urban businesswomen.[14] In doing so, it also argues that elite women's engagement with estate accounting was just one aspect of their wider involvement in managing and improving landed estates in the period between c. 1700 and 1830. The chapter thus enriches both the literature on women and accounting – which has largely ignored upper-class women and their contribution to estate economies – and work on gender and landed estates more generally, a body of material which in discussing landowners' role in managing and improving the agricultural landscapes of Georgian England has almost always assumed that the landowner in question was a man.[15] What follows is split into four sections. The first introduces elite women's bookkeeping, briefly discussing their role in household accounting before moving on to outline the sources available to those studying their contribution to estate accounting. It also introduces the women whose individual stories and experiences make up the main body of the chapter. The second section explores propertied women's engagement in estate accounting in more detail, examining the books kept by a number of single, married and widowed women and reflecting on important questions about the nature of the accounts they kept and the channels by which they acquired the necessary skills to do so. The third section examines questions of auditing and accountability as they relate to both the women themselves and their senior servants. The fourth reflects on the idea that accounting was a crucial tool in attempts to improve estate finances, exploring the contribution that elite women's accounting made to efforts to clear debts and increase profits via enclosure, associated agricultural improvements or urban development. The final section of the chapter offers some concluding comments.

13 Kirkham and Loft, 'The Lady', 75.

14 Christine Wiskin, 'Businesswomen and Financial Management: Three Eighteenth-Century Case Studies', *Accounting, Business and Financial History* 16:2 (2006), 143–61.

15 On estate accounting see David Oldroyd, *Estates, Enterprise and Investment at the Dawn of the Industrial Revolution* (Aldershot, 2007); Christopher Napier, 'Aristocratic Accounting: The Bute estate in Glamorgan 1814–1880', *Accounting and Business Research* 21:82 (1991), 163–74. On estate management more generally, see Sarah Webster, 'Estate improvement and the Professionalisation of Land Agents on the Egremont Estates in Sussex and Yorkshire, 1770–1835', *Rural History* 18 (2007); J. R. Wordie, *Estate Management in Eighteenth-century England: The Building of the Levison-Gower Fortune* (London, 1982); T. J. Raybould, 'Systems of Management and Administration on the Dudley estates, 1774–1833', *Business History* 10:1 (1968), 1–11; David Spring, *The English Landed Estate in the Nineteenth Century: its Administration* (Baltimore, MD, 1963).

Elite Women's Bookkeeping

As the conduct literature of the period makes clear, the wives of both middle-class and elite men were expected to have an oversight of the domestic household. Responsibilities typically included the hiring and management of servants, the education of children and the provisioning of the household.[16] The ideal wife demonstrated prudence and an economy in keeping with her husband's wealth and many married women would have had responsibility for at least some aspects of household accounting.[17] This could include keeping a basic record of the sums laid out on food and other household necessities, making arrangements to settle bills run up with traders and looking over the cash books kept by senior servants, the latter particularly the case in larger households. Many married women would also have been responsible for accounting for how their pin money – sums paid to a woman by her husband and agreed as part of the marriage negotiations – was spent. While the precise arrangements for accounting varied from household to household, day to day spending was usually recorded in a pocket or memorandum book, with items later copied into a larger volume of accounts often containing both personal and household items. Even young unmarried women were encouraged to keep a record of daily personal expenses, typically in small volumes published specifically for the purpose and known as ladies' pocket books.[18] As Vickery notes, these female-authored financial records survive in some numbers in archives offices across the country, though many more must have been lost or destroyed in the intervening two centuries.[19]

Yet if household accounts, memorandum books and pocket books survive in some numbers for both middle-class and elite women, female-authored estate accounts and ledgers are rather more difficult to identify. This is in part because for married women estate accounting by and large fell within their husband's sphere of responsibility, but it also stems from the difficulties in uncovering women's hidden histories: the ledgers kept by landowning women have sometimes been miscataloged as their steward's account books, while those kept by women on behalf of absent husbands or sons do not always clearly identify their author.[20] At the same time, widows' estate management has often been written out of family histories, going unrecorded in both

16 Vickery, *Gentleman's Daughter*, pp. 127–60; idem, 'His and Hers', passim.

17 See, for example, Charles Allen's *The Polite Lady: Or a Course of Female Education* (London, 1769), which recommended that daughters learn to be 'be a complete mistress of the four simple rules of arithmetic, the rule of proportion, and a plain method of book-keeping' (cited in Edwards, 'Accounting Education', 50).

18 Batchelor, 'Fashion and Frugality'.

19 Vickery, *Gentleman's Daughter*, p. 133; Kirkham and Loft, 'The Lady', 76. On factors affecting the survival of account books, see Vickery, 'His and Hers', 21–2.

20 On the gendering of household accounting and consumption, see Vickery, 'His and Hers'.

printed and manuscript genealogies. In focusing on the descent of title and arms, the genealogical histories written by John Burke and others have elided women's estate management, often assuming that estates followed title and giving little space to women's management of property under jointure or other more individualised arrangements. One brief case study will suffice to exemplify this tendency.

The widowed Lady Elizabeth Dryden managed the Canons Ashby estate in Northamptonshire for more than twenty years after her husband's death in 1770. Yet Burke's *Peerage* makes no mention of her, noting only that when Sir John Dryden died without issue the baronetcy expired and the estates devolved upon his niece, another Elizabeth Dryden.[21] The younger Elizabeth Dryden – known to the family as Betsy – had been adopted by the Drydens in 1761 specifically with the intention of making her Sir John's heiress.[22] Betsy married John Turner Esq. in 1781, but contrary to the entry in Burke's *Peerage* the couple did not inherit the Dryden family estates until the death of her aunt in 1791. By then the elder Elizabeth Dryden had managed the property for more than two decades, as the family archive reveals. During this time she carefully recorded the rents and other profits she received in two account books, balancing the sums against her annual outgoings for the farms and adding a series of memoranda about the tenancies on the estate.[23] Although they were until relatively recently miscatalogued as her steward's accounts, the two account books are undoubtedly written by Dryden herself. We know it was she who penned the accounts because a contemporary letter records that she suffered a stroke in 1790, a circumstance which tallies with the sudden deterioration of the handwriting at this point in the account books.[24] That she persisted in keeping the accounts is also testament to the grit and determination with which she approached the task of recording and auditing the estate's finances.

Nor was Dryden alone in keeping accounts for the property she managed. This chapter draws on account books belonging to fifteen gentle and aristocratic women as a means of assessing propertied women's contribution to the financial management of Georgian landed estates. The account books were identified as part of a larger project on elite women's role in estate management and agricultural improvement in the long eighteenth century. Key details of

21 John Burke, *Peerage and Baronetage* (London, 1839), p. 335.

22 On which see Briony McDonagh, 'Women, Enclosure and Estate Improvement in Eighteenth-Century Northamptonshire', *Rural History* 20:2 (2009), 143–62, especially 147–8; Mark Rothery and Jon Stobart, 'Merger and Crisis: Sir John Turner Dryden and Canons Ashby, Northamptonshire, in the Late Eighteenth Century', *Northamptonshire Past and Present* 65 (2012).

23 Northamptonshire Record Office (hereafter NRO), D(CA) 321 and 322. There are also further loose pages from one of the books at D(CA)/351.

24 NRO, D (CA) 1054.

their authors are summarised in Table 2 below and some general comments made here. Most were women of independent means – widows or unmarried women who owned or otherwise controlled property – though there are also one or two married women discussed here. All resided in a country house, sometimes with access also to a London townhouse, and all would have thought of themselves as upper class rather than middle class. Some were titled and managed large estates running to several thousand acres or more, while others came from the lower reaches of the gentry and controlled as little as a few hundred or a thousand acres, perhaps with additional income from mining or other sources. Many were widows, although, regardless of whether they were single, married or widowed at the time we meet them here, many had inherited as heiresses. Others did not strictly speaking own the property but controlled landed estates under jointure arrangements or as guardians to young sons. Still others were the purchasers of estates or managed land on behalf of absent husbands. Geographically their estates were scattered across England from Cornwall to County Durham, with a significant number of women owning property in south and south-west England or the Midlands, a product of the parameters of the larger research project.[25] Thus, while their class and gender united them, they were otherwise a diverse group in terms of wealth, geography and acreage held.

The accounts themselves were as varied as their authors. Some were large volumes, or collections of volumes, covering multiple aspects of personal, household and estate accounting in great detail, while others were much smaller books covering, for example, only rents, sales and farm expenditure. Some covered just one or two years, while others covered several decades. Most were written in the period between about 1775 and 1850, though there are also a handful of earlier eighteenth-century examples discussed here. Not all the account books were strictly speaking female-authored: most were written by the women themselves, though some were produced by an estate steward on his mistress's behalf to be later audited or otherwise used by her. In other cases, a female landowner wrote some of the accounts herself while her estate steward or land agent kept the rest. It is clear in many cases that there were once other accounts books written by or for the women in question but that these have been subsequently lost or destroyed. Thus we know from other sources that both Anne Lister and Elizabeth Montagu kept accounts for the mines on their estates and while the books cannot now be found among their surviving papers some discussion of their bookkeeping is included here. It is to the account books and the stories of the women who wrote them that we now turn.

25 Few of the women discussed here came from northern England, and none from East Anglia or the north-west.

Table 2. Female landowners keeping accounts and featured in the text

Name and main property	Alive	Approx. age on coming into property	Route to landownership	Marital status whilst managing property	Approx. no. of years managing property	Surviving accounts kept by subject	Years covered by accounts	Evidence subject audited accounts
Anna Maria Agar of Lanhydrock (Cornwall)	1771–1861	27	Inherited from uncle	Widowed	63*	No	Most years 1811–54	Yes
Judith Baker of Elemore (Durham)	1726–1810	48	Widow acting on behalf of son	Widowed	36	Yes	1774–1810	
Lady Olivia Bernard Sparrow of Brampton Park (Huntingdonshire)	c. 1778–1863	27	Controlled property under jointure arrangements	Widowed	58	No – estate Yes – charity	Various accounts c. 1803–63	Yes
Mary Clarke of Chipley (Somerset)	c. 1656–1705	n/a	Married woman managing estate on behalf of/in collaboration with absent husband	Married	15+	Yes (along with husband & steward)	1690s	
Lady Anne Cust of Belton (Lincolnshire)	c. 1694–1779	40	Controlled property under jointure arrangements and as guardian to children. Later inherited Belton estate from brother.	Widowed	45	Yes	1734–59	
Lady Elizabeth Dryden of Canons Ashby (Northamptonshire)	d. 1791	60+	Controlled property under jointure arrangements	Widowed	21	Yes	1770–91	

* This included a short period between 1804 and 1811 when Agar was married and her husband owned and managed the estate. She retained considerable control during this period, however (see, for example, their marriage settlement: Courtney Library, Truro, HJ/1977/44).

Table 2 cont.

Elizabeth Hood of Butleigh Wootton (Somerset)	1770–1855	18	Inherited from father	Single/ married/ widowed	67	Yes	c. 1787–1808	
Amabel Hume-Campbell, Baroness Lucas of Crudwell (from 1797) and Countess de Grey (from 1816), of Wrest Park (Bedfordshire)	1751–1833	46	Inherited from mother	Widowed	36	No (letters & diaries only)	–	Yes
Mary Vere Hunt of Lanhydrock (Cornwall)	1696–1758	45	Inherited from brother	Widowed	17	No	1744, 1749	Yes
Anne Lister of Shibden (West Yorkshire)	1791–1840	35	Inherited from uncle	Single	14	Some (now lost)	–	
Lady Jane St John Mildmay of Dogmersfield (Hampshire)	c. 1765–1857	43	Inherited from father, great uncle & aunt. Later controlled large estate as widow 1808–57	Widowed	49	No	1808–21 1824–33	Yes
Jane More Molyneux of Loseley (Surrey)	1729–1808	48	Inherited from sister	Single	31	Yes	Various accounts 1777–94	Yes
Elizabeth Montagu of Sandleford (Berkshire)	1718–1800	57	Inherited from husband	Widowed	25	Some (now lost)	–	Yes
Elizabeth Prowse of Wicken (Northamptonshire)	1733–1810	34	Controlled property under arrangement with mother-in-law	Widowed	43	Yes	1768–71 1774–84	Yes
Elizabeth Somerset, duchess of Beaufort, of Badminton and Stoke Gifford (Gloucestershire)	c. 1713–99	43	Controlled property as son's guardian. Also inherited from brother.	Widowed	Badminton 9 Stoke Gifford 29	Some (as guardian to 5th duke)	1756–66	Yes

Estate Accounting

While the two account books for Canons Ashby were written by Elizabeth Dryden in her widowhood, Elizabeth Hood (née Periam) kept the accounts for her estate at Butleigh Wootton (Somerset) not just as a widow but also as a young unmarried woman and a wife. Aged just eighteen, Hood inherited the Wootton estate from her father John Periam (d. 1788) and later married Alexander Hood, a captain in the Royal Navy who was killed in command of the *HMS Mars* six years later.[26] The estate was a small one: in 1806 the rental brought her just over £1000 a year, plus smaller sums for bark, corn and livestock and regular dividends from her funds in stocks.[27] The core of the estate inherited from her father amounted to no more than 600 acres in 1772, but Hood spent more than £11,000 on purchasing land and houses in the neighbourhood and her son's portion of the estate – held by him whilst she still owned the rest of the estate – amounted to nearly 1700 acres in 1846.[28]

The account book which she inherited with the estate had been started by her father in 1745 and used to record his annual rental, receipts and disbursements alongside various memoranda. Periam also left her a smaller notebook in which he recorded his expenses at university and the Inns of Court in the 1730s, along with details of his purchases in the neighbourhood of Wootton and his improvements to the house and estate. Hood continued her father's account and memoranda books, keeping the receipts and disbursements until 1808 – by which time she had filled the volume and presumably started a new, now lost, account book – and adding notes about her own purchases and improvements. Her husband's poor health meant that he spent the first few years of their marriage with her in Somerset, but – having established a separate estate in her property prior to their 1792 marriage – it was her who kept the estate accounts.

Entries in the account book suggest that she had begun to keep the accounts prior to her father's death in late 1788. A rental of 1786 was written into the book by Hood, then sixteen, in the neat, overly elaborate handwriting of an adolescent. She began keeping the receipts and disbursements in August 1787, though her father continued to add occasional items to the accounts, most notably in the spring of 1788.[29] The decision to turn the account book over to Hood probably reflects her father's failing health, but presumably also

26 SHC, copy marriage settlement of Elizabeth Periam and Captain Alexander Hood, 5th July 1792.

27 SHC, estate account book of John Periam (with additions by Elizabeth Hood), 25, 108 and 139 [and unpaginated, 29 July 1804].

28 SHC, estate account book of John Periam (with additions by Elizabeth Hood), 22–5; DD/AH/50/7/3 and 14/4/2.

29 SHC, estate account book of John Periam (with additions by Elizabeth Hood), 22 and 108–11.

the desire on the part of an elderly estate owner – Periam was then seventy-four – to ensure that his young heiress knew how to manage the estate and keep the necessary financial records. Her only brother had died before her own birth and Hood was brought up as the heiress to the estate, but we can only guess at exactly what lessons her father provided for her. She was certainly sent to Wells School from the age of ten, where she was probably introduced to bookkeeping.[30] Many genteel girls would have learnt the basics of household accounting at home from their mothers, governesses or tutors, but girls' schools also taught arithmetic and bookkeeping and there were also instructional texts on accounting aimed specifically at women.[31]

Perhaps just as important as the schooling Hood received was the 'on the job' training in estate accounting and management her father provided her with. Given his early instruction in the law and his five decades spent running the Wootton estate, John Periam was surely able to impart to his daughter something of the legal, financial and agricultural knowledge necessary to run a small landed estate. In keeping the accounts for the last year of her father's life, she effectively served her apprenticeship. Thus the occasional crossings out that appear in the pages for 1787 and 1788 seem to reflect the ongoing process of learning how to keep the accounts and the couplets written inside the book's front cover – quoted at the beginning of this chapter – presumably reflected something of the lessons her father had taught her as a young woman.

Other women also took on bookkeeping on behalf of ailing or absent relatives. Lady Anne Cust made entries in her husband's account book from as early as 1732 and increasingly frequently from spring 1734, presumably because he was by then unwell and she acted as his amanuensis.[32] Sir Richard Cust died in summer 1734 and Lady Anne took over the account books. Her lawyer wrote to her in the weeks following her husband's death advising her to keep three account books: one for her jointure property and her newly purchased estate at Grantham, one for the younger children's property and legacies, and one for the remainder of the estate, which now belonged to her eldest son.[33] She held mixed portfolios of land, government stock and mortgages, but seems to have had a preference for land as an investment.[34] While the accounts kept by Hood were relatively simple charge and discharge accounts, Lady Anne's used the terminology of debtor and creditor and represented a rather more complex system of accounting, if one she had admittedly inherited with the books.

30 SHC, account and memorandum book of John Periam (with additions by Elizabeth Hood).

31 Edwards, 'Accounting education', 45; Allen, *The Polite Lady*, p. 13.

32 Lincolnshire Archives (hereafter LA), BNLW 4/6/19/5.

33 LA, BNLW 4/1/10/4/1.

34 LA, BNLW 4/1/10/4/2.

By contrast, Elizabeth Prowse (née Sharp) introduced a sophisticated system of estate accounting on her modestly sized estate at Wicken (Northamptonshire). Prowse grew up in a moderately wealthy clerical household, the daughter of Thomas Sharp, archdeacon of Northumberland and granddaughter of the archbishop of York, John Sharp.[35] We know nothing of her education, but, like Elizabeth Hood, she probably learnt the basics of household accounting from her mother. At the age of sixteen or seventeen her brother William Sharp, later surgeon to George III, urged her parents to allow her to live with him in London as his housekeeper, a good indication that she by then had the necessary bookkeeping skills to manage a small metropolitan household.[36] They refused, but she later lived with another brother, James, remaining in his house for almost three years until her marriage in April 1762. Her brother too was then unmarried and she apparently acted as his housekeeper, a role which almost certainly included keeping the household accounts. Sharp had just bought himself into the partnership of an iron manufactory in Leadenhall Street, London and his household included the clerks employed in the business next door. Given that the business accounts have not been located, it is impossible to say exactly what Prowse's contribution might have been to keeping them. Yet having spent nearly three years living in a commercial household like Sharp's, hers was potentially a very different experience of business and accounting to that of Hood and many other propertied women.

When Prowse married in April 1762 it was to her cousin George Prowse, the son of a Somerset MP who owned land there and in Northamptonshire. They lived in London with his family during the first years of their marriage, but in 1764 George's father granted them the 2,200-acre Wicken estate on the Northamptonshire-Buckinghamshire border. Three years later both George and his father were dead and Prowse found herself a childless widow who was required to quickly apply the skills she had learnt in supervising a household to running the wider estate.[37] It was exactly this kind of progression from personal to household to business accounting which the author of *Advice to the Maidens of London* imagined for her readers, noting that 'shee that is so well versed in this as to keep the accounts of her Cash right and dayly entred in a book fair without blotting, will soon be fit for greater undertakings'.[38] Neither the household or estate accounts for the period before George Prowse's death have survived, but three volumes of personal, household

35 Gloucestershire Archives (hereafter GA), D3549/14/1/2 part 3 (hereafter cited as Prowse, 'Memoir'), pp. 2–3; *ODNB*, 'Sharp, Thomas (1693–1758)'.

36 Prowse, 'Memoir', pp. 4–5.

37 Briony McDonagh, '"All towards the improvements of the estate": Mrs Elizabeth Prowse at Wicken, 1764–1810', *Custom, Improvement and the Landscape in Early Modern Britain*, ed. R. W. Hoyle (Ashgate, 2011), p. 267.

38 *Advice to the Maidens of London*, p. 3.

and estate accounts kept by Elizabeth Prowse in the first decade and a half of her widowhood are preserved in the Northamptonshire Record Office.[39] They begin in May 1768, nine months into her widowhood, when her brother James Sharp helped her set up the accounts, ruling the pages, adding the headings and writing in the first year's entries. Sharp and his wife visited Wicken frequently in 1768 and Prowse spent time in their Leadenhall Street home by return, family visits which no doubt provided the opportunity for Prowse to learn all she needed to know about keeping the accounts.

At year-end in May 1769 Prowse assumed full responsibility for the accounts and the remainder of the volumes are completed in her neat, open hand. As was the case in the accounts of Elizabeth Hood, there were some early crossings out as Prowse got to grips with the organisation of the ledgers. Yet, despite this early confusion, the ledgers as a whole represent a highly organised and methodical record of the estate's finances on a par with – or even superior to – many of the accounts kept by estate stewards.[40] They also demonstrate elements of double-entry bookkeeping. Prowse referred to the accounts as 'ledgers', used the terminology of debtor/creditor and treated the home farm, stable, house and estate as separate financial entities, so that produce from the farm that was used in the house or stables appear as a debit in one account and a credit in the other. Items in the accounts were meticulously cross-referenced against other entries in the volume and against entries in a separate series of cash books.[41] Prowse was scrupulous in ensuring that entries were made under the correct heading: when, in 1776, she forgot to charge hay produced on the farm to the coach horse stables where it had been eaten she chastised herself for her mistake, writing in her ledger that 'next year I must be more particular & have an account what is used in that stable'.[42] That the accounts were organised using elements of double-entry bookkeeping is perhaps not surprising given that it was her brother, the owner of a substantial business, who set up her accounts. While many landed estates continued to use charge-discharge accounting into the twentieth century, merchants and traders were – according to accounting historians such as John Richard Edwards – more likely to use double-entry bookkeeping than landowners and stewards.[43]

39 There was presumably also a fourth volume covering the years 1771–74 and perhaps also later volumes, but these have not survived.

40 See for example, NRO, 364p/67, fols 28, 36–7.

41 Only one cash book now survives: NRO, 364p/70, which covers the period from 1 May 1774 to 31 August 1781. The cash books were single-entry cash accounts.

42 Ibid., fol. 10.

43 Mae Baker and Caroline Eadsforth, 'Agency reversal and the steward's lot when discharge exceeds charge: English archival evidence, 1739–1890', *Accounting History* 16.1 (2011), 89; John Richard Edwards, 'Accounting on English Landed Estates during the Agricultural Revolution – a Textbook Perspective', *Accounting Historians Journal* 38.2 (2011), 11–12. See also Edwards,

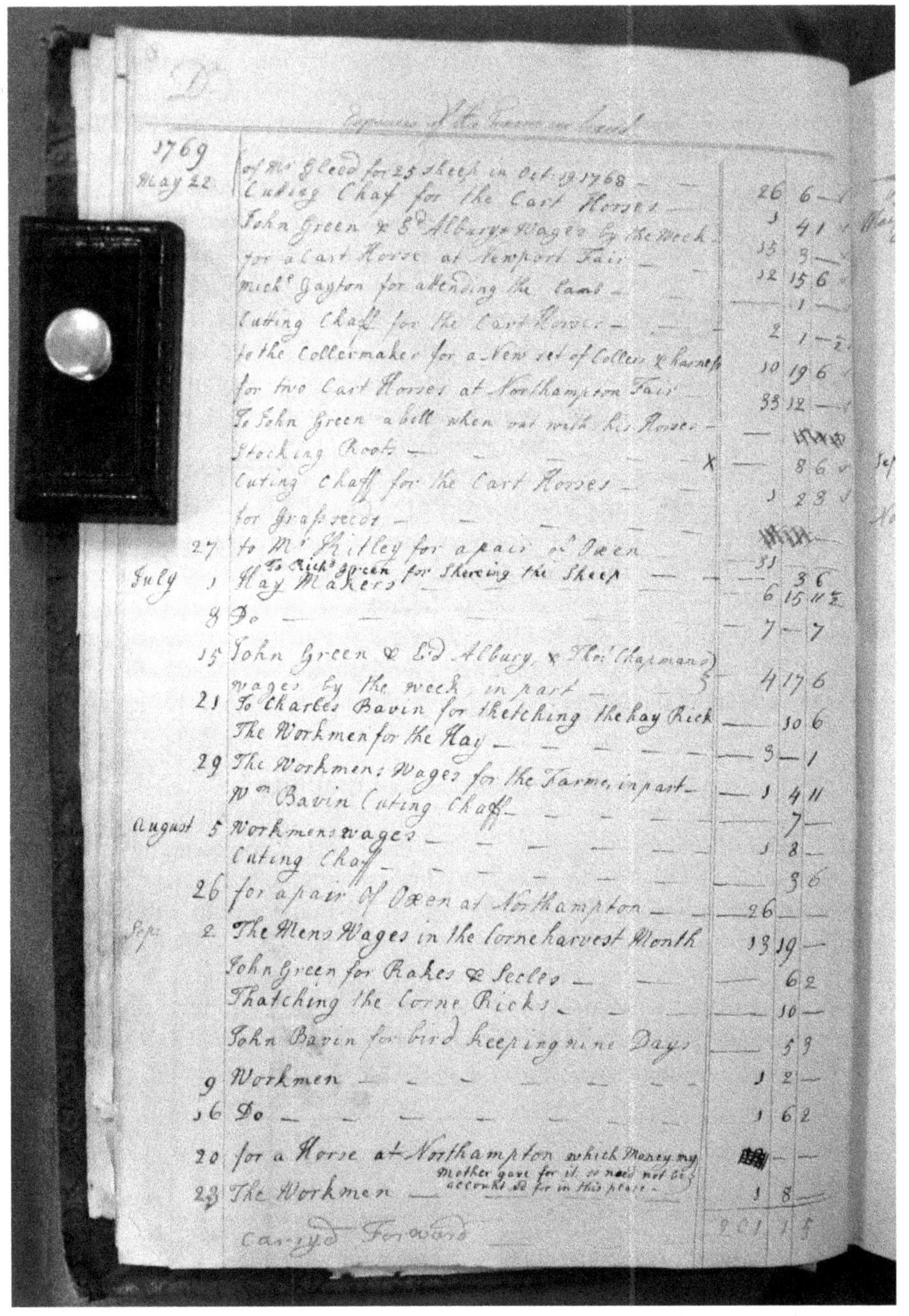
Dr

Date	Item	£	s	d
1769 May 22	of Mr Gleed for 25 sheep in Oct 19 1768	26	6	—
	Cuting Chaf for the Cart Horses	1	4	1
	John Green & Ed Albury's Wages by the Week	15	3	—
	for a Cart Horse at Newport Fair	12	15	6
	Richd Gayton for attending the same		1	—
	Cutting Chaff for the Cart Horses	2	1	—
	to the Collermaker for a New set of Collers & harness	10	19	6
	for two Cart Horses at Northampton Fair	33	12	—
	To John Green a bill when out with his Horses	—	[illegible]	
	Stocking Roots	—	8	6
	Cuting chaff for the Cart Horses	1	2	3
	for Grass seeds	[illegible]		
27	to Mr Whitley for a pair of Oxen	31		
July 1	To Richd Green for Shereing the Sheep		3	6
	Hay Makers	6	15	11½
8	Do	7	—	7
15	John Green & Ed Albury & Thos Chapman wages by the week in part	4	17	6
21	To Charles Bavin for thetching the hay Rick	—	10	6
	The Workmen for the Hay	3	—	1
29	The Workmens Wages for the Farme in part	1	4	11
	Wm Bavin Cuting Chaff		7	—
August 5	Workmens wages	1	8	—
	Cuting Chaff		3	6
26	for a pair of Oxen at Northampton	26	—	—
Sep 2	The Mens Wages in the Corne harvest Month	13	19	—
	John Green for Rakes & Seeles		6	2
	Thatching the Corne Ricks		10	—
	John Bavin for bird keeping nine Days		5	3
9	Workmen	1	2	—
16	Do	1	6	2
20	for a Horse at Northampton which Money my mother gave for it so need not be accounted for in this place	[illegible]	—	—
23	The Workmen	1	8	
	Carryd Forward	201	1	5

Figure 7. A page from the ledgers of Elizabeth Prowse (NRO, 364p/67). Note the two different hands, with the header completed by James Sharp and the main text written by Elizabeth Prowse. Reproduced courtesy of Northamptonshire Archives.

The main ledgers and Prowse's own cash books were further augmented by a series of cash books kept by Prowse's senior servants. None of these now survive, but it is clear from entries in the ledgers that Prowse carefully audited the books kept by the estate steward, housekeeper and cook. She periodically copied entries from their cash books into the main ledger, cross-referenced these against entries elsewhere in the volume, signed off the servants' accounts and settled any outstanding sums.[44] Notably, Prowse's stewards were local men rather than lawyers or professional land agent firms managing multiple estates.[45] She did occasionally employ London-based solicitors: for example, a lawyer called Lally drew up the tenants' new leases in March 1768 and later provided legal opinions and advice.[46] Yet it was Prowse, not her steward, who retained control of the estate and its finances. Having seemingly learnt the basics of household accounting in her parents' house as a young woman, later been exposed to more commercially orientated forms of bookkeeping in her brother's business household in the capital and herself learnt how to keep complex double-entry books in the first year of her widowhood, Prowse was well placed to run her modestly sized Northamptonshire property. Throughout the more than four decades she owned Wicken she maintained close personal oversight of the estate finances, a task she obviously took extremely seriously. She was also the driving force behind a series of agricultural, social and religious improvements undertaken during the forty-three years she managed the estate.[47]

Accounting and Accountability

Both charge-discharge accounts and double-entry bookkeeping allowed the landowner to check the steward's honesty and effectiveness and thus safeguard her interests.[48] Textbooks on estate management often recommended that the gentry and aristocracy learn to keep accounts for precisely this reason.[49] Dishonest stewards were, however, seen by some as a particular risk for propertied women, who were thought to be less financially literate than their male peers. As Matthew Quin argued in his 1776 *Rudiments of Book-keeping*, women had been 'debarred by custom from a necessary

'Accounting Education', 49, on texts on double-entry and single-entry bookkeeping for merchants and stewards.

44 See, for example, NRO, 364p/67, fols 29, 45–59.

45 NRO, 364p/67, fol. 40; Prowse, 'Memoir', p. 37.

46 Prowse, 'Memoir', p. 27; NRO, 364p/68, fols 200 and 207.

47 On this point see McDonagh, 'All towards the improvements', 270–86.

48 Napier, 'Aristocratic accounting', 173. See too Jacob Soll, *The Reckoning: Financial Accountability and the Making and Breaking of Nations* (London, 2014), p. xv.

49 Margaret R. Hunt, *The Middling Sort: Commerce, Gender and the Family in England, 1680–1780* (Berkeley, CA, 1996), p. 59.

knowledge of accounts', yet an understanding of bookkeeping was essential if they were to 'know the real state of their own affairs'.[50] Single women and widows without some knowledge of accounting stood 'defenceless … against the attacks of the insinuating flatterer; the deceit of the seeming friends, and the fraud of sagacious agents', while wives with absent or infirm husbands who were incapable of inspecting their clerk's accounts potentially brought suffering on their families. Quin ultimately wanted to sell copies of his text, hence his deliberate marketing to women, yet he was by no means the only author to recommend that women learnt basic bookkeeping skills. While most accounting textbooks were aimed at men – typically merchants, lawyer's clerks, stewards and occasionally landowners – a handful of authors recognised the benefits to women of being able to keep accounts, even if their accounting practice was primarily seen as taking place within the domestic arena of household management.[51]

The women discussed in the previous section all kept their own estate accounts, but propertied women who did not themselves keep the estate accounts might still check over and sign off books kept by their steward or land agent, sometimes with the help of a solicitor or auditor. They thus had input into the financial management of their estates even where writing the accounts was the routine responsibility of the steward. Amabel Hume-Campbell, Baroness Lucas, of Wrest Park (Bedfordshire), Elizabeth Somerset, dowager duchess of Beaufort, who lived at Stoke Gifford (Gloucestershire), Mary Vere Hunt and her granddaughter Anna Maria Agar, both of Lanhydrock (Cornwall), and Lady Jane St John Mildmay of Dogmersfield (Hampshire) all audited accounts kept on their behalf by stewards or estate agents, typically adding their signature to the final page of each years' accounts, a task which might be undertaken either in London or on their return to their country estate.[52] Lady Olivia Bernard Sparrow of Brampton Park (Huntingdonshire) apparently did similarly, while the bluestocking and landowner Elizabeth Montagu examined only the abstracts of accounts which her northern agent brought down to London on an annual basis, but carefully went over the detailed accounts kept at Denton (Northumberland) on her trips there in 1775, 1778, 1783 and 1786. She also apparently kept some of the accounts for northern coal mines herself.[53]

50 Matthew Quin, *Quin's Rudiments of Book-Keeping* (London, 1776), p. 68 (cited in Edwards, 'Accounting education', 51).

51 Edwards, 'Accounting education', 50–1; Connor, *Women, Accounting & Narrative*. See also *Advice to the Maidens of London*.

52 Bedfordshire Archives, L30/11/132/5 and 7; Cornwall Record Office (hereafter CRO), CL/650, accounts for 1744 and 1749, and CL/734/70; Gloucestershire Archives, D2700/QB3/1/3, 3/2/5 and QP/3/1/5; Badminton House, FMK/5/1–4; Hampshire Record Office, 46M72/E6, /E13 and /E15; West Yorkshire Archives Service, WYL150/7/8/25, 46 and 169.

53 Spring, *The English Landed Estate*, pp. 86–8; Beckett, 'Montagu', 152, 153 and 156.

The thoroughness of the audit provided by these women no doubt varied according to the individual landowner's knowledge, skill and interest. Elizabeth Prowse, for example, was clearly a meticulous bookkeeper with a tight rein on the estate finances and an eye on her steward's books. The same was true of Anna Maria Agar and the dowager duchess of Beaufort, both of whom carefully annotated the various accounts and bills they were sent, sometimes closely questioning their stewards about the costs incurred on their behalf. Other women were perhaps more dependent on auditors or solicitors to guide them through the process and for some accounting and estate management was clearly an undesirable – if also unavoidable – responsibility. Both Mary Vere Hunt and Elizabeth Montagu complained about the inconvenience to which estate management and accounting put them.[54] Yet careful scrutiny of the accounts was essential in that it helped to identify dishonesty on the part of the estate steward or other principal servants. Elizabeth Montagu dismissed her Northumberland agent in 1786 after financial irregularities were revealed in the accounts, while Anna Maria Agar dismissed the surveyor and land agent William James in part because of his erratic accounting.[55] Mary Clarke of Chipley (Somerset) sacked her bailiff after she became suspicious that he was defrauding the estate and took on the role herself. She complained to her absent husband – on whose behalf she managed the estate – that the bailiff had not only left the estate in great 'confusion and disorder' but had 'not bought nor sold nor managed anything of yours almost that he has not made a profit to himself'.[56]

Olivia Bernard Sparrow dismissed her land agent and solicitor Alexander Haldane after she became convinced that he had falsified the accounts in order to conceal the theft of £7,000.[57] Sparrow was a wealthy widow controlling estates in Huntingdonshire, Cambridgeshire and Essex that together yielded a gross income of over £11,000 a year in 1830 and 1846, and thus a major landowner compared to women such as Hood and Prowse. Sparrow managed the estate for nearly sixty years from the death of her husband in 1805 to her own death in 1863, rebuilding the house at Brampton Park in c. 1820 and engaging in a diverse range of religious and charitable works on her estates.[58]

54 CRO, CL/1300; Beckett, 'Montagu', 153.

55 Beckett, 'Montagu', 156; Gwyn Howells, 'Anna Maria Agar: The Restoration of the Robartes Dynasty, 1798–1844', *Lanhydrock Journal* 5 (2005–6), 21.

56 Letters 28 and 29 October, 2 and 11 November 1696; cited in Bridget Clarke, *The Life and Correspondence of Edward Clarke of Chipley, 1650–1710* (a transcription of the Clarke letters prepared for Somerset Record Office in 2007 and available online at http://www.nynehead.org/index.php/history/nynehead-history), part III, 30, 32 and 35. See also letter 23 April 1696; cited in Clarke, part II, 131–2 on Mary's suspicions that the bailiff was defrauding them when selling their beasts at market and the profits he made from grazing the Clarke's sheep on his own land.

57 Spring, *The English Landed Estate*, p. 88.

58 Victoria County History (hereafter VCH), Hunts III, 12–20; Cambridgeshire County Record Office, Huntingdon (hereafter CCRO), MB13/1, MB21/5.

While she kept some of the accounts herself – including the charity accounts – she also relied heavily on Haldane and other agents to keep the main estate accounts. Haldane claimed that Sparrow was the victim of a 'delusive panic', but the truth of the matter is now difficult to determine, not least because the roles of receiver and auditor were combined in the person of Haldane and any external audit of the estates was reliant solely on Sparrow.[59] Yet Haldane was not the only employee Sparrow dismissed, having sacked her steward William Dent in the early 1850s after accusing him of 'one subterfuge after another' undertaken in order to avoid paying up the rents from her Essex estates.[60] Sparrow may have been naturally paranoid, but she also seems to have been the victim of poorly organised estate accounting which left her vulnerable to the dishonesty of her stewards and senior estate staff. Clearly she would have benefited from a better knowledge of accounting practice along the lines advocated by Quin.

Yet estate accounts and associated financial records were also crucial documents for a second notion of accountability in that they helped a female landowner to account to her heir and wider family for her management of the estate.[61] It is clear that propertied women often intended their accounts and other papers to act as a record for future generations of landowners and stewards. Elizabeth Prowse, for example, kept two small notebooks for the two estates she managed, filling the volumes with detailed notes about taxes, quit rents, local charities, presentations to the vicarage, common rights and encroachments on the estate.[62] She later used the volumes to construct her memoirs, which as a result contain numerous references to matters of estate management, but the notebooks were also intended to provide her heirs with important information – or, as she termed it, 'Notice [and] Security' – about the Wicken and Grafton Park estates.[63]

Both Elizabeth Hood and Jane More Molyneux seem to have ascribed a similar function to their account and memorandum books. Along with details of family births, marriages and deaths, Hood's account books include detailed notes on a wide range of estate matters, including purchases and exchanges, improvements, surveys and leases, land in hand and common rights. Such memoranda were in part intended for the benefit of her son, who also added occasional memoranda to the books during his mother's lifetime.

59 Spring, *The English Landed Estate*, p. 88.

60 CCRO, M68/4.

61 On charge-discharge accounting as a system for personal accountability see Edwards, 'Accounting on English Landed Estates', passim. On accounts as what we might term 'memory work', see Anne Hughes '"The accounts of the kingdom": Memory, Community and the English Civil War', *Past and Present* 230:11 (2016), 311–29.

62 NRO, 364p/501 and /61. The book is wrongly attributed to Elizabeth (Betsy) Mordaunt (née Prowse) in a typed note at the front of the volume.

63 NRO, 364p/61.

In the event, he died before his mother – an event which she sadly noted as 'to my great grief & incomparable loss' – and the estate was inherited in 1855 by her grandson.[64] Jane More Molyneux too wrote huge numbers of notes and memoranda on a range of topics relating to the house and estate at Loseley, including suspected encroachments, customary rights and silviculture. She also wrote detailed instructions for maintaining the house and gardens and kept a volume containing 'An account of repairs done at Losely [since] it came into my possession', which she noted was kept 'for my own perusal and satisfaction', even whilst other memoranda were clearly intended to be of use to her heirs.[65] Thus the accounts and memos served both as an *aide memoir* for Molyneux and her staff and as a repository of information that she envisaged would be used to those that came after her (Molyneux herself was childless and the estate was eventually inherited by her brother's illegitimate son). They were also a record of her management, providing irrefutable evidence that she had prudently administered the family property so as to improve its financial position, and in doing so fulfilled her duty of stewardship.

Yet if keeping accounts and other estate records was on the one hand about providing an audit trail so as to demonstrate that one had fulfilled one's responsibilities as landowner, bookkeeping also provided landowners with opportunities to understand their estates and direct their management in a way which would not have been possible without such a comprehensive knowledge of estate finances. This was perhaps of particular significance to female landowners, who were less likely than either their male peers or their stewards to have previous hands-on experience of farming or estate management. They were also less likely than landowning men to have grown up on the estate they subsequently managed: some heiresses were brought up to inherit the family property and hence had a long-standing familiarity with their estates, but most widows managing their dead husbands' estates would not have known the property prior to their marriage. As such, detailed knowledge of the estate finances had the potential to change the balance of power between propertied women and their stewards and agents, as well as between the female landowners and their male relatives and heirs. A propertied woman with a strong understanding of the estate finances and a good overview of the various parts of the estate, its agricultural policy and its staff was in a much better position to push through her own ideas if she were to encounter resistance from either her staff or family relations. Thus, rather than being an instrument of patriarchy and a way of controlling and constraining women, as in Stephen Walker's analysis, bookkeeping had the

64 SHC, account and memorandum book of John Periam (with additions by Elizabeth Hood) and estate account book of John Periam (with additions by Elizabeth Hood); VCH Somerset 9, 82–102.

65 Surrey History Centre (hereafter SuHC), LM 811/1–138, 826/37 and /68–120, 1087/3/14, 1087/4/2–10 and 2060.

potential to empower elite women, to make them the decision-maker on the estate rather than simply its custodian, a point also made by Vickery in relation to household and personal accounting.[66] Accounting allowed women to 'know their Estates' and it was by having such an overview that propertied women might become 'fully and completely mistress of the whole business'.[67] At the same time, bookkeeping offered both an intellectual exercise and a sense of achievement for those involved. As the author of *Advice to the Maidens of London* noted, 'though Arithmetic set my brains at work, Yet there was so much delight in seeing the end, and how each question produced a fair answer and informed me of things I knew not'.[68] As such, we can begin to understand why elite women might be prepared to take on the time-consuming and sometimes tedious task of keeping estate accounts, as well as why women such as Jane More Molyneux took such personal satisfaction and pride both in bookkeeping and in managing the estate more generally.

Accounting, Innovation and Improvement

The preceding section has pointed to be multiple functions of accounting. By keeping or auditing estate accounts, landowners could check the honesty and effectiveness of their staff, demonstrate to relatives and heirs that they themselves were effectively managing the estate and provide those that inherited the property with the necessary information to continue to successfully administer the business. Yet accounting was 'a tool of management as well as a system of reckoning', allowing landowners to improve the financial position of landed estates and create – as well as maintain – wealth and social capital.[69] Large businesses were near impossible to run without adequate 'data management tools' and annual accounts provided information on cash flow, allowing a landowner to judge how much he or she had to invest in estate improvements.[70]

Jane More Molyneux, for example, was a committed accountant whose bookkeeping seems to have been motivated by a desire to return the estate to

66 Vickery, *Gentleman's Daughter*, pp. 127–60 and 'His and Hers', 21. See also J. Maltby and J. Rutterford, 'Editorial: Women, Accounting and Investment', *Accounting, Business & Financial History* 16:2 (2006), 135.

67 The first quote comes from *Advice to the Maidens of London*, p. 1 (where the term 'estates' strictly referred to women's financial resources, not solely their real property) and the second a letter to Anna Maria Agar from her steward, February 1799 (quoted in Jacqueline Collins, 'The role of the steward as shown by the correspondence between Anna Maria Hunt and William Jenkin', *Lanhydrock Journal* 1 (2001), 34.

68 *Advice to the Maidens of London*, p. 3.

69 Sidney Pollard, *The Genesis of Modern Management: A Study of the Industrial Revolution in Great Britain* (London, 1965), p. 216.

70 Soll, *The Reckoning*, p. 20; Napier, 'Aristocratic accounting', 173.

a sound financial footing. She inherited the 1,550-acre Loseley Park estate in Surrey in 1777 after the deaths of her two brothers and older sister, holding it until her own death in 1802 and remaining unmarried throughout. As her father's fourth or fifth child she cannot have expected to inherit Loseley and take on its management, and she presumably received none of the informal guidance of estate management provided to women such as Elizabeth Hood.[71] Yet Molyneux approached her task with vigour and dedication, keeping the household and estate accounts for Loseley throughout the 1770s and 1780s and writing a huge number of memoranda about the house and estate, as well as carefully annotating and filing bills and receipts. She was thus an enthusiastic if not always expert accountant who kept books on a scale that vastly outstripped Elizabeth Hood's efforts.

Her brother had been an extravagant young man who had lived beyond his modest means, running up debts and doing little to care for the estate. By the time Molyneux inherited, the house was in a parlous condition. The roof was in a particularly bad state and in July 1778 she bought two dozen pans 'to catch the drips'. More pans and buckets were purchased in the following years and Molyneux supplied her staff with detailed written instructions identifying the worst of the leaks and specifying that the snow which inevitably blew into the building in the winter must be immediately 'swept up & carry'd away'. The house also seems to have been overrun with vermin.[72] Proper repairs to the roof were obviously entirely beyond her means and although ad hoc work was carried out by a mason and carpenter, the entire west wing was eventually demolished in 1835.[73]

Yet if Molyneux could do little to stop the rot in the west wing, she did succeed in putting the estate finances and much of the estate property in a considerably improved position. She worked hard to pay off the debts left by her brother over the first five years of her management, economising where she could on the cost of housekeeping, giving up her life interest in property and manorial rights in Haslemere and selling land in Wales in order to settle the debts.[74] Soon after coming into her inheritance she commissioned a valuation of the estate and surveys of the house and tenant farms, making careful notes on the repairs that were needed.[75] She capitalised heavily on the estate's timber, cutting down large numbers of trees, some of which were used in repairs in the house and farms and the rest sold to raise much needed

71 J & S Russell, *The History Of Guildford* (Guildford, 1801), p. 81.

72 SuHC, LM 826/120.

73 SuHC, LM 826/120, 1087/4/3 and 'List of Buildings of Special Architectural and Historic Interest'.

74 SuHC, LM 1087/4/2–4; LM/358/88/1; Jane Hitch, *The Household and Estate Management of Loseley Estate under Jane More-Molyneux 1777–1802* (report at SuHC, 1980/81), pp. 20–1.

75 SuHC, LM/807–8; 826/122, 125–6; 1327/24.

funds.[76] She also leased out the home farm and demesne lands, keeping just thirty-five acres in hand.[77] Yet Molyneux was by no means liquidising the estate's assets for her own personal gain. Instead she did what she could to invest in the estate, planting acorns and oak, ash and elm saplings to replace the trees that were cut or blown down, investing in hedging and fencing on various parts of the estate and planting fruit trees in the orchard.[78] She also repaired furniture, reframed pictures, decorated parts of the house and repainted the railings in front of the house.[79] By leasing out the demesne she both produced a modest income that could be put towards the debts and repairs and reduced her own liability for repairs to the home farm. Her strategy was to combine prudent housekeeping with the repayment of debts and careful investment in the estate, including much needed repairs to Loseley House – a strategy underpinned by Molyneux's meticulous bookkeeping, careful archiving of financial materials and endless note-taking. By the early 1790s the house – like the estate finances – was in a much improved state.[80] Having put things in order and done much to secure the financial wellbeing of future generations of the family, Molyneux chose to lease out what remained of the land in hand, including the house and gardens.[81] She moved to a house in Conduit Street, London, where she resided for the rest of her life and from where she continued to audit the Loseley steward's accounts.[82]

While the perilous condition of the house and farms at Loseley may have been relatively unique – most landowners did not have to instruct their stewards to regularly survey the exterior of the great house for stonework that might fall and injure someone! – the precarious financial situation Molyneux encountered was far from unusual amongst the gentry and aristocracy of Georgian England.[83] As David Cannadine has argued, 'debt was a common – although not all-pervasive – feature of estate management' in both the eighteenth and the nineteenth centuries. Extravagant landowners who lived beyond their means, multiple long-lived dowagers and large numbers of younger children each requiring portions could place heavy demands on estate finances, as could mortgages taken out by previous owners.[84] Those who inherited estates with crippling debts might choose to tackle them

76 SuHC, LM 358/89–91, 93, 102 and 104, 826/29.
77 SuHC, LM 826/18.
78 SuHC, LM/826/24–26 and 1087/4/3.
79 SuHC, LM 1087/4/3.
80 See, for example, the yearly surpluses recorded in the steward's accounts for the late 1780s (SuHC, LM 1087/4/13).
81 SuHC, LM 358/110/1.
82 SuHC, LM 1087/4/13–14.
83 SuHC, LM 825.
84 David Cannadine, 'Aristocratic Indebtedness in the Nineteenth Century: The Case Re-opened', *Economic History Review* 30:1 (1977), 645 and 628.

by reducing spending, selling off assets or increasing profits, the latter of particular potential on as-yet-unimproved properties. Landowners might of course undertake to do all three, but, whatever path they chose, accurate accounting was central to decision-making about the future of the estate. Two brief examples of women actively engaged in managing and improving the estate finances will serve here.

Elizabeth Somerset, duchess of Beaufort, was another landowner who found that a clear overview of estate finances was crucial to attempts to improve her property. The duchess was widowed in 1756 and took on estate management on behalf of her young son. Her husband's elder brother, the third duke, had run up significant debts and as part of the attempt to improve family finances the duchess reorganised accounting practice on the estate from 1760 onwards. The restructured ledgers for Badminton included abstracts of profits and losses, providing her with a much clearer overview of which parts of the estate were profitable and which were not, allowing her to rein in overspending, sell off assets and increase profits. By 1766 the Badminton estate was again running at a modest profit and by the time it was fully settled on her son, the 5th duke, in 1777, things were further improved. Her successes at Badminton meant that when she inherited her brother's Stoke Gifford estate in 1770 she quickly introduced the same accounting practices as were used at Badminton, and this even whilst the existing steward remained in post.

Anna Maria Agar too worked hard to maximise estate incomes and clear inherited debts on her estate at Lanhydrock (Cornwall). These totalled £68,000, equivalent to more than £6 million in today's money, but she cleared the debts within fifteen years of inheriting, thanks to her careful management of estate finances, a willingness to experiment and her marriage to a wealthy younger son of an aristocrat. As a result of her early and sustained efforts to improve estate finances and the success of her later investments, the estate Agar handed on to her son was in a much better financial position than when she inherited it six decades earlier.[85]

Other women too improved the value of their estates by developing both the agricultural and non-agricultural aspects of estate economies. Amabel Hume-Campbell, Sarah Dawes of Escrick (East Riding of Yorkshire), Jane Ashley of Ashby St Ledgers and Elizabeth Prowse of Wicken (both Northamptonshire) all increased their rentals by enclosing land, rationalising farm layouts or otherwise investing in capital improvements such as drainage works and farm buildings – as revealed by their account books, correspondence and memoirs.[86] Elsewhere mining provided the potential

85 On the duchess of Beaufort and Anna Maria Agar, see Briony McDonagh, *Elite Women and the Agricultural Landscape* (Abingdon, 2017), pp. 45–8.
86 McDonagh, *Elite Women*, pp. 39–100.

for income. As has already been mentioned, Judith Baker kept meticulous accounts for the family's lead, coal and alum mines in County Durham, while Anne Lister of Shibden Hall (West Yorkshire) developed the coal mines on her estate and – like Elizabeth Montagu – kept the (now-lost) colliery accounts.[87] Many of these women undertook improvements not because the estate faced crippling debts – as was the case for Beaufort and Agar – but from a commitment to growing profit margins on modestly successful estates and thus producing surplus income that could be ploughed into the wider accoutrements of power. Others were motivated by a more general commitment to good stewardship – that is, to managing the estate for the benefit of future generations of landowners and tenants – and to wider discourses of improvement circulating in Georgian society. Whatever their motivations, good accounting practice was of central importance to attempts to improve estate finances and profit from the latest agricultural innovations and non-agricultural opportunities.

Conclusions

This chapter has offered a new perspective on female-authored financial records, focusing on the estate accounts, rent ledgers and other financial papers kept by gentle and aristocratic women, specifically those who – as a result of inheritance, widowhood or other circumstances – found themselves managing sizeable landed properties. The women studied here owned estates across England and included in their number married women managing property on behalf of absent husbands and sons, as well as both unmarried heiresses and widows. All were from the upper strata of society, but they were otherwise a diverse group in terms of relative wealth, acreage owned and primary source of estate income. While the discussions necessarily focus on the experiences of a relatively small number of women, taken together they provide good evidence of elite women's contribution to the financial apparatus that allowed landed estates to function, revealing a great deal about the careful supervision of estate business exhibited by the women as well as their solid understanding of estate matters. Importantly, landed estates were much larger and more diverse businesses than many of the small urban businesses on which the published literature focuses, even whilst there were of course also important differences between urban businesses and landed estates. While the division of responsibility between propertied women and estate stewards awaits more detailed exploration elsewhere, it is nevertheless clear that elite women were often the leading decision-maker on the estate – whether those decisions

87 Berry, 'Prudent Luxury'; Jill Liddington, 'Gender, Authority and Mining in an Industrial Landscape: Anne Lister 1791–1840', *History Workshop Journal* 42 (1996), esp. 59–71.

related to the financial aspects of estate management, to agricultural practice or to the wider moral economies of landed estates. They were – to borrow the words of Anna Maria Agar's steward – 'fully and completely mistress of the whole business'. To suggest that estates managed by women were simply kept ticking over until they could be restored to male hands is to vastly underestimate the energy and commitment with which some female landowners took on the task of estate management.

This is not to argue that elite women necessarily conducted the business of estate management on gender-neutral lines, as Wiskin argued was the case for small businesswomen.[88] Gender mattered, perhaps particularly for married women, whose relationships with property was shaped – if not wholly determined – by the strictures of coverture (on which see the introduction to this volume). It also impacted on their relationships with both estate staff and family members. As the chapter makes clear, elite women were less likely than their male peers to have prior experience of estate management at the point they took on these responsibilities or to have benefited from specific training in estate management or accounting. Some, such as Hood and Prowse, clearly received at least some tuition from fathers or brothers, but for other women the only option was to try to apply their experience keeping household or personal accounts to the task of estate accounting. In such circumstances detailed knowledge of estate finances and a good overview of management practices on the estate could change the balance of power between a propertied woman and her male staff and relatives, helping her to assert her authority, hold her steward to account and negotiate with male relatives or trustees. Thus bookkeeping functioned as a source of power for propertied women rather than an instrument of patriarchy, as in Walker's argument – a means of empowering themselves in a world in which they were otherwise profoundly disadvantaged.

Elite women's contribution to landed estate accounting is explored here as just one aspect of gendered experiences of property ownership, estate management and landscape improvement. Accounting was, of course, one of the few aspects of estate management that could be effectively carried out within the house. Yet gentle and aristocratic women were also involved in other more 'hands on' aspects of estate management, including negotiating with tenants and neighbouring freeholders, pushing forward plans for enclosure, experimenting with new crops, techniques and machinery, and even occasionally personally collecting rents.[89] Carrying out these responsibilities necessarily required women to regularly walk or ride over their properties, as the diaries and memoirs of individuals such as Lady Lucas and Elizabeth Prowse make abundantly clear.[90] Country-house women were certainly

88 Wiskin, 'Businesswomen', 143.

90 See, for example, WYL150/7/8/25 and /26; Prowse, 'Memoir'.

neither practically or imaginatively confined to a private, domestic sphere: nor were aristocratic women who ran landed estates quite the 'rarity' scholars once perceived them to be. Studying their account books thereby helps us to reassess elite women's intellectual and practical engagements with the land, as well as to recognise their role in shaping the rural landscape as we see it today. Yet we must also recognise that these individuals' relationships with the land were not only gendered, but also classed: they looked upon land and other property as *owners*, usually with more or less capacity to control its appearance and use. In this, their encounters with the land were not only very different from those further down the social hierarchy – whose relationship to it as tenants, commoners or labourers has been fruitfully explored by Flather, Heggie and Spicksley elsewhere in this volume – but also materially impacted on the experiences of those others (via the elite's ability to control access to the land and its resources, for example). In this sense, the account books written and audited by propertied women offer us important insights into the crucial role played by these individuals in both shaping the early modern landscape *and* the making of modern property relations.

Acknowledgements

The research was funded by a Leverhulme Trust Early Career Fellowship and an Arts and Humanities Research Council Fellowship. I am grateful to those who made comments on the draft, including Jennifer Aston, Amanda Capern and Sarah Shields, as well as all those who have who asked questions and offered comments when I presented this and related research at conferences, seminars and workshops. Short sections of this chapter previously appeared in Briony McDonagh, *Elite Women and the Agricultural Landscape, 1700–1830* (Abingdon, 2017) © 2018 Briony McDonagh. Reproduced with permission of The Licensor through PLSclear.

7

Negotiating Men: Elizabeth Montagu, 'Capability' Brown, and the Construction of Pastoral

STEPHEN BENDING

> When a Wife, I was obedient because it was my duty, & being married to a Man of sense & integrity, obedience was not painful, or irksome, and in early youth a direction perhaps is necessary if the sphere of action is extensive; but it seems to me that a new Master, & new lessons, after one's opinions & habits were form'd, must be a little awkward, & with all due respect to ye superior Sex, I do not see how they can be necessary to a Woman unless she were to defend her Lands & tenements by Sword or gun. I know, that by Fees to Lawyers, I laid out 36:000 in a purchase of Land, with as good assurance of ye title; and by ye help architects, Masons &c, I have built as good a House in Portman Square; & am now, by ye assistance of ye celebrated Messrs Brown & Wyatt, embellishing Sandleford within doors, & without as successfully, as if I was Esquire instead of Madame. All that I have mention'd has been effected in little more than 5 years, few Gentlemen in ye Neighbourhood have done more.
>
> Elizabeth Montagu to Elizabeth Carter, Sandleford, 11 July 1782[1]

Writing seven years after the death of her husband, the wealthy socialite and Bluestocking Elizabeth Montagu could look back over a period in which she had managed coalmining estates in Denton, built a new London townhouse in Portman Square, begun remodelled her country house at Sandleford in Berkshire, and set in process the work of relandscaping its pleasure gardens. To achieve this a husband was far from necessary, but the assistance of professional men was, and it is Montagu's engagements with a predominantly male world of architecture and landscape design that I want to explore in this essay.

1 Huntington Library manuscript MO 3530. All subsequent references taking this form refer to the Montagu Papers in the Huntington Library, California, and I would like to record my thanks to the Huntington for the fellowship which allowed me to undertake the research on which this essay is based.

Focusing on the period in which Sandleford was transformed by 'Capability' Brown – and drawing on Montagu's wide-ranging correspondence – this essay investigates the relationship between a powerful Bluestocking and a professional male designer – but a designer whose death in 1783 meant that the transformation of the estate took place largely in his absence.

Unlike Brown – whose limited verbal archive means that he continues to remain something of an enigma – Montagu has left us an extraordinarily articulate and sustained correspondence. Brown's appearances here, too, are nothing if not brief, but those appearances are nevertheless illuminating, not perhaps for what they tell us of Brown himself, but for the way in which Brown and the group of amateur and professional designers, on whom Montagu drew, operated in her imagination and for her sense of self, both public and private. Montagu's correspondence in fact offers us a remarkable account both of how a landowner might feel about her landscape and of how those feelings might be managed. However, her insistence that Sandleford was a 'Brown' landscape also raises questions for us about what she buys from Brown, what she buys into and what she resists as she set about constructing a 'pastoral' landscape in late eighteenth-century England.

Perhaps the most famous (and certainly the most wealthy) Bluestocking of the late eighteenth century, Montagu was always aware of her status as a landowner and of her fame as a city socialite.[2] She was acutely aware, too, of the ways in which both she, and her landscape, would be viewed and interpreted by men.[3] Up until her husband's death in 1775 a substantial part of what Montagu had to negotiate was when she would be at Sandleford and when her husband's interest and agenda would allow her to be elsewhere. With Edward's death, negotiating with men about Sandleford did not cease, but it did take a different form. I have written elsewhere about Montagu's close – male – landowning friends in the period up until the mid-1770s – primarily the earl of Bath and George Lord Lyttelton – but it is the period after their deaths which is the focus of this essay. From the early 1780s to the mid-1790s Montagu employed a distinguished group of (largely) professional men and, as her correspondence records, this entailed economic and practical negotiations about the transformation of the house and gardens at Sandleford, even as those negotiations were underpinned by issues of taste. The figure who stands out in this period, however, is 'Capability' Brown, and not only because – by early in 1783 – he was dead. Indeed, even dead, Brown

2 For Montagu's building projects and business activities see Barbara Brandon Schnorrenberg, 'Mrs. Montagu and the Architects', *Eighteenth-Century Women: Studies in their Lives, Work, and Culture*, ed. Linda Troost, vol. 4 (New York, 2006), and Elizabeth Child, 'Elizabeth Montagu, Bluestocking Businesswoman', *Reconsidering the Blue Stockings, Huntington Library Quarterly* 65:1–2 (2002), 153–73.

3 See Stephen Bending, *Green Retreats: Women, Gardens and Eighteenth-Century Culture* (Cambridge, 2013), chapter 3.

played perhaps the most important role in the landscape Montagu continued to develop in the 1780s and 1790s.

In the years before the death of Montagu's husband, the estate at Sandleford was widely perceived as unexpectedly old-fashioned for a woman of Montagu's wealth and city celebrity. Within weeks of Edward Montagu's death, however, and with a huge income now fully her own, Elizabeth Montagu began what would be a twenty-year project of reshaping the house and gardens of Sandleford, and she did so with the aid not only of Brown but of that most fashionable – if notoriously lazy – of architects, James Wyatt.[4] As the decades progressed she turned to Joseph Bonomi for the interiors of the house; after Brown's death she employed his successors Samuel Lapidge and William Eames; along the way she leaned on the support of her close friend, and ex-courtier, Leonard Smelt; while, by the 1790s, as age began to catch up with her, she increasingly relied upon her nephew and heir, Matthew Montagu. Montagu rightly saw herself as the dominant figure in these relationships, but while wealth and widowhood gave Montagu substantial freedoms, they also required her to adopt a number of characteristic strategies in order to negotiate views both of her landscape and of herself.

As my opening quotation suggests, Montagu was of course aware of something close to modern stereotypes of feisty women resisting male oppression; but it is not – quite – the position she adopts. In large part that is because, from at least 1775, she had the confidence of a landowner in her own right. She felt limited need to apologise for her power, and instead joined with her male counterparts in a shared culture of landowning. In this she could lay claim to the practicalities of economics alongside a normalised – and moralised – set of expectations about elite aesthetics which ranged from classical learning to contemporary literature, and from Greek, Roman and gothic architecture to European landscape painting and the fashionable language of the picturesque.[5]

Drawing predominantly on Montagu's manuscript letters at the Huntington Library, the following pages set out first the evolution of her garden project at Sandleford and second a set of interconnected issues which for Montagu are central to her understanding of both what her garden was and what it was for. Broadly, we might say that Montagu arranges these ideas in terms of: pastoral stasis, the experience of process and the significance of her other properties; spending, as a display of financial responsibility;

4 For Wyatt see John Martin Robinson, *James Wyatt, 1746–1813: Architect to George III* (New Haven, CT, 2013).

5 For the wider context of Montagu as a landowner see J. V. Beckett, 'Elizabeth Montagu: Bluestocking Turned Landlady', *Huntington Library Quarterly* 49:2 (Spring 1986); and for the most compelling discussion of Montagu's engagement with labour at Sandleford see Steve Hindle, 'Representing Rural Society: Labor, Leisure, and the Landscape in an Eighteenth-Century Conversation Piece', *Critical Inquiry* 41 (Spring 2015), 615–54.

domestic retreat, understood in relation to public display (fundamental to the choice of employing Brown); and, closely linked to this last, a sophisticated display of taste – and of self – which combines classical and literary models with financial planning and which repeatedly articulates itself in relation to alternative landscapes and accounts of place.

The evolution of the garden

Part of the problem with writing about Sandleford as a 'Brown' landscape – as garden historians have discovered – is that Brown says so little and that Montagu says so little of him. One result of this is that Sandleford – and Montagu – tend to appear only in passing in even the most recent studies of Brown's work.[6] However, by freeing ourselves from garden history's usual obsession with design features and dates, by turning instead to Brown's place in Montagu's imagination and by exploring Brown's position in relation to the other professional and non-professional landscapers and architects with whom Montagu worked we can gain some valuable insights into what a Brown landscape might be for a powerful woman landowner. Always articulate, Montagu's letters offer us a detailed record of a woman landowner imagining and creating the landscape she inhabits and, in this sense, it is Montagu's letters – quite as much as Brown's design – that tell us about a 'Brown' landscape. The letters offer us a glimpse, that is, of what Brown meant to a sophisticated woman landowner, and of how a landscape designed by one, and developed by the other, functioned in an owner's imagination.

Despite my casual dismissal of design features and dates as ends in themselves, it nevertheless remains helpful to begin with an outline of Sandleford's evolution.[7] The years 1781 to about 1795 saw the major phase of development overseen by Montagu, and her letters help us to piece together an outline of changes in the landscape from one year to the next.

Brown first appeared at Sandleford in July 1781 and, while he made further brief visits up until his death in 1783, details about construction work are limited. With little to go on, historians of Brown make Sandleford the occasion for anecdotes about the insanity of one of Brown's foremen, or find little to say beyond it being just another small-scale, domestic landscape in the

6 See David Brown and Tom Williamson, *Lancelot Brown and the Capability Men: Landscape Revolution in Eighteenth-Century England* (London, 2016), p. 186.

7 The evolution of Sandleford after about 1785 has remained oddly sketchy in modern histories, in part because scholars of Brown lose interest after the death of Brown and in part because the careful work of Sybil Wade in her unpublished *Sandleford Priory: The Historic Landscape of St. Gabriel's School* (April 1997) did not have access to the Huntington Library's Montagu Papers.

'pastoral' style.[8] However, while most of the landscape Brown designed was not realised until several years after his death, it is this landscape – Brown's landscape after Brown – that particularly interests me here, because Montagu so insistently continues to refer to it as Brown's and yet she is so obviously the moving force in its creation from this point on.

Perhaps most crucial to the design established in early meetings between the two was Montagu's insistence on, and Brown's formulation of, a project which could be completed over many years.[9] Montagu wrote to her friend Elizabeth Vesey in 1781 that Brown has assured her he would make a plan that 'I might execute the whole, or part … as I pleased'. After the initial payment to Brown of £500, expenditure on the improvements went on well into the 1790s. As we will see, while Montagu went on to claim that 'It is pity the noble genius of Mr Brown should be restrained by ignoble considerations' of money, her insistence both on Brown's genius and on the work being funded only from income become crucial parts not only of what Sandleford looked like but of how it enabled its owner to feel about the landscape she was creating.[10]

With the death of Brown, supervision of the landscaping was taken over by Samuel Lapidge – one of Brown's associates – and later, in the 1790s, by William Eames; concurrently, the house itself was being remodelled – more slowly than Montagu wished – by the fashionable architect James Wyatt. In May 1785 work was under way on a new approach road to the house, but the landscaping of the new pleasure grounds had been delayed by bad weather; by June of that year both the gardens and the house were 'in a more busy state than a hive of bees'; by August some of the London carpenters had already completed their work on the interiors, and by October, while many of the new rooms were not finished, the elegantly fitted up drawing room provided Montagu with good views of the new lake, 'fashioned by the Grace forming hand of the great Capability Brown'.[11] By May 1786 the pleasure gardens were in a fit state for 'sauntering', but the house continued to need major works, including repairs to the front wall, a new roof and plaster and slate for the new rooms. All of this continued late into 1786, with Wyatt working on the

8 See, for example, Dorothy Stroud, *Capability Brown* (London, 1975; first published 1950), pp. 195–7; Edward Hyams, *Capability Brown and Humphry Repton* (New York, 1971), pp. 104–6; Jane Brown, *The Omnipotent Magician: Lancelot 'Capability' Brown, 1716–1783* (London, 2011), pp. 294–7. The exceptions here are Rosemary Baird, *Mistress of the House: Great Ladies and Grand House 1670–1830* (London, 2003), pp. 190–6; and Wade, *Sandleford Priory*.

9 For Brown's working practices and his management of labour, see Brown and Williamson, *Lancelot Brown and the Capability Men*.

10 Montagu to Vesey, Sandleford, 31 July 1781, MO6565.

11 See Montagu to Carter Sandleford 9 June [1785], MO 6106; Montagu to Carter Sandleford 26 August 1785, MO 6113; Montagu to Sarah Scott, Sandleford 18 October 1785, MO 6117; Montagu to Carter, Sandleford, 1 November 1785, MO 3598.

dining room and the dressing room, but with Montagu declaring that, despite the arrival of fashionable visitors, the place was not fit to be seen.[12]

While work continued on the house, by 1787 attention had turned to new plantations, and especially to the expansion of ponds leading down to the river. And, while Wyatt continued – slowly – with designs for the interiors, Montagu was also by this point taking landscaping advice from her friend Leonard Smelt. It was Smelt who encouraged Montagu to extend 'a piece of Water down to our little River, the bounds of which we intend to enlarge', with the aim of making a small pond appear as the continuation of Brown's original lake.[13] Most of this landscaping work was completed by November of 1787, but it was at this point that Montagu ran into complications: having assumed that she could simply purchase the land she needed at the southern edge of the estate to extend her pleasure grounds and river, Montagu found her neighbours had no wish to sell; and by 1788 she recognised that her attempt to complete Brown's landscape had transformed into a much longer-term venture. Though 'desirous, anxious, ambitious, avaricious to obtain what will enable me to compleat Mr Browns plan', she concluded that even 'a handsome compensation' might not be enough for her neighbours to agree to her acts of enclosure.[14] Despite these setbacks, however, work continued, particularly on the eastern side of the estate, close to Greenham Common, with new walks being created and a gothic front door finally in place, but with one crucial aspect of the design still unfinished: Wyatt's 'intolerable neglect and delays' meant that the mirrors for the antechamber – intended to reflect the arched branches of the grove outside – were still not in place.[15]

By the end of the 1780s, and on into the 1790s, with work on the house slowly continuing, Montagu brought in another associate of Brown's, William Eames, to mark out the land needed close to the river, but with thirty acres required to create the grass walks, meadows and sunk fences, along with two six-foot waterfalls, and with most of this land belonging to landowners outside London (and apparently outside her influence), Montagu was warned that the project would not only take a long time to achieve but would be

12 See Montagu to Vesey Sandleford 31 May 1786, MO 6608; Montagu to Carter Sandleford 22 June 1786, MO 3605; Montagu to Elizabeth [Charlton] Montagu Sandleford, 23 July 1786, MO 2959; Montagu to Carter Sandleford 26 July 1786, MO 3607; Montagu to Sarah Scott, Sandleford 26 July 1786, MO 6132; Montagu to Vesey Sandleford 26 July 1786, MO 6610; Montagu to Carter, London, 26 October 1786, MO 3614; Montagu to Sarah Scott, London, 14 November 1786, MO 6140.

13 See Montagu to Carter, Sandleford, 8 September 1787, MO 3630; Montagu to Sarah Scott, Sandleford 12 September 1787, 'Mr Smelt much encouraged me to this operation as which he thought it might be done for an L100, from ye favourable state of ye ground & nature of ye soil', MO 6150.

14 See Elizabeth Montagu to Matthew Montagu, ?April ?1788, MO 3889.

15 For Wyatt's 'intolerable neglect', see Elizabeth Montagu to Matthew Montagu, Sandleford 27 August 1788, MO 3904.

'very costly'.[16] Feeling her age, and increasingly handing responsibility for the estate to her nephew, Matthew Montagu, her letters lose their focus on the designing and organising of landscape, though they continue to express her pleasure in the pleasure gardens that she had created and to articulate her sense that those gardens represented a crucial account of herself.

While the outline of the garden's evolution I have just set out suggests continuous development, it is important to recognise that Montagu experienced this alongside periods of stasis, of waiting and of absence. What is significant here, too, is that these moments result in part from another fundamental element of Montagu's life at Sandleford, which is that she was only there from time to time, and that the imagining of future time and the responsibility of passing on an inheritance sit alongside periods of more immediate pleasure. It is to this experience of landscape over time and to questions of self-representation that we should now turn, because – alongside the economics and the organisation of labour – it's this that helps us to understand what Montagu was buying from Brown.

Pastoral Pleasures

Perhaps the most obvious thing that Montagu bought from Brown was an idea, and that idea – or set of ideas – is most easily explained in relation to the term 'pastoral'.[17] It is the word she uses most frequently to explain Brown's creation and while there is a tendency – not least amongst modern garden historians – to assume pastoral's conventions are so well known as to require little thought, Montagu gave almost nothing little thought, and nowhere is that more the case than when she set about negotiating her position in relation to one of polite culture's most readily available but complex accounts of the country.[18]

A classic account of pastoral might say that it draws upon a city vision of leisure, a vision which suppresses labour and the realities of rural life in

16 For Eames finishing 'what the great Brown had planned' see Montagu to Sarah Scott, Sandleford 4 November 1789, MO 6194; Montagu to Sarah Scott, Shooters Hill, 9 July 1790, MO 6200; and Elizabeth [Charlton] Montagu to Matthew Montagu Sandleford 27 October 1790, MO 2859.

17 For Montagu's merging of pastoral with georgic – crucial to her vision of Sandleford – see especially Nicolle Jordan, 'From Pastoral to Georgic: Modes of Negotiating Social Mobility in Elizabeth Montagu's Correspondence', *Eighteenth-Century Women: Studies in Their Lives, Work, And Culture*, ed. Linda Troost (New York, 2011), pp. 103–30

18 For a subtle overview of pastoral and georgic see David Fairer, 'Persistence, Adaptations and Transformations in Pastoral and Georgic Poetry', *The Cambridge History of English Literature, 1660–1780*, ed. John Richetti (Cambridge, 2005), pp. 259–86; but see also Michael McKeon, 'The Pastoral Revolution', *Refiguring Revolutions: Aesthetics and Politics from the English Revolution to the Romantic Revolution*, eds Kevin Sharpe and Steven N. Zwicker (Berkeley, CA, 1998), pp. 267–89.

favour of the kind of personal ease and meditative possibilities associated with classical ideas of *otium*. As a fantasy of rural life made possible by wealth and by the exploitation of the poor, eighteenth-century pastoral has been repeatedly demystified by critics and historians as a kind of empty frivolousness, or at best a kind of knowing false-consciousness. My aim here is not to challenge that reading – which seems to me incontrovertible – but rather to explore in more detail why pastoral might remain powerfully seductive for a woman acutely aware of her position as a landowner and of the labour on which she depends. That is, while Montagu's insistence on pastoral can look like the cynicism of convention, we can still ask how it operates for a woman landowner in the late eighteenth century. And rather than start from the kind of conventional definition of pastoral I have just set out, we might instead see Montagu's letters as providing their own definition of what pastoral feels like, and why it matters.

In 1781 Montagu wrote to her friend Elizabeth Carter that the 'great Mr Brown' had sent her a plan for improvements to the grounds directly visible from the house: 'with very little expence it will form a sweet scene in the humble and simple character of pastoral'. We can return to Brown's greatness in a moment, but it is worth tracing Montagu's repeated use of this term pastoral over the following decade. With the early work underway in 1782 Montagu returns to the term, and claims that Brown is forming:

> ... a lovely pastoral – a sweet Arcadian scene. In not attempting more, he adapts his scheme to the character of the place and my purse. We shall not erect temples to the gods, build proud bridges over humble rivulets, or do any of the marvellous things suggested by caprice, and indulged by the wantonness of wealth.[19]

This characterisation of Sandleford as pastoral continues well into the 1790s. By the summer of 1785 Montagu was writing – again to Carter – that, after the 'hurry and bustle' of life in London:

> The beauties of Sandleford never present any thing to ye mind but the humble delights of the Pastoral life; but when I return to them after many months spent in a populous city, I feel myself as delighted as a Robin red breast seems to be when he escapes at ye return of spring from the confinement which the rigours of the Winter induced him to accept ... .[20]

In the summer of 1786 she wrote to another close friend, Elizabeth Vesey, both of the genius of Brown and of a view from her new bow window where

19 Quoted in Stroud, *Capability Brown*, p. 196.

20 Montagu to Elizabeth Carter, Sandleford June 1785, MO3587; Montagu's echo of Milton's 'one in populous cities pent' of course underlines that sense of Sandleford as a pastoral retreat from the city.

'each window of the Bow presents a most delightful pastoral scene';[21] while in the late summer of 1792 she again returned to the theme, writing to Carter that

> Our Pastoral Scene here has been much embellish'd by the glowing Tints of Sunshine, & the evening by the clear soft light of the moon. My Constitution will not allow me to take moonlight walks in the open air, but my Eating Room & Drawing Room are beautifully illuminated by moon, & stretch to ye length of an 112 Feet, & the Woods & Water in prospect make my pensive walk soberly delightful.[22]

The insistence on pastoral is, then, nothing if not pronounced, and it invites us to think about just why it plays such an important part in Montagu's account of Sandleford. As my combination of quotations suggests, pastoral for Montagu represents a group of closely connected ideas, with the term frequently used in conjunction with claims about private pleasure, about money, about the absence of ostentatious show and about a life distinct from the city. All of these claims can of course be dismissed as the standard conventions of pastoral, but Montagu's use of them moves her beyond some empty form of words. Notably, while that language of pastoral 'scenes' – whether framed by a bow window or by a connoisseurly language of tints, prospects and shifting light effects – might suggest that butt of modern criticism, the dissociated consumer of landscape, that is not, quite, what is happening here. It is certainly the case that Montagu experienced Sandleford, at times, in terms of stasis, of solitude and of untroubled ease, all of which might be framed as forms of pastoral pleasure. Characteristically, she wrote in the 1790s of having passed 'every morning in sauntering on foot or lolling in my Whiskey', and of 'enjoying the tranquillity of retirement, but also the pleasure of rural life in the highest perfection; every meadow breathing fragrance, every Grove resounding with Vocal harmony; every shrub adorned with blossoms'.[23] It is also the case that such pleasure was, at times, expressed by Montagu herself in ostentatiously literary terms. Often away from Sandleford, Montagu's experience of her country estate might be recognised as pastoral in another way, too, in that her understanding of rural pleasure was framed by her knowledge of, and identification with, city sophistication. For all this, however, Montagu's letters work hard to resist some easy sense of literary dissociation or thoughtless pleasure even as they acknowledge its lure;[24] and her challenge to the literary, and to its fantasies of ease, is achieved not only

21 Montagu to Elizabeth Vesey Sandleford 26 July 1786, MO 6610.

22 Montagu to Elizabeth Carter Sandleford 10 August 1792, MO 3704.

23 Elizabeth Montagu to Matthew Montagu, Sandleford, 3 October 1790, MO 3677; Elizabeth Montagu to Elizabeth Carter, Sandleford, 27 June 1794, MO 3728.

24 See, for example, Elizabeth Montagu to Elizabeth Carter, Sandleford 14 September 1790, MO 3676, where she writes of 'perfect leisure' in the country being illusory; or, for its conscious

by her focus on the practicalities of landscape construction but by repeatedly returning to questions of wealth and landowning, and their proper use.

One way of understanding how Montagu positions herself in relation to pastoral is to turn to her engagement with one of its most famous motifs, Ovid's tale of Baucis and Philemon. She returns to this story of rural hospitality at various moments in her letters, and her use of the tale's juxtaposition of humble dwellings and magnificent architecture mirrors the way in which she both embraces and resists pastoral's literary conventions as a model for her own experience at Sandleford. Thus, for example, we find her writing to her friend Vesey in 1785:

> I am glad to find your taste for a Cottage does not abate, for if you will come to Sandleford with me next Summer, I think I shall be able to find you a Cottage in this neighbourhood as pleasant, & as humble, as that of Bauces & Philemon before the quality of Olympus visited there, & bade proud Turrets rise & eclipse the comfortable chimney, and hide the lowly roof where hospitality received, & entertain'd the Guest.[25]

If this seems just a 'literary' flight of fancy, however, Montagu's repeated use of the motif suggests that she found in it a useful shorthand for the pastoral pleasures of Sandleford as 'not the city' but also as a place lacking in ostentation. Indeed, the trope of the humble cottage allows Montagu to emphasize one of Sandleford's most striking features, or rather one of its most striking absences: unlike many of the gardens created from the middle of the eighteenth century onwards, Sandleford had never turned to the fashionable use of temples and monuments as markers for intellectual and emotional engagement, or – less generously – as the markers of a pleasurable vision unconcerned by utility or productivity. But what the Baucis and Philemon reference also does here, of course, is demonstrate another mode of enjoying those same pleasures: architectural emphases on pleasure are not necessary because pleasure is to be found in responsible hospitality and intellectual engagement rather than in mere show. Such a formulation should remind us, in turn, of another distinctly 'literary' model on which Montagu might be playing here, that most influential of English country house poems, Ben Jonson's 'To Penshurst', with its famous opening line, 'Thou art not, Penshurst, built to envious show'.[26] Jonson's negative defence of an unfash-

balancing of rural life and fantasies of its pleasures, Elizabeth Montagu to Matthew Montagu, Sandleford, 21 July 1795, MO 3970.

25 Montagu to Vesey, Sandleford, 24 October 1785, MO 6604.

26 For this, and for the long tradition of country house poetry, see especially G. R. Hibbard, 'The Country House Poem of the Seventeenth Century', *Journal of the Warburg and Courtauld Institutes*, 19 (1956), 159–74, and Raymond Williams, *The Country and the City* (London, 1973), chapter 3.

ionable house, his rejection of expense and show and his embrace of forms of hospitality felt to be under threat might all seem powerfully relevant for Montagu's country estate; but they also highlight the sleight of hand taking place in Montagu's repeated assertion that at Sandleford pastoral also means 'humble'. As we will see, hospitality certainly becomes a crucial part of how she justified her wealth, but Montagu's emphasis on the 'humble' landscape of her pleasure grounds also becomes a means of sidestepping the very obvious expense of turning an old abbey into a fashionable new house, and of doing so with the aid of some of the most famous architects and designers of her day. Sandleford was certainly modest in size when compared with many of the estates that Montagu knew; 'humble', however, seems something of a stretch.

But it is less, perhaps, the scale of Sandleford that is important here than its relation to Montagu's other estates: the newly built, very expensive and nothing if not ostentatious house in Portman Square; and Denton, the colliery estate near Newcastle. Montagu had moved into her new London house shortly before work at Sandleford began, and it was a house designed to be in keeping with her status as the 'Queen of the Blues'.[27] Denton, inherited by Edward Montagu, was nothing of this kind, but its coal provided a huge part of Montagu's ongoing wealth.[28] Set between city glamour and a northern estate framed throughout Montagu's correspondence almost entirely in terms of business and dirt, Sandleford is crucial in allowing Montagu not only to distance herself from business but also to claim an alternative identity to that of the fashionable city woman with her diamonds and her great house.

Sandleford was, then, 'humble' in comparison to Portman Square, but Montagu still had to work hard in her correspondence to justify her sustained – and at various points substantial – spending in the country. Here, too, the manoeuvres made available to her by pastoral proved helpful; and what her letters show us in turn is just how rich the language of pastoral can be when attempting to explain what landscape feels like. Notably, for all of the language of pastoral retreat, Montagu was acutely aware that Sandleford was becoming a tourist site, despite – she claimed – her best intentions: letters from the 1780s regularly record her shying away from her front door because unexpected visitors have arrived from Winchester and beyond. In a letter to Vesey, written in the summer of 1786, Montagu expressed her hope that her friend would visit so that together they could 'take many a noon day wander, & evening Walk in grounds embellishd by the genius of Brown, & dine where

27 For a recent account of the house in Portman Square, see Rosemary Baird, *Mistress of the House: Great Ladies and Grand Houses, 1670–1830* (London, 2003).

28 For her views on 'the black hole at Denton' in comparison to Sandleford see, for example, Montagu to Carter, Sandleford, 6 August 1786, MO3608; see also, however, Montagu to Carter, London, 29 May 1782, MO 3527, where she stresses the distinction between house and home.

the taste of Mr Wyatt appears in all the noble simplicity of character'. And, after playing off Arcadian visions against the rustic 'nymphs' she has 'weeding & picking up stones' in the garden, she complained of yet another party of 'Ladies & Gentlemen who ask leave to see my House' despite its unfinished state meaning that 'a Brick kiln, a Carpenters shop, & a stone Cutters yard are just as fit to be seen'. It was a complaint she repeated within days in letters to Scott, to Carter and to her niece.[29] Laying the blame squarely on such visitors, Montagu claims, here at least, 'I always hoped that Sandleford, tho pleasant to the inhabitants, wd never be fine enough to attract Travellers, but alas! curiosity loves to take a peep even at small, & trifling objects. Strangers come to Sandleford, & my dear Vesey does not come ... '.[30]

With Brown, Wyatt and Bonomi all employed at Sandleford, 'small, and trifling' once again seems less than convincing, but it remains in keeping with Montagu's more insistent claims about the 'humble' nature of her pastoral vision and with her attempt to shape Sandleford as a landscape for the domestic and emotional pleasures of friendship.

More problematic, perhaps, for all the talk of Sandleford being paid for only out of annual income, that income was huge, and even Montagu admitted that the costs at times were embarrassingly high.[31] Writing to her sister Sarah in July 1788, Montagu recounts the primate of Ireland's praise for Sandleford, but then continues:

> I believe had he given his opinion concerning the expence of its improvements he wd not have expressd the same approbation. You may be sure I did not by any confession lead him to ye knowledge of this disagreable circumstance but his sagacity might lead him to suspicions that the sums I have laid out upon it wd have made some figure in Bank or S[outh] S[ea] Stocks. However I am so obstinate in my folly & indiscretions, that I shall lay out some of my superfluous money every year in planting & improving the grounds around me, as there are seasons in which it will be of use to ye poor who want work, as well as a source of pleasure & amusement to me, & some advantage to my Heirs. I am too old for vanity in dress, or pomp of

29 See Montagu to Elizabeth [Charlton] Montagu Sandleford, 23 July 1786, MO 2959; she repeats the story in Montagu to Carter Sandleford 26 July 1786, MO 3607, and Montagu to Sarah Scott, Sandleford 26 July 1786, MO 6132.

30 Montagu to Vesey Sandleford 26 July 1786, MO 6610.

31 As a widow Montagu's income rose from about £7000 per annum to near £10,000 by the time of her death; in 1789 she wrote, 'When thousands are concerned I am cautious, but hundreds if a little indiscreetly spent, are mere peccadillo's in Oeconomy', though, characteristically, she continued 'At this time I consider pounds shillings pence in a more serious light than when I am in the proud & opulent City. My poor neighbours by ye hard winter are sadly distressed & the naked & the hungry are continually presenting to me their miserable forms, which cannot be rejected', Montagu to Matthew Montagu Sandleford 11 June 1789, MO 3914.

equipage, & luxury of ye table I despise. I shall not build any more which is the most expensive improvement.[32]

In part, what Montagu acknowledges here is not simply that building work is expensive but that architecture is also more obviously a work of artifice and a display of wealth. Carefully defining the continuation of her pleasure in relation to the landscape rather than the house, and setting all of her improvements in the context of family inheritance, Montagu highlights for us here another set of moves which revolves around her understanding and utilisation of pastoral. Carefully distancing herself from mere displays of wealth or the indulgence of luxury, Montagu's 'folly & indiscretions' appear as no such thing in part because they are grounded in her 'natural' landscape. This, too, is something of a repeated motif in her letters, and especially in letters to her (much less wealthy) sister. Thus, for example, when responding to Scott's letter about a visit to the famous gardens at Piercefield (or Persefield), close to Tintern Abbey, Montagu addressed both the beauty of Valentine Morris' gardens and his notorious excess. Piercefield, she wrote,

> presents you with all that is sweet & gentle in the Pastoral Scenes, enobled by Rocks, & Mountains, & renderd venerable & respectable by views of Chepstow Bridge & Tintern Abbey. It is strange that a situation so favourable to sober thought, & dignity of mind did not raise Mr Morris above the paltry ostentation, frivoulous Vanity, & expensive luxury, which brought ruin in their train. But as Milton says, *The mind is its own place*, An ambitious Man wd be forming schemes of greatness if thrown on a Desert Island; & ye vain Man wd be getting pompous equipage & gorgeous apparel in the Pastoral Life of Arcadia.[33]

The criticism of Morris for his failure to understand the pastoral landscape he has created is of course a defence of Montagu's own position, and one which turns again on questions not only of money but of character. Morris's spending on gardens and lavish hospitality marks the disjunction between pastoral as mere fashion and pastoral as the proper use of wealth. And it is in this context of spending, of landscape and of character that we can now turn to Montagu's employment of 'Capability' Brown.

Process and Stasis: The Genius of Brown

In some sense, of course, the answer to what Montagu was buying from Brown is straightforward. As a landowner, she paid money to Brown for a fashionable commodity. However, Montagu was acutely aware not only

32 Elizabeth Montagu to Sarah Scott, Sandleford, 24 July 1788, MO 6169.

33 Montagu to Sarah Scott Sandleford 14 June 1786, MO 6129.

of her wealth but of how others might seek to frame her in relation to it. One easy attack – to be found in numerous satires – was to align professional landscape designers and their patrons with both upstart wealth and vulgarity. And that attack – despite his many titled patrons – was certainly one aimed at Brown. Notably, by the 1780s, the garden writer and politician George Mason had mounted a scathing attack on Brown as a mere mechanic producing little more than mass-produced landscapes hardly distinguishable from one another. Mason's answer was to insist that only gentlemen could landscape their own estates, because only such men could possibly understand the genius of the place.[34] For Mason, Brown – with his brief visits and his distinctly similar-looking plans – appeared to be everything that was wrong with modern garden design.[35] Montagu clearly rejected such criticism, and by commissioning Brown she explicitly championed his genius, his vision of pastoral landscape and the methods he used to create it.

While Montagu's exchange with her sister about Valentine Morris and his misunderstanding of pastoral highlights her own insistence that pastoral marks the absence of ostentation, her use of the term – and crucially of its motifs – suggests a more complex account of its pleasures. Pastoral may be the occasion for 'sober thought, & dignity of mind', but it is also the occasion for sensual delight and easy pleasure. The question of how to justify such pleasure becomes a central part of Montagu's thinking about Sandleford, and we can understand both the significance of Brown and one of Montagu's most important ideological manoeuvres here if we return to the tale of Baucis and Philemon and to the ways in which Montagu utilises it.

In the late summer of 1783 – deep in business at her coalmining estate at Denton – Montagu turned to Ovid's myth once again in a letter to her friend Vesey, writing:

> When I am at Sandleford I shall earnestly wish you to see it, but at present, you wd not find it alter'd as you imagine. The commands of Jupiter soon Elevated Baucis & Philemons Cottage to an edifice of great eminence & dignity; and castles in ye air are soon raised to as great height, but when a House is to be alterd by the means of ye hammer & ye Saw, & places are to be smoothd, & levelld by the pick axe & ye spade, it requires a long time to change their form & character to ye degree you suppose. Mr Wyatt had mere mortal Bricklayers, stone cutters, & Carpenters, at command, & Mr Brown only a parcel of day labourers under his direction. The Front of the House, & ye approach to it, remain as yet just as when you were at Sandleford: the eating Room, & drawing room are completed. The ground

34 For this account of gardening see Tim Mowl, *Gentlemen and Players: Gardeners of the English Landscape* (Stroud, 2000) and Tim Richardson, *The Arcadian Friends: Inventing The English Landscape Garden* (London, 2007).

35 George Mason, *An Essay on Design in Gardening* (London, 1768; revised version 1795).

> to the South is much improved, & a little rivulet that used to trickle between the ground on ye East of ye Wood, is now enlarging, so that it will assume the appearance of a River by next Spring. Then, according to the Plan & intentions of Mr Brown, the improvements towards the front of ye House will be begun. Mr Wyatts people are now making such alterations as will give me a noble bed chamber, & dressing room, both of which will have yt southern aspect & a most beautiful view. The other alterations must be delayd till another Autumn, if I was to undertake more now, the House would not be habitable next Summer, & as I cannot flatter myself, at my age, with a long succession of Summers, it wd be improvident to banish myself from Sandleford when I most delight to spend that season.[36]

Such detailed accounts of progress to the house and garden are a stock element of Montagu's letters from the early 1780s onwards and are as much a part of her experience of Sandleford as those moments of delight and of untroubled pleasure that she repeatedly records while enjoying the beauty of her gardens.[37] The relation between these kinds of practicality and easy pleasure, however, is worth exploring. Not simply a riposte to her friend Vesey's reputation for flights of fancy, Montagu's letter to her friend employs a number of characteristic moves as she attempts to justify her building work at Sandleford. Notably, Montagu's swift movement from castles in the air to bricklayers, stonecutters, carpenters and day labourers may seem a straightforward rejection of fantasy; but we can understand it better, perhaps, as an attempt to hold on to pleasures informed – indeed created – by literary traditions even as those traditions are recognised to have little relation to the physical world. Insisting on the down-to-earth practicalities of building and landscaping, even as she conjures up her favoured tale of classical mythology, Montagu resists – without finally undermining – pastoral's powerful fantasies of pleasure. While in Ovid's tale grand new buildings emerge as a result of supernatural powers, Montagu's estate is the result of labour and human activity. The sleight of hand here, of course, is that while the tale of Baucis and Philemon is conventionally used to align happiness with a humble life, Montagu uses it to justify large-scale spending on a house and garden, to align that spending with practicality rather than fantasy and to claim the estate as humble rather than ostentatious. In this sense, Montagu's willingness to embrace practicality and process was what enabled her to take pleasure from a 'pastoral' landscape that we might otherwise expect to obscure labour in

36 Montagu to Elizabeth [Vesey] Handcock, Denton, 27 September 1783, MO 6579.

37 See, as one example among very many, her letter to Edward Montagu, Sandleford, 5 August 1762 'The garden is delightfully sweet … I passd almost every hour in the garden, never were the zephirs more gentle & pleasing, the wood was delightfull', MO 2457; and for Montagu's engagement with pleasure and problems it represents, see Stephen Bending, 'Pleasure Gardens and the Problems of Pleasure', *Moving Worlds* 17:1 (2017), 14–28.

favour of ease. And it is in this context, too, that we can begin to understand Brown's significance for Montagu in the remaking of the Sandleford estate.

Montagu's early acknowledgement of Brown's genius continued after his death, and if anything became more important as an account of the landscape she was creating. In the summer of 1786 she wrote to Vesey of her pleasure in imagining walking through grounds 'embellishd by the genius of Brown', a gesture which we might – to be sure – dismiss as just another of those loose claims about genius and the genius of the place so often employed about English garden design throughout the eighteenth century.[38] Montagu's agenda is rather more specific, however, as we can see if we turn to another letter to Vesey written that same summer. After inspecting the 'alterations and improvements that had been made during six months absence', Montagu went on to align Brown's genius with something beyond a mere fashionable phrase. Writing of her enjoyment of bird song in this new landscape, she continued:

> we have ye fullest Band of these musicians I ever knew in any place, whether owing to the season, or that they like ye pleasure grounds adorned by the genius of ye great Mr Brown I do not know, but I rejoice they have settled here...[39]

The gesture is of course light-hearted, but it nevertheless offers an account of Brown's genius in which money disappears from view because it is literally naturalised, it has been transformed into 'nature', and that transformation once again resists any vulgar notion of endlessly exchangeable commodities unattached to rural life. Light-hearted or not, this is a move that Montagu repeatedly makes, and it is one linked closely both with 'pastoral' and with her sense of landscape as an ongoing process of creation. Indeed, one of her characteristic ploys when writing of Sandleford is to merge the language of pastoral stasis, of untroubled pleasure, with an insistence on process over time, and this too becomes a means of resisting any characterisation of her as a mere sightseer in her own landscape. In an important sense, then, we might also say that this is what Montagu bought from Brown when he provided her with a plan which 'I might execute the whole, or part ... as I pleased': the plan allowed for stasis even as it set out a process of development, and it assumed pleasurable ease even as it required complex organisation and negotiation.

Though it is not neatly so, one of the manoeuvres that emerges in Montagu's letters of the 1780s and 1790s is a tendency to differentiate between Brown's genius as a landscape designer and the work of her architects, as well

38 For which see John Dixon Hunt and Peter Willis (eds), *The Genius of the Place: The English Landscape Garden 1620–1820* (Cambridge, MA, 1975).

39 Montagu to Vesey Sandleford 26 July 1786, MO 6610; and Montagu to Vesey Sandleford 31 May 1786, MO 6608.

as between skilled London craftsmen and the work of local labourers on the estate; and, just as the house is often used in Montagu's letters as an occasion to view the landscape, so Montagu's architects tend to play a subordinate role to the genius of Brown. Notably, both Wyatt and Bonomi – for all of their abilities – are far more closely aligned by Montagu with the changing world of fashion, and her concern is that they should offer her architectural designs which are at once of the moment and that will pass a long-term test of taste. Inevitably that meant classical and gothic, and she worried about the misstep taken by friends who remodelled their houses in some more faddish form.[40]

On the rare occasion when Montagu does use the term 'genius' about Wyatt, it is not – quite – the compliment it seems. Writing to her niece (also named Elizabeth Montagu) of the flurry of activity taking place in the summer of 1786, Montagu places her own energies, and her ability to organise, at the centre of events:

> ... the arrival of Messrs Evans & Lapidge on Friday evening, & of the great Wyatt on Saturday morning, has furnishd employment for every moment of my time. To apply ye genius of Mr Wyatt, to awaken the dullness of Mr Lapidge, & point out employment for the industry of Mr Evans, you will guess must engross all my faculties, & all my hours, & it is with much art & contrivance that I have managed leisure enough to tell you I have no leisure at all; which I think the greatest evil in human life except having no business ... .[41]

Wyatt may be 'great', and he may have 'genius', but Montagu's phrasing is nothing if not arch, and the important distinction here is that, along with the dullness of Lapidge (clearly no 'Capability' Brown in Montagu's eyes) and the mechanical diligence of Mr Evans, the overseer of works, Wyatt's genius must be focused by Montagu herself. In this, just as at the great London house in Portman Square, Montagu recognises that her choices in architecture and interior decoration will be judged by the world as an account of her taste. It should be no surprise to us, then, that she repeatedly asserts her (intellectual) ownership of both town and country houses; at Sandleford, however, that leaves us with 'my house', but 'Brown's landscape'.

All of this returns us to the question of why Brown's genius remains so important for Montagu, and why it appears in her letters to be of a different

40 See, for example, her views on Lady Portsmouth's house near Whitchurch, Hampshire: 'The House is a very large, & commodious Habitation, & the Furniture of it rich & brilliant: many yards of Sattin, many a feet of gilding, much flounce, & furbelow of trimming in bed, & Curtains present themselves to your eye, but the Architect, & upholsterer, have not been guided by Grecian or Gothic taste, & I fear future times will give their works as little praise & attention as they have paid to the past', Elizabeth Montagu to Matthew Montagu, Sandleford, 8 August 1792, MO 3954.

41 Montagu to Elizabeth [Charlton] Montagu Sandleford, 23 July 1786, MO 2959.

order from that of her architects. As we have seen, the choice of Brown did not necessarily come without its criticism, and Montagu's withering characterisation of Samuel Lapidge's 'dullness' suggests that she too could dismiss landscape gardeners as mere mechanics. In her early years at Sandleford Montagu was heavily involved in designing parts of the estate, with Edward in particular praising her eye for landscape alterations. We should not, then, assume that the employment of Brown marks an inability on Montagu's part. We might conclude that it acknowledged a shortage of time for a woman who spent much of the year in London; we might also conclude that – just as with Wyatt and Bonomi – Montagu was simply buying in the most fashionable figure of the day. But we might think about other kinds of motivation here too.

With an all too easy association to be made between a landscape and its owner, with the most influential works of the period assuming that owners would (and perhaps should) be male, and with her own awareness of how she might be framed by the fashionable society in which she moved, Montagu's insistence that Sandleford was 'Brown's landscape' suggests – rhetorically at least – a kind of separation which she may have found helpful even as she announced her delight in its pleasure.[42] Rather than being acutely personalised, 'Brown's landscape' had the potential, at least, to keep Montagu out of sight, to resist a reading of the garden as a mere parade of self or as the haughty vision of the city lady.

What complicates any such sense of distancing, however, is that Montagu was inevitably still associated with the garden that she owned; that even before it was finished it had become fashionable to visit the country estate of Mrs Montagu; and that a number of her friends went out of their way to make a connection between Montagu's character and the character – or genius – of the garden.

Certainly, Montagu's close friend Leonard Smelt sought to emphasise the shared genius of garden and owner when he described Sandleford in the following terms:

> My Balloon shall suspend Its flight over Sandleford – I see the Genius of the Place, in Her little Car, traversing all its Environs – I see new Creations arise in every part, and Beauty, in Her most elegant dress, attending every step she takes – Nature, exhausted with her Visitors, puts on Her most engaging Attire, and a Smile of ineffable pleasure diffuses a Sunshine which gilds the Winter day, and softens the garish Summers noon-tide blazes – No proud, massy Greek or Roman structures obtrude themselves upon Her fair Surface. The humble necessaries of Man, avail themselves of shelters most similar to Her own productions – Her Groves direct the Column & the

42 Most notably, of course, Horace Walpole's hugely influential *Essay on Modern Gardening*, for which see Hunt and Willis, *Genius of the Place*.

> Arch, and are so interwoven with the fabric as scarce to be distinguish'd from It – Happy combination which gives to the possessor all the merits of health with the greatest sublimity of thought, and to all who are admitted the highest pleasure the human mind is capable of tasting … .[43]

A number of manoeuvres in Smelt's letter are worth registering here. Notably, Smelt offers a combination of winter and summer as a classic image of timeless pastoral, and pastoral as meditative retreat; but the letter also stresses the lack of structures in the garden, the absence of show and the genius of its owner. Indeed, Smelt's emphasis on the lack of architectural features at Sandleford goes further even than Montagu in her account of its humble nature: aligning the gothic exterior of the house with natural forms, in Smelt's overview both the house and the money spent on remodelling it disappear from sight, becoming simply another part of the natural scene. Brown's genius may have remade the physical landscape at Sandleford, but it has made it in Montagu's image, and she represents the true genius of the place.

As a series of compliments to Montagu and her landscape this may seem rather laboured, but it highlights for us the balancing act that Montagu is attempting with the aid of Sandleford: the estate is clearly recognised by Smelt as an image of its owner, but this kind of bodying forth also represents a problem for a public woman seeking to stress the virtues of a humble domestic life. And whereas Smelt's effusive letter can focus on Montagu the genius, it is much more awkward for Montagu to do that herself. In this context, then, distancing herself from the garden's design and insisting, instead, on the genius of Brown suggests that Montagu might have been drawn to this kind of rhetorical separation because it is also a separation between the public self-display of a Bluestocking and the domestic life of a private woman. That is, by framing Sandleford as a 'Brown' landscape, Montagu could effectively distance herself from a direct acknowledgement of the garden as self-image even as her letters insist on that connection in other ways, and even as it is recognised as such by others. We might say, then, that the employment of a male designer at Sandleford ultimately acts as a means of asserting a feminine identity; and we might say, too, that Montagu – like many other women gardeners – focused on her experience of the garden, rather than on its design, as a demonstration of that private domesticity.[44] With this in mind we can return one final time to the question of what Montagu bought from Brown.

Like all of Brown's clients, Montagu was buying not simply a landscape design but a form of project management which would enable that design

43 Leonard Smelt to Elizabeth Montagu, Langton, Yorks, 6 November 1784, MO 4984.
44 See Bending, *Green Retreats*.

to be completed.[45] Rather than simply handing over capital in return for a finished product, the long-term nature of the project played an important part in creating the imagined character and purpose of the estate. Indeed, because landscape gardens take years to create, and because they are so closely associated with the identity of their owners, part of what Montagu was buying was an account of herself which could in turn be shaped over time. As we have seen, Brown's death in 1783 meant that the project had to be taken over much more directly by Montagu herself, and the terms on which the process of landscape management and design were agreed was itself a vital part of how Montagu imagined both herself and her estate. We need to make another distinction here, however. In Montagu's letters 'Sandleford' tends to denote the estate as a whole – that is, both the house and landscape – but the landscape held a particular charge both for the pleasures that it offered and for the nature of the labour employed in its creation and maintenance. Montagu bought from Brown a plan that was at once a physical design and a mode of employment and it is the latter, I am suggesting, that proved so attractive to her: on the one hand her 'humble' estate might be defined by the undramatic visual landscape of the Berkshire–Hampshire border; on the other, Montagu's Sandleford was the patrician employment and support of those labourers who made the landscape around her.

It is here, too, that the distinction between architecture and landscape becomes most apparent: while the architectural aspects of the project relied upon skilled labour, often brought in from London on short-term contracts, the reshaping of Sandleford's landscape relied upon long-term labour by local inhabitants. In Montagu's letters the use of these poor labourers is not simply mentioned in passing, but plays a central role in the story that Montagu is able to create. In the more than twenty years that it took to develop 'Brown's' landscape, Montagu can tell both herself and her friends a tale of construction in which labour is not simply part of the narrative of Sandleford's creation but a central part, too, of its justification, and even of its pleasure.[46] Again, what is important here is that, rather than announcing the purchase of a commodity, Montagu insists on highlighting the payment of labourers, and that insistence in turn allows her to characterise financial exchanges as moral transactions.

While building work has its seasons too (Montagu repeatedly complained, for example, of how long plaster was taking to dry), the landscape's development was driven both by the natural growth of new plantations and by the

45 Brown and Williamson argue that it was the skills of organisation and man-management that characterised Brown's entire career and that were particularly prized by his clients: *Lancelot Brown and the Capability Men*, p. 139 and passim.

46 See, for example, Elizabeth Montagu to Sarah Scott, Sandleford, 4 November 1789, MO 6194. For the influence of georgic, with its emphasis on labour, in Montagu's pastoral language see Jordan, 'From Pastoral to Georgic'.

gendered and seasonal cycles of rural labour.[47] Throughout the year Montagu could rely on local women to work on those parts of the garden traditionally reserved for their labour – notably weeding, stone-picking and the like – and she appears to have been unusual in drawing also on the labour of the infirm and the old in the creation of her gardens.[48] Inevitably, however, the more heavy labour of landscape improvement was undertaken by men. Acutely aware of the need for this manpower during good harvests, Montagu would at times put her improvements on hold as a result, waiting for the summer season of farm labour to be over.[49] But, more significantly in terms of how she imagined and justified the pleasure gardens that she created, Montagu was also insistent on a moral responsibility to employ the poor – especially during periods of hardship – as, for example, when she wrote to Carter after the poor harvest of 1785:

> I have an Army at work in the Pleasure Grounds, for the poor Labourers cann[ot] get employment , & beg so hard for work I cannot refu[se] them, tho I can hardly afford such weekly expence, & shd prudently have proceeded peu à peu, if their distress had not been so urgent. I never knew the poor people so wretched as at this time. There was a short harvest, there is little grain to thresh, & few Turnips to hoe.[50]

Three years later – after another short, wet harvest – she looked back on the creation of her landscape and again offered a vision of moral responsibility rather than selfish pleasure, writing that

> There is great distress amongst the poor in this neighbourhood for want of employment. My improvements here for some years gave support to many, & if I could afford it I wd lay out a large sum every year in planting & adorning all around Sandleford, not merely for the pleasure of ye eye, but to give bread to the industrious who want means to obtain it.[51]

47 For building work being better suited to the autumn (but more importantly not encroaching on Montagu's summer visits), see, for example, Montagu to Carter, Sandleford July 26 1786, MO 3607.

48 See, for example, Elizabeth Montagu to Elizabeth Carter, Sandleford, 6 September 1789 'I have however 18 ... feeble Persons at work on my pleasure grounds, which is some help to them. In harvest time I employ only this set of people. It is hurtful to ye Farmers to take ye able from their work & it is doing no good to such as can get other business. I think it would be detestable not to endeavour to make one's vanities & luxuries of some use', MO 6189. For the classic account of gendered labour at harvest time, see, Michael Roberts, 'Sickles and Scythes: Women's Work and Men's Work at Harvest Time', *History Workshop* 7 (1979), 3–28.

49 See, for example, Montagu to Carter, Sandleford, 8 September 1787, MO 3630; and on the same topic Montagu to Sarah Scott, Sandleford 12 September 1787, MO 6150.

50 Montagu to Carter, Sandleford, 1 November 1785, MO 3598.

51 Montagu to Elizabeth [Charlton] Montagu, Sandleford, August 1788, MO 2974.

Acknowledging the 'pleasure of the eye', Montagu insists on a larger vision of the estate, and in doing so offers us an account once again of Sandleford as process as much as stasis, of moral responsibility as much as selfish pleasure, and we might see Brown's visual and economic plan as a crucial means of enabling that view.

It is in this context of personal pleasures and the landowner's responsibility to the poor that we can understand one last account of pastoral – and the one for which Montagu was most famous – which is the transformation of harvest festival feasts at Sandleford into something distinctly more politicised.[52] Commissioning the remodelling of Sandleford in the decade following Oliver Goldsmith's withering account of London money turning a community into a desert, a village into a mere landscape, Montagu seems to have been acutely aware of the need to resist the kind of attack made in *The Deserted Village*.[53] A frequent visitor to Nuneham – sometimes claimed to be the estate Goldsmith had in mind – her emphasis on responsible stewardship and charitable support for the poor (much like the Harcourts at Nuneham) suggests both her knowledge of how she might be publicly framed and her particular urge to resist that idea of land as a commodity to be bought and sold for private pleasure alone.[54] While she was quite comfortable with acts of enclosure – a central target of Goldsmith's poem – and fretted that her plans for an expansion of the gardens into Greenham Common were being held up by her neighbours, like her friends the Harcourts she championed a form of moral economy which was looking increasingly old-fashioned by the end of the century.[55]

Just as the Harcourts mounted annual festivities as Nuneham – in which the most virtuous labourers would be rewarded with ribbons for their hats and repairs to their houses – so Montagu increasingly used open-air feasts to cement her account of Sandleford's pastoral character. A description from 1788 is characteristic: 'Yesterday an 105 boys dined under the Trees, then sung Psalms, & made *the Grove Vocal with their makers praise*. It is a delightfull

52 For Montagu's charitable activities, not just at Sandleford, see Edith Sedgwick Larson, 'A Measure of Power: The Personal Charity of Elizabeth Montagu', *Studies in Eighteenth-Century Culture* 16 (1986), 197–210.

53 The claim, much repeated, is made in Mavis Batey, 'Nuneham Courtenay: An Oxfordshire 18th-Century Deserted Village', *Oxoniensia* 33 (1968), 108–24. For a first-hand account of the annual festivities see Lady Anne Hadaway's *Travel & Tour Guide for England* (incomplete manuscript, 1791), Huntington Library MS, ST vol.359.

54 Preparing for a visit to Nuneham, she wrote that she expected to spend 'three or four days very agreeably in the regions of Virtue, talents, & taste. The attention Ld & Lady Harcourt give to the Religion & morals of the poor, & their liberal encouragement of their industry, & compassionate relief of their necessities, are most pleasing objects of contemplation', Montagu to Elizabeth Carter, Sandleford, 2 September 1791, MO 3691.

55 For Montagu's failure to see enclosure as itself leading to hardship for the rural poor, see Hindle, 'Representing Rural Society', 645–6.

thing to see an 105 human Creatures happy & so easily made so, by a few joints of roast meat, pyes & plumb puddings.'[56] And the following summer – with the same events in progress – we find her making another characteristic move in attempting to distinguish her activities from empty aristocratic splendour. Writing to her niece of her absence from court on the king's birthday, she claimed

> The old character of a Lady Bountifull becomes me better than ye glittering Court robes, so I celebrate ye day in an antique style, an 150 boys have already been singing God Save ye King as they passed the Lawn to ye Grove, & as soon as ye rest arrive for all my Guests are not yet come, Roast & boild beef, mutton, pudding, & pyes, will be served up to them on long tables in ye Grove.[57]

While it is hardly a revelation to claim harvest festival traditions as reassertions of landowning power structures – Herrick's most ambiguous of poems, 'The Hock-Cart', had done that as far as back the 1640s – Montagu's regular feasts (alongside more quotidian – if equally patrician – support at the kitchen door) allowed her to justify the personal pleasures of a garden alongside the landowner's responsibility to the poor, and to do so by insistently merging labourers with landscape, pastoral pleasure with personal responsibility.

Alongside her descriptions of the visual and sensual pleasures of the landscape, these accounts of rural festivities take up an increasing part of Montagu's letters from Sandleford in the late 1780s and 1790s, and, far from hiding labour from the landscape, they are used to insist on its centrality. In a letter to Carter in the late summer of 1788 Montagu made that connection plain, writing:

> I was particularly mortified by ye wet weather last Friday, as it was our Harvest home feast, & I always interest myself in its festivity. When I consider that for my profit the poor Labourers have plowd, sowed, & reaped, I do not think mere wages acknowledgement enough, & I wish to give to them & their Wives, & children, a liberal treat & friendly entertainment so at my Farm Beef, mutton, plumb pudding, & pyes are prepared for them all, & as the company comes up to ye number of more than an 100, the dinner served up on tables under ye canopy of Heaven passes more agreeably than under ye low roof & within the narrow circumscribed walls of an humble Farm House. When Montagu was a little boy I used to make

56 Elizabeth Montagu to Elizabeth [Charlton] Montagu, Sandleford, 27 July 1788, MO 2973; and for the conscious juxtaposition with aristocratic pastoral, see Montagu to Matthew Montagu, Sandleford August 1788 'I know your benevolent heart would have taken more pleasure in my Sunday scholars dinners than in the luxurious & superb fêtes champetres that have been given by the rich & proud, to the rich & proud', MO 2974.

57 Elizabeth Montagu to Elizabeth [Charlton] Montagu, Sandleford, 4 June 1789, MO 2979.

> him sit at the head of ye Table, & lead up the Dance at night, in order to give him more sympathetick feelings for his poor neighbours, & if I have half a dozen years longer, my eldest Grandson shall fulfil ye same offices; & I heartily wish they may have the same good effect on his heart it has had on his Fathers.[58]

By the 1790s these feasts extended to the Sunday School boys and girls on the king's birthday, took place in sight of the main house and, as orchestrations of rural happiness, were also sharpened by Montagu's acute awareness of events in France.[59] While in 1782 – as my opening quotation suggests – she could confidently celebrate her achievements after the death of her husband, by 1790 she was forced to question the inheritance she expected to pass on to her heir, writing to her sister: 'I have built, I have planted, I have adopted. Shall les sans Cullotte inhabit, enjoy, inherit my possessions?'[60] If Montagu's question was safely rhetorical, we might still note that these rural festivities continued to expand both in their scale and their inclusivity, and that their mention in Montagu's letters tends to come close on the heels of news from the French republic.[61]

From a comfortable modern perspective we can of course dismiss Montagu's absolute insistence on property rights and her increasingly elaborate festivities as just another demonstration of patrician landowners maintaining an inequitable system and ensuring the continuing poverty of the poor. Indeed, Montagu was hardly unaware of the limits of her endeavours; and we might balance the apparent confidence found in my opening quotation against a re-examination of her achievements in a letter to her sister of 1790:

> You are very polite in allowing my operations to be *something*, but they are of narrow extension, for ye benefit of myself, & Heirs[.] I have built Houses, & embellish'd grounds, & the employment these things have given to the poor laborious part of Mankind have been useful, but the Mechanick who has improved the construction of a Plough, or a Wheelbarrow, has been much better employd than yr Humble Servant with her Architects, &c, whose exertions benefit her self & … a small number of others.[62]

58 Elizabeth Montagu to Elizabeth Carter, Sandleford, 23 & 25 September 1788, MO 3647.
59 Registering the events in France, and Montagu's peculiar status at Sandleford, her friend Frances Boscawen wrote to her in 1791: 'I shall venture to address you at your sweet Priory, persuaded that you have by this time resum'd your venerable Function of Lady Abbess now so rare that perhaps you are the only one in the The Kings Dominions of Great Britain France & Ireland that fear no Brigandage, no Insult, no Municipality, or National Guard, but enjoy your own Possession & the Pleasure of your surrounding Flock', Frances Boscawen to Elizabeth Montagu, Rosedale House 29 July 1791, MO 551.
60 Montagu to Sarah Scott, c.1790, MO 6212.
61 See, for example, Elizabeth Montagu to Elizabeth Carter, Sandleford, 22 July 1792, MO 3702.
62 Elizabeth Montagu to Sarah Scott, Sandleford, 13 September 1790, MO 6203.

However, Montagu's complex vision of Sandleford as a place of heightened pleasure and of laborious processes also suggests that we might move beyond accounts of pastoral as no more than the wilful fantasy of a blind elite or the selfish egotism of the rich.[63] Equally, while it may be tempting to separate the literary from the economic and practical concerns of a landowner, that is not what Montagu does. Rather, if labour is repeatedly framed by those literary conventions of pastoral which would seem to separate the viewer from the scene, that labour – and its hardships – is constantly acknowledged not only as the process which creates landscape but as the basis for responsible pleasure. And, while the rural feasts of the late 1780s and 1790s are perhaps the most obvious example of a self-serving vision of the landowner's rural happiness, what I have been attempting to map out alongside physical changes to the estate is a more expansive reading of a pastoral landscape made possible both by Brown and by what Montagu imagined Brown's landscape to be.

For Montagu, financial and legal concerns, along with the organisation of labour, run in tandem – rather than at odds – with visions of pastoral and its implications of an untroubled timelessness; and what Montagu bought from Brown – or, better, what Brown enabled Montagu to create – was a state of mind, a set of ideas, a mood, all of which relied upon, and celebrated, the long-term employment of labour. Beyond the traditional justification that spending money provides work for the poor – though work which is not, or should not be, seen – Montagu's letters from the 1780s and 1790s suggest an attempt to make that work, and payment for that work, a part of her 'pastoral' vision.[64] Rather than being incidental, repeated accounts of labour, by the untrained, the disabled and the poor, become a part of Sandleford's narrative identity, a part of the story that both Montagu and Sandleford tell, and a part of the pastoral landscape that Montagu bought from Brown. If that labour is folded back into the natural cycles of rural life, it is nevertheless made a crucial and visual part of a landscape which – thanks to Brown and his 'pastoral' – could offer Montagu both separation from self-display and a means of self-expression, both private pleasures and a public mode of accounting for herself.

63 For a reading of this manoeuvre in terms of georgic see Jordan, 'From Pastoral to Georgic'; and for a carefully balanced view of Montagu's stance see Hindle, 'Representing Rural Society'. As Hindle demonstrates, there were certainly plenty of contemporary responses to Montagu that stressed the cynicism and hypocrisy of her position.

64 The context here is, of course, John Barrell, *The Dark Side of the Landscape: The Rural Poor in English Painting, 1730–1840* (Cambridge, 1980) and Ann Bermingham, *Landscape and Ideology: The English Rustic Tradition, 1740 –1860* (Berkeley, CA, 1986).

8

Women's Involvement in Property in the North Riding of Yorkshire in the Eighteenth and Nineteenth Centuries

JOAN K. F. HEGGIE

This chapter aims to advance knowledge about women's involvement with property transfer and the wider property market in the eighteenth and nineteenth centuries. The findings arise from a pilot study using the Register of Deeds for the North Riding of Yorkshire,[1] a rich but under-utilised resource that allows the systematic, if not perfect, quantification of women's involvement with property, as well as some insight into their status in society.[2] Index Ledgers[3] and related Deeds Registers were selected for the study covering two five-year periods, 1785–89 and 1885–89, and containing 5,032 and 14,481 unique transactions respectively.[4] This chapter provides detailed insight into women's involvement with property during these two moments in

1 At almost 3.7 million acres, the County of York was by far the largest county in England in 1831. However, when taken as individual Ridings, the North Riding was the fourth largest 'county' in England, covering more than 1.3 million acres and surpassed only by the West Riding of Yorkshire, Lincolnshire and Devon. See W. J. Weston, *Cambridge County Geographies: The North Riding of Yorkshire* (Cambridge, 1919). A map showing the original boundaries of the three Ridings of Yorkshire and their modern-day equivalents can be found at: http://www.genuki.org.uk/big/eng/YKS#Maps, accessed 12 April 2018.

2 This pilot study was partly funded by a Carnevali Small Research Grant Reference WPH/MG (November 2014) from the Economic History Society. I wish to thank Margaret Boustead, Chief Archivist of the North Yorkshire County Record Office and her team, who provided full access to the original records. I am also grateful to research assistant Karen Ellwood, whose contribution to the project has been vital to its success.

3 The correct name for these ledgers are Books of Reference; however, as they are more commonly referred to as Index Ledgers, this term is the one utilised within this chapter.

4 Index of Lands Volume 9 (1784–90) relates to a seven-year period and contains 6,868 unique transactions (31,966 lines). The data presented in this chapter refers only to 1785–89 to allow a direct comparison with the 1885–89 Index; data related to 1784 and 1790 has been removed.

time,[5] as well as capturing the impact of the Married Women's Property Acts of 1870 and 1882[6] and of changes to the method of recording and indexing transactions introduced in 1885. The results presented are not a quantification of women's property ownership *per se*, but of the number of women involved with property during the periods examined and their proportion in relation to men transacting in the same periods. The study uses marital status as the primary method of analysis to ascertain differences in property involvement behaviour between women and across time.

The chapter is structured around four key thematic findings. Firstly, analysis reveals distinctive patterns of female property involvement by gender and marital status, as well as between rural, coastal and industrial townships. Secondly, while there was clear concentration of women's involvement within the categories of conveyancing, mortgages and indentures, their participation across these categories differed significantly by marital status. Of all marital status categories, unmarried women's participation with property increased the most and almost half of all married women's property transactions in 1885–89 were carried out independently of their husbands. Thirdly, there was a growth of women-to-women transactions both within and across the two periods, again with varying patterns of participation by marital status. Finally, registration of female wills increased, suggesting a growth in the number of women who owned property at death in the North Riding of Yorkshire. The study provides a new resource to examine the complex and varied ways that women and men participated in the property market in both the eighteenth and nineteenth centuries, including a unique dataset of 6,755 individual women that will support further scholarship in this area.

Deeds Registers are incredibly rare in England, the three Ridings of Yorkshire and Middlesex being the only counties to introduce them during the eighteenth century, despite many legislative attempts.[7] Acts of parliament

5 The 1885–89 Index of Lands Ledger was selected for the pilot study as it was the inaugural index following the introduction of a new system in 1885 and had the least number of transactions within it; thereafter indexes grew exponentially in every five-year period. It was also subsequent to the 1882 Married Women's Property Act. The second period, exactly one hundred years earlier, was selected to ensure that the people transacting within it were of a different generation. Examining both eighteenth- and nineteenth-century records enabled scrutiny of the impact of legislation, which affected married women's relationship to property.

6 Married Women's Property Act 1870 (33 & 34 Vict. c. 93) and the Married Women's Property Act 1882 (45 & 46 Vict. c. 75).

7 See John Wilson, *A Practical Treatise on the Statutes for Registering Deeds and Other Instruments in the Counties of Middlesex and York with Precedents of Memorials* (London, 1819), p. 1, and W. E. Tate, 'The Five English District Statutory Registries of Deeds', *Historical Research* 20 (1944), 97–105. It is recognised that a land registry existed from the seventeenth century for the area known as the Bedford Level; however, it is considered to be very different from the county registries of Middlesex and the three Ridings of Yorkshire. See Tate, 'The Five English District Statutory Registries of Deeds'; C. A. Archer and R. K. Wilkinson, 'The

required the implementation of a Register of Deeds in each of the three sub-divisions of the County of York from the early eighteenth century, legislation which remained in force until the late twentieth century.[8] Although the registration of property transactions was never compulsory, the practice 'became customary', with little evidence of avoidance.[9] Collectively across the three Ridings, these ledgers contain millions of full copies or memorials of original records related to freehold and leasehold property transactions, such as affidavits, bargain and sale, conveyances, deed polls, indentures, leases and releases, mortgage documents, settlements and wills.[10] The North Riding's Register of Deeds is generally acknowledged as the most complete.[11] Named within these documents are hundreds of thousands of women who were involved in property transactions, but of whom little is known.

Erickson's work on early modern women and property posited that the 'most important component of wealth was not wages, but inheritance, whether that inheritance be made up of real or personal estate', and that '[V]irtually every death and every marriage involved a transfer of property.'[12] Understanding more about how such inheritance was experienced in a

Yorkshire Registries of Deeds as Sources of Historical Data on Housing Markets', *Urban History Yearbook* (1977), 40–7 and Francis Sheppard and Victor Belcher, 'The Deeds Registries of Yorkshire and Middlesex', *Journal of the Society of Archivists* 6 (1980), 274–86.

8 Yorkshire (West Riding) Land Registry Act, 1703 (2 & 3 Ann, c. 4, 5 Ann, c. 18 and 6 Ann, c. 35); Yorkshire (East Riding) Land Registry Act, 1707 (6 Ann, c. 62); and Yorkshire (North Riding) Land Registry Act, 1734 (8 Geo. 2, c. 6). Deeds Registers cover the periods: East Riding 1708–1974, held at Beverley; West Riding 1704–1970, held at Leeds; and North Riding 1736–1970, held at Northallerton.

9 Archer and Wilkinson, 'The Yorkshire Registries of Deeds', 40–7 and Sheppard and Belcher, 'The Deeds Registries of Yorkshire and Middlesex', 277. See also Peter Roebuck, 'The Irish Registry of Deeds: A Comparative Study', *Irish Historical Studies* 18 (1972), 61–73, which demonstrates that the Irish system operated under a similar customary practice.

10 Archer and Wilkinson, 'The Yorkshire Registries of Deeds', 40–7 estimated that there are more than eight million entries across the three Ridings, with well over half of these pertaining to the West Riding alone (it having 11,844 volumes of Registers). See also Sheppard and Belcher, 'The Deeds Registries of Yorkshire and Middlesex', 285. Copyhold property was excluded from the need for registration in the Register of Deeds because such property was administered through the manorial courts and inheritance rights were predetermined. However, copyhold land could be converted to freehold status by the lord of the manor using an enfranchisement clause in the conveyance document or by compiling a separate Deed of Enfranchisement. Such documents were included in the Register of Deeds and their frequency of registration increased during the latter half of the nineteenth century after the passing of the Copyhold Act 1852 (15 & 16 Vict. c. 51), which permitted tenants to demand enfranchisement. Archer and Wilkinson, 'The Yorkshire Registries of Deeds', 40–7 and Sheppard and Belcher, 'The Deeds Registries of Yorkshire and Middlesex', 274–86.

11 There are eighty-nine Index of Lands Ledgers and 2,328 Deeds Registers for the North Riding covering the period from 1736 to 1970. Compilation of Index of Lands ceased in 1966. The Index of Parties continued until 1970.

12 Amy L. Erickson, *Women and Property in Early Modern England* (London, 1995), pp. 3–4.

practical sense helps clarify the impact on a woman's economic status. Her work concludes that, although male and female children inherited 'on a remarkably equitable basis' from their parents (in value), it was more usual for boys to inherit real property, while their sister were more likely to receive bequests of personal property.[13] Consequently, as women inherited less freehold and copyhold property, they had less to dispose of within their lifetime or at death.[14] Involvement with leasehold land and property, considered 'chattels real', on the other hand, was more common for women and enabled them to manage their property with some autonomy. In all cases, however, the degree to which a woman was able to own, manage and bequeath property was dependent on her marital status.

Until the late nineteenth century women's relationship to property fundamentally changed upon marriage. While single women had the same legal rights as men to own property and widows were protected by the right of dower,[15] married women had no legal identity; it was 'covered' by that of her husband. Unless the wife's property, both real and personal, was put into a separate estate 'for her sole and separate use',[16] her husband had the right to control all property brought to the marriage, including bequeathing it in a will to others.[17] It was only upon the death of her husband that the woman, as a widow, was 'reborn as [an] independent actor[s]' and regained control of her lands.[18] A separate estate enabled a wife's property to be protected, as

13 Real property was originally defined as pertaining to freehold property only and subject to common law. Personal property, or 'chattels', referred to moveable or realisable goods, such as money, furniture and clothing. Copyhold land was subject to manorial law. Leasehold land, being a category subject to a set time-span, was classified as somewhere between real property and personal as 'chattels real'. See Erickson, *Women and Property*, pp. 19 and 23–4.

14 See also R. J. Morris, *Men, Women and Property in England, 1780–1870* (Cambridge, 2005), p. 234.

15 A third of a husband's estate was traditionally granted to the widow to maintain her for the remainder of her life; another third to be divided between all surviving children and the remainder classed as 'dead man's third', as it could be used to pay the debts of the deceased. See Leonore Davidoff and Catherine Hall, *Family Fortunes: Men and Women of the English Middle Class, 1780–1850* (London, 1987). See also Morris, *Men, Women and Property in England*, pp. 380–1.

16 A. A. Tait, 'The Beginning of the End of Coverture: A Reappraisal of the Married Woman's Separate Estate', *Yale Journal of Law & Feminism* 26 (2014), 167. The separate estate did not have to contain land; it could be made up of any assets. A separate estate trust could be set up at any point before or after marriage, but were most common as part of a marriage settlement.

17 A husband could dispose of all moveable property, but could not dispose of copyhold or freehold property without his wife's consent, as he was holding it on her behalf. Nevertheless, he had the right to receive and spend the profits from such land. See Lee Holcombe, *Wives & Property: Reform of the Married Women's Property Law in Nineteenth-Century England* (Toronto, 1983), pp. 18–19.

18 David R. Green and Alastair Owens, 'Gentlewomanly Capitalism? Spinsters, Widows, and Wealth Holding in England and Wales, c. 1800–1860', *Economic History Review* LVI (2003), 510–36.

such assets were unavailable to her husband. Tait argues that separate estates trusts 'allowed the married woman a way around the rules of coverture because the wife did not legally own the property ... the trustee held legal title while the wife held equitable title'.[19] Married women were also limited in what they had the right to bequeath.[20] 'The clearest indication of an uncontested separate estate is the survival of a married woman's will',[21] and five such wills were registered during the 1785–89 period. The 1870 Married Woman's Property Act gave limited property rights to women who married after that date, mainly related to the control of her personal property, including bequeathing property in her will without requiring her husband's consent.[22] Although the 1870 Act was considered a shadow of the original ambitious demands submitted by reformers, Combs argues that the changes implemented through this legal change, however limited, enabled women who married after 1870 to 'shift their wealth-holding away from real property to personal property' and into 'forms of property that they could both own and control'. Her study concludes that, compared to women married before 1870, such women 'owned a larger share of household wealth'.[23] The subsequent decade of attempted reform tried to address the shortcomings of the 1870 Act and change the rights of married women to hold and to control property separately from their husbands. The Married Women's Property Act 1882 addressed this by providing 'an equitable marriage settlement upon every married woman who did not have one' and setting out 'the rights that married woman were to have with respect to their separate property'.[24] Both of these acts of parliament influenced how women across all marital categories were enabled to be involved with property.

Various studies have used wills and probate documents to assess women's property holding at death. These are ably summarised in Morris's study of the middle class in Georgian and Victorian Leeds, which also draws attention to the changes in practice regarding the conventions of inheritance. Whereas in the eighteenth century it was more likely that the dominant model of primogeniture would privilege the oldest male child with real property at the age

19 Tait, 'The Beginning of the End of Coverture', 167.

20 See Susan Staves, *Married Women's Separate Property in England, 1660–1833* (Cambridge, MA, 1990), as cited in Green and Owens, 'Gentlewomanly Capitalism', 516. A wife could will 'paraphernalia' – clothing, ornaments brought to the marriage or received from the husband during their time together – but otherwise required her husband's consent, which could be revoked at any time prior to going through probate. See Holcombe, *Wives and Property*, p. 23 and Erickson, *Women and Property*, pp. 139–40.

21 Erickson, *Women and Property*, p. 139.

22 M. B. Combs, 'Wives and Household Wealth: The Impact of the 1870 British Married Women's Property Act on Wealth-Holding and Share of Household Resources', *Continuity and Change* 19 (2004), 141.

23 Combs, 'Wives and household wealth', 141–3.

24 Holcombe, *Wives and Property*, pp. 202–3.

of majority, Morris argues that the growing middle classes were responsible for 'a drive towards the almost total use of partible inheritance for all types of property', based mainly on the need to mitigate risk to their wealth and to keep the wealth within the family. It could be argued that a more equitable inheritance model benefited female family members more obviously in real terms, granting them access either to funds of their own or to annuities from trusts set up to protect the income.[25] Viewpoints differ within the literature on this latter point: Davidoff and Hall viewed the increase in using trusts to control women's assets as 'part of a move away from the common law right of widows to traditional dower' and the subsequent loss of her absolute right to inherit,[26] but which, by the very nature of separating legal ownership from the beneficiary, left most women, not just married women, in a position of ultimate dependence on the benevolence and financial acumen of male relatives or family friends.[27] This study, however, is not drawing solely on end of life documents, but rather on a range of official papers demonstrating the variety of ways that women (and men) were involved with property during their life, including as vendor, purchaser, borrower, lender, trustee, executor/ trix and testator/ trix. This approach maximises the potential to learn more about women's participation in the property market and demonstrates the importance of seeking out alternatives to statutory records to contextualise women's lives.

Methodology

This study first focused on women in general and their involvement with property compared to men transacting in the same period. As can be seen in Table 3, the 1785–89 database contains 23,232 lines of data (where each line represents a person's name), originally recorded in eleven Deeds Registers and related to 5,032 unique transactions. The 1885–89 dataset contains 52,741 lines of data, originally recorded in thirty Deeds Registers and related to 14,481 unique transactions. Women, as a group, constitute 17.65 per cent of transactions in the 1785–89 dataset and 13.44 per cent of the 1885–89 dataset. The average number of transactions per annum increased from 1,006 in the eighteenth century to 2,896 in the nineteenth century, while the average number of parties involved in a transaction fell from 4.62 to 3.64.

Transcription of the two Indexes into a database and concurrently coding for gender could not, by itself, provide a complete overview of women's involvement with property during the selected periods. Both ledgers contained

25 Morris, *Men, Women and Property in England*, pp. 367–81.

26 Davidoff and Hall, *Family Fortunes*, p. 209.

27 See also Morris, *Men, Women and Property in England*, pp. 380–1.

Table 3. Breakdown of datasets by line, gender and unique transactions

	1785–89		1885–89	
Total number of lines	**23,232**		**52,741**	
Female	4,101	17.65%	7,088	13.44%
Male	19,101	82.22%	42,885	81.31%
Not Applicable	30	0.13%	2,748	5.21%
Unknown	0	0.00%	20	0.04%
Number of unique transactions	5,032		14,481	
Ave. unique transactions per annum	**1,006**		**2,896**	

broadly similar core data, namely: township, a three-part unique reference number and the name(s) of the parties; however, there were key differences which affected data collection. Legislation requiring *every* person involved in a transaction to be listed in the Index was introduced in 1885, meaning that the 1785–89 Index was missing data needed for the study.[28] The Latin word 'uxor' after a male party's name indicated that his wife was involved in the same transaction. Similarly, a symbol denoting 'and others' was used to highlight the presence of additional unlisted parties. Both of these notations confirmed the presence of additional women, the details of whom had to be extracted from the relevant documents in the Deeds Registers and added to the datasets *before* analysis by gender could be carried out. This exercise established the number and names of all men and women transacting during these periods, as well as the number of unique transactions,[29] as can be seen in Table 3.

In coding for gender, the categories used in this study were: *Female*, *Male*, *Not Applicable* (e.g. companies, banks and building societies) and *Unknown* (for ambiguous forenames, or where initials had been used). Marital status categories used were: *Married*; *Spinster*; *Widow*; *Infant/<21 years*; and *Not stated*. By referring to the relevant documents in the Deeds Registers, each woman's marital status was recorded. Where married women featured,

28 See C. J. Haworth, *The Yorkshire Registries Acts, 1884 & 1885* (London, 1907). Legislation governing the registration and indexing of documents required that separate indexes be maintained listing transactions both by 'Township' (Index of Lands) and by 'Party' (Index of Names). However, for transactions prior to 1885 only the first named party was included in the Index of Names, rendering it meaningless for a study of this type. Using the 'Index of Lands' for both periods ensured the greatest amount of data was captured. See also Sheppard and Belcher, 'The Deeds Registries of Yorkshire and Middlesex', 278.

29 Each transaction has a unique reference number but can contain multiple parties and cover more than one township. To identify the true number of transactions, the data had to be controlled for these factors.

their husbands' occupations were also recorded in the dataset to provide a convention by which to assess a basic level of economic and class status:[30] for example, Sarah Kilvington Jackson, wife of the Reverend Thomas Norfolk Jackson, Clerk in Holy Orders of Acomb in the County of York.[31] Although a large proportion of such men are described only as Esquire or Gentleman, a wide variety of male occupations are listed[32] and the data demonstrates that women from all economic classes were participating in property transactions during these periods. Examples include Rebecca Waddy, wife of Henry Waddy, Labourer of Scarborough;[33] Ann Raper, wife of Christopher Raper, Inn Keeper of Thirsk and formerly the widow and relict of William Pickard, Yeoman of Tollerton, deceased;[34] and The Honourable Marcia Amelia Mary Lane Fox, eldest daughter of the Right Honourable Sackville George Lord Conyers, Baron Conyers.[35] For spinsters and widows, the convention included listing the name, marital status and usual residence, followed by any additional information about their relationship to others.

Qualitative data was extracted from the documents in the Deeds Registers and added to the datasets to provide an enhanced snapshot of every woman. This helped to 'locate' each one, both geographically and as an individual transacting property at a specific point in time. Such data included her place of residence, occupation, details of previous marriages, names of family members and wider social networks, such as Annie Boyes, Spinster of Scarborough in the County of York; Niece of Susannah Paper, Widow of Scarborough.[36] Lastly, details about women's inherited rights to real and personal property were added to the dataset to provide the context within which her involvement with the property might be better understood.[37] A good example of how these conventions help to build an individual snapshot and might assist in clarifying a woman's position within a transaction is demonstrated here:

30 Davidoff and Hall, *Family Fortunes*, pp. 229–34.

31 North Yorkshire County Record Office, Northallerton. *North Riding Register of Deeds*, 1887, 13/471/209.

32 The variety of male occupations also demonstrates that the Registers of Deeds could serve as a new and interesting source for a prosopographical study of men living in the eighteenth and nineteenth centuries who were involved in property in the North Riding of Yorkshire. See K. S. B. Keats-Rohan, 'Biography, Identity and Names: Understanding the Pursuit of the Individual in Prosopography', *Prosopography Approaches and Applications: A Handbook*, ed. K. S. B. Keats-Rohan (Oxford, 2007).

33 *North Riding Register of Deeds*, 1785, BX/548/833.

34 *North Riding Register of Deeds*, 1786, BZ/384/551.

35 *North Riding Register of Deeds*, 1886, 11/232/103.

36 *North Riding Register of Deeds*, 1886, 11/976/444.

37 Although sometimes used interchangeably, for the purposes of this paper, a 'devisee' is considered to be someone inheriting real estate and a 'legatee' is someone inheriting personal estate, such as money, jewellery or household items.

> Susanna Watson, Spinster of Park Gate, Fylingdales; Daughter and residuary devisee named in the last will and testament of Elizabeth Harding, Widow of Park Gate in Fylingdales, deceased, formerly Elizabeth Coverdale and subsequently Elizabeth Watson, who was one of the daughters and a devisee named in the last will and testament of William Coverdale the Younger, Yeoman of Hawsker in the Parish of Whitby, deceased.[38]

By including information about Susanna's mother, Elizabeth, and her rights to inherit property from her father's estate, rather than that of either of her deceased husbands, the document connects the property in question to that lineage.[39]

Women with occupations represented a very small percentage of the female subsets of data (1785–89 – 0.17 per cent; 1885–89 – 1.1 per cent), but include women such as Sarah Hodgson, Widow and Milliner of the City of York,[40] Mary Davis, Cheesemonger and Co-Partner in trade with James John Davis of Newcastle upon Tyne[41] and Fanny Jackson, Coal Dealer of Middlesbrough.[42] The documents list women in trades such as shopkeeper, grocer, draper, fancy dealer and wine and spirit merchant, as well as those in professions such as teaching and nursing. Several women were lodging housekeepers or innkeepers, but only one identified as a domestic servant.[43] Four unique women stated occupations in the 1785–89 dataset, only one of whom did not give her marital status. A century later, however, the marital status of women with occupations was less likely to be recorded; of the forty-nine unique women with occupations listed, 61 per cent had no marital status shown.[44] These figures, however, should not be considered a true reflection of women's *actual* participation in paid or unpaid work or in family businesses. As Capern argues, women's relationship to work is more complex than men's, often requiring further investigation or supplementary documentation to identify and make sense of. In addition, legal and societal conventions positioned woman's marital status as the dominant descriptor, ensuring that the variety and complexity of women's participation in the

38 *North Riding Register of Deeds*, 1787, CC/189/331.

39 Additionally, the use of the word 'residuary' illustrates that, in addition to Susanna inheriting a share of her mother's estate in her own right as a daughter of Elizabeth, she has inherited a further share(s) by outliving other named devisees.

40 *North Riding Register of Deeds*, 1787, CB/113/150.

41 *North Riding Register of Deeds*, 1785, BY/144/208.

42 *North Riding Register of Deeds*, 1885, 1/135/51.

43 Other female occupations included a butcher, a farmer, a tobacco manufacturer and a professional singer.

44 See also Morris, *Men, Women & Property in England*, p. 234, where such women are described as having what he calls their 'own economic title'.

labour market were hidden from view.[45] Many academics, such as Davidoff and Hall, Humphries, and Hill, have argued that official records, especially the Victorian censuses, consistently under-reported women's work. However, this position has been challenged more recently by Higgs and Wilkinson, who argue that these documents, when correlated to local sources, actually provide a reliable source of data on women's work.[46] For the purposes of this study, however, it is recognised that the occupational data is unlikely to be truly representative of the total number of women involved in business or paid employment, as official documentation tended to use women's marital status as the dominant descriptor.

Findings

Gathering accurate marital status data for all women in both datasets provided the means to address research questions regarding coverture as an impediment to property involvement and whether changes could be discerned over time for differing marital status categories. The significance of this was to understand the context within which any changes to established patterns and behaviours occurred and to highlight anomalies. Both datasets were analysed first by gender and then by marital status.

As can be seen in Table 4, men's involvement as a group with property remained constant across the periods at c. 80 per cent. Women's involvement in general, however, reduced from 17.65 per cent in the 1785–89 period to 13.44 per cent a hundred years later. This shows that women as a group were more likely to be involved in property transactions in the eighteenth century, despite legislation aimed at removing impediments to married women's involvement in property. When data was controlled for uniqueness by gender,[47] Table 4 shows that women's involvement increased within each period in percentage terms from 17.65 per cent to 30.62 per cent, and from 13.44 per cent to 19.33 per cent respectively, but decreased between the periods. Eighteenth-century

45 Amanda Capern, *The Historical Study of Women: England, 1500–1700* (Basingstoke, 2010), pp. 118–19.

46 See Davidoff and Hall, *Family Fortunes*. Also Sara Horrell and Jane Humphries, 'Women's Labour Force Participation and the Transition to the Male-Breadwinner Family, 1790–1865', *The Economic History Review* 48:1 (1995), 89–117, and Bridget Hill, 'Women, Work and the Census: A Problem for Historians of Women', *History Workshop Journal* 35 (1993), 78–94, as cited in Edward Higgs and Amanda Wilkinson, 'Women, Occupations and Work in the Victorian Censuses Revisited', *History Workshop Journal* 81 (2016), 17–38.

47 A control for uniqueness was needed to remove duplications related to those people and organisations involved in multiple transactions and avoid conflating everyone with the same name into one person: e.g. all Mary Smiths of Scarborough would be considered to be the same person unless a differentiating characteristic was introduced, such as marital status, name of husband, or residence.

Table 4. Breakdown of datasets by period, gender and unique people

	1785–89				1885–89			
	No. by Gender		Unique by Gender		No. by Gender		Unique by Gender	
Female	4,101	17.65%	2,296	30.62%	7,088	13.44%	4,459	19.33%
Male	19,101	82.22%	5,195	69.28%	42,885	81.31%	18,115	78.53%
Not Applicable	30	0.13%	8	0.11%	2,748	5.21%	482	2.09%
Unknown	0	0.00%	0	0.00%	20	0.04%	13	0.06%
	23,232		**7,499**		**52,741**		**23,069**	

unique women were involved in an average of 1.79 transactions each; in the nineteenth century, this figure had reduced to 1.59 transactions. This shows, however, that the number of unique women participating in the property market in the nineteenth century had increased, but that they were involved in fewer transactions than their eighteenth-century counterparts. This is a different pattern from that of men, whose involvement, when controlled for uniqueness, decreased within each distinct period. This statistic illustrates that, although an increasing number of women were engaging in property, men were still much more likely to be involved in multiple transactions. In addition, unlike women, the percentage of unique men involved *increased* across periods, from 69.28 per cent in 1785–89 to 78.53 per cent in 1885–89. Similar to unique women, the number of unique men participating in the property market in the nineteenth century increased, but they were involved in fewer transactions than their eighteenth-century counterparts (ave. 3.68 in 1785–89 and 2.37 in 1885–89). The difference in results between the two gender groups was caused by women's participation growing at a slower pace than men's and their involvement in fewer multiple transactions. Transactions involving third-party organisations, such as companies, building societies and banks, increased significantly in the nineteenth century (by a factor of 60.25). The data shows that each unique organisation was, on average, involved in 5.7 transactions in 1885–89, more than either men or women, demonstrating the importance of the growing building society movement and the impact of joint stock companies on the property market.

Table 5 indicates the breakdown of the female dataset for each period by marital status, both for women in general and for unique women. Over half of women involved in property transactions in the 1785–89 period were married and this proportion increased to 52.61 per cent when controlled for uniqueness. This is a surprising result considering that married women were

Table 5. Breakdown of female datasets by marital status and unique females

	1785–89				1885–89			
	No. of all females		No. of unique females		No. of all females		No. of unique females	
Married	2,086	50.87%	1,208	52.61%	2,048	28.89%	1,336	29.96%
Spinster	721	17.58%	403	17.55%	2,256	31.83%	1,399	31.37%
Widow	1,272	31.02%	670	29.18%	2,580	36.40%	1,569	35.19%
Infant <21 years	1	0.02%	1	0.04%	2	0.03%	1	0.02%
Not stated	21	0.51%	14	0.61%	202	2.85%	154	3.45%
	4,101		**2,296**		**7,088**		**4,459**	

not able to own property during this period independently of their husbands, unless administered as a separate estate.[48] Nevertheless, the inclusion of these women demonstrates that there was a legal requirement to include and acknowledge wives as parties within the property documentation where the wife had originally owned the property or was inheriting the property. By doing so, husbands were restricted in their ability to act independently of their wives in certain property transactions.[49] In the 1885–89 dataset married women's involvement dropped considerably to 29.96 per cent, appearing to contradict the intended benefits of increased legal empowerment of married women provided through changes to the law in 1870 and 1882, which gave married women the same rights over property as unmarried women. Three separate factors appear to be contributing to this effect. The first concerns married women's inclusion within property transactions in the eighteenth century for legal reasons where, in reality, they had no decision-making

48 See Tait, 'The Beginning of the End of Coverture', 165. The 1785–89 period falls within the legal restrictions of coverture as experienced by married women, where having a separate estate was the only means to 'circumvent the law of coverture'. The later period falls after the implementation of the Married Women's Property Acts 1870 and 1882, when married women were legally entitled to transact alone and to bequeath their real (landed) property. See also Coombs, 'Wives and household wealth', 141, and Holcombe, *Wives and Property*, pp. 202–4.

49 Erickson makes the point that freehold land or property owned by the wife at the time of marriage technically remained in her name and could not be disposed of without her agreement. However, her husband was entitled to any income generated by the property and under no obligation to share it with her. See footnote 5 in Tait, 'The Beginning of the End of Coverture', 167.

power, as such transactions were subject to the laws of coverture. The second concerns the numbers of married women participating in property transactions in the nineteenth century, which reduced in volume (2,086 to 2,048), rather than increased, as might have been expected over time. The third is the period selected for the pilot study, 1885–89; analysis suggests that it is too close to the dates of legislative change to see a more meaningful effect on married women's participation.

Closer examination of the data for married women in 1785–89 reveals that 2,086 married women transacted during this period, but only 1.39 per cent did so without their husband being involved in the transaction.[50] This supports the claim that married women's participation was limited in law by coverture and controlled in practice by their husbands. The exception was when property was placed into a separate estate to be administered on the woman's behalf by trustees. While the volume of married women involved with property in 1885–89 is analogous (2,048), the number of women participating independently of their husbands had significantly increased to 45.47 per cent. Therefore, although the percentage share of married women in general and of unique women reduced from the eighteenth-century dataset to the nineteenth-century dataset, it can be argued that married women's participation was more meaningful in the latter period, given that they were acting independently of their husbands and of any third party. These findings reinforce that both the Married Women's Property Act 1870 and subsequent 1882 legislation were beginning to make an impact by rendering married women capable of 'acquiring, holding, and disposing by will or otherwise, of any real or personal property as her separate property, in the same manner as if she were a feme sole, without the intervention of any trustee'.[51]

Data for the 1885–89 period shows that there is more parity of involvement across the three main marital status groups, particularly when controlled for uniqueness. Widows as a group have remained the most static across marital status categories, increasing by 6 per cent. They constitute just under a third of unique women in the 1785–89 dataset (29.18 per cent) and are the largest group by marital status in the 1885–89 dataset (35.19 per cent). Spinsters' involvement, on the other hand, increased the most, from 17.58 per cent in the eighteenth-century data to 31.37 per cent by the late 1880s, highlighting the growth in investment opportunities available for unmarried women not just in property but also in money lending (mortgages), shares, bonds and

50 See Holcombe, *Wives and Property*. The transactions including these twenty-nine women are undergoing analysis currently to establish if these are separate estates. See also Tait, 'The Beginning of the End of Coverture'.

51 The Married Women's Property Act, 1882, 45 & 46 Vict. 75, as quoted in Tait, 'The Beginning of the End of Coverture', 213.

other annuities.[52] Other factors also contributed to the increase in spinsters' involvement in property. By the end of the nineteenth century unmarried women of all social classes were less dependent on marriage for financial security,[53] and the age at which they married increased.[54] Growing numbers of women were in paid work of some kind or, in the case of middle-class women, were looking for new ways of making their disposable income work for them.[55] Even for those women from middle- and upper-class families used to living on annuities, the nineteenth century provided ever-expanding opportunities for investment, such as in railway shares or utility companies.[56] In addition, the flourishing building society movement and the increasing demand for housing offered the means by which mortgages for even modest properties could be purchased as investments.[57]

Women's involvement with property differed from township to township, in part caused by gender demographics, types of industry and levels of female employment in each area. The coastal town of Scarborough, although the largest in the North Riding until the late nineteenth century, had little opportunity for expansion until the arrival of the railways during the Victorian era. The corresponding increase in visitors was significant for women's employment, heavily involved as they were in the service sector.[58] Middlesbrough's rapid growth in the first half of the nineteenth century,[59]

52 See Green and Owens, 'Gentlewomanly Capitalism?' 511. Also Coombs, 'Wives and Household Wealth', 141, who argues that ' ... women married after the 1870 Married Women's Property Act shifted their wealth-holding away from real property to personal property'.

53 Green and Owens, 'Gentlewomanly Capitalism?' 511.

54 Martha Vicinus, *Independent Women: Work and Community for Single Women 1850–1920* (London, 1985), pp. 26–7.

55 See Green and Owens, 'Gentlewomanly Capitalism?' and Janette Rutterford, David R. Green, Josephine Maltby and Alastair Owens, 'Who Comprised the Nation of Shareholders? Gender and Investment in Great Britain, c. 1870–1935', *Economic History Review* 64 (2011), 154–87.

56 Holcombe, *Wives and Property*, pp. 34–5.

57 Colin Pooley and Michael Harmer, *Property Ownership in Britain c. 1850–1950: The Role of the Bradford Equitable Building Society and the Bingley Building Society in the Development of Home Ownership* (Cambridge, 1999), as quoted in David Green, Alastair Owens, Josephine Maltby and Janette Rutterford, 'Men, Women, and Money: An Introduction', *Men, Women, and Money: Perspectives on Gender, Wealth, and Investment 1850–1930*, ed. Green, Owens, Maltby and Rutterford (Oxford, 2011), pp. 1–30.

58 For mention of the nineteenth-century expansion of the town to the north shore see 'The Borough of Scarborough', *A History of the County of York North Riding: Volume 2*, ed. William Page (London, 1923), pp. 538–60. https://www.british-history.ac.uk/vch/yorks/north/vol2/pp538–560, accessed 22 April 2018.

59 As Asa Briggs points out, ' ... within the reign of Queen Victoria itself, Middlesbrough grew from a very tiny rural community to a very large town of over 100,000'. No other English town 'grew from nothing faster'. See Asa Briggs, 'Middlesbrough: The Growth of a New Community', *Middlesbrough: Town and Community, 1830–1950*, ed. A. J. Pollard (Stroud, 1996), pp. 1–31.

although similarly driven by the same expansion of the railways, did not afford women the same opportunities for employment. The demand for labour within male-dominated heavy industries, such as iron and steel making, shipbuilding and ironstone mining, had a significant impact on the town's gender demographics.[60] Compared to similarly sized towns, Middlesbrough's female employment rates were the lowest.[61] Women's involvement in property transactions in the nineteenth-century dataset was anticipated to be lower in industrial townships than in other established communities, such as rural and coastal towns, or in places dependent on other types of industry, such as maritime.

Comparative analysis of selected township data as shown in Table 6 supports this hypothesis, but also adds some insight into changing patterns by location across time.[62] All nineteenth-century industrial townships (marked **) reflect lower levels of female property involvement than other types of township, even Middlesbrough, whose population by 1885 had overtaken Scarborough's to establish it as the largest town in the North Riding, and which commanded the highest number of property transactions of any township. Yet, despite this phenomenal level of growth, female participation was lower than in Scarborough. This was not caused solely by increased male participation, although that did grow, but by a significant increase in third-party involvement from, for example, iron, steel and mining companies, and where inward migration was high. This pattern of growth reflects the slower pace of change in Middlesbrough's demographics and the lack of employment opportunities for women. In all industrial townships, the percentage share of property transactions involving third-party organisations was high in comparison to all other townships except Linthorpe and Thornaby, which are analysed below.

Larger and better-established townships, such as Scarborough and Whitby, experienced the impact of industrialisation differently. Similarly to Middlesbrough, the percentage share of female participation reduced significantly in Scarborough, but the volume of women doubled. Although the volume of men involved in property transactions in Scarborough grew

60 See Chapter 3, 'Demography and Urban Growth', in Minoru Yasumoto, *The Rise of a Victorian Ironopolis: Middlesbrough and Regional Industrialization* (Woodbridge, 2011). The male to female sex ratio for Middlesbrough was 105 in 1851, increasing to 117 in 1871 but dropping back to 109 in 1881. This drop was due in large part to the decrease in demand for iron and the ensuing depression.

61 David Taylor, 'The Infant Hercules and the Augean Stables: A Century of Economic and Social Development in Middlesbrough, c. 1840–1939' in *Middlesbrough: Town and Community, 1830–1950*, ed. A. J. Pollard (Stroud, 1996), pp. 53–80.

62 It is appreciated that the low number of entries in some townships in the 1785–89 dataset (e.g. eight entries for Middlesbrough) render the gender participation figures meaningless for comparison purposes; however, they have been included for illustrative purposes.

Table 6. Breakdown of datasets by township and gender

Township	Total Number of Entries	Female		Male		Not Applicable		Total Number of Entries	Female		Male		Not Applicable	
	1785–89							1885–89						
Eston**	22	2	9.09%	20	90.91%	0	0	570	46	8.07%	482	84.56%	42	7.37%
Middlesbrough**	8	2	25.00%	6	75.00%	0	0	8,289	944	11.39%	6,639	80.09%	699	8.43%
Normanby**	20	2	10.00%	18	90.00%	0	0	807	70	8.67%	680	84.26%	57	7.06%
Skelton**	6	2	33.33%	4	66.67%	0	0	339	25	7.37%	276	81.42%	38	11.21%
Falsgrave	146	26	17.81%	120	82.19%	0	0	2,183	262	12.00%	1,839	84.24%	82	3.76%
Linthorpe	15	2	13.33%	13	86.67%	0	0	2,995	370	12.35%	2,299	76.76%	326	10.88%
Thornaby	23	6	26.09%	17	73.91%	0	0	1,894	302	15.95%	1,445	76.29%	147	7.76%
Guisborough*	103	13	12.62%	90	87.38%	0	0	499	76	15.23%	403	80.76%	20	4.01%
Northallerton*	230	34	14.78%	196	85.22%	0	0	399	62	15.54%	330	82.71%	7	1.75%
Pickering*	679	101	14.87%	578	85.13%	0	0	729	119	16.32%	595	81.62%	15	2.06%
Redcar***	42	5	11.90%	37	88.10%	0	0	423	64	15.13%	342	80.85%	17	4.02%
Scarborough***	1,422	400	28.13%	1,022	71.87%	0	0	6,536	998	15.27%	5,287	80.89%	248	3.79%
Whitby***	723	175	24.20%	548	75.80%	0	0	1,079	192	17.79%	847	78.50%	40	3.71%

* denotes market township; **denotes 19th-Century industrial township; *** denotes coastal township

by a factor of five, the increase in percentage share grew by just under 8 per cent. In Whitby, on the other hand, while the number of women increased slightly, the percentage share of female involvement decreased. Male involvement increased in volume by nearly a third, but by less than 3 per cent by percentage share. The rise in the 'Not Applicable' category in both these instances reflects the growing involvement of building societies, which, unlike industrial companies that purchased land for works or workers' housing, enabled individual women to purchase land for investment purposes. Marital status may also be a factor here, as many widows relocated to coastal towns after the death of their husbands. In addition, the fishing/sea-going trade was a high-risk occupation, hence the inclusion in the dataset of many wives and widows of mariners.[63] As the development and expansion of Scarborough progressed throughout the latter half of the nineteenth century and the railway companies espoused its virtues as a place to go to take the air, many affluent families invested in second properties in the town. This expansion of the property market required many more women to work in hotels, schools, domestic service and businesses which serviced these female clients and their children, such as milliners, drapers and haberdasheries. As the expansion of the town provided women with more opportunities to earn a living, similarly the opportunities for investment also increased. Overall, the data shows that, although the participation of women in coastal towns was quite disparate in the eighteenth century, the percentage share was reasonably similar across this category in the 1885–89 period.

Falsgrave, Linthorpe and Thornaby were large townships that were, by the nineteenth century, on the outskirts of significant urban or industrial conurbations, namely Scarborough, Middlesbrough and Stockton-On-Tees. As these towns expanded, Falsgrave, Linthorpe and Thornaby became *de facto* suburbs, desirable for the land, which facilitated the building of spacious housing for the growing middle classes away from the grime of industry, as well as workers' housing for local industries. Although this provided excellent opportunities for women to invest in property or exploit their land-holdings for development, inevitably it also attracted male investors and developers who, as the data shows, were much more likely to participate in multiple transactions. In addition, third-party involvement differed in these townships. Male involvement was higher and third-party involvement lower in Falsgrave than in both Linthorpe and Thornaby which, owing to their location near large industrial conurbations, were also themselves sites of inward business investment.

The patterns of female involvement with property are the most consistent across time in well-established market townships, such as Northallerton and

63 See, for example, Helen Doe, *Enterprising Women and Shipping in the Nineteenth Century* (Woodbridge, 2009).

Table 7. Breakdown of female datasets by marital status and type of transaction, 1885–89

Marital Status	Conveyance/ Re-conveyance		Indenture		Mortgage/Transfer of mortgage	
Infant/ <21 years	0	0.00%	0	0.00%	0	0.00%
Married	690	31.96%	676	31.56%	394	24.86%
Not stated	55	2.55%	35	1.63%	25	1.58%
Spinster	702	32.52%	699	32.63%	545	34.38%
Widow	712	32.98%	732	34.17%	621	39.18%
Total	2,159		2,142		1,585	

Pickering. Although the volume of transactions changes considerably from the eighteenth-century data, the level of participation is relatively steady at c. 14–16 per cent. Redcar's and Guisborough's female participation rates are the only ones to increase over time. Both of these townships also have similar levels of third-party involvement, reflecting their proximity to ironstone mines, railways and iron companies.

The following section of the chapter draws on data available only in the 1885–89 dataset related to type of transaction.[64] Although over 120 different types of transaction were recorded in the Deeds Registers, women's involvement was limited to about half this number. When wills and codicils are excluded (c. 5.5 per cent of female transactions), the vast majority of the remainder fall into three main types: Conveyances and Re-Conveyances (30.46 per cent); Indentures (30.22 per cent) and Mortgages/ Transfer of Mortgages (22.36 per cent). Table 7 shows the breakdown of these types of transaction according to marital status.

While participation in conveyances is relatively equally spread between the three main marital status categories, widows are the most likely to be involved in a mortgage transaction. While this might be expected, these statistics cannot indicate whether the widow was the borrower or the lender; this requires each mortgage document to be examined individually. Equally, it is important to recognise that over a third of women participating in a mortgage transaction were unmarried (34.38 per cent) and almost a quarter were married (24.86 per cent), reinforcing the argument that, while legal changes promised married women greater autonomy, marriage was still a barrier to women's involvement in specific types of transaction. As can be seen in Table 8, only six women were involved in more than twenty

64 From 1885 onwards the Index Ledger included the type of transaction.

Table 8. Breakdown of unique female participation by type of transaction, 1885–89

Number of transactions	Conveyance	Re-conveyance	Mortgage	Transfer of mortgage	Indenture	Total
26–30	3	0	0	0	0	3
21–25	1	0	0	0	2	3
16–20	0	0	0	1	0	1
11–15	0	0	1	0	1	2
6–10	7	0	5	2	7	21
5	4	0	4	0	4	12
4	20	0	8	5	24	57
3	31	2	33	9	50	125
2	154	20	64	28	182	448
1	1,027	249	674	246	1,080	3,276
Total	1,247	271	789	291	1,350	3,948

transactions during this period, none of them married, and their patterns of involvement were not uniform.

The most prolific were the Skinner women, sisters Hannah Georgiana Skinner and Elizabeth Walker Skinner, and their cousin, Hannah Skinner, who each participated in thirty transactions during this five-year period. The Skinner women were all unmarried and, at the time of these transactions, in their fifties and sixties.[65] They transacted together, bound by the conditions of their respective fathers' wills[66] to act as devisees and trustees in the sale of real estate, which they had jointly owned. They were mostly involved in conveyances, selling land in Thornaby township for housing development at a time when many new streets were being laid out to house workers for expanding industries. Rachel Robinson Cross from Scarborough, the widow

65 Hannah Skinner (1826–1905), daughter of William Skinner, banker of Stockton-on-Tees; Hannah Georgiana Skinner (1828–1916) and Elizabeth Walker Skinner (1838–1920), daughters of George Skinner, earthenware manufacturer of Stockton-on-Tees. Source: Case study research: Skinner.

66 George and William Skinner were sons of William Skinner Senior, originally from Whitby, who moved to Stockton-on-Tees in 1815 to set up the Skinner, Atty & Holt Bank, later purchased by the National Provincial Bank in 1836. William Skinner Junior became a partner in the bank but also invested in land in Thornaby with his brother George, an earthenware manufacturer. George died in 1870, leaving the Thornaby lands to two of his daughters, Hannah Georgiana and Elizabeth Walker Skinner. When William Skinner the younger died in 1876 his share of the Thornaby land passed to his unmarried daughter Hannah. From this point on, the women transacted together. Case study research: Skinner.

of a physician, was involved only in indentures, with twenty-one transactions. These transactions related mainly to property that she inherited from her unmarried brother, a ship owner, who had inherited a considerable amount of property from their father.[67]

Several women were involved only in mortgages; two women transacted in four mortgages and twelve women were involved in three separate mortgage transactions. Elizabeth Hanson, wife of William James Hanson, Accountant of Middlesbrough, was involved in the highest number of mortgages (eleven), as well as seven conveyances of property in Middlesbrough. This is a similar pattern of property involvement as that of Annie Grubb Dalton, wife of George Grubb Dalton, Builder of Middlesbrough, who was also taking advantage of the demand for terraced housing and homes for the middle classes. Annie was involved in eight conveyances and five mortgage transactions. However, the data for the 1885–89 period shows that, despite 224 women being involved in multiple transactions and 448 in two transactions, the vast majority (82.98 per cent) were involved in only one transaction during this five-year period. This might suggest that women were predominately involved in transactions related to their own use, rather than for investment purposes.

Across both datasets, transactions involving women but no men were identified as being of particular interest in order to understand more about autonomous decisions being made, as well as whether there were different patterns of involvement according to marital status. Only fifteen women-to-women transactions appear in the 1785–89 period, none involving married women. The majority of these transactions name two parties and none contain more than three parties. Widows constitute 83.87 per cent of these transactions, with the balance being unmarried (9.67 per cent) or undeclared (6.45 per cent). Several of the transactions name parties who are related to one another, such as the Indentures CE/321/505 and CE/322/506,[68] where 'Ann Preston, Widow, Relict and Devisee for Life named in the last Will and Testament of Israel Preston late of the same place Gentleman Deceased' sets out for each of her daughters, Elizabeth and Mary, both spinsters, the details of land and property that would be devised to them after her death. In the 1885–89 period 137 women-to-women transactions were listed, rising from nineteen in 1885 to over thirty per annum in 1889.

As can be seen in Table 9, women-to-women entries cluster by type of transaction in a similar pattern to that previously described: Conveyances/Re-conveyances; Indentures; and Mortgages/Transfer of Mortgages.[69] The

67 Case study research: Rachel Robinson Brown Cross.

68 *North Riding Register of Deeds*, 1789, CE/321/505 and CE/322/506.

69 More detailed analysis of Mortgages and Transfer of Mortgage transactions will be carried out to demonstrate that women were both lending and borrowing money, both from individuals

Table 9. Breakdown of women-to-women transactions by year and marital status

	1785–89						
	1785	1786	1787	1788	1789	Total	
Married	0	0	0	0	0	0	0.00%
Not stated	1	0	1	0	0	2	6.45%
Spinster	0	0	1	0	2	3	9.68%
Widow	3	9	8	0	6	26	83.87%
Total	4	9	10	0	8	31	
	1885–89						
	1885	1886	1887	1888	1889	Total	
Married	10	13	14	25	22	84	26.42%
Not stated	0	2	0	2	1	5	1.57%
Spinster	28	19	29	21	35	132	41.51%
Widow	12	13	30	24	18	97	30.50%
Total	50	47	73	72	76	318	

vast majority (78 per cent) contain only two parties, with a further 14.6 per cent containing three parties. The remainder have between four and six parties. The breakdown by marital status is as follows: Married: 26.42 per cent; Not stated: 1.57 per cent; Spinster: 41.51 per cent; and Widows: 30.50 per cent. These figures demonstrate both a growth in these types of transaction and a distinct change in married women's and spinsters' participation. Unlike the eighteenth-century period, where they do not feature at all in such transactions, married women are involved in more than a quarter in the 1885–89 period. The increase in spinsters' participation is also of interest. Although they represent 31.83 per cent of all transactions and 31.37 per cent of unique women, the data demonstrates that over 40 per cent of women-to-women transactions during 1885–89 involved spinsters, a considerably higher figure than married women or widows. This provides an indicator that unmarried women during 1885–89 were investing in property differently from their married or widowed counterparts and choosing to transact more frequently with other women. Hannah, Agnes and Jane Wearing, Spinsters of Preston, were involved in two transactions with Louisa Annie Ventress, the wife of Joseph Ventress, Ironmonger of Stockton-on-Tees. The Wearing

and from institutions such as building societies.

sisters loaned money to Louisa by way of a mortgage to purchase a small piece of land and dwelling house in Kings Road, North Ormesby.[70] The Register of Deeds as a resource could be utilised for a much larger study to explore this aspect of women's participation in the property market more fully over a longer period.

Female wills and codicils were also of interest to this study as, unlike other repositories of wills, there was no requirement to register these documents unless real estate was involved. A total of 288 women's wills were transcribed in full. Forty-four of these fall in the 1785–89 period, an average of eight per annum and representing 1.92 per cent of the unique women in this dataset. The remainder (244) were registered during the 1885–89 period, an average of almost fifty per annum or 5.47 per cent of unique women. This increase reinforces the growth in women's involvement with the property market across time while also providing a means to quantify property ownership at death by gender.[71]

The breakdown of female wills by marital status is shown in Table 10 below. Full copies of a will and any codicils did not have to be registered in the Register of Deeds – a memorial was sufficient – although the original will or a certified full copy had to be produced at the time of registration.[72] As Table 10 illustrates, the majority of all wills recorded in the Register of Deeds during the periods studied were written by widows. Five married women left wills in the 1785–89 period, and future analysis will establish if these transactions relate to property that was part of a separate estate.[73] Nine women left wills, but their marital status was not recorded. Of these, five had occupations: three were innkeepers, one a grocer and one a draper and shopkeeper. At ten pages, the longest will is that of Ann Allan, Spinster of Blackwell Grange in the Parish of Darlington in the County of Durham. Ann inherited from her grandfather, George Allan of Blackwell Grange, but died unmarried. She bequeathed her considerable estates, including those located in the County of York, to her cousin, James Allan the Elder, Gentleman of Darlington.[74]

In addition to the disposal of real and personal estates, many wills are detailed in their composition and demonstrate a considerable level of thoughtfulness. Mary Appleton, a Spinster from Northallerton, left detailed

70 *North Riding Register of Deeds*, 1885, 5/1090/473.

71 The Yorkshire Registries Acts 1884 & 1885 required that wills were registered within a specific period by an authorised person, namely the executor/ executrix/ trustee. Not all wills provided details of the property in question but the recording of even the most basic information regarding the real estate of the deceased in the Deeds Register was an important step in the subsequent transference of property rights (and responsibilities) from one person to another. See Haworth, *The Yorkshire Registries Acts*.

72 Haworth, *The Yorkshire Registries Acts*, p. 31.

73 See Tait, 'The Beginning of the End of Coverture'.

74 *North Riding Register of Deeds*, 1785, BU/92/32.

Table 10. Breakdown of female wills by marital status

	1785–89				1885–89			
	Copy will	Memorial will	Total		Copy will	Memorial will	Total	
Married	1	4	5	11.36%	12	14	26	10.66%
Not stated	0	0	0	0.00%	2	7	9	3.69%
Spinster	4	7	11	25.00%	22	45	67	27.46%
Widow	5	23	28	63.64%	48	94	142	58.20%
Total	10	34	44		84	160	244	

instructions to her executor regarding the payment she wished to give to the women who would be required to look after her in her final days and lay out her body ready for burial: 'And in further Trust also to pay thereout to two women if such are imployed [sic] in sitting up with me in my last illness each a handsome reward for their trouble according to the discretion of the said William Squire not exceeding five pounds each'.[75] Arguably, this level of planning and detail is more prevalent in wills of never married or single women, who might have to rely on strangers, rather than family, to look after them at their death.[76]

Conclusion

The main purpose of this pilot study was to establish the efficacy of using a new resource, the Registers of Deeds, in advancing knowledge about how women were involved with property transfer and the property market in the late eighteenth and nineteenth centuries. The initial findings presented in this chapter demonstrate its worth. Every document related to property ownership and transfer presented to the Registry during these periods was recorded routinely and systematically, providing a new opportunity for researchers to examine a much wider cross section of the population than is possible through estate collections or purely by using wills and probate documents, which cannot be guaranteed to hold information about land and buildings. The datasets refer to 19,513 unique property transactions containing 75,973 names. Included within that number is a subset of 6,755 unique women, whose involvement with land and property across the North Riding can now be quantified and interrogated. The inclusion of supplementary qualitative

75 *North Riding Register of Deeds*, 1787, BU/135/57.
76 Amy Froide, *Never Married: Singlewomen in Early Modern England* (Oxford, 2005).

data enabled analysis to take into account information about their family history, marital status, occupation, social networks and inheritance rights.

The percentage of unique women involved in property transactions was 30.62 per cent in 1785–89 and 19.33 per cent in 1885–89. Although married women represent over half the unique women in the early dataset, only a small number transacted without their husbands, indicating that the property in question was probably part of a separate estate. Otherwise, their inclusion in transactions was not representative of their legal power to make decisions over the property in question. Married women's participation, at 29.96 per cent, was more meaningful in the latter period, given that they were acting independently of their husbands and of any third party. While the percentage of widows increased only slightly in a century, the proportion of unmarried women involved with property almost doubled. The industrialisation of the North Riding of Yorkshire during the eighteenth and nineteenth centuries and the subsequent growth in population and infrastructure had a significant impact, bringing with it new opportunities for women to invest disposable income in joint stock companies and building societies. Women in general were also marrying later in life and were under less pressure to marry for financial security.[77] Overall, the data shows that there is more parity across marital status categories in the nineteenth-century data, notwithstanding that legislative changes were only just beginning to make an impact to married women. At the same time, the laws regarding married women's involvement with property were being challenged, with the result that, by 1883, married women were no longer a legal nonentity, but were treated as if a *feme sole*, with the rights to make autonomous decisions.

The wealth of data available from these property documents demonstrates how the Register of Deeds can provide new opportunities for those studying women's (and men's) social and economic history from the eighteenth century onwards. The study illustrates how quantitative and qualitative data can be used to advance knowledge about women's wider involvement with

77 It is outside the scope of this study to establish whether the age at marriage for women in Middlesbrough was lower than women from other parts of the county because of its swift growth as an industrial town; however, studies indicate that this is likely to be the case. See, for example, N. F. R. Crafts, 'Average Age at First Marriage for Women in Mid-Nineteenth-Century England and Wales: A Cross-Section Study', *Population Studies* 32 (1978), 21–5, which calculated that the estimated median age at first marriage of women in the North Riding of Yorkshire was 23.9 years in 1861. Crafts also concluded that the impact of industrialisation on marriage age was 'significant and negative' but unlikely to have a large impact on average age over time (he calculated a 0.4 fall in mean age over a fifty-year period). Nevertheless, Crafts' data shows that, the more industrialised the county, the lower the age at marriage. The West Riding was the most industrialised and had the lowest median age at 23.3 years, followed by the East Riding at 23.6 years. As illustrated earlier in this chapter, the North Riding was much more rural and less industrialised than its neighbouring counties, which explains why the North Riding had the highest estimated median age.

property, rather than focusing on purely ownership. There is potential for other research, such as propospographical studies of male occupations or class-based property holding, as well as fulsome information on the genealogical connections between individuals, family networks and the history of specific properties within the County of York. As such, this resource will be of great interest to other academic researchers, as well as local, regional, family and architectural historians. The core datasets have been made available online to enhance accessibility and promote use of this important resource by the general public.[78] Given the rarity of such resources and the potential to view the results of this study as 'representative' of a larger population, future studies could include further analysis of the geographical diaspora of women transacting property to provide a means of understanding more about women's involvement with property nationally.

78 The core datasets include all data transcribed from the original Index Ledgers. This data has been made available in a public search engine at http://www.registerofdeeds.org.uk. It is the intention to make the full datasets available to other researchers at the end of the study via an appropriate repository.

9

Invisible Women: Small-scale Landed Proprietors in Nineteenth-century England

JANET CASSON

Until recently it was widely believed that women in the nineteenth century had very little personal stake in land, and this view was reflected by many in the patrician ruling elite at the time. Lord Derby, speaking in 1871 about 'the question of ownership of the soil' at the annual meeting of the Manchester and Liverpool Agricultural Society, commented that in the 1861 Census 30,000 people had returned themselves under the heading of landowner, of whom 15,000 were women.[1] Derby commented 'We know that half of the land is not in female hands, and that probably not one-tenth of our landowners, if so many, are women.' He slightly understated the case. In the long eighteenth century women were involved in the ownership of 10.3 per cent of land, as has been shown by McDonagh, and my own work on the nineteenth century is broadly confirming of this figure, as will be seen.[2]

A majority of female landowners in the nineteenth century inherited their property. The majority of men who held large estates had usually inherited them too and often found that their management of their land was restricted by the requirements of dependent family members, marriage settlements, dowries and mortgages. It is therefore unclear whether the position of women landowners was really very different from that of men.

Until recently, it was also believed that until the 1882 Married Women's Property Act married women could not hold land in their own right, and that only spinsters and widows could own land. However, this is an over-simplification. Prior to the act, the default legal position with regard to

1 Sir T. H. Sanderson and E. S. Roscoe (eds), *Speeches and Addresses of Edward Henry XVth Earl of Derby K.G.* (London, 1894), vol. 1, pp. 139–40.

2 Briony McDonagh, *Elite Women and the Agricultural Landscape 1700–1830* (Abingdon, 2017), Chapter 2, Table 2.1; Janet Casson, 'Women's landownership in England in the nineteenth century', in Mark Casson and Nigar Hashimzade (eds.), Large Databases in Economic History: Research methods and case studies, (Routledge, Abingdon, 2013), pp. 200-221.

married women was determined by the common law principle of coverture, in which a married woman ceased to exist as a legal entity. Coverture resulted from the belief that by marriage the couple became 'two peoples but one flesh', automatically conferring the dominance of the husband and granting him full authority over his wife and her property.[3] A married woman could own real property but she lost any independent control of the management of the property and the use of any rents and profits associated with it; these were all transferred to her husband. There was a safeguard to prevent a husband selling his wife's land in that the wife had to be independently interviewed by a lawyer and give her consent formally and alone. Under common law, a married couple owning shares in a property along with others only got one share between them because they were legally regarded as one person. However, if real property had been conveyed to both the husband and wife – in other words, a tenancy by entireties – then they could own it jointly.[4]

The constraints of common law were mediated by equity dispensed by the court of Chancery. It therefore became possible to establish personal trusts.[5] By creating a trust a contract was established, valid in equity, though not in common law, that allowed a woman to own property, real or personal, independently of her husband for her 'sole and separate use'. With careful wording, such a trust could provide a married woman with considerable control over her separate property.[6] By 1850 10 per cent of all married women were believed to have some form of settlement and by 1863 a 'Banker's Daughter' was giving advice that 'no prudent woman should marry without this provision'.[7]

This chapter shows how legal provisions for the ownership of land by women worked in practice. It also dispels the assumption that only wealthy women held land and challenges the belief that where a woman did own land a man must have been involved as a co-owner. The evidence to disprove these assumptions is provided by detailed case studies of ten nineteenth-century women landowners, each of whom owned a single plot of land. The decision to focus the chapter on such small-scale landed proprietors stems from the

3 For a fuller discussion of coverture see Tim Stretton and Krista J. Kesselring, 'Introduction: Coverture and Continuity', *Married Women and the Law of Coverture in England and the Common Law World*, eds Tim Stretton and Krista J. Kesselring (Montreal/Kingston/London, 2013), pp. 3–23.

4 Lee Holcombe, *Wives and Property, Reform of the Married Women's Property Law in Nineteenth-Century England* (Toronto, 1983), pp. 19–24.

5 Leonore Davidoff and Catherine Hall, *Family Fortunes: Men and Women of the English Middle Class 1780–1850* (Abingdon, revised edition, 2002), p. 209.

6 J. H. Baker, *An Introduction to English Legal History* (London, 1971), pp. 258–9.

7 Holcombe, *Wives and Property*, p. 46; A Banker's Daughter, *A Guide to the Unprotected in everyday matters relating to property and income* (London, 1863), p. 96.

fact they were not fully acknowledged by Derby or the compilers of the 1873 Return of Owners of Land, and because they have generally been overlooked by other researchers.[8] One of its aims is also to bring to light more qualitative detail about the female landowners in a series of biographical sketches.

Historiographies of female land ownership

The lack of a central register of landowners and the belief that women's ownership of land was minimal have both contributed to a deficiency of research into female landowners. Research into women's property has often, therefore, concentrated on their financial assets, as illustrated by the work of Carlos and Neal, Laurence, and Newton and Cottrell among others.[9]

Nevertheless, a few studies have focused on female land ownership. Berg, Lane and Combs are among those who have investigated women's land ownership using wills or related documents.[10] Wills, however, can create a 'wealth bias', because they were made by people who had assets, and a 'death bias', because they were often written when such people were no longer economically active and had disposed of some of their property. In addition, wills are affected by testators' motives, such as avoiding taxes and controlling inheritance. Finally, women are often underrepresented with regard to wills because, before the Married Woman's Property Act of 1882, a married woman could not make a will without her husband's permission unless she had separate property protected by a trust or settlement.[11] These studies are also vulnerable to criticism on the grounds that they involved searching through the source material seeking out the women who owned land. The

8 Great Britain, Local Government Board, *England and Wales (Exclusive of the Metropolis): Return of Owners of Land, 1873*, 2 vols (London, 1875); John Bateman, *The Great Landowners of Great Britain and Ireland*, with an introduction by David Spring (Leicester, 1971, reprinted by the Humanities Press, New York).

9 Ann M. Carlos and Larry Neal, 'Women investors in early capital markets, 1720–1725', *Financial History Review* 11:2 (2004), 197–224; Anne Laurence, 'The emergence of a private clientele for banks in the early eighteenth century: Hoare's Bank and some women customers', *The Economic History Review* 61:3 (August 2008), 565–86; Lucy Newton and Philip L. Cottrell, 'Female Investors in the First English and Welsh Joint-Stock Banks', *Accounting, Business & Financial History* 16:2 (July 2006), 315–40.

10 Maxine Berg, 'Women's Property and the Industrial Revolution', *Journal of Interdisciplinary History* 24:2 (Autumn 1993), 233–50; Penelope Lane, 'Women, Property and Inheritance: Wealth Creation and Income Generation in Small English Towns, 1750–1835', *Urban Fortunes: Property and Inheritance in the Town 1700–1900*, eds Jon Stobart and Alastair Owens (Aldershot, 2000), pp. 172–94; Mary Beth Combs, '*Cui Bono*? The 1870 British Married Women's Property Act, Bargaining Power, and the Distribution of Resources Within Marriage', *Feminist Economics* 12:1–2 (January–April 2006), 51–83.

11 Holcombe, *Wives and Property*, pp. 21, 25, 43.

samples of women so obtained were relatively small and the number of people who had to be investigated in order to generate the discussed sample was not normally recorded. Such 'looking for women' can reinforce the bias in favour of wealthier women.

Robin used enclosure awards and maps and Seeliger and Davey used tithe maps and apportionments but the studies were restricted to small geographical regions and short time periods.[12] McDonagh's recent study used enclosure bills, acts and awards as well as supporting primary sources from across England for the period 1700–1830.[13] She assembled a database of over 13,000 plots owned by 700 women and several thousand men and analysed what land they owned and how they managed their property, even whilst she primarily concentrated on seventy wealthy elite women with sizable rural estates. Rubinstein used the 1873 Return of Owners of Land and Bateman's reassessments to study land ownership by wealthy men and included a seven-page appendix on sixty-three very wealthy women, but he unfortunately gave no information about the properties that they owned.[14]

Methodology

This chapter utilises information generated from a large study of 23,966 plots of land recorded in canal and railway books of reference over the whole nineteenth century. Instead of searching for women, the study recorded details of a representative sample of plots and identified those owned by women. This method avoided the biases discussed above. The books of reference have a number of other advantages. Their information is very reliable because they were legal documents that were scrutinised by both parliament and members of the public. In addition, their geographical coverage was representative, drawn from many counties across the country, rural and urban, and detailed, disaggregating to parish and township level. They enable landownership in adjacent parishes to be examined. The socio-economic range of the owners is comprehensive, as canal and railway development, with its accompanying compulsory purchase, was widespread. Finally, the information links plots to their owners, lessees and occupiers, whereas in most other sources only

12 Jean Robin, *Elmdon: Continuity and change in a north-west Essex village 1861–1964* (Cambridge, 1980); Sylvia Seeliger, 'Hampshire Women as Landowners: Common Law Mediated by Manorial Custom', *Rural History* 7:1 (1996), 1–14; B. J. Davey, *Ashwell 1830–1914: The decline of a village community* (Leicester, 1980).

13 McDonagh, *Elite Women*, Chapter 2.

14 W. D. Rubinstein, *Men of Property: The Very Wealthy in Britain since the Industrial Revolution* (London, rev. 2nd edn, 2006), pp. 250–6; Great Britain, Local Government Board, *Return of Owners of Land, 1873*; Bateman, *The Great Landowners*.

occupiers were listed.[15] The methodology further identified if women were acting on their own or with others, and also compared the uses and characteristics of the land owned by women with those of the land owned by men. Organised by region and by time period, the study was designed to account for regional differences and track changes over time.

The quantitative analysis that was carried out on the resultant database revealed that women were on average involved in the ownership of 12.4 per cent of plots but that there were regional variations.[16] The figure that emerged is broadly confirming of that found by McDonagh for the long eighteenth century: *viz.* 10.3 per cent of her land sample. McDonagh also discovered regional variations and that women owned 11.4 per cent of the individual plots of land in her sample.[17] So, two large datasets, covering 1700–1900 between them, show that women's land ownership was remarkably consistent across two centuries.[18]

The study of the 23,966 plots identified 639 individual women, of whom 348 (54.5 per cent) could be profiled. A striking feature of this profiling was that, while a large number of the plots were owned by wealthy women who owned many plots, there were also many women that appeared in their specific book of reference owning only one plot and for whom subsequent profiling produced no evidence of substantial property elsewhere. These women were overlooked by nineteenth-century writers and, to some extent, women's ownership remains largely unacknowledged today. As McDonagh discovered for her period, such individuals 'are too often almost impossible to recover in the archives'.[19] These are the invisible women and they are the focus of this chapter because it has been possible to find biographical information about them using online resources as well as standard archive material.

This chapter showcases ten women who were involved in the ownership of eight separate plots of land. Six of the eight plots were held by individual women and two were held jointly by pairs of sisters. Two plots were selected in each of the four regions to give a broadly representative picture of small-scale landownership by women in each region. For each woman the books of reference gave the name of the parish in which their plot was situated,

15 Peter H. Lindert, 'Who Owned Victorian England? The Debate over Landed Wealth and Inequality', *Agricultural History* 61:4 (Autumn 1987), 25–51.

16 Janet Casson, 'Women and Property: a study of women as owners, lessors and lessees of plots of land in England during the nineteenth century as revealed by the land surveys carried out by the railway, canal and turnpike companies' (PhD diss., University of Oxford, 2013). For additional analysis see Janet Casson, *Women in Control? Ownership and Control of Land by Women in Nineteenth Century England*, forthcoming.

17 McDonagh, *Elite Women*, Chapter 2.

18 Ibid. Casson, 'Women and Property'; For additional analysis see Casson, *Women in Control?*

19 McDonagh, *Elite Women*, Chapter 2.

their name and those of any co-owners and the uses of the land. This enabled an ownership pattern to be determined and the number of plots owned by a particular woman to be counted. Ownership was allocated to one of four categories: sole ownership, ownership with other women and no one else, ownership where men were co-owners, and ownership where institutions were co-owners.[20]

Further research was carried out using a wide range of additional primary sources to build profiles of all the female owners named in the books of reference and to link them to 'their' land. The UK census collection 1841–1911 provided a rich source of information, including details of place and date of birth, parents and siblings, employment, marriage, information about spouses and children, widowhood and change of residence. The Church of England, nonconformist and civil records of baptisms, marriages, deaths and burials in the UK and Ireland provided the obvious specific details, but could also indicate father's occupation, previous marriage and literacy. Wills, accessed via the England and Wales Prerogative Court of Canterbury Wills 1384–1858 provided information about the immediate and extended family and sometimes indicated that the land had passed to the woman by inheritance. Entries in the UK Extracted Probate Records 1269–1975 and National Probate Calendar (Index of Wills and Administration) 1858–1966 gave details of a woman's wealth at death. Local, regional and family histories occasionally provided clues about the single plot owners.

Other primary sources consulted included Poll Books and Electoral Registers; Land Tax Records, 1780–1832; the *London Gazette*; city and county Directories and Gazetteers; tithe maps and apportionments; and Chancery records. Secondary sources were consulted in order to amplify and contextualise the information gathered from the primary sources. The range of secondary sources consulted included *The Return of Owners of Land 1873*; John Bateman's *Landowners*; the Oxford Dictionary of National Biography; Victoria County Histories; Burke's *Peerage and Landed Gentry*; the National Heritage List for England;[21] The Peerage;[22] History of Parliament;[23] and Find a Grave Index for England and Wales.[24] However, these sources, especially the secondary ones listed here, were more useful in profiling the women who owned multiple plots than in profiling the 'invisible' women who held insufficient land to appear in the sources named above.

20 For a full explanation see Casson, *Women in Control?*

21 https://historicengland.org.uk/listings.

22 http://thepeerage.com.

23 http://www.historyofparliamentonline.org/.

24 Many of the sources, including wills, were accessed via the Ancestry UK website at https://www.ancestry.co.uk. Such references will not be cited individually, although individual wills are identified and cited.

Table 11. Women's plot ownership across the four regions

	Regions			
	Oxfordshire	Yorkshire	Durham	London
Percentage of plots owned by women	14.7	12.4	12.0	8.9

Table 12. Comparative regional analysis of the ownership of plots by subgroups of women owners expressed as a percentage of all plots owned by women

Ownership category	Regions			
	Oxfordshire	Yorkshire	Durham	London
Sole owner or with women co-owners	57.8	39.4	39.4	55.1
With men of the same name	11.5	31.5	23.3	16.8
With specified husband	8.2	21.5	24.3	1.8

Regions

Four regions were subject to detailed study: Oxfordshire and London in the south of England and West Yorkshire and County Durham in the north. The region centred on Oxfordshire (but including land from the adjacent counties of Berkshire, Buckinghamshire, Gloucestershire, Northamptonshire, Warwickshire and Worcestershire) was selected because it was a predominantly rural agricultural area. West Yorkshire was chosen because it had a large textile industry based around Bradford, Halifax, Huddersfield, Leeds and Wakefield. Additionally, it had large coal reserves, an accompanying iron industry based in the south and links to the coast via the inland docks at Goole. The region experienced rapid urbanisation during the nineteenth century but still retained a viable agricultural economy with arable farming in the east and mixed farming elsewhere.[25] County Durham was selected because it was a coal-mining area and the records were in excellent condition because of the area's importance to railway development, being the site of some of the earliest railways. London was chosen because it was the metropolis and railway schemes were selected that went into the central area and radiated out in all directions.

25 Arthur Raistrick, *West Riding of Yorkshire* (Hodder and Stoughton, 1970), pp. 20–1.

Women's landownership in Yorkshire and Durham was about average, but that in Oxfordshire was above average at 14.7 per cent and in London below average at 8.9 per cent.

In each region at least 39 per cent of women were sole owners or owned with other women and these were the predominant ownership categories for women who held land in the south of England. However, women landowners in the northern regions of Yorkshire and Durham held 47 per cent of their plots with specified husbands or men who bore the same surname.

Women's ownership of plots also varied according to plot use and the pattern of variation differed across the regions.[26] Importantly, there was a long-term multiregional trend towards a greater involvement of women in the ownership of land during the century. This was tempered, however, by a significant decline in women's land ownership in Yorkshire and Durham after the 1870 Married Women's Property Act. In Oxfordshire women's ownership declined slightly after the 1870 Act but significantly after the 1882 Married Women's Property Act. In London, women's ownership of land rose after the 1870 Act and fell after the 1882 Act. The 1870 Act did not affect the law relating to married women's ownership of real estate. However, it allowed married women to invest in approved schemes including government annuities, public stocks, building societies and savings banks and to keep the capital plus the interest derived from it as separate property. Some women seem to have taken advantage of the new investment opportunities after 1870 rather than invest in land. The 1882 Act gave married women the same property rights for land as unmarried women. Financial investments, however, are easier to manage than land and after 1882 women in Oxfordshire and London seem to have chosen them.

Representation

The ten women selected for the biographical study were chosen to illustrate the diversity of women's experience of landownership even though they were small-scale landed proprietors. They were drawn from all four regions and span the entire period from 1801 to 1893. They owned in rural and urban areas, including a rapidly developing industrial new town. They owned a range of property, including houses, a bakehouse, gardens, arable fields, a market garden and a street. They also encompassed the four ownership categories: Ann Hogg, Henrietta Baddiley, Elizabeth Galpin and Georgiana Paine were sole owners; Elizabeth and Mary Hale were co-owning sisters; Bessy (Elizabeth) Hick, Margaret Oliver and Jane Gibson co-owned with

26 See Casson, 'Women and Property', for details.

Table 13. Women's ownership categories and marital status

Ownership category	Marital status		
	Unmarried	Married	Widow
Sole			Ann Hogg Henrietta Baddiley Elizabeth Galpin Georgiana Paine
Co-owning with women	Elizabeth Hale[a] Mary Hale[a]		
Co-owing with men		Margaret Oliver[b] Jane Gibson	Bessy Hick[b]
Co-owing with institutions			Martha Greenwell

[a] and [b] denote sisters

men; and Martha Greenwell co-owned with an institution. The selected women included spinsters, widows and married women.

Margaret Oliver of Yorkshire and Jane Gibson of County Durham were married women when listed as owners but in neither case was their then husband also listed as an owner, although Jane was referred to as a trustee for the will of William Richardson, who was her first husband. However, both women were listed as landowners for railway schemes that were promoted after the introduction of the 1882 Act, which allowed wives to own, buy and sell all forms of real and personal property as their 'separate property'.[27] The act overcame the disparity between common law and equity by prioritising equity, but it did not interfere with settlements already in operation and it did not affect ability of a family to set up trusts if required. Jane may have already benefited from a trust and it is possible that Margaret may have benefited as a result of the 1882 Act.

Oxfordshire Women

In Oxfordshire there were 145 profiled women, of whom 19 per cent owned just one plot. Sixty-four per cent of those single-plot women were sole owners, 7 per cent co-owned with women and 29 per cent co-owned with men. Three women represent Oxfordshire: the Hale sisters, Elizabeth and Mary, who were co-owners, and Ann Hogg, who was a sole owner.

27 Married Women's Property Act 1882 c.75 (45 and 46 Vict.).

Elizabeth Hale (d. 1838) and Mary Hale[28]

In 1836 two inhabitants of the small Thames-side agricultural village of Sutton Courtenay, Berkshire, were about to experience a cultural shock. The Oxford and Great Western Union Railway was surveying a route through the parish and a paper mill was being built by the river. Although these were not the first large constructions to have occurred, the Saxons having built a large causeway because of flooding, the railway would cut through the centre of the village and potentially disrupt the lives of Elizabeth and Mary Hale. The spinster sisters co-owned and occupied a plot containing a house, outhouse and garden. Their father, Cornelius Hale, was a yeoman farmer who had bought land in the village. On his death in 1804 he left £500 to each of his daughters, Elizabeth, Mary, Susannah and Ann; £150 to his son John, and the land to his son Cornelius. Elizabeth's will, written in 1824, left all her land in Sutton Courtenay to her sister Mary Hale and made cash bequests to her brother Cornelius and sister Susanna Pullen. Elizabeth died in 1838. Mary's date of death is unknown.

Ann Hogg (1793–1866)[29]

In 1853 Aylesbury, Buckinghamshire, was a thriving market town which already had good transport links thanks to the canal (1814) and the railway (1839). However, the Wycombe and Oxford Railway was promoting a branch line to Aylesbury and one plot on the route, containing a house, bakehouse and garden, was owned by Ann Hogg, *née* Stephens. Ann was born in Hulcott, a village to the north of Aylesbury, and had married widower Thomas Hogg, a farmer and corn dealer, in St Mary's Church, Aylesbury, in 1818. They had two children, Thomas and Betsey. By 1837, when Thomas senior wrote his will, the family had moved from Aylesbury to Nash, a village in the parish of Whaddon Bucks. Thomas owned real estate in several parishes and made provision for his three sons and two daughters from his first marriage as well as for Ann and her children. When Thomas died in 1838 Ann inherited the household effects in their dwelling at Nash outright. However, the farmland and all the farming equipment in Nash was left in trust to her for her lifetime so long as she remained a widow, so that she could continue supporting herself and her children. Thomas also left an estate in Aylesbury in trust for Ann's widowhood with the rents to be paid

28 Oxford and Great Western Union Railway from Oxford to join intended Great Western Railway, the line to go from Oxford via Abingdon to Didcot, 1836, Oxfordshire Record Office (ORO), PD2/5; Will of Elizabeth Hale, The National Archives (TNA), Kew, England, *Prerogative Court of Canterbury and Related Probate Jurisdictions: Will Registers*, PROB 11/1899; Will of Cornelius Hale, PROB 11/1408.

29 Wycombe and Oxford Railways with branch to Aylesbury with land between Chinnor and Oxford, 1853, ORO, PD 2/70; Will of Thomas Hogg, PROB 11/1189.

to her and her children. Her co-trustees were Philip Hogg (her step-son), and two male friends of her husband's. In 1841 Ann was described as a farmer living in Nash with Thomas, Betsey and Philip. By 1851 Ann was living 'On the Green' at Great Horwood, Buckinghamshire, with Betsey, and both were described as 'annuitants'. It is not clear if the 1853 property was part of her husband's estate or one she had bought herself, but probably the latter, as she was the sole owner. In 1861 Ann was living in Principal Street, Whaddon, Buckinghamshire, with Betsey and her husband John Bonham, a butcher, and their three young sons. Ann died in 1866.

Yorkshire Women

There were 100 profiled women in Yorkshire, of whom 27 per cent were single plot owners. Forty-four per cent of those women were sole owners, 52 per cent co-owned with men and 4 per cent co-owned with institutions. Three women represent Yorkshire: Henrietta Baddiley, a sole owner, and sisters Bessy Hick and Margaret Oliver, who co-owned with a man.

Henrietta Baddiley (1814–1902)[30]

In 1879 an arable field owned by Henrietta Baddiley in the parish of Felkirk in the Hemsworth district of the West Riding of Yorkshire was on the potential route of the Hull, Barnsley and West Riding Junction Railway. Henrietta was born in Lancaster to army lieutenant John Wilkinson and his wife Mary. In August 1841 she was married by licence in Huddersfield to John Hounsfield, a butcher. By 1851 they were living in Brierley, one of Felkirk's townships, where John was both trading as a butcher with two apprentices and farming 132 acres with two labourers. John died in April 1856 aged forty-seven, and was buried at the church of Felkirk St Peter with Brierley St Paul. Two years later Henrietta remarried in the same church to farmer James Baddiley, a thirty-eight-year-old widower with three small children. They remained in the area, living in the nearby village of South Kirkby, where James farmed eighty acres with the help of several labourers. James died in 1872 and was buried in All Saint's South Kirkby. At probate his effects were 'under £4000'. Henrietta went to live in King's Road, Wheatley, Doncaster, where she died in 1902, leaving effects of £47 5s 4d. She was buried at South Kirkby with her second husband. Henrietta's land was probably inherited from her first husband.

30 Hull, Barnsley and West Riding Junction Railway, 1879, West Yorkshire Archive Service Wakefield (WYASW), QE20/1/1879/9.

Bessy (Elizabeth) Hick (1838–1914)[31] and Margaret Oliver (1843–1928)[32]

In 1886 the Great Northern Railway was planning a route through Wakefield, in the West Riding of Yorkshire, a thriving market town and a centre for coal mining. Wakefield was also an important transport hub, with several turnpike roads, three canals, a railway and an inland port that specialised in trading in grain and textiles. It was also establishing itself as a prominent civic hub. The new route crossed a field owned by siblings Bessy Hick, Margaret Oliver and William Hartley. Their parents were William Hartley, a corn miller, and his wife Margaret. In 1851 the siblings were with their parents, their sister Mary and several servants in Ouzlewell Green, Wakefield. Bessy married corn miller Henry Hick in Holy Trinity, Rothwell, in February 1861. The couple were to have three children, but in April 1861 they were living in Bolton upon Dearne, South Yorkshire, with one servant. By 1871 Bessy and Henry, now described as a wine merchant and maltster, were in Crown Point House, Hunslet, Leeds. Henry had retired by 1871 and the family had moved to The Mansion House, Whitkirk. Henry died in 1883 leaving a personal estate of £5,323 16s. Bessy and her eldest daughter remained in Whitkirk, but they had moved to Scarborough by 1901 and to Ilkley by 1911. Bessy died in 1914. She left £391 15s and was buried in Rothwell with Henry.

At the 1861 census the remaining siblings were still living with their parents. William senior died in 1868, leaving an estate of 'under £7000'. His widow and children were his executors. Margaret had married farmer Thomas Oliver in Holy Trinity, Rothwell, in July 1864, and they eventually had eight children. In 1871 Margaret and Thomas were living in Carlton Hall, Ardsley, Wakefield, where Thomas was employing three men to farm 138 acres. Thomas died in September 1899, leaving an estate of £2,741 2s 2d. Margaret remained in Charlton Hall with the family, including her only son Thomas, who was farming the land by 1901. By 1911, however, Margaret and five of her unmarried daughters were living in Roundhay, Leeds. Margaret died there in 1928, leaving £876 1s 1d.

Durham Women

In County Durham there were fifty-eight profiled women, of whom 24 per cent were single plot owners. Fifty per cent of those women were sole owners, 14 per cent co-owned with women, 29 per cent co-owned with men and 7 per cent co-owned with institutions. Two women represent Durham: Martha Greenwell, who co-owned with an institution, and Jane Gibson, who co-owned with a man.

31 Great Northern Railway (Halifax High Level and North and South Junction Railway), 1886: WYASW, QE20/1/1886/2.

32 WYASW, QE20/1/1886/2.

Martha Greenwell (1815–1877)[33]

In the early nineteenth century the rural parish of Stranton contained three townships, one of which, Stranton, contained a twelfth-century church and sixty-eight houses. From the 1830s the area underwent dramatic changes because of the industrial development of the West Dock, which was built in Stranton parish because there was insufficient space within the old town and parish of Hartlepool. The West Dock area became a new town known as West Hartlepool and, as people moved in to take advantage of the new opportunities and the population of Stranton parish increased, the parish councillors, many of whom were volunteers, were unable to cope with the additional responsibilities. This situation improved in 1857, when West Hartlepool got its own governing body, the Board of Improvement Commissioners. They upgraded the rural tracks and built new roads, one of which was Throston Street, in the heart of the dock-side development. In 1873 the Hartlepool and Cleveland Junction Railway Company proposed a line into the dock. The route crossed Throston Street, which was co-owned by Martha Greenwell, Joseph Bell, Thomas Matthews, Richard Bowser, Thomas Mossman and the North-Eastern Railway Company. Martha Greenwell was born in the village of Bishop Middleham, Durham, the eldest child of John Fletcher, a blacksmith, and his wife Maria, and she lived with them and her six siblings until her marriage in 1845. Martha married William Greenwell, a local agricultural labourer, and in 1851 they were living in the village with three children and other family members. By 1861 Martha and William had six children and had moved to the Old Hart Road, West Hartlepool, with Martha's eighty-year-old father and her brother Robert. They seem to have taken advantage of the opportunities in the new town, as William and Robert were working as stone quarriers. William moved further up the social ladder, being described as a farmer with an estate of 'under £100' when he died in 1870 aged fifty-eight years. Martha was William's executrix and Joseph Bell, a mason of Coxhoe Durham and one of the co-owners of Throston Street, was an executor. Martha was listed as a farmer of twenty-three acres in 1871 and was living in Hart Road, Stranton, with five children, a grandson and a nephew. The family had invested in farming and in the expanding urban infrastructure of West Hartlepool, as shown by Martha's co-ownership of Throston Street. Martha died in the winter of 1877.

33 Hartlepool and Cleveland Junction Railway, Railway 1, 1873, Durham Record Office (DRO), QDP/313/2; Robert Wood, *West Hartlepool: The Rise and Development of a Victorian New Town* (Hartlepool, 1996), pp. 82, 84, 86, 94–5; William Page (ed.), *The Victoria History of the County of Durham*, vol. 3 (London, 1928), p. 365; Ordnance Survey Landranger 93, Middlesbrough and Darlington area.

Jane Gibson (1841–1904)34

In 1893 the route of the proposed Durham Coast Railway passed through the parish of Stranton and crossed a plot containing a house, garden, yard and outbuildings occupied by William Spark and co-owned by Jane Gibson and William Vaile, trustees of the will of the late William Richardson. Jane Gibson was born in the small village of Well, North Yorkshire, to railway labourer John Spence and his wife Mary. Her father soon moved the family to Stranton to take advantage of the railway development at the West Dock. The township of New Stanton[35] started with a few houses between Stranton and Hartlepool sometime in the thirteenth to fifteenth centuries. By the early nineteenth century there was a mill and an inn, but the area underwent rapid development as the West Dock complex expanded and complementary industries such as Bastow's foundry and engineering works were built. In 1851 Jane, her parents and two siblings were living in Mill Street, having joined the 1,000 immigrant workers who had settled in New Stranton. The township was eventually incorporated into West Dock/West Hartlepool during the 1850s. In April 1861 Jane was working in West Hartlepool as a servant for shipbroker John Sutcliffe and his family, who had recently moved from Bradford. Jane married labourer William Richardson in winter 1863, but at the 1871 census she and their two children were at 13 Princess Street, West Hartlepool, with her mother and stepfather, George Staindrop, a joiner. Boarding with the family was a widowed actress from London called Mary Millar, who was possibly appearing at the newly opened Theatre Royal. By 1881 William and Jane were running an inn on Lynn Street, West Hartlepool, aided by their son John, a barman called William Gibson from Rutland, and an eighty-year-old Irish domestic servant. Running an inn on Lynn Street was a prudent move, as it was the town's main business, shopping and entertainment thoroughfare and the site of the covered market. William died in May 1886, leaving an estate of £392 1s 6d to be administered by Jane and William Vaile,[36] a railway porter from West Hartlepool. In spring 1888 Jane married William Gibson, the inn barman. Jane and William seem to have retired from running the inn, because in the 1891 and 1901 censuses they were living in Reed Street, West Hartlepool, and William was listed as a labourer. Initially they were joined by Jane's son, who had become a widower, but subsequently they were joined by two of her daughter's children. Jane died in the spring of 1904.

34 Durham Coast Railway, 1892, DRO, QDP/408/2.

35 Wood, *West Hartlepool*, pp. 40–4, 48, 85; *Hartlepool History Then and Now*, website available at http://www.hhtandn.org, accessed 23 April 2018.

36 William had married Jane's mother Mary in 1884 as her third husband when she was fifty-nine and he was forty-two.

London Women

In London there were forty-five profiled women, of whom 29 per cent were single plot owners. Sixty-nine per cent of those women were sole owners, and 31 per cent co-owned with men. Two women represent London: Elizabeth Galpin and Georgiana Paine

Elizabeth Galpin (1741–1818)[37]

In 1801 an iron railway was proposed to run from Croydon to the River Thames at Wandsworth, with a collateral branch leading from a corner of Mitcham Common to the hamlet of Wallington in the parish of Beddington, Surrey. One of the plots on the route was a piece of agricultural land in Bygrove Mead Mitcham owned by Elizabeth Galpin. In 1801 Mitcham was a predominantly rural parish known for its Physic Gardens: specialised market gardens which grew medicinal herbs and aromatic plants including lavender, chamomile, peppermint and liquorice. The parish's industrial area was based on the banks of the Wandle River and contained works for the bleaching and printing of calico and silk, and several snuff mills.

Elizabeth Galpin was born to John Caslake and his wife Sarah and baptised in St Mary's Church Putney in January 1741. In May 1767 she was married by licence to farmer James Galpin in the church of St Peter and St Paul, Mitcham. Both were literate and signed the register. James died in 1789 and was buried in Mitcham church on 1 May. His will was undated and unwitnessed, so on 15 May John Watney of Wimbledon and Samuel Caslake of Putney swore affidavits to the effect that the document purporting to be James Galpin's last will and testament was indeed in his handwriting and contained correct information about his family. James left bequests of land and money to his two sons, James and Samuel, and money to his four daughters, Mary, Sarah, Eleanor and Ann. He left his 'horses, cows, sheep and everything else' to Elizabeth, who was his executrix. She obtained probate on 18 May 1789. Galpin's Farm was one of the largest in the area and Elizabeth Galpin of Kennet Square, Mitcham, was listed in the Surrey Land Tax records for 1798 and 1800 as an owner paying tax of 11s 9d. She was also listed as an occupier of land owned by several other people. She died in September 1818 and was buried in the churchyard at Mitcham at a time when the church was dilapidated and about to be demolished.[38]

37 Croydon to the River Thames at Wandsworth, 1801: Surrey History Centre (SHC), QS6/8/7/2, Will of James Galpin, TNA, PROB 1/1179; Surrey Land Tax returns of 1798 and 1800; Pollard's Hill Merton, available at http://www.merton.gov.uk, accessed 24 November 2014; Samuel Lewis, *Topographical Dictionary of England* (London, 1840), 4th edn, vol. 3, p. 287; It seem that James and Elizabeth had two other sons, John and William, but they were not mentioned in James's will.

38 The church was rebuilt between 1819 and 1822 and the base of the Saxon tower was retained.

Georgiana Paine (b.1810)[39]

In 1836 a railway was promoted to run from Hyde Park, Middlesex, to Richmond, Surrey. Along its route was a market garden owned by Georgiana Paine and leased and occupied by Richard Attwood. Richmond was a royal manor that had been acquired in the early fourteenth century by Edward I, who made the first park. Subsequent monarchs added further parkland and built a palace. As a result of several centuries of royal residence and patronage the village itself contained good-quality housing, several high-quality inns, a wide range of places of worship and a theatre. It also had good schools and several well-endowed alms houses. So, with the addition of good transport links, including a bridge over the Thames and well-maintained highways, Richmond in 1836 was a prime location with 7,000 inhabitants.

Georgiana Paine was born in 1801 to Mary Upton and baptised in January 1801 at Isleworth, Middlesex. On 20 December 1806 George Paine, a butcher from Richmond, Surrey, wrote his last will and testament. He owned real estate in Richmond, which he left for the use of his 'dear wife' Maria Paine for her life. He then requested Maria to 'appropriate such part thereof as she shall think necessary or proper toward maintaining and educating and bringing up Georgina Upton the daughter of Mary Upton widow and my reputed daughter' until she was twenty-one. After Maria's death the land was to pass to Georgiana. George appointed his brother Edward to be Georgiana's guardian. In the will George also specified that the house and premises that he used for his butcher's trade were to go to his nephew, William Paine, if Georgiana did not live to be twenty-one.[40]

On 1 December 1821 Georgiana was married by banns to a merchant, Edward Paine (1784–1822), at the church of St Antholin, Budge Row, in the City of London. Edward was seventeen years her senior. In June 1819 he had sailed to Van Diemen's Land as a free settler to seek his fortune via a scheme instigated by the Colonial Office. Edward had landed at Hobart in October 1819 and had claimed his promised grant of land. He then set about collecting information about the various opportunities for trading before returning to England at the end of 1820 to further his business connections and find a wife, as there were few women in the colony. Georgiana was Edward's first cousin, since his uncle was the George Paine who was her reputed father. Georgiana was also Edward's second cousin, because Mary Upton, her mother, was a member of the Paine family prior to her marriage. Edward and Georgiana

39 Hyde Park to Richmond, 1836, SHC, QS6/8/194; Will of George Paine, TNA PROB 11/1179; information about Georgiana Paine and Edward Paine available at https://www.wikitree.com/wiki/Paine-1205, accessed 24 April 2018; Van Diemen's Land was not called Tasmania until 1 January 1856; Lewis, *Topographical*, Vol. 3, pp. 587–8.

40 In the 1827 Surrey Land Tax Georgiana was listed as the owner of a house in George St Richmond rented by W. H. Paine, and in the 1841 census W.H. Paine was listed as a butcher living in George Street.

left London on the *Deveron* on 13 February 1822 to settle in Van Diemen's Land with other members of their extended family, namely Edward's cousin Rosalie, her husband John Deane and their children. The group arrived in Hobart on 19 June 1822. However, on 8 July 1822 Edward Paine drowned in an accident on the river Derwent when the boat in which he was travelling capsized. Edward's death was reported in the *Hobart Town Gazette* on 13 July and in the same edition Georgiana stated her intention to apply for letters of administration of Edward's estate and retained John Deane as her lawyer. Georgiana gave birth to Edward's posthumous son in October 1822, and named the child Edward. She appears to have married another distant relative, Matthew Paine, in Brighton, Van Diemen's Land, in 1844.

Discussion

Based on the information about their father's occupation, when known, none of these women were from the wealthy upper class. Elizabeth and Mary Hale and Henrietta Baddiley could be regarded as middle class, being daughters of a yeoman and army officer respectively. Bessy Hick and Margaret Oliver were daughters of a corn miller, Martha Greenwell was a blacksmith's daughter and Georgiana Paine was a butcher's daughter; they were all children of skilled artisans. Jane Gibson, the daughter of a railway labourer, may be deemed working class. The information from probate records also suggests that none of these women were wealthy. Henrietta Baddiley left £47 5s 4d on her death in 1902; Bessy Hick left £391 15s on her death in 1914 and Margaret Oliver left £876 1s 1d when she died in 1928; and several of the others do not appear in the probate records. The women were landowners of small parcels of property. Nevertheless, their ownership of such property was probably economically important as part of their income.

For each of these women the ownership of real estate, whilst important to their perception of their own status, was probably insufficient to improve their social standing in the wider community because of the small amount of property held. Status for women in the nineteenth century was usually determined by that of their father and then their husband. Using information obtained during profiling, an assessment has been made as to whether or not these women increased their status during their lifetimes, irrespective of their landholding. Martha Greenwell, whose father was an artisan, was probably regarded as losing status when she married an agricultural labourer. However, she married someone with entrepreneurial skills who was farming his own land when he died, so, overall, her status increased. Jane Gibson's father and first husband were labourers, but her husband went into inn keeping and left almost £400 and property on his death, so Jane's social status had increased by the end of her first marriage, although it is unclear if she maintained that status through her second marriage. Georgiana Paine also improved her status as a result of her inheritance from her 'reputed father' and her first marriage to an older merchant, although her subsequent life is unknown.

Henrietta Baddiley, an army officer's daughter, probably lost status when she married a man who was both a butcher and a farmer, although he seems to have left property, as did her second husband, a farmer. Elizabeth and Mary Hale seem to have maintained their status as daughters of a yeoman and Elizabeth left significant bequests on her death. Bessy Hick and Margaret Oliver also appear to have maintained a similar social status. The occupations of fathers of Ann Hogg and Elizabeth Galpin are unknown, but they both married farmers, so it is possible that each retained their initial status or possibly moved upwards.

The number of siblings in a family seems to have had little impact on the marriageability of these women, as Martha Greenwell, who had five brothers and a sister, was able to marry an entrepreneurial labourer. The size of the parental family almost certainly dictated the amount a daughter inherited from her father's estate, although not how such an inheritance was shared: for example, the four sisters of the Hale family received equal cash bequests on the death of their father.

Where a husband predeceased a wife, as was the case for both Bessy Hick and Margaret Oliver, his estate had to be shared between the widow and the children and therefore, contrary to popular opinion, some women may had more influence when their husband was alive than after his death, when the estate was shared with the children.[41]

Conclusions

This chapter has helped throw light on a group of women whom a predominantly patriarchal nineteenth-century society dismissed and discounted because it wanted to believe that land, usually still regarded as the main source of wealth, was owned by a fairly small group of rich and powerful men who, because of their experience in running estates, felt empowered to run the country through parliament. It is true that as the century progressed there was a greater awareness that some men made a lot of money from industry and commerce, but such men often reinforced the patriarchal norms and acquired land in recognition of its aid in social mobility. It is also true that there had always been an awareness that land occasionally passed to an heiress. What nineteenth-century society had difficulty in recognising was that some very ordinary women owned small plots of real property and that they were confident in their ownership and wished for it to be acknowledged. The case studies illustrated in this chapter help to ensure that such women are no longer 'invisible'.

41 This is the subject of ongoing research by Jennifer Aston and is discussed further in her chapter in this volume.

10

More than Just a Caretaker: Women's Role in the Intergenerational Transfer of Real and Personal Property in Nineteenth-century Urban England, 1840–1900

JENNIFER ASTON

This chapter will explore women's role in the acquisition, enjoyment and intergenerational disposal of real and personal property in nineteenth-century urban England. It expands upon the examination of female business owners as autonomous managers of business enterprises seen in my recent monograph *Female Entrepreneurship in Nineteenth Century England: Engagement in the Urban Economy*.[1] Analysis of the existing historiography and a series of case studies of the probate records of men and women from Victorian England explores the way that female ownership of property (both real and personal) could mark a distinct period in both the female lifecycle and the lifecycle of the property itself. This analysis will establish the ways in which women came into possession of real and personal property; the ways in which they used it; who they chose to bequeath their land or personal property to; and the way in which they did this – for example, absolutely or in trust. This will enable a firmer understanding of how women's agency and posthumous financial strategies shaped the towns and cities of nineteenth-century England.

The historiography of female economic agency in nineteenth-century England began almost as soon as the century had passed, with Alice Clark and Ivy Pinchbeck publishing their seminal works on women and industrialisation.[2] Although these founders of women's economic history disagreed

1 Jennifer Aston, *Female Entrepreneurship in Nineteenth-Century England: Engagement in the Urban Economy* (London, 2016).

2 Alice Clark, *The Working Life of Women in the Seventeenth Century* (London, 1919); Ivy Pinchbeck, *Women Workers and the Industrial Revolution 1750–1850* (London, 1930).

on the exact chronology of events, both argued that the industrialisation that was widely perceived to have dramatically and irrevocably changed the economic landscape of Britain in the nineteenth century had, inadvertently, also permanently altered the social and economic opportunities available to women. They also argued that, prior to industrialisation, women were able to acquire the skills and knowledge of trade and business because it was happening in (or very close to) their home. Therefore they were able to combine other domestic tasks, such as childrearing, cooking and cleaning, with economic activity. The separation of home and work as a result of industrialisation severed this relationship and subsequently the easy opportunity for women to access the world of trade.

This idea was further developed in Leonore Davidoff and Catherine Hall's hugely influential *Family Fortunes: Men and Women of the English Middle Class 1780–1850*, first published in 1987, which tied the separation of home and work to social standing. They used a series of microstudies from Birmingham, Exeter and East Anglia to argue that, by 1850, a woman who remained active in the public world of work could not simultaneously perform the middle-class rituals and duties that were required of her in the private domestic world. This is not to say that her assets were not utilised; she was expected to provide free or below-market-rate finance to her male family members and it was also assumed that unmarried female family members would provide domestic labour, acting as unpaid housekeepers in exchange for a respectable place to live.[3] Davidoff and Hall's 'Separate Spheres' theory, together with the idea that the mid-nineteenth century marked a turning point in social and economic opportunities for women, became so engrained that many historians stopped looking for any other interpretations. Moreover, women who were discovered participating in 'masculine' activities such as property ownership, land holding, politics or business tended to be seen as performing public extensions of their domestic duties, either as caretaker–owners for minor children or through philanthropic roles within prison reform and school regulation.[4]

The end date of 1850 employed by Davidoff and Hall is indicative of a wider chronological divide within the historiography. Prior to this date the focus is very much on the decline of a 'golden age' of opportunity for women and their experiences under an industrialised and patriarchal society. In contrast, the post-1850 literature tends to focus on women's struggle to escape the domestic sphere, the fight for political emancipation and access to the

3 Leonore Davidoff and Catherine Hall, *Family Fortunes: Men and Women of the English Middle Class, 1780–1850* (London, 1987, 2002).

4 Aston, *Female Entrepreneurs*, pp. 34–5.

professions.[5] This artificial chronological divide has led to a historiographical view of the long nineteenth century described by Beatrice Craig as a 'U' with perceived 'golden ages' at either end and a low slump of limited opportunity and agency in the middle.[6] There has been a substantial amount of work published in recent years, not least by many of the authors included in this volume, which has reshaped the nineteenth-century 'U'. Rather than being seen as occupying peripatetic existences in relation to the men in their lives, women are now located in a long narrative of independent female agency.[7]

This chapter will add to this body of work by examining the role that women played in transferring the 'real' property of bricks and mortar, of businesses, of cold hard cash, and of household items. This will illustrate the way that women used the probate process to shape the urban landscape, exert their authority and transfer the material goods that turned a house into a home. Beginning with an examination of women's legal status in the nineteenth century, it will argue that women were frequently the architects of the family economic strategy who, through the ownership and transfer of belongings, created and strengthened familial and friendship networks, thus cementing both the economic and social futures of their loved ones. It moves the historiography forward not simply by adding to our understanding of women's lives but by repositioning the female experience in the mainstream narrative of nineteenth-century England.

Sources and Methodology

In order to explore the way that women received, enjoyed and disposed of property before the Married Women's Property Acts, I have selected a sample of previously unexamined male and female wills proved in mid

5 Jane Rendall, *Women in an Industrializing Society: England 1750–1880* (Oxford, 1990); June Purvis (ed.), *Women's History: Britain 1850–1945, An Introduction* (London, 2002).

6 Béatrice Craig, *Female Enterprise Behind the Discursive Veil in Nineteenth-Century Northern France* (London, 2017).

7 Hannah Barker, *The Business of Women: Female Enterprise and Urban Development in Northern England 1760–1830* (Oxford, 2006); Maxine Berg, 'Women's Property and the Industrial Revolution', *Journal of Interdisciplinary History* XXIV:2 (1993), 233–50; Margot C. Finn, *The Character of Credit: Personal Debt in English Culture 1700–1914* (Cambridge, 2003); A. C. Kay, *The Foundations of Female Entrepreneurship: Enterprise, Home and Household in London c.1800–1870* (London, 2009); Stana Nenadic, 'Gender and the Rhetoric of Business Success: The Impact on Women Entrepreneurs and the "New Woman" in Later Nineteenth-Century Edinburgh', *Women's Work in Industrial England: Regional and Local Perspectives*, ed. Nigel Goose (Hatfield, 2007), pp. 269–88; Nicola Phillips, *Women in Business 1700–1850* (Woodbridge, 2005); Amanda Vickery, 'Golden Age to Separate Spheres? A Review of the Categories and Chronology of English Women in History', *The Historical Journal* 36:2 (June 1993), 383–414.

nineteenth-century Birmingham. The sample consists of thirty-seven wills, thirty male and seven female dating from 1858. They were the first batch of wills to be granted probate by the newly formed Court of Probate at Birmingham, which was one of thirty registries established by the Court of Probate Act 1857. Therefore, the only connecting factors between the documents examined are the year that the executors applied for probate and the fact that they applied to the Birmingham court, although all of the testators lived in the Midlands. Selecting the last wills and testaments from the mid-nineteenth century was a deliberate decision designed to compare and contrast male and female testamentary behaviours in a time well before the Married Women's Property Acts gave married women the legal right to inherit and to dispose of their property freely. The documents in the sample were analysed to reveal the marital status of the testator and the items they bequeathed. Further biographical information was gathered from the wills and used alongside other records, including census returns, newspapers, Birth, Marriage and Death Indexes and trade directories, to reconstruct the familial and friendship networks that surrounded the testators and offer some insight as to their decision-making process. This analysis enables the direct comparison of men's and women's wills, offering the opportunity to examine the way that women inherited and how they disposed of property, and, in doing so, challenge some of the gendered arguments surrounding men, women and probate.

David Green estimates that approximately 32 per cent of all regional testators were female, which means that this sample is slightly under-representative in terms of the male:female ratio. Furthermore, in a time when only 8 per cent of the population made a last will and testament, the men and women examined in this chapter belong to an elite group regardless of how modest their estates might appear. The vast majority of testators, both male and female, sought to benefit their loved ones. If someone died intestate then their estate would either go to a spouse or, if they were unmarried or their spouse had predeceased them, then it would be divided between the deceased's biological descendants. Therefore, it should not be assumed that the desires and instructions of the men and women in the following pages were any different to those who did not put pen to paper; the underlying assumption was that assets would be transferred (one way or another) to the younger generations. As such, there is value in using these records to shine light on the way that women directed the intergenerational transfer of real and personal property in the nineteenth century. However, before examining the wills themselves, it is first necessary to understand the legal context within which they were written.

The Legal Status of Women

Research into nineteenth-century women in their capacity as business owners has shown how closely the middle-class lifecycle was interwoven with the opportunity to advance one's social and economic prosperity.[8] Yet, although female business owners may have acted in the same way as their male counterparts when they were able to, for much of the nineteenth century married women were forced to act within a specific set of legal circumstances that ostensibly restricted their ability to exercise full control over their property before and after death. Unlike men, whose legal identity remained the same regardless of their relationships, the law regarded women in terms of their marital status; they were spinsters, wives and widows, sometimes multiple times over, and each of these identities carried with it a different set of legal parameters for women to navigate. Therefore, considering the ways in which marital status affected women's ability to acquire, control and dispose of property is imperative to understanding the implications of their actions.

Both before and after the Married Women's Property Acts of 1870, 1882 and 1893, any unmarried woman over the age of twenty-one was legally considered – in terms of property ownership at least – as equal to men. They were technically free to buy, own, enjoy and bequeath real and personal property as it suited them, and, as David Green has argued, many unmarried women used this economic power to benefit other unmarried women, particularly younger female relatives such as nieces.[9] Yet the legal and financial freedom that unmarried women might appear to have possessed was somewhat tempered by the societal expectation that they would continue to occupy a domestic role within the wider family, providing unpaid domestic support as well as below-market-rate financial support to family firms in return for a place in the household and the security that could provide.[10]

In stark contrast to their unmarried sisters, prior to 1870 married women were restricted by the common law practice of 'coverture', a legal device that saw a woman's legal identity literally subsumed into that of her husband upon their marriage. Under coverture, a wife was legally unable to buy, raise credit, and receive the income from real estate or her own enterprise, or dispose of her belongings according to her own wishes without the express permission of her husband. Significantly, even in cases where a husband did consent to his wife making a last will and testament, his permission could be

8 R. J. Morris, *Men, Women and Property in England, 1780–1870: A Social and Economic History of Family Strategies amongst the Leeds Middle Classes* (Cambridge, 2005); Aston, *Female Entrepreneurship*.

9 D. R. Green, 'Independent Women Wealth and Wills in Nineteenth-Century London', *Urban Fortunes: Property and Inheritance in the Town 1700–1900*, eds Jon Stobart and Alistair Owens (Aldershot, 2000), p. 219.

10 Davidoff and Hall, *Family Fortunes*, pp. 272–316.

withdrawn at any time until probate was granted, thus making the execution of her wishes entirely dependent on his good nature. Once married, it was very unlikely that anything other than death would legally part the couple. Before the Divorce and Matrimonial Causes Act was passed in 1857, divorce was prohibitively expensive to all but the wealthiest in society, requiring an act of parliament to legally dissolve the union. Even after 1857, divorce was still very difficult for a woman to achieve as, whilst a husband had only to prove that his wife had committed adultery, a wife had to prove that her husband had:

> … been guilty of incestuous adultery, or of bigamy with adultery, or of rape, or of sodomy or bestiality, or of adultery coupled with such cruelty as without adultery would have entitled her to a divorce á mensâ et thoro [judicial separation], or of adultery coupled with desertion, without reasonable excuse, for two years or upwards.[11]

Proving these misdemeanours was no easy task and, despite legislative reforms, still a financial impossibility for the vast majority of the female population. Desertion alone was also not considered an acceptable reason for a divorce to be granted; under coverture this meant that a husband could be absent for many years and upon his eventual return would be legally entitled to assume control of any assets his wife had accumulated in the meantime. The Divorce and Matrimonial Causes Act 1857 offered some protection from this situation under an 'Order for the Protection of Property'. Under this legislation a wife could apply to the courts to protect any belongings or assets that she had acquired during the period of her husband's absence. In January 1858 the *Leeds Mercury* reported on the first application heard in Leeds and commented that the court expected to hear many more applications in the coming months.[12]

Of course, the restrictions of coverture as described above are very much the worst-case scenario and not all marriages were unhappy; indeed, some husbands and wives deliberately used coverture to manipulate the legal system.[13] Yet the legal bias against married women was clear, and it was a problem that both men and women were acutely aware of. Over the previous centuries a system of marriage settlements and trusts had developed that operated in parallel to coverture, which allowed families to give their female children the use and income from land or property but without the right to

11 Text of Divorce and Matrimonial Causes Act 1857, paragraph 27, reproduced in Horace Nelson, *Selected Cases, Statutes and Orders* (London, 1889).

12 *The Leeds Mercury*, Thursday, 21 January 1858, in Aston, *Female Entrepreneurship*, p. 132.

13 Jennifer Aston and Paolo di Martino, 'Risk, Success, and Failure: Female Entrepreneurship in Late Victorian and Edwardian England', *Economic History Review* 70:3 (August 2017), 837–58; Phillips, *Women in Business*, p. 68.

sell or otherwise dispose of it.[14] The intention was to ensure the financial security of female offspring and preserve the capital sum without the risk that a feckless or irresponsible husband would appropriate it or that the property would be subsumed into his family if the woman died.

Of course, there were points in the lifecycle other than marriage where a woman might expect to receive property, namely upon the death of her parents. In this situation property and hard cash would frequently be bequeathed in the 'belt and braces' form of a trust that was created by the testator/testatrix expressly for the beneficiary's 'own sole and separate use' during their lifetime. The will would then also contain further instructions as to what should happen after the death of the initial beneficiary. Such a legal creation meant that either the beneficiary would be able to use the land or property itself to generate an income, or alternatively, they could receive a regular (usually quarterly) payment of the interest generated by the investment of a capital sum. This was highly effective in that it generated revenue whilst simultaneously keeping the property, whatever its form, intact. This epitomizes the middle-class Victorian desire to ape the aristocracy, to found dynasties, preserve estates and continue social and economic progress.[15]

The role of women as recipients of trusts is well covered in the feminist literature, with many – most notably Leonore Davidoff and Catherine Hall – arguing that trusts were in effect a legal stranglehold on the ability of women to gain any meaningful financial independence, as they removed the opportunity for women to access and invest capital in the same way as their male relatives.[16] R. J. Morris has explored the importance of trusts to the formation and maintenance of the middle-class businessmen of Leeds and these same values of preservation and longevity underpinned the actions of their economically active female counterparts.[17] The role of women as creators of trusts has received much less attention. However, evidence from female business owners in Birmingham and Leeds reveals that they protected their estates, both small and substantial, by creating trusts for male and female beneficiaries alike, and in this respect it was economics rather than gender that dictated their actions.[18] Arguably, in the pre-1882 period at least,

14 Amy Erickson, *Women and Property in Early Modern England* (London, 1993); Briony McDonagh, *Elite Women and the Agricultural Landscape, 1700–1830* (Abingdon 2017), Chapter 2.

15 Morris, *Men, Women and Property*, p. 130.

16 Catherine Hall, *White, Male and Middle Class: Explorations in Feminism and History* (Oxford, 1992), p. 177.

17 Aston, *Female Entrepreneurship*, p. 196.

18 Ibid., pp. 195–201.

it can be argued that a trust was a way to protect vulnerable men *and* women as much as to restrict them.[19]

The watershed moment for married women and property transfer was the passing of the Married Women's Property Act of 1870, which, although riddled with loopholes, marked the first time in English legal history that all married women retained a separate legal identity from their husband upon marriage.[20] This legislation gave married women the right to retain ownership of property that they owned before their marriage, to acquire and manage property during their marriage, and to dispose of it according to their own wishes and without the danger of their husband revoking consent. The extent to which these acts were the great equaliser of economic opportunity is highly debatable. Although some studies suggest that the Married Women's Property Acts had a marked impact on female investment in railway land and in property transactions more generally, research into female business ownership shows a relatively stable level of activity across the nineteenth century, suggesting that the acts did not incentivise women to enter trade.[21]

Reform of married women's property rights was happening at the same time as reform of bankruptcy law, and the subsequent results were not entirely what the legislators had hoped for. As discussed above, under coverture married women had no independent legal identity and therefore could not sue or be sued. A married woman's lack of legal status was problematic in the world of business, both to the married women themselves and to other (male) traders. This was for two key reasons: first, it was very difficult for women to raise credit from formal credit sources; and, second, although married women were able to trade, and did so very successfully throughout the eighteenth and nineteenth centuries, any credit advanced to them by smaller local creditors was done so in the knowledge that it would be very difficult to claim it back. However, the passing of the Married Women's Property Acts gave married women a legal status that they had not previously had, and this *should* have opened them up not just to the possibility of earning but to the negative consequences of engaging in the market place. The Bankruptcy Acts of 1883 and 1890 maintained the position of married women as a special category who could not be sued by creditors or found bankrupt, except in cases where the wife had declared herself to be trading completely separately to her husband. Therefore, although married women were now able to keep

19 Maxine Berg argues that this is true of the provinces: see Berg, 'Women's Property and the Industrial Revolution', 233–50.

20 For further discussion see Anne Laurence, 'Women and the Transmission of Property: Inheritance in the British Isles in the 17th Century', *Dix-septième siècle* 244:3 (2009), 435–50.

21 Aston, *Female Entrepreneurship*; Xuesheng You, 'The Missing Half: Female Employment in Victorian England and Wales', *The Online Historical Atlas of Occupational Structure and Population Geography in England and Wales 1600–2011*, available at https://www.campop.geog.cam.ac.uk/research/occupations/outputs/onlineatlas/, accessed 18 September 2018.

any income generated through their own trade and make formal credit agreements it was still very easy for them to escape the consequences of bankruptcy. The Board of Trade regularly commented on this inequity in its annual reports, citing the frequent abuse of the system by husbands and wives who deliberately traded apart on paper and sold or transferred assets between them to afford the protection of the wife's legal status when the business failed. Despite the Board of Trade's displeasure at the special status of married women under bankruptcy law, the uneasy situation remained until the wide-ranging bankruptcy law reforms of 1913 finally viewed married women trading as the same as *femme soles*.[22]

Evidence of married and unmarried women trading under their own name can be observed in surviving trade cards, newspaper advertisements and trade directories from seventeenth-, eighteenth- and nineteenth-century England. This and, additionally, the lack of a sudden increase in women (married or otherwise) entering the marketplace in the years following 1870 suggests that women traded *in spite* of the pre-1870 legal system, not *because* of the changes brought in under the Married Women's Property Acts.[23] This in turn indicates that the changes in the legal status of married women bestowed under the Married Women's Property Acts were not enough to entice those who were not already predisposed to trade to follow that path.

The final stage in the female lifecycle, and arguably the most important in terms of autonomy and financial freedom for married women, was that of widowhood. Widowhood could be a complicated concept for nineteenth-century society, just as it is for historians observing it through a twenty-first-century lens. Widows were simultaneously technically free from the legal control of their father and late husband(s), able to exercise the powers of their unmarried counterparts, and yet potentially limited in their autonomy by the conditions of their inheritance. As Beatrice Moring and Richard Wall have argued, widows are nearly always seen as old, passive and poor, existing on the fringes of their children's family – and, in the case of childless widows, more isolated still.[24] Widows might well have inherited their late husband's estate for their sole and separate use without any caveats, but far more likely would be the scenario where the widow was given full use and enjoyment of her inheritance during her lifetime, but with the condition that upon her death the estate would be divided according to the husband's last will and testament. This was primarily a tool to ensure that any children of that particular union would be provided for, rather than the estate being

22 For a wider discussion of women and bankruptcy law see Aston and di Martino, 'Risk, Success, and Failure'.

23 Erickson, *Women and Property*; Barker, *The Business of Women*; Phillips, *Women in Business*; Kay, *The Foundations of Female Entrepreneurship*; Aston, *Female Entrepreneurship*.

24 Beatrice Moring and Richard Wall, *Widows in European Economy and Society 1600–1920* (London, 2017), Introduction.

subsumed by the offspring of a second or even third marriage. The higher male mortality figure meant that a wife was likely to outlive her husband and, with only rudimentary contraception available, further children were an almost inevitable result of a young remarriage.

There is some evidence of testators creating trusts even when they possessed only very small estates. However, the cost of creating and administering such a device (not to mention the value of the return) meant that trusts tend to appear in the probate records of larger estates.[25] Contemporary legal advice argued against primogeniture and in favour of providing for all children so as not to leave younger children destitute. However, it was also recognised that being able to keep a portion of capital intact would allow for the maximum return. Trusts were a form of compromise, allowing for the advancement of the younger generation while protecting the vulnerable members of the family, be they a widow or otherwise. This was a form of posthumous control, and with the right circumstances could result in the deceased holding financial influence for many decades after their death. Yet these were also practical documents and they had to be workable in the real world otherwise all that would be achieved would be the starvation and ruin of the testator's family.

An important part of many women's experience of widowhood would have been the formal assumption of financial responsibility for themselves and their household. For some, this would have meant continuing to work just as they had done before their widowhood; others would have perhaps had to downsize in order to be able to live comfortably on the investment income from trusts. For a significant minority, however, widowhood represented a new stage in their working lives, the move from being partner in a family business to being the named owner, and possibly also the day-to-day manager. As recent research from the Midlands and Northern England has shown, women frequently took over their late husband's firm and operated it using their own name even when there were adult sons who, on the face of it, should have assumed control and allowed their mother to maintain or attain the social status associated with withdrawal from trade.[26] The exact numbers of widows who did assume control of a family firm is unknown, but analysis of trade directory entries suggests that this was a commonplace event, with most firms coming into female possession through inheritance (usually from a husband but occasionally from another family member or friend).[27]

25 Davidoff and Hall, *Family Fortunes*, p. 209.

26 Barker, *The Business of Women*; Phillips, *Women in Business*.

27 Aston, *Female Entrepreneurship*, p. 111.

Evidence from the Wills

Crucially, we only know about the business activities of those widows who changed the working name of the firm to their own; many more may have chosen to continue using their late husband's name for the sake of continuity, just as some sons chose to after they inherited from their mother. Furthermore, analysis also reveals that women tended to operate the businesses for longer than the man from whom they had inherited the firm.[28] This indicates that wives must have had either direct experience of the work required to operate the business themselves, thus debunking the fundamental underlying tenet of the 'Separate Spheres' theory, or had the business nous to appoint appropriate managers who could handle the day to day running of the business and generate enough profit to cover the expense of their hiring.

The way that widows were able to engage with the family firm would have been reliant on the wording of their late husband's last will and testament. As mentioned above, these documents had to allow the deceased's family to maintain their financial security and so had to be flexible whilst also protecting the testator's estate. Some husbands specified that their widow should continue the family firm on their own account: for example, Beer Seller James Buckley gave his business to his wife Mary Ann for 'her own use, benefit and enjoyment absolutely'.[29] Others appointed their wife in the role of mentor. James Dawes, a 'Licensed Victualler and Pump Maker', stated that his wife should continue to operate the pump-making business, employing his nephew Alfred until he reached the age of twenty-three. If, when he reached that age, Alfred had 'conducted himself in the said Business to the satisfaction of [executors] then I bequeath the said stock in trade and business of Pump Maker to the said Alfred Dawes absolutely'. If Alfred did not conduct himself well then Ann would continue in her role as owner and operator of the firm until such a time that he did, or one of them died.[30]

In both of these scenarios the widows were free to make business decisions as to the running of the firms, or, as Thomas Tempest Robinson, a confectioner from Coventry, phrased it, to trade 'without being answerable or accountable for any losses'.[31] For some widows, such as Ann Buckley, this included expanding the cloth cap manufacturing that she inherited from her husband, building a substantial purpose-built factory and opening a new branch of the firm in London, while for others, such as Maria Hipkiss, this meant changing the focus of the business from that of a general provision merchant to a coal

28 Ibid.

31 Last will and testament of Thomas Tempest Robinson, proved at Birmingham on 8 April 1858.

distributor.[32] The terms of a husband's last will and testament could prevent a widow from disposing of the firm she had taken over and built up in the way that she might have wanted. However, it is probable that her and her late husband's periods of ownership were in fact just individual pieces of a much longer-term financial strategy, one that was not dictated by gender but which operated to ensure that each subsequent generation would have financial security. Button maker Edward Darleston left his 'all and every trade, stock in trade, working tools, household furniture, chairs, goods, chattels and effects whatsoever and whensoever' to his wife Mary. He included the express wish that they were for her own use and benefit for her life, 'not doubting that she will use her best exertions to provide for the good and welfare of my children until they shall become of full age'. Edward directed that after Mary's death everything should be sold and the money split between their seven children.[33] It is easy to forget that family units frequently worked together to achieve the same ends; a trust dictating terms of the continuation of business can be viewed as a way to protect the family's primary source of income whilst allowing an able actor (namely the widow) to act otherwise freely in a potentially vulnerable period of transition.

The role that women played as owners of and investors in real estate has come under greater scrutiny in recent years, specifically in terms of women as owners and managers of great estates, as investors in railway land and as investors in urban real estate.[34] It is becoming increasingly obvious that, far from being 'hidden', women had a clear and prominent public presence, whether it was riding-out to survey land use, manufacturing and selling their wares or renting rooms to tenants. In undertaking these activities, in expanding businesses and then passing them on, the women were playing a vital role not just in the intergenerational transfer of property but also in the shaping of the physical landscape of Victorian towns and cities. There was a female presence on virtually every commercial street in nineteenth-century England, including in the most fashionable arcades; women acted as business proprietors and as property owners, altering the cityscape as they did so.[35]

Table 14 shows that the vast majority of the male wills sampled were

32 Aston, *Female Entrepreneurship*, p. 109.

33 Last will and testament of William Edward Darleston, proved at Birmingham on 24 August 1858.

34 Jennifer Aston, Amanda Capern and Briony McDonagh, 'More Than Bricks and Mortar: Female Property Ownership as Economic Strategy Mid-Nineteenth Century Urban England' (*Urban History* 46 (2019), DOI:10.1017/S0963926819000142;); McDonagh, *Elite Women*; J. P. Casson, 'Women and Property: a study of women as owners, lessors and lessees of plots of land in England during the nineteenth century as revealed by the land surveys carried out by the railway, canal and turnpike companies' (DPhil diss., University of Oxford, 2013); Joan Heggie, this volume.

35 Hannah Barker, *Family and Business During the Industrial Revolution* (Oxford, 2017).

Table 14. Marital status of testators by sex

Sex	Married	Widowed	Legally divorced/separated	Not Stated
Male	27	0	1	2
Female	3	4	0	0

those of married men, and it is likely that the two where marital status was not stated were unmarried. Marital status is given for all of the female testators, which is unsurprising given that – in 1858 – marital status very much determined the way that women could use the probate process. The last will and testament of one of the male testators, Frederick Hollis Appletree, states that he is legally separated from his wife through a Deed of Separation and had made specific provision for her spousal support. The exact date when this arrangement was formalised is not given in the will, but Frederick's other bequests give much more detail about his complicated domestic arrangements and the way he intended they be dealt with after his death.

Frederick Hollis Appletree was an upholsterer and cabinet maker who lived in Bordesley Green, on the outskirts of Birmingham. He married Louisa Warren (b. 1791) in 1827 and together they had several children, of whom three, Louisa (b. 1828), Amelia (b. 1830) and Henry (b. 1831), survived to adulthood. The first two bequests in Frederick's last will and testament are to Amelia and Henry, with each receiving substantial parcels of land and property in Bangor (Amelia) and Birmingham (Henry).[36] Both of these bequests were made using the same language, with no special provision made to protect Amelia's inheritance from any future husband. Perhaps Frederick assumed that she was unlikely to marry, although given that she was only twenty-two at the time he made the will this seems a risky strategy. He did, however, provide cash bequests for his three sisters under the proviso that the sums were given for their 'own use and benefit' and could not be used to service any debts belonging to their husbands.

As mentioned above, the date that Frederick and his wife Louisa were granted a Deed of Separation is unknown, but the next bequest in Frederick's last will and testament reveals that his housekeeper Hannah Massey (sometimes known as Hannah Jackson) was to have full use of his dwelling house for her lifetime. Furthermore, with the exception of his wine, books, bookcases and large paintings (which were bequeathed to son Henry and

36 Last will and testament of Frederick Hollis Appletree, proved at Birmingham on 3 August 1858. His eldest daughter Louisa disappears from the archival records after the 1851 census and is not mentioned in Frederick's Last will and testament, so it is likely that she died between March 1851 and August 1852, when Frederick's will was written.

a brother in law), Hannah would receive all of his other household goods absolutely, that is to say without any conditions and restrictions as to their use and disposal. The reason for this generous bequest becomes apparent as one reads that, after Hannah's death, the right to reside in the said dwelling house would pass on to Hannah's minor son, Frederick Appletree Massey. In addition to this, Frederick Hollis Appletree also created two trusts. The first gave instruction for a capital sum of £350 to be invested and the resulting payments used for the clothing and maintenance of Frederick Appletree Massey until he reached the age of twenty-one. If Frederick should reach this age, the capital would be withdrawn from the trust and a sum of £1,000 would be added, creating a new capital sum of £1,350. This money was to be used for his 'advancement' in life, thus ensuring he was able to enter business or a profession and allowing Frederick Hollis Appletree to posthumously provide for his illegitimate son. By referring to the Deed of Separation in his last will and testament, Frederick Hollis Appletree was making sure that the legal basis of his last will and testament was established unequivocally, and all his loved ones – legitimate or otherwise – were looked after.

Establishing a concrete legal position was especially important for married women who were attempting to write wills before the Married Women's Property Acts so as to ensure that their wishes were carried out and free from outside influences. The methods for bestowing property and money on married women whilst keeping it out of their husband's grasp and the ways that women could accumulate wealth have both been the focus of a great deal of study, but the ways in which women then passed that property on in the nineteenth century have been examined less frequently.[37] Mary Barton lived in Birmingham, where she drew her income through receiving rents from properties that she let. She wrote her last will and testament on 27 April 1858 and the first line reads:

> This is the Last will and testament or Writing Testamentary of me Mary Barton of Camden Street, Birmingham now or formally wife of John Barton, one time of Great Hampton Street Birmingham aforesaid Silver Plater as to whose decease I am uncertain … .[38]

In writing this, Mary reveals that, although she did not have a formal Deed

37 There are a few notable exceptions to this: Morris, *Men, Women and Property*, Chapter 6; Aston, *Female Entrepreneurship*, Chapter 5; Penelope Lane, 'Women, Property and Inheritance: Wealth Creation and Income Generation in Small English Towns, 1750–1835', *Urban Fortunes: Property and Inheritance in the Town, 1700–1900*, eds Jon Stobart and Alistair Owens (Aldershot, 2000); D. R. Green, 'Independent Women, Wealth and Wills in Nineteenth-Century London', *Urban Fortunes: Property and Inheritance in the Town, 1700–1900*, eds Jon Stobart and Alistair Owens (Aldershot, 2000).

38 Last will and testament of Mary Barton, proved at Birmingham on 2 June 1858.

of Separation like Frederick Hollis Appletree and his estranged wife Louisa, she was living apart from her husband and the two had clearly been out of communication for some time. Simply establishing estrangement, however, was not enough to enable Mary to dispose of her belongings without the fear that John might turn up one day and exercise his right as a husband to her assets. Therefore, her will goes onto state that

> under or by virtue of the Indenture dated the twenty seventh of December one thousand eight hundred and forty-five between my father and mother Joseph Hobs and Susanna his wife of the first part, myself of the second part and James Allen and Samuel Guest of the third part. And of an Indenture dated the twenty fourth day of March one thousand eight hundred and forty-six made between myself and the said James Allen and Samuel Guest of the other part. Powers are given or reserved to me to appoint such sums as are mentioned in the same Indentures … .

From this statement, we learn that Mary was one party in not one but two indentures, each of which gave her rights to dispose of the assets, namely eleven leasehold messuages detailed within them. Although the relationship that James Allen and Samuel Guest shared with Mary is not specified, it is interesting to note that Mary's mother Susannah is named as another party in the agreement, thus suggesting that the said property may have descended through the maternal line – circumstances that might have been more commonplace than previously assumed.[39] Mary therefore used her will to establish her legal right to hold her property in her own name and to make a last will and testament to dispose of it, despite the fact she may (or may not) have been married at the time of writing. She and her solicitor went further, however, and demonstrated their legal shrewdness by listing the rest of her belongings, including building society shares and furniture, and explaining that Mary had purchased them all with the proceeds of, and subject to, the conditions of her trust. This meant that her husband would have no legal claim over these items – or her ability to dispose of them – if he were to suddenly reappear.

It was particularly important for Mary to establish her legal position given the potential for conflict between her wishes and those of her estranged husband; however, two other married women in the sample also used their last will and testament to demonstrate their legal testamentary ability. The first of these, Hannah Haydon (formerly Hannah Bashford *née* Swann), was the widow of John Bashford, a retail brewer from Birmingham, who married William Haydon (who was also a retail brewer), from Balsall Heath. She used her last will and testament to prove her right to dispose of leasehold

39 Heggie, 'Women's Involvement in Property', pp. 201–225 in this volume.

Table 15. Content of last will and testament by sex

	Trust		Property		Cash		Land		Business		Household goods		Clothes	
Male	11	37%	19	63%	14	47%	8	27%	18	60%	25	83%	3	10%
Female	5	71%	4	57%	3	43%	2	29%	0	0%	5	71%	0	0%

land, nine messuage tenements and dwelling houses and their accompanying outbuildings and workshops.[40] The land and buildings came to her through a marriage settlement dated December 1857, the same month that Hannah wrote her will and just one month before her death. It seems likely that the land was settled on her at her second marriage by her own family, as her brother Thomas Swann was one of the trustees of that trust as well as being the trustee of the trust created in Hannah's will and her executor. Along with a man named Thomas Coates, who is described as a friend, Thomas Swann was responsible for selling all of Hannah's property and converting it to cash, which was invested to create a trust. Hannah does not appear to have had any children from either of her marriages – or at least none that survived to adulthood – and she instructed that the trust be split into four shares, with Sarah Caswell claiming one share, her grandniece Emma Greenwood (who lived with her) one share, and her brother Thomas Swann the remaining two shares. All beneficiaries were relations from her own family rather than either of her late husbands.

Table 15 shows that, despite the concerns held by some historians that trusts were a patriarchal way to constrain female economic agency, they were actually a tool that was utilised by women just as often (in fact, in this sample, more frequently) than men. The wills examined here are just a tiny snapshot of probate behaviour in nineteenth-century England; however, examination of the four trusts created by the women reveals that they were confidently engaging in probate behaviour held as typical of middle-class men, including restricting access to the capital sums.

One such widow was Mary Wood, who lived on Cannon Street, Birmingham. In her last will and testament, written in January 1852, she directed that her brother Jonathon Grant would receive all her household goods and furniture for his own use. In addition to this he would receive a sum of £200, which would be advanced to him at the amount of twelve shillings per week.[41] Mary does not state why she was unwilling to bequeath Jonathon his relatively modest inheritance as a one-off payment, but she was by no means unique. Mary Barrs, a married woman, had the right to dispose

40 Last will and testament of Hannah Haydon, proved at Birmingham on 10 February 1858.

of £2,600 under her marriage settlement and £4,000 under her late father's will, although she does note that this second amount had been reduced to £3,900 because of a bad investment.[42] She chose to use the £2,600 to create a trust, the income of which should be paid to her husband until his death, at which point £1,000 of the capital sum was to be reinvested to create a trust for the benefit of her brother's widow Matilda until she died, or until she married again. Mary's last will and testament went on to direct that the remaining £1,600, together with the £3,900 from her late father's estate, should be divided in unequal cash sums between her nieces and nephews. In 1841 Mary married for the first time at the age of fifty-eight.[43] She had no children with new husband William Barrs, and indeed it is only through the 1851 census return and their marriage certificate that we know his name at all; he is not mentioned by name at any point in Mary's will, nor did he act as one of her executors. Instead, Mary used her last will and testament to keep her assets within her family, giving William access to only a limited stream of income (notably not drawn from the full value of the estate), thus keeping her estate intact for the next generation of *her* family.

This behaviour is mirrored in the wills of some men in the sample. Butcher John Bundley directed that his property should be held in trust for the benefit of his wife during her lifetime or until she remarried, after which time it should all be sold and divided between their two daughters.[44] Similarly, licensed victualler James Miller directed that all his real and personal estate should be placed into trust for his wife and then split equally between their son and daughter.[45] Other men, though, bequeathed their estates without condition. Steam engine manufacturer Matthew Robinson bequeathed everything including his trade to his wife.[46] Baker and flour dealer Thomas Whitmore and victualler William Hopkins both also bequeathed everything to their wives with no conditions; significantly, none of the women examined in this sample did the same.[47]

While it is worth noting the number of similarities between the content of male and female wills in Table 15, there is one glaring difference: not one of the seven female wills makes mention of a business enterprise. This is, however, something of a red herring. Of the seven female written wills examined only one does not refer to property, land or an independent source of wealth such as a marriage settlement. Four of the women owned rental property portfolios, the running of which arguably constitutes a business enterprise in just the same way as a trade does. This highlights the difficulties

44 Last will and testament of John Bundley, proved at Birmingham on 20 June 1858.

45 Last will and testament of James Miller, proved at Birmingham on 13 February 1858.

46 Last will and testament of Matthew Robinson, proved at Birmingham on 18 November 1858.

47 Last will and testament of Thomas Whitmore, proved at Birmingham on 20 December 1858; Last will and testament of William Hopkins, proved at Birmingham on 1 June 1858.

encountered by historians who attempt to measure female economic activity; so much of their work is concealed behind their everyday activities, or happened in a way that escaped formal recording practices, that we find only the very faintest footprints in the archive today.[48]

Women as 'Things' People

One consequence of the historiography overlooking women as property owners and underestimating their agency under probate law is the assumption that women would not have had any control over the building they were living in, or the way in which they received and spent their income. This, together with the focus on women as curators of the interior domestic space, has meant that historians have tended to focus on women as collectors of domestic items, as hoarders of the material culture that so frequently defines the nineteenth century; silverware, hair brushes, jewellery, clothes, musical instruments, books, furniture and other assorted trinkets. R. J. Morris has argued that women, particularly widows, were 'things' people: that is, they were far more likely than men to bequeath specific items in their wills and they were more likely to engage in this behaviour with their female relatives.[49] Underlying this analysis is the unspoken but implicit assumption that these female written wills were dealing with the sentimental, 'softer' side of life, the relationships that created a family network but which, ultimately, were not as important as the public world of business, employment and money.

The only female will in the sample not to make any mention of income at all is that of widow Sarah Battelle. She was born in St Croix in the Caribbean in 1785 and the 1851 census shows that she lived with one of her four daughters (also a widow) and three granddaughters in Leamington Spa.[50] Sarah's family were heavily involved in the sugar plantations of St Croix. She was the daughter of a planter and the widow of another; her late husband, Cornelius Durant Battelle, owned the Little Princess Plantation in St Croix.[51] Although Sarah moved to England following his death, their daughter Judith Tower Battelle had married Sir Robert Innes Grant, who owned several plantations, including Little Princess, in 1825, and together they remained in St Croix and continued the business. The sudden emancipation of the slaves of St Croix

48 Bridget Hill, 'Women, Work and the Census: A Problem for Historians of Women', *History Workshop* 35 (Spring 1993), 82; Jane Humphries, 'Women and Paid Work', *Women's History: Britain 1850–1945, An Introduction*, ed. June Purvis (London, 2002), p. 91.

49 Morris, *Men, Women and Property*, pp. 100–1.

50 *1851 England Census* [online database, www.ancestry.co.uk], Class: HO107; Piece: 2072; Folio: 405; Page: 14; GSU roll: 87337–87338.

51 O. Davis, 'Little Princess, A Typical V.I Estate', University of Florida Digital Collections, available at http://ufdc.ufl.edu/CA01300919/00133, accessed 27 June 2019.

in 1848 had apparently pushed the Grant family into financial hardship. However, it is important to note that Grant received two payments of £5,414 14s 2d and £418 2s 6d in compensation for the release of 149 men and women who were enslaved on plantations he owned in British Guiana and Jamaica, the equivalent of approximately £6 million today.[52] After arriving in England Sarah lived first with one daughter, Cornelia, on the Isle of Wight, and then with another, Anna, in Leamington Spa.[53]

Sarah's last will and testament epitomises the idea of a wealthy widow being a 'things' person. The document is a hugely detailed description of her household and personal belongings, amounting to some seventy-six individual bequests, seventy-one of which were 'things'.[54] She does not refer to any personal financial income or trusts and, aside from three small cash bequests to her granddaughters and servant, the only other financial asset she lists is a bond of unspecified value from Sir Robert James Grant, her son-in-law's father. Despite the family's decline in fortune, at the time of her death Sarah called a substantial four-storey, double-fronted Georgian townhouse home, and her last will and testament speaks to the luxury that surrounded her. She lists several sets of silver cutlery, including three canteens for twelve, sweetmeat forks, a marrow spoon and a cheese scoop, plus large silver waiters, candlesticks and two tea urns. Items are often described in detail: for example, daughter Cornelia Cotton was to receive the large silver waiter 'with the swirly edges', the 'soup ladle with the shell pattern' and (perhaps most intriguingly of all), ten tablespoons and two gravy spoons decorated 'with crest of cat'.[55] This vast collection of silver and tableware constituted the bulk of Sarah's estate. She referred to only one item of furniture – a mahogany wardrobe – suggesting that either she rented a furnished house or perhaps that she had already gifted such items in her lifetime.

Sarah did, however, include several items of jewellery that she tried very hard to divide equally between her four surviving daughters, Judith Towers Grant, Anna Murray, Elizabeth Stedman Fergusson and Cornelia May Cotton – her fifth daughter, Sarah Gordon Battelle, having died in 1827. She owned two gold seals on chains, one with her married initials of 'S.B.' and one with her maiden initial of 'S.G.', one of which was bequeathed to Judith and the other to Elizabeth and Cornelia, depending on which of them would like to

52 'Robert Innes Grant 9th baronet of Dalvey', Legacies of British Slave-ownership database, available at http://wwwdepts-live.ucl.ac.uk/lbs/person/view/6310, accessed 17 August 2018.

53 Ancestry.com. *1841 England Census* [online database, www.ancestry.co.uk], Class: HO107; Piece: 406; Book: 11; Civil Parish: Freshwater; County: Hampshire; Enumeration District: 8; Folio: 10; Page: 2; Line: 10; GSU roll: 288806; Ancestry.com. *1851 England Census* [online database, www.ancestry.co.uk], Class: HO107; Piece: 2072; Folio: 405; Page: 14; GSU roll: 87337–87338.

54 Last will and testament of Sarah Battelle, proved at Birmingham on 18 August 1858.

55 Last will and testament of Sarah Battelle, proved at Birmingham on 18 August 1858.

own it and which would rather have a cash sum of £25. The two seals were obviously made and bought or gifted especially for Sarah, but other items reveal a much longer chain of ownership. Sarah bequeathed a locket to Judith, 'containing the hair of Judith Towers her great grandmother-in-law, her grandmother Sarah Gordon, and myself'. Anna was to receive two rings, 'one with a single pearl containing the hair of her grandmother Anna Battelle, the other the hair of her great grandmother Sarah Towers'. Elizabeth also received a ring, this one containing the hair of Sarah's friend, a Mrs Kelly. Finally, Cornelia was to receive a brooch 'containing the hair of her great grandfather James Towers and his sister Agnes Allen' and a ring with a small diamond 'containing the hair of her cousin Gysbert Behagen'.[56] Mourning jewellery, particularly those that had hair integrated into the design, was the height of early nineteenth-century fashion and Deborah Lutz argues that creating and sharing these items was both an expression of longing for the deceased loved one and an allusion to the medieval worship of relics.[57] Certainly, it appears that Sarah Battelle deliberately used jewellery to construct a familial narrative that would link her descendants to her ancestors in a tangible way. Indeed, by including her own hair in a locket along with that of her own grandmother and mother Sarah was giving her eldest daughter a literal piece of three generations of her maternal line. As discussed above, Sarah Battelle's last will and testament is the only one in the sample to include such vast lists of 'things'; however, it should be noted that her estate was initially valued at £4,000, which indicates that there was a financial as well as a sentimental necessity to her detailed testamentary instructions. Yet, interestingly, as Table 15 shows, a higher percentage of male testators included bequests of household goods and the most intimate of personal items, clothes, are mentioned in only three wills in the sample, and all are male.

In some respects, Sarah Battelle's last will and testament exemplifies what the historiography has suggested we would find in a woman's will in that it contains a large number of personal items, yet it also contradicts expectation. Table 16 shows the value of the estates proved before the Birmingham Court of Probate in 1858 and we can see that Sarah's estate of £4,000 was not just significantly higher than both the male and female average but was therefore much wealthier than the estates which did not follow the 'female' pattern of describing domestic chattels and personal possessions in great detail.[58] In

56 The cousin Sarah refers to was the grandson of Gysbert Behagen, who was a Danish merchant and director of the Danish Asia Company. They were related through Nancy Towers, who was Gysbert's mother and Sarah's aunt. The island of St Croix had been bought by the Danish Asia company in 1733 and, with the exception of some disruption 1801–15, it remained under their ownership until it was sold to the United States in 1916.

57 Deborah Lutz, 'The Dead Still Among Us: Victorian Secular Relics, Hair Jewelry, And Death Culture', *Victorian Literature and Culture* 39:1 (2011), 129.

58 Sample: 37 last wills and testaments proved in Birmingham in 1858.

Table 16. Values of male and female estates

Sex	Highest value	Lowest value	Average value
Male	£6,000.00	£20.00	£904.00
Female	£4,000.00	£100.00	£950.00

short, personal and household items could be just as financially important as real estate, land and businesses. This emphasises the importance of looking beyond gender when examining the potential diversity of wealth portfolios, thus allowing for the full impact of property ownership in all its forms to be considered.

Analysis of this small sample of mid-nineteenth-century wills, coupled with other recent studies, shows that women (both married and unmarried) were able to exercise considerable financial and testamentary agency. Asa Briggs' seminal work on nineteenth-century material culture reveals the importance placed on the acquisition of domestic items by the middle classes; the items displayed in people's homes were chosen not just for their practical or aesthetic value but as part of a complex performance of social and economic status.[59] Sarah Battelle was a wealthy woman who came from a wealthy family and her last will and testament offers a glimpse into the last wishes of a woman who was shaping the future of her small dynasty using the tools at her disposal: household items and personal jewellery. As well as the shrewd financial decisions made by women such as Sarah Barrs, Hannah Haydon and Mary Wood, both men and women were able to transfer the concept of 'home' in an imagined way by bequeathing items that can be too easily dismissed as sentimental trinkets, albeit with some financial value attached. In placing greater importance on the inclusion of either real estate, land and business premises or personal and domestic goods we risk losing sight of the importance that Victorians of both sexes placed on the active management of their wealth and assets. Examining the last wills and testaments of men and women together allows us to consider the way that men and women were able to use the probate process to physically shape the world of their descendants. Similarly, bequests of tableware, furniture and other personal apparel detailed by male and female testators imposed layers of identity on the homes, and potentially even the bodies, of beneficiaries. Monogrammed silver, portraits of the testator and their forbears and bespoke jewellery all add to an intimate performance of identity and personal connection that in some cases could last for several generations, creating a simultaneously real and imagined space.[60]

59 Asa Briggs, *Victorian Things* (London, 1988).

60 S. E. James, *Women's Voices in Tudor Wills, 1485–1603: Authority, Influence and Material Culture* (London, 2016) examines the relationship between possession and probate in the earlier

Conclusion

This chapter argues that women played a crucial role in the intergenerational transfer of work and home in both a literal and an imagined way. An assessment of the historiography and close reading of provincial mid-nineteenth-century probate records reveals very little evidence to support the notion that women at any stage of their lifecycle were economically passive. Indeed, as David Green states, 'Gentlemanly capitalism may, indeed, have driven the British economy forward, but the wealth so generated frequently ended up in women's hands.'[61] The women examined in this chapter have demonstrated that they played a key role in the long-term economic strategy of their birth family by utilising the legal system regardless of their marital status. If they did marry, they could become instrumental economic agents directing the establishment, expansion or continuation of firms, buying and selling real estate and speculating on the financial markets. Property, land and trusts were not static entities. Buildings were developed, expanded, improved, demolished and rebuilt under each of their owners, financial portfolios diversified, invested, grew and sometimes shrank; all of these things happened whether the owner was male or female. Women were normally life partners in every sense of the term. They helped to create the business or profession, in many cases they worked in it themselves and, when the husband died (which frequently happened before the death of the wife), the wife assumed the role of widow and could choose also to take control of the familial reins in place of sons, regardless of whether they had come of age. Women could change the course of the firm, expanding and relocating as they saw fit, before eventually transferring the enterprise to the next generation. The women made these decisions alone in order to fulfil the economic purpose and responsibility of the head of the family. In doing so, they would be creating security of both home and work in much the same way as the men observed in R. J. Morris's study of Victorian Leeds.

The contents of the home, namely those domestic items so frequently linked with women, were actually of concern to both sexes, with a higher proportion of men directing who should receive their personal and household belongings.[62] Objects such as silverware, jewellery, furniture and artwork were purchased, inherited and accumulated over a lifetime before being carefully bequeathed to family and friends in a complex performance designed to

period. Meanwhile, the importance of household items in Victorian novels is discussed in works such as John Plotx, *Portable Property: Victorian Culture on the Move* (Princeton, NJ, 2008) and Deborah Wynne, *Women and Personal Property in the Victorian Novel* (London, 2016).

61 D. R. Green, 'Independent Women, Wealth and Wills in Nineteenth-Century London', *Urban Fortunes: Property and Inheritance in the Town, 1700–1900*, eds Jon Stobart and Alistair Owens (Aldershot, 2000), p. 196.

62 See Table 14.

strengthen networks and ensure remembrance, whether through wearing, observing or using the belongings. The importance of this cannot be overestimated. Although land, property and stock portfolios carry an obvious financial value, as Geoffrey Crossick succinctly put it, 'to treat property primarily in terms of its total financial valuation is to neglect some of the most socially significant of its influences'.[63] It is, however, important that in assigning significance to domestic items we do not disregard the fact that women could and did possess property of every description, and in doing so used its sentimental and financial value to shape the world around them.

Probate documents also reveal that married women were able to navigate the inherently biased pre-1870 legal system regardless of their marital status. Although receiving property in trust did restrict access to the capital sum, married women were able to exploit the security of legal devices such as trusts and, as in the case of Mary Barton, protect themselves and their standard of living. The last wills and testaments examined in this chapter show that male and female testators utilised the tools of the legal profession to both look after their own beneficiaries and ensure that their wishes were carried out. This post-mortem control is seen in the probate behaviour of men and women alike and treads a fine line between ensuring that the capital of the estate was not exploited, squandered or subsumed whilst also giving the beneficiaries enough freedom to actually benefit from the bequest. The women examined in this chapter were more than passive guardian–caretakers; they were frequently more restrictive than their male counterparts, favouring their biological family over their spouse and never bequeathing property or land absolutely. The women were not only actively creating their estates through property purchase, business ownership and the creation of family heirlooms such as hairwork mourning jewellery but were also architects of intergenerational wealth strategies designed to protect their wide-ranging assets, providing for their beneficiaries and strengthening familial and friendship networks for another generation.

63 Geoffrey Crossick, 'Meanings of Property and the World of the Petit Bourgeoisie', *Urban Fortunes: Property and Inheritance in the Town, 1700–1900*, eds Jon Stobart and Alistair Owens (Aldershot, 2000), p. 50.

Afterword

AMY LOUISE ERICKSON

It is worthy of note that in 2019 a book on the significance of female landholding, constituting 'a rebuttal to any implicit or explicit suggestion within the existing historiography that women were insignificant as landowners in early modern and modern history', should even be required. Why would anyone think that women did not own and rent land as well as use it? At least through the seventeenth century, most English men lived directly off the land in the sense that they worked in agriculture.[1] But farming required the labour of an entire family. Unmarried men, or women who were farmers, invariably had adult children or hired help. Even those involved in crafts and trades used the products of the land (leather, wood, wool, metal). More than 80 per cent of the population lived in communities of fewer than 5,000 people in 1700, and still in 1800 more than 70 per cent did so.[2] So *most* people lived in rural areas where land was the principal form of wealth and offered a means of making a living through lease or labour, even if one did not own it. After all, *everyone* had to make a living.

This year is the centenary of Alice Clark's *Working Life of Women in the 17th Century* (1919), which expounded at length on the ways in which early modern women made a living, working outside as well as inside the home. The first three chapters are 'Capitalists', 'Agriculture' and 'Textiles', all of which are integrally related to land use. *Working Life* was not read only by scholars but was advertised in the main newspapers alongside other economic and feminist research from Routledge.[3] Clark herself was a businesswoman,

1 Leigh Shaw-Taylor and E.A. Wrigley, 'Occupational Structure and Population Change', *The Cambridge History of Modern Britain*, eds Roderick Floud, Jane Humphries and Paul Johnson (Cambridge, 2014), Table 2.2, 59.

2 E. A. Wrigley, *Energy and the English Industrial Revolution* (Cambridge, 2010), Table 3.2, 61.

3 See advert on p. 20, *Times Literary Supplement*, Thursday, 11 December 1919.

not an academic.[4] Two decades earlier, Charlotte Carmichael Stopes' *British Freewomen* had gone through three editions in the 1890s, expounding the history of women's property ownership and therefore entitlement to the franchise.[5] A century ago *everybody* was more aware of the nexus between property and power in society and politics. Property was more of a political issue *because* of female exclusion from the citizenship rights in a voting system based on property.

The recent celebrations of the centenary of women's suffrage in Britain should bring to mind the significance of women's entitlement to property. In 1919 the vote was extended only to women over the age of thirty who were registered occupiers (or married to a registered occupier) of property to a certain value. The age and property restrictions were imposed to counter-balance the extension of suffrage to all men by the *removal* of their property qualification, in the belief that the number of landless men and propertied women over thirty was equivalent. That belief proved incorrect (5.2 million men and 8.4 million women were added to the electorate in 1919) but women remained safely in the minority, at 40 per cent of the electorate. Women who were under thirty, or over thirty living with family members or as servants, or in furnished rooms, were excluded. That amounted to 5 million people, or one-third of all adult women, who remained voteless for another eight years.[6] But clearly a majority of women had control over some form of land in the early twentieth century.

If the literature of 'first-wave' feminism abated in the decades after partial suffrage was achieved in 1918, it revived in the 'second wave' after 1969, when Clark's *Working Life* was reprinted. Research on women's economic activity grew exponentially in the 1990s. For at least thirty years it has been systematically and repeatedly demonstrated that women acquired land along with other types of asset through inheritance, purchase and marriage – the same means by which men acquired property. And although the documentary record provides much more evidence on landholding than on labouring in the landscape, historians have also elaborated women's economic activities – working in the fields, picking up raw wool and delivering spun yarn, laundering, marketing, selling as pedlars or in shops, gathering fuel, moving from place to place in search of work – all of which required women to use land that they did not own.

4 On Clark, see Tim Stretton, 'Alice Clark's Critique of Capitalism', *Generations of Women Historians: Within and Beyond the Academy*, eds Hilda L. Smith and Melinda S. Zook (London, 2018).

5 On Stopes see Hilda L. Smith, '"No Leisure for Myself": C. C. Stopes and British Freewomen', *Generations of Women Historians: Within and Beyond the Academy*, eds Hilda L. Smith and Melinda S. Zook (London, 2018).

6 Mari Takayanagi, 'Women and the Vote: the Parliamentary Path to Equal Franchise 1918–28', *Parliamentary History* 37 (2018), 168–85.

Despite the proliferation of scholarship, women continue to feature in the historiography of land ownership primarily as 'bearers of assets to advantageous matches or as potential drains on family estates as a result of long widowhoods', in the words of Deborah Wilson, talking about Ireland.[7] As Briony McDonagh, Amanda Capern, Jennifer Aston and Hannah Worthen discuss in the introduction to this volume, the accepted narrative among most historians and among the wider public is still one of 'separate spheres' depicting a public male world of ownership, business, political activity and mastery and a private female world of household, children, interiors, domesticity and subordination. There are elements of truth in these associations, but as social description the dualist notion is not merely inadequate but serves a patriarchal political purpose (as discussed below).

The idea of separate spheres is closely associated with the two legal theories of primogeniture in inheritance, which prioritised the eldest son over other children, and coverture in marriage, which recognised the husband as the representative of the wife. These two principles, possibly the most persistent in English law over centuries, support the idea that men dominated the public, political sphere and women were relegated to a subordinate role in the domestic sphere.[8] But interpreting the impact of these principles is much more complex than reciting their main features. Primogeniture was applied to freehold land only at the death of the owner if s/he had not already sold or otherwise disposed of the property. In other words, the eldest son had an expectation of – but not a right to – the land. Perhaps ironically, among those with the inferior tenure of copyhold, eldest sons had a firmer right to inherit. But because of the high concentration of land in few hands, most land was not owner-occupied, and increasingly over time many more people leased land, in which case transfer at death was governed by the terms of the lease, not the sex of the lessee. Furthermore, although primogeniture in the first instance directed land to the eldest son, more than one-third of marriages did not produce any son,[9] and in that case, primogeniture directed land to daughters jointly. (The importance of inheritance through the maternal line is seen in several chapters in this volume.) In any event, most people did not own land, and moveable property was divided equally among all children, both according to law and among those who left wills detailing their wishes. But if daughters inherited, their control over property was compromised at their marriage.

7 Deborah Wilson, *Women, Marriage and Property in Wealthy Landed Families in Ireland, 1750–1850* (Manchester, 2008), p. 2.

8 On the persistence, dysfunctionality and patriarchal purpose of the legal fiction of coverture, see Tim Stretton and Krista J. Kesselring, 'Introduction', *Married Women and the Law: Coverture in England and the Common Law World*, ed. Stretton and Kesselring (Montréal/Québec/London, 2013), pp. 8–9.

9 Introduction (p. 5).

Coverture transferred ownership of all a woman's movable assets to her husband, and is the reason that English women took their husbands' names for 500 years before it became fashionable elsewhere in Europe in the nineteenth century.[10] The close association between the name and the property is illustrated by the practice of women retaining their surname, as in the case of Anne Clifford, or a husband taking his wife's surname where she held significant wealth and his was lesser. The one form of property that a married woman did *not* lose to her husband was her real estate, which he managed but did not own.[11] Should he wish to alienate the land, she had legally to be separately examined by independent parties to ascertain her agreement. These essays differ on how much autonomy this legal requirement gave to wives: compare, for example, the chapters of Joan Heggie and Janet Casson. But it is safe to say that, as wives, women managed much more property than they owned. Gentry and aristocratic houses were the major employers, or factories, of their day, as Anne Clifford and Elizabeth Montagu suggest (as the chapters by Jessica Malay and Stephen Bending).[12] In theory, elite women's land ownership and management should be more obvious in retrospect than that of more ordinary women.

Marriage was important for both sexes because it joined two inheritances to establish a working unit.[13] But it was particularly important for men because of the permanent economic advantages gained. Most households were headed by a married man (and his wife); among the minority of households headed by a single person, women predominated. English tax listings consistently show that 15–20 per cent of all household heads were women, which means they must have been at least the tenant if not the owner of their house and land, and that they supported themselves and their families. Married women too were highly likely to be involved in gainful employment.[14] While women were over-represented among paupers, as a result of lower wages and coverture, only a tiny proportion of female household heads were paupers. Most women, like most men, were not household heads. At any given time throughout this period around half of all

10 A. L. Erickson, 'Coverture and Capitalism', *History Workshop Journal* 59 (2005), 4.

11 Technically, a married woman also retained her 'pin money' but this had to be specified in a contract and applied to such a small proportion of the population that it can be safely ignored in the context of discussing larger patterns.

12 The most complete exploration of the manorial economy is Jane Whittle and Elizabeth Griffiths, *Consumption and Gender in the Early Seventeenth-Century Household: The World of Alice Le Strange* (Oxford, 2012).

13 A. L. Erickson, 'The marital economy in comparative perspective', *The Marital Economy in Scandinavia and Britain, 1400–1900*, eds Maria Ågren & A. L. Erickson (Aldershot, 2005), pp. 3–20.

14 A. L. Erickson, 'Married women's work in eighteenth-century London', *Continuity & Change* 23 (2008), 267–307.

adult women were unmarried and so not subject to coverture (although, as widows, they may have been previously).[15]

So, while the principles of primogeniture and coverture dominated property transfer, their influence was modified, limited and subverted in a myriad of ways. Within a patriarchal system women inherited land and property – as daughters because parents were concerned for their welfare and their prospects, and as widows because everyone alive at the time knew that a man's wealth derived at least equally from his wife. Barbara Hanawalt posited a 'self-limiting patriarchy', established by custom to limit legal injustice.[16] There remains today one last redoubt of primogeniture: the British aristocracy. The English crown abolished primogeniture in 2013, allowing the eldest child of either sex to inherit, but the hereditary peerage (who constitute nearly an eighth of the total number of seats in the House of Lords) still descends in the male line.[17] Five aristocratic daughters took a case to the European Court of Human Rights in 2018 as part of the 'Daughters' Rights' campaign.[18] The peerage is a very small and perhaps unsympathetic group of people, but it includes some of the country's largest landowners.

It is estimated that in 1700 one-quarter of 1 per cent of the population owned 50 per cent of the land in England. To put that in perspective, today just over one-half of 1 per cent of the population owns nearly 70 per cent of Britain, so it is safe to say that there has been little significant change in landholding.[19] The vast majority of the population moved around on land that they did not own in 1500, as they still do. It is not possible to estimate with any precision what proportion of women controlled land or what proportion of land was controlled by women outside of single place studies because – as the authors of the introduction point out – there has never been a central register of landholding in England. So it is equally impossible to make the same calculations for men.

The essays in this collection employ different sources in different places to understand women's relationship to land. Mostly that relationship is visible in terms of landholding, since that is what tends to be documented most securely, but land use can also be deduced. Some essays in this collection use well-known sources in innovative ways: Judith Spicksley reads early

15 Amy M. Froide, 'Hidden Women: Rediscovering the Singlewomen of Early Modern England', *Local Population Studies* 68 (2002), 26–41.

16 B. Hanawalt, *The Wealth of Wives: Women, Law and Economy in Late Medieval London* (Oxford, 2007).

17 Sarah Gordon, 'The British Aristocracy must solve its Downton Abbey Problem', *Financial Times*, 11 January 2019.

18 BBC, 'Daughters in legal bid for House of Lords seats', 16 July 2018, available at https://www.bbc.co.uk/news/uk-44844335, accessed 27 June 2019. For the campaign, see http://daughtersrights.co.uk/, accessed 27 June 2019.

19 Kevin Cahill, *Who Owns Britain?* (Edinburgh, 2002).

modern wills not only for bequests of land but also for the animals which imply use of land, and Jennifer Aston uses modern wills to identify trusts set up by women for men, whereas trusts are usually associated with the female legatee; Amanda Flather reads court depositions for descriptions of space and movement; and Briony McDonagh interprets account books as ego-documents of ownership. Four essays explore one individual's account of her land: Jessica Malay reads Anne Clifford's diaries for the way in which she constructs and projects lordship; Amanda Capern interrogates Arabella Alleyn's record of abduction and rape to claim her inheritance; Jon Stobart surveys Sophia Newdigate's account of her tours; and Stephen Bending reviews Elizabeth Montagu's relationship with her country estate. Two essays exploit previously unused sources: Joan Heggie on the eighteenth-century Registers of Deeds and Janet Casson with the canal and railway companies' records of compulsory purchase. The Register of Deeds that Heggie examines was created only for Yorkshire and Middlesex: it recorded not ownership but conveyances or land transfers, and its use was customary rather than mandatory. The twentieth-century Land Registry similarly records only sales, but while it has achieved 80 per cent coverage of land in the United Kingdom it remains inaccessible behind a prohibitively expensive pay wall, so is impossible to analyse.[20]

Despite extensive historical research on women's property and women's labour, the idea of a historic gendered separation of spheres has so successfully permeated popular culture that every country house which mentions ownership by a woman describes her as 'exceptional', or 'of independent views and strong character', as in the case of the internet historian described by Capern. And it is still common to find museum exhibition references to women being 'confined to the home' until the twentieth century. Sometimes an exception is made for 'poor women' who 'were forced to work outside the home'. On this criterion, more than 95 per cent of the population might meet the definition of 'poor'. Certainly there were *ideas* of a masculine public sphere and a feminine private sphere, but the rigidity of this schema cannot adequately describe a population in continual motion.

As Amanda Flather underlines, virtually all space was – as it still is – used in different ways at different times by different people. Elite women's frequent movement across the landscape is vividly illustrated in this collection by Anne Clifford's regal progresses between her Westmorland houses (Malay), the regular movement of Arabella Alleyn's abductors between Kent and Yorkshire to keep her away from rival factions (Capern), Sophia Newdigate criss-crossing the counties of southern England and Derbyshire to see great houses (Stobart) and Elizabeth Montagu's regular travel from the west end

20 Guy Shrubsole, 'Utopian thinking: to "take back control" of England, we must find out who owns it', *The Guardian*, 20 March 2017.

of London some sixty miles to Sandleford in Berkshire over a period of fifty years (Bending). On a smaller and more quotidian scale the deponents in Essex church courts in Flather's chapter also moved continuously, from house to fields, to church, to markets, and sometimes to migrate. We cannot know how much migration was temporary and how much was permanent, but among court deponents women reported migration as often as men did.[21] In both rural and urban areas migration was common: in most places around one-third of the population moved away from the parish of birth and in many cities more than half of the population had been born elsewhere.[22] Among those without land, migration to where employment was available offered an opportunity to make a (better) living. Over the four centuries examined here the growth of cities and increasing occupational complexity meant more ways to make a living in new trades and different ways to store value, in financial investments as well as land.

What is actually known of the complexity of early modern communities and labour markets makes clear that primogeniture, coverture and the idea of a male breadwinner were the machinery of a patriarchal system designed to consolidate male predominance. The mechanisms lasted and succeeded because the dysfunctional principles were adapted and elided. In this volume covering four hundred years we can identify some variation in sources, in laws and in geography. A great deal of literature has been devoted to the development of strict settlements in tail male from the sixteenth century, married women's separate estate from the late seventeenth century and the Married Women's Property Acts in the nineteenth century. But the relative disempowerment of women seems remarkably persistent. As the introduction documents, women today are still less likely than men to own land and other property and more likely to live in poverty. Claiming female agency in the past – that most marriages were economic partnerships, that widows were left in substantial control, or that daughters generally inherited if not equally then at least considerably – does not negate the powerful structure of patriarchy which empowered men in inheritance and marriage. Judith Bennett posited a 'patriarchal equilibrium' in terms of the static gender wage gap over five centuries, and property transfer is another prime example of long-term patriarchal equilibrium.[23]

That long-term continuity in control of assets is the reason why the idea of separate spheres is dangerous. An image of two historically separate spheres which have merged in an egalitarian present is an illusion which serves to

21 Peter Clark, 'Migration in England during the late 17th and early 18th centuries', *Past and Present* 83 (1979), 57–90.

22 Ian Whyte, *Migration and Society in Britain 1500–1830* (Basingstoke, 2000), esp. Chs 2–3.

23 Judith M. Bennett, 'Patriarchal equilibrium', *History Matters: Patriarchy and the Challenge of Feminism* (Philadelphia, PA, 2006).

preserve the patriarchal status quo. It encourages the assumption that the status of women was bad in the past so should not be expected to be perfect in the present. If the past was quite similar to the present, then questions must be asked about why women are still so disadvantaged relative to men of the same social group. Why is it difficult for historians broadly and the general public to see the women in the landscape – as workers and as owners? How is it that people continue to be surprised by women landholders, to underestimate their prevalence and influence, and to assume a male landscape in which female ownership or labour seem exceptional? One of the ways that patriarchal stories come to dominate perceptions is the number of repetitions they are awarded, the number of times that story is told. Probably women used land in largely the same ways as men, as an asset for family support and advancement (although they may have gambled less of it away). There are many questions to be investigated about how different and how similar women and men were as owners, as tenants and as labourers. But the first step is to see two sexes to start with.

The inability to see women as economic agents is a cognitive error or bias – a trick of the brain, based on cultural stereotypes, which overrides logical thought.[24] It is still the case that a book on land may be written without reference to women, and yet it does not require the word 'men' in its title. But a book on women's use of land must have 'women' in the title. This linguistic marking creates the illusion that the book on 'land' is a 'broader history' – that 'men' cover both sexes, as Hilda Smith once put it – while the book on 'women and land' is a 'niche field'.[25] That illusion is based on the cultural stereotypes of public and private that most people live with, the caricatures of primogeniture and coverture. Psychological studies over the past two decades have demonstrated how we all, women as well as men, depend on cultural stereotypes that in professional environments favour men: in assessing *curricula vitae*, for example, we will rank the same *curriculum vitae* as more impressive with a man's name on it than a woman's name. We also prefer European names to non-European names.[26] We use different language to talk about women and men, which ascribes natural genius to men and diligent

24 For an elaboration of the mechanisms of cognitive biases, albeit without reference to gender, see Daniel Kahneman, *Thinking, Fast and Slow* (London, 2011).

25 Hilda L. Smith, *All Men and Both Sexes: Gender, Politics and the False Universal in England, 1640–1832* (Philadelphia, PA, 2002).

26 For example, Marianne Bertrand and Sendhil Mullainathan, 'Are Emily and Greg More Employable than Lakisha and Jamal? A Field Experiment on Labor Market Discrimination', *American Economic Review* 94 (2004), 991–1013. For a full discussion of the literature, see Danica Savonick and Cathy N. Davidson, 'Gender Bias in Academe: An Annotated Bibliography of Important Recent Studies', LSE Impact Blog, available at https://blogs.lse.ac.uk/impactofsocialsciences/2016/03/08/gender-bias-in-academe-an-annotated-bibliography/, accessed 27 June 2019.

study to women.[27] Academics exhibit the same male preference in teaching and citation practices: male-authored work is disproportionately likely to be included in a class reading list or footnoted in a publication, by female as well as male academics.[28]

These cognitive biases based on cultural stereotypes repeatedly override the careful analysis of the historical record, which shows a counter-intuitive picture. And the stereotypes reinforce the patriarchal story. The only function that is served by insisting on the ubiquity of primogeniture and coverture in the old days, and on the reification of the male breadwinner norm, is to keep the disadvantaged grateful for the progress of history.

Amanda Capern refers to the sanitisation of family histories which have interpreted abduction and rape as 'either an agreement eventually reached or even female complicity in a forced marriage'. She calls this 'a form of historiographical forgetting' (p. 117). The omission from the historical 'mainstream' of the extensive research on women and property and work is also a form of historiographical forgetting. Research on cognitive bias dates from the 1970s, and implicit bias has become widely known in the 2010s, but as early as the 1940s anthropologists identified 'genealogical amnesia' or 'structural amnesia', whereby people tend to remember only those links that are socially important. This phenomenon was observed in a wide range of cultures, including our own: 'in the genealogies of the strongly patrilineal British peerage, the ascending male lines are much more memorable than the associated distaff lines'.[29]

Our structural amnesia in respect of women and land has two obvious effects: repeated surprise at the discovery of female agency; and an inability to analyse the persistence of patriarchal structures. The fact that men were the great majority of landowners and landholders was made possible by the active exclusion of daughters from inheritance and of wives from control. Women are therefore integral to the structure of land ownership and land use,

27 There are many academic studies, but the most vivid demonstration is Ben Schmidt's interactive analysis of the linguistic corpus of the Rate My Professor website, available at http://benschmidt.org/profGender, accessed 27 June 2019.

28 The best-known work on citations is in male-dominated fields such as economics, as Marianne A. Ferber and Michael Brün, 'The Gender Gap in Citations: Does It Persist?', *Feminist Economics* 17 (2011), 151–8, and international relations, as Daniel Maliniak, Ryan Powers and Barbara F. Walter, 'The Gender Citation Gap in International Relations', *International Organization* 67 (2013), 889–922. But even more interesting is similar findings in librarianship, where women are over- rather than under-represented. See Malin Håkanson, 'The Impact of Gender on Citations', *College & Research Libraries* 66 (2005), 312–22. For reading lists, https://blogs.lse.ac.uk/impactofsocialsciences/2018/01/31/male-authors-outnumber-their-female-counterparts-on-international-relations-course-reading-lists-by-more-than-five-to-one/, accessed 27 June 2019.

29 John Barnes, 'Postscript: Structural Amnesia', *Models and Interpretations: Selected Essays* (Cambridge, 1990), p. 227, from an essay originally published in 1947.

not just as an architectural detail on the facia but as the foundation of the whole building.

In the attempt to complicate simplistic stories of primogeniture and coverture, and from a desire to give credit for ingenuity and financial management where it is due, many historians have emphasised female agency. Insofar as claims of agency allow a perception of 'exceptionality', they perpetuate cultural bias by assuming that other women were oppressed but not these particular ones. Insofar as they are universalised, they run the risk of assuming that patriarchy was less effective because really women had agency. If the patriarchal structure is underplayed, then a historian may be accused of positing a pre-capitalist or pre-industrial 'golden age'. This is a means of dismissal as powerful as the assumption of universal oppression. What must be explained is how the structure and the agency co-existed, and why the equilibrium that Bennett used to describe gendered wage differentials persists in property ownership too.

The Married Women's Property Acts and women's suffrage were only achieved after hard-fought political campaigns, lasting more than half a century in the case of suffrage. In the words of Martin Luther King, Jr, 'Change does not roll in on the wheels of inevitability, but comes through continuous struggle.' The first step towards change is recognising what has *not* changed for the last five hundred years in women's relationship to land. The essays in this book help us to do that.

Select Bibliography

Archer, Rowena E., '"How ladies ... who live on their manors ought to manage their households and estates": Women as Landholders and Administrators in the Later Middle Ages', *Woman is a Worthy Wight: Women in English Society c. 1200–1500*, ed. P. J. P. Goldberg (Stroud, 1992), pp. 149–81.

Aston, Jennifer, *Female Entrepreneurship in Nineteenth-Century England: Engagement in the Urban Economy* (London, 2016).

Aston, Jennifer and Paolo di Martino, 'Risk, Success, and Failure: Female Entrepreneurship in Late Victorian and Edwardian England', *Economic History Society* 70:3 (August 2017), 837–58.

Aston, Jennifer, Amanda Capern and Briony McDonagh, 'More than Bricks and Mortar: Female Property Ownership as Economic Strategy in Mid-Nineteenth Century Urban England', *Urban History* 46:4 (2019).

Barker, Hannah, *The Business of Women: Female Enterprise and Urban Development in Northern England 1760–1830* (Oxford, 2006).

Barker, Hannah, *Family and Business During the Industrial Revolution* (Oxford, 2017).

Bennett, Judith M., *History Matters: Patriarchy and the Challenge of Feminism* (Philadelphia, PA, 2006).

Berg, Maxine, 'Women's Property and the Industrial Revolution', *Journal of Interdisciplinary History* XXIV:2 (1993), 233–50.

Bohls, Elizabeth, *Women Travel Writers and the Language of Aesthetics, 1716–1818* (Cambridge, 2004).

Bonfield, Lloyd, *Marriage Settlements 1601–1740: The Adoption of Strict Settlement* (Cambridge, 1983).

Butler, Judith, *Gender Trouble: Feminism and the Subversion of Identity* (London, 1991).

Cahill, Kevin, *Who Owns Britain?* (Edinburgh, 2002).

Capern, Amanda L., 'Early Modern Women Lost and Found: Case Studies in the Selection and Cataloguing of Historical Sources and the (In)visibility of Women', *Women's History Notebooks* 5:2 (1998), 15–22.

Capern, Amanda L., *The Historical Study of Women: England, 1500–1700* (Basingstoke, 2010).

Capern, Amanda L., 'The Landed Woman in Early-Modern England', *Parergon* 19:1 (2002), 185–214.

Carlos, Ann and Larry Neal, 'Women Investors in Early Capital Markets, 1720–1725', *Financial History Review* 11:2 (2004), 197–224.

Casson, Janet, 'Women's Landownership in England in the Nineteenth Century', *Large Databases in Economic History: Research Methods and Case Studies*, eds Mark Casson and Nigar Hashimzade (Abingdon, 2013), pp. 200–21.

Churches, Christine, 'Women and Property in Early Modern England: A Case-Study', *Social History* 23:2 (1998), 165–80.

Combs, Mary Beth, 'Cui Bono? The 1870 British Married Women's Property Act, Bargaining Power, and the Distribution of Resources Within Marriage', *Feminist Economics* 12:1–2 (January – April 2006), 51–83.

Combs, Mary Beth, 'Wives and Household Wealth: The Impact of the 1870 British Married Women's Property Act on Wealth-Holding and Share of Household Resources', *Continuity and Change* 19 (2004), 141–63.

Connor, Rebecca Elisabeth, *Women, Accounting, and Narrative: Keeping Books in Eighteenth-Century England* (London, 2004).

Craig, Béatrice, *Female Enterprise Behind the Discursive Veil in Nineteenth Century Northern France* (London, 2017).

Crawford, Patricia, 'A Decade in the Life of Elizabeth Harvey of Taunton 1696–1706', *Women's History Review* 19:2 (2010), 245–57.

Crawford, Patricia, 'Women and Property: Women as Property', *Parergon* 19:1 (2002), 151–71.

Davidoff, Leonore and Catherine Hall, *Family Fortunes: Men and Women of the English Middle Class, 1780–1850* (London, 1987).

Dunn, Caroline, *Stolen Women in Medieval England: Rape, Abduction, and Adultery, 1100–1500* (Cambridge, 2013).

Eckerle, Julia A., *Romancing the Self in Early Modern Englishwomen's Life Writing* (New York, 2013).

English, Barbara, *The Great Landowners of East Yorkshire 1530–1910* (Hull, 1990).

Erickson, Amy, 'Coverture and Capitalism', *History Workshop Journal* 59 (Spring 2005), 1–16.

Erickson, Amy, 'The Marital Economy in Comparative Perspective', *The Marital Economy in Scandinavia and Britain, 1400–1900*, eds Maria Ågren & A. L. Erickson (Aldershot, 2005), pp. 3–20.

Erickson, Amy, 'Married Women's Work in Eighteenth-Century London', *Continuity & Change* 23 (2008), 267–307.

Erickson, Amy, *Women and Property in Early Modern England* (London, 1993).

Foster, Shirley and Sara Mills (eds), *Women's Travel Writing* (Manchester, 2002).

Froide, Amy, *Never Married: Singlewomen in Early Modern England* (Oxford, 2005).

Froide, Amy, *Silent Partners: Women as Public Investors during Britain's Financial Revolution, 1690–1750* (Oxford, 2017).
Garside, Charlotte, 'Women in Chancery: An Analysis of Chancery as a Court of Redress for Women in Late Seventeenth-Century England' (PhD diss., University of Hull/The National Archives, submitted 2018).
Green, David and Alastair Owens, 'Gentlewomanly Capitalism? Spinsters, Widows, and Wealth Holding in England and Wales, c. 1800–1860', *Economic History Review* 56:3 (2003), 510–36.
Green, David, Alastair Owens, Josephine Maltby and Janette Rutterford (eds), *Men, Women, and Money: Perspectives on Gender, Wealth, and Investment 1850–1930* (Oxford, 2011).
Hall, Catherine, *White, Male and Middle Class: Explorations in Feminism and History* (Oxford, 1992).
Hanawalt, Barbara, *The Wealth of Wives: Women, Law and Economy in Late Medieval London* (Oxford, 2007).
Harris, Barbara J., *English Aristocratic Women, 1450–1550: Marriage and Family, Property and Careers* (Oxford, 2002).
Hill, Bridget, 'Women, Work and the Census: A Problem for Historians of Women', *History Workshop* 35 (Spring 1993), 78–94.
Holcombe, Lee, *Wives & Property: Reform of the Married Women's Property Law in Nineteenth Century England* (Toronto, 1983).
Horrell, Sara and Jane Humphries, 'Women's Labour Force Participation and the Transition to the Male-Breadwinner Family, 1790–1865', *The Economic History Review* 48:1 (1995), 89–117.
Humphries, Jane, 'Enclosures, Common Rights, and Women: The Proletarianization of Families in the Late Eighteenth and Early Nineteenth Centuries', *Journal of Economic History* 50:1 (1990), 24–31.
Hunt, Margaret R., *The Middling Sort: Commerce, Gender and the Family in England, 1680–1780* (Berkeley, CA, 1996).
King, Peter, 'Customary Rights and Women's Earnings: The Importance of Gleaning to the Rural Labouring Poor', *Economic History Review* 44:3 (1991), 461–76.
Kirkham, Linda and Anne Loft, 'Gender and the Construction of the Professional Accountant', *Accounting, Organizations and Society* 18:6 (1993), 507–58.
Korda, Natasha, 'Coverture and its Discontents: Legal Fictions On and Off the Early Modern English Stage', *Married Women and the Law: Coverture in England and the Common Law World*, eds Tim Stretton and Krista J. Kesselring (Montréal, 2013), pp. 45–63.
Lane, Penelope, 'Women, Property and Inheritance: Wealth Creation and Income Generation in Small English Towns, 1750–1835', *Urban Fortunes: Property and Inheritance in the Town 1700–1900*, eds Jon Stobart and Alastair Owens (Aldershot, 2000), pp. 172–94.

Laurence, Anne, 'The Emergence of a Private Clientele for Banks in the Early Eighteenth Century: Hoare's Bank and Some Women Customers', *The Economic History Review* 61:3 (August 2008), 565–86.

Liddington, Jill, 'Gender, Authority and Mining in an Industrial Landscape: Anne Lister 1791–1840', *History Workshop Journal* 42 (1996), 58–86.

Lindert, Peter H., 'Who Owned Victorian England? The Debate over Landed Wealth and Inequality', *Agricultural History* 61:4 (1987), 25–51.

McDonagh, Briony, '"All towards the improvements of the estate": Mrs Elizabeth Prowse at Wicken, 1764–1810', *Custom, Improvement and the Landscape in Early Modern Britain*, ed. R. W. Hoyle (Farnham, 2011), pp. 263–88.

McDonagh, Briony, *Elite Women and the Agricultural Landscape, 1700–1830* (Abingdon, 2017).

McDonagh, Briony, 'Women, Enclosure and Estate Improvement in Eighteenth-Century Northamptonshire', *Rural History* 20:2 (2009), pp. 143–62.

Malay, Jessica L. (ed.), *Anne Clifford's Autobiographical Writing 1590–1676* (Manchester, 2018).

Malay, Jessica L. (ed.), *Anne Clifford's Great Books of Record* (Manchester, 2015).

Maltby, Judith and Janette Rutterford, 'Editorial: Women, Accounting and Investment', *Accounting, Business & Financial History* 16:2 (2006), 133–42.

Massey, Doreen, *Space, Place and Gender* (Oxford, 1994).

Mills, Sara, *Discourses of Difference: An Analysis of Women's Travel Writing and Colonialism* (London, 1991).

Moring, Beatrice and Richard Wall, *Widows in European Economy and Society 1600–1920* (London, 2017).

Morris, R. J., *Men, Women and Property in England, 1780–1870: A Social and Economic History of Family Strategies Amongst the Leeds Middle Classes* (Cambridge, 2005).

Murray, Mary, 'Primogeniture, Patrilineage and the Displacement of Women', *Women, Property, and the Letters of the Law in Early Modern England*, eds Nancy E. Wright, Margaret W. Ferguson and A. R. Buck (Toronto, 2004), pp. 121–36.

Okin, S. M., 'Patriarchy and Married Women's Property in England: Questions On Some Current Views', *Eighteenth-Century Studies* 17:2 (1983–84), 121–38.

Payling, S. J., 'The Economics of Marriage in Late Medieval England: The Marriage of Heiresses', *Economic History Review* 54:3 (2001), 413–29.

Phillips, Nicola, *Women in Business, 1700–1850* (Woodbridge, 2006).

Pinchbeck, Ivy, *Women Workers and the Industrial Revolution 1750–1850* (London, 1930).

Rendall, Jane, *Women in an Industrializing Society: England 1750–1880* (Oxford, 1990).

Seeliger, Sylvia, 'Hampshire Women as Landowners: Common Law Mediated by Manorial Custom', *Rural History* 7:1 (1996), 1–14.

Sharpe, Pamela, *Adapting to Capitalism: Working Women in the English Economy, 1700–1850* (Basingstoke, 1996).

Sharpe, Pamela, 'Gender in the Economy: Female Merchants and Family Businesses in the British Isles, 1600–1850', *Histoire Sociale* 34:68 (2001), 283–306.

Sharpe, Pamela, 'A Woman's Worth: A Case Study of Capital Accumulation in Early Modern England', *Parergon* 19:1 (2002), 173–84.

Shoemaker, Robert B., 'Gendered Spaces: Patterns of Mobility and Perception of London's Geography, 1660–1750', *Imagining Early Modern London: Perceptions and Portrayals of the City from Stow to Strype, 1598–1720*, ed. Julia Merrit (Cambridge, 2001), pp. 144–65.

Smith, Hilda L. and Melinda S. Zook (eds), *Generations of Women Historians: Within and Beyond the Academy* (London, 2018).

Spence, Richard T., *The Lady Anne Clifford* (Sutton, 1997).

Spicksley, Judith (ed.), *The Business and Household Accounts of Joyce Jeffreys, Spinster of Hereford, 1638–1648* (Oxford, 2012).

Spicksley, Judith, '"Fly with a duck in thy mouth": Single Women as Sources of Credit in Seventeenth-Century England', *Social History* 32:2 (May 2007), 187–207.

Spicksley, Judith, 'Women, "Usury", and Credit in Early Modern England: The Case of the Maiden Investor', *Gender and History* 39:2 (2015), 247–75.

Spring, Eileen, 'The Heiress-at-Law: English Real Property Law from a New Point of View', *Law and History Review* 8:2 (1990), 273–96.

Spring, Eileen, *Law, Land and Family: Aristocratic Inheritance in England, 1300–1800* (Chapel Hill, NC, 1993).

Staves, Susan, *Married Women's Separate Property in England, 1660–1833* (Cambridge, MA, 1990).

Stobart, Jon, *Travel and the British Country House* (Manchester, 2017).

Stobart, Jon, Andrew Hann and Victoria Morgan, *Spaces of Consumption: Leisure and Shopping in the English Town, c.1680–1830* (London, 2007).

Stretton, Tim, *Women Waging Law in Elizabethan England* (New York, 1998).

Tait, Allison, 'The Beginning of the End of Coverture: A Reappraisal of the Married Woman's Separate Estate', *Yale Journal of Law & Feminism* 26 (2014), 165–216.

Vicinus, Martha, *Independent Women: Work and Community for Single Women 1850–1920* (London, 1985).

Vickery, Amanda, *The Gentleman's Daughter: Women's Lives in Georgian England* (New Haven, CT, 1998).

Vickery, Amanda, 'Golden Age to Separate Spheres? A Review of the Categories and Chronology of English Women's History', *Historical Journal* 36:2 (1993), 383–414.

Vickery, Amanda, 'His and Hers: Gender, Consumption and Household Accounting in Eighteenth-Century England', *Past and Present* 1:1 (2006), 12–38.

Walker, Stephen, 'Accounting Histories of Women: Beyond Recovery?', *Accounting, Auditing & Accountability Journal* 21:4 (2008), 580–610.

Walker, Stephen, 'Identifying the Woman behind the "Railed-in Desk": The Proto-Feminisation of Bookkeeping in Britain', *Accounting, Auditing & Accountability Journal* 16:4 (2003), 606–39.

Ward, Jennifer (tr. and ed.), *Women of the English Nobility and Gentry 1066–1500* (Manchester, 1995).

Whittle, Jane, 'A Critique of Approaches to "Domestic Work": Women, Work and the Pre-Industrial Economy,' *Past and Present* 243:1 (2019), 35–70.

Whittle, Jane, 'Enterprising Widows and Active Wives: Women's Unpaid Work in the Household Economy of Early Modern England', *Journal of the History of the Family* 19:3 (2014), 283–300.

Whittle, Jane, 'Housewives and Servants in Rural England: Evidence of Women's Work from Probate Documents', *Transactions of the Royal Historical Society* 15 (2005), 51–74.

Whittle, Jane, 'Inheritance, Marriage, Widowhood and Remarriage: A Comparative Perspective on Women and Landholding in North-east Norfolk, 1440–1580', *Continuity and Change* 13:1 (1998), 33–72.

Whittle, Jane and Elizabeth Griffiths, *Consumption and Gender in the Early Seventeenth-Century Household: The World of Alice Le Strange* (Oxford, 2012).

Whittle, Jane and Mark Hailwood, 'The Gender Division of Labour in Early Modern England,' *Economic History Review* (2019, forthcoming).

Worthen, Hannah, 'Supplicants and Guardians: The Petitions of Royalist Widows during the Civil wars and Interregnum, 1642–1660', *Women's History Review* 26:4 (2017), 528–40.

Worthen, Hannah, Briony McDonagh and Amanda Capern, 'Gender, Property and Succession in the Early Modern English Aristocracy: the Case of Martha Janes and her Illegitimate Children', *Women's History Review* (forthcoming).

Wright, Nancy E., Margaret W. Ferguson and A. R. Buck (eds), *Women, Property, and the Letters of the Law in Early Modern England* (Toronto, 2004).

Young, Hannah, 'Gender and Absentee Slave Ownership in Late Eighteenth- and Early Nineteenth-Century Britain' (PhD diss., University College London, 2017).

Index

Page numbers in **bold** refer to tables; page numbers in *italics* refer to figures.

abduction of heiresses 100–26
female complicity in 105, 126
historiography of 105
punishment of offenders 103
satires 103–5, 107
academic bias 275
account books 149–75
accounting textbooks 164–5
Act Books 39
adultery 249
Advice to the Maidens of London (1678) 149, 161, 169
aesthetics 136–7, 142–8, 178
affordable housing 3, 4
Africa, landownership 19
Agar, Anna Maria **157**, 166, 172
agricultural landholders, definition 18
agricultural work/workers 38–42, 46–9, 196, 267
alehouses 35
alimony 10, 120–1
Allen, James 258
Alleyn, Arabella, abduction of 100–26
Alleyn Manuscript 100–9
The Case of Arabella Lady Howard 10
death of Arabella 123
domestic violence 118–23
Alleyn, Edmund 109–10, 111
Alleyn, Frances 109, 112–13
will of 110–11
Alleyn, John 113
ancient monuments/sites 133, 141
Anglicans 108
annuities 59
Appleby by-election 94–6
Appleby Castle 84, 85, 89, 91, 97–8, 99
Appleton, Mary 222–3
Appletree, Frederick Hollis, will of 256–7
Arbury Hall 142
Archer, Elizabeth 40
Archer, Rowena 75
architecture 138–9, 141, 191–2
aristocracy
estate accounting 152–75
and female inheritance 51
pastoral landscape, construction of 176–200
primogeniture 271
and property accumulation 74–5
residences of 130, 132
see also country house visiting; elite women
art appreciation 139–40
Atkinson, Robert 83
autobiography
Arabella Alleyn 100–26
gendering of 125
historical value of 101–2
Aylesbury, Buckinghamshire 235

Baddiley, Henrietta 236, 242, 243
Badminton estate 172
bailiffs 166
Baker, Judith 152, **157**
ballads 41
ballrooms 140
bankruptcy 7, 251, 252
baptism registers 41
Barrs, Mary, will of 260
Barton House 142, 143
Barton, Mary, will of 257–8
Baskerville, Thomas 43
Batelle, Sarah 261–4
Baucis and Philemon myth 185, 189, 190

Baynes, Adam 88
beauty, of buildings and landscape 144
  see also aesthetics
Beckett, John 150
Bending, Stephen 26
Bennet, Henry, 1st earl of Arlington 94, 95
Bennett, Judith 51–2
Berry, Helen 152
biases, cognitive/cultural 274–5, 276
biblical references 84–5
Birdbrook manor 123
Birmingham, probate data 247, 254–66
Blount, Anne 109
Board of Trade 252
Bohls, Elizabeth 129, 143
Bonomi, Joseph 178, 191–2
bookkeeping 151, 154–6, **157–8**, 168–9
  double-entry bookkeeping 162, 164
Books of Reference (Index Ledgers)
  property transaction data 201, 206–25
  women's landownership 229–43
Bracegirdle, Anne 104
Braddick, Michael 32
Brampton Park **157**
Briggs, Asa 264
broadside ballads 41
Brough Castle 89, 99
Brougham Castle 80, 88–9, 91, 98, 99
Broughton, Elizabeth 37
Brown, Lancelot ('Capability' Brown) 177–80, 182, 183, 188–200
Browne, Joane 68–9
Bruce, Edward, Lord Kinloss 81
Buckley, Ann 254
Buckley, Frances, will of 62
Buckley, James 254
Bundley, John, will of 260
Bunworthe, William, will of 59–60
Burke, Edmund 143, 144
businesses, female ownership/operation of 11–17, 24, 254–5
  see also work activities
Butleigh Wootton estate **158**, 159–60
Buxton, Derbyshire 145

Cahill, Kevin 20
Camden, William 131
Campbell, Colin 130
canal building 229
Cannadine, David 171
Canons Ashby estate 155, **157**
Carter, Elizabeth 183, 184, 196
cash books 154, 164
cash gifts 72–3
castles, Anne Clifford's rebuilding/progresses 87–92, 97–9
Catholics 108, 109
caves 145–6
census data 226, 231
Centlivre, Susannah 104
charge-discharge accounting 162, 164
charitable works, Anne Clifford 89, 92–3
Charles I 86
Charles II 94
Chatsworth 137
Chester diocese
  formal lending with land 74
  land bequests 66
  landholding by spinsters *63*, *64*, *70*
  leases 67
  livestock holding *70*, *73*
  wills and probate inventories, spinsters' **55**
children
  abduction of 100–26
  care of 36–8
  fatal accidents 42
  guardianship of 110–11, 112
  illegitimacy 257
Chippenham, Wiltshire 52
Chipping Ongar market 46
church courts 39
church records 231
Churches, Christine 7, 53
Cibber, Susannah 104–5
Civil Wars, British 83, 86, 106
Clark, Alice 244–5, 267–8
Clarke, Mary **157**, 166
classical mythology 185, 189, 190
Clifford, Anne 2, 26, 77–99, 270, 272
  'authorising presence' 87, 90, 99
  biblical references of 84–5
  castle progresses 90–2, 97–9
  castle rebuilding 87–9
  charitable works 89, 92–3
  correspondence 176–200
  Her Great Books of Record 77, 85, 88, 93, 97
  monument building 90
  patronage network 93, 96, 99
  political strategy of 96–7
  tenants, relations with 82–7, 88
Clifford, Francis, 4th earl of Cumberland 81, 82, 83

Clifford, George, 3rd earl of Cumberland 5, 77, 81
Clifford, Henry 81–2, 83
Clifford, Margaret 5
Cliveden House 143
cloth trade 42, 46
clothes washing 36
co-parceny 58, 61
coal mining 165, 173, 186, 232
codicils 222
cognitive biases 274–5
Combs, M. B. 205
common land/rights 46–7, 48
common law 58, 227
communal work 43
Compton, James, 3rd earl of Northampton 94
conveyances **218**, **219**, 220
Cooke, Martin, will of 60
cooking 34
country house visiting 127–8, 130, 131–2, 136–7, 140, 147, 186, 187
'Country Studies' report on Gender and Land Rights 19
countryside, tourism 129, 142
County Council Act (1888) 16
coverture 6–7, 54, 226–7, 248–9, 270, 271
cows 47, 71–2
Craig, Beatrice 246
Cranfield, Frances, countess of Dorset 93
credit 251, 252
Cross, Rachel Robinson 219–20
Crossick, Geoffrey 266
cultural bias 276
cultural stereotypes 274, 275
Cust, Anne **157**, 160
customary duties/rights 78

dairy trade 44, 45
  see also milking work
Dale, Alice 68
Dalton, Annie Grubb 220
Dance, Henry, will of 60
Darleston, Edward 255
data sources *see* historical sources
Davidoff, Leonore 15–16, 245, 250
  and Catherine Hall, *Family Fortunes: Men and Women of the English Middle Class, 1750–1850* (1987) 15–16, 245
Dawes, James 254
de facto ownership 10
de Veteripont, Idonea 81, 89
de Veteripont, Isabella 81
debt 7, 171
Deed of Separation 256–7
deeds 56
Deeds Registers, property transaction data 201–25
defamation cases 39, 40
Denton estate 165, 186
Derby, Lord 226
Derbyshire, tourism 133, 143–6
desertion 249
developing countries, female landholding 18
dishonesty, estate accounting 166–7
divorce 249
dock-side development 238, 239
Dolan, Frances 107
domestic goods, bequests of 262–4, 266
domestic violence 118–23
domestic work 33–8
Done, Jane, will of 65
double-entry bookkeeping 162, 164
Dovedale, Derbyshire 146
dowers 9, 10, 54
Dryden, Elizabeth 155, **157**
Dryden, Elizabeth (Betsy) 155
Dryden, John 155
Dunn, Caroline 102, 105
D'Urfey, Thomas 107
Durham Coast Railway 239
Durham, County, women plot owners **232**, 233, 237–9
Durham diocese
  formal lending with land 74
  land bequests 66
  landholding by spinsters 63, 64, 70, 72
  leases 66, 67
  livestock holding 70, 72, 73
  wills and probate inventories, spinsters' **55**
'dutche worke' 46

Eames, William 181
Earle, Peter 11
early modern period
  spatial dynamics of gender relations 29–50
  spinster landholding 51–76
elections, Appleby by-election 94–6
elite women 26, 272
  see also aristocracy
Elizabeth I 86, 87, 98

Emerson, George, will of 60
employment *see* work activities
enclosure 48, 197
'England's Eliza' (Heywood) 98
English, Barbara 5–6
engrossing offence 45–6
enslaved people, release of and owner compensation 262
entrepreneurs 12
equity 54, 227
equity law 116
Erickson, Amy L. 8–9, 15, 52, 54, 203
Essex, work activities 33–50
 Hatfield Peverell 110
 Register of Deeds 201–25
estate accounting/management 13, 26, 149–75
 bookkeeping 151, 154–6, **157–8**, 162, 164, 168–9
 fraud 166–7
estates trusts 205
Eston, North Yorkshire **216**
estrangement 258
Extracted Probate Records 231

Fades, Henry 49
Falsgrave, North Yorkshire, **216**, 217
family firms 254–5
family histories 231, 275
FAOUN *see* Food and Agricultural Organization of the United Nations
feme sole 224
Ferguson, Margaret 4–5
festivities 197–9
Ffuller, William 34
Fielding, Henry 105
fields, as hazardous places for women 47–8
fieldwork 38, 39, 40
Fiennes, Celia 43
financial investments 13–14, 233, 255
fines 82
fishing industry 217
Flather, Amanda 27
Food and Agricultural Organization of the United Nations (FAOUN) 18, 19
food and drink, shopping for 34–6
forced marriages, Arabella Alleyn abduction 100–26
forestalling offence 45–6
formal lending 73, 74, 75
Fothergill, Nicholas 82
franchise 16–17, 268, 276
fraud 166–7
free bench 10
French Revolution 199
Froide, Amy 14
furniture, bequests of 262–3, 266
future research 27–8

Galpin, James 240
gardens
 land bequests 67
 pastoral landscape, construction of 176–200
 tourism 137
Garside, Charlotte 8
gender relations
 and autobiography 125
 contemporary inequalities 17–21
 estate accounting/management 149–75
 and inheritance 60
 land/property ownership/rights 2–4, 17–21
 spatial dynamics of 29–50
Georgian period, estate accounting/management 149–75
Gibson, Jane 234, 239, 242
gifts of land 65
gleaning 40–1, 49
Goldsmith, Oliver 197
Goodall, John 87
Gordon, Anna 105
Gothic architecture 138–9, 141
grain dealers 45–6
Grand Tour 128, 130, 136, 141
Gray, Dorothy 66–7
grazing rights 71
Great Books of Record (Clifford) 77, 80–1, 85, 97
Great Northern Railway 237
Green, David R. 247, 265
Greenwell, Martha 238, 242, 243
guardianship 15, 110–11, 112
Guest, Samuel 258
Guisborough, North Yorkshire **216**, 218

Haldane, Alexander 166, 167
Hale, Elizabeth 235, 242, 243
Hale, Mary 235, 242, 243
Hall, Catherine 15–16, 245, 250
Hammond, Lieutenant 80
Hampshire, mortgages of land 69
Hanawalt, Barbara 271
Hanbury, William 141

Harris, Barbara 2, 7, 51, 74
English Aristocratic Women, 1450–1550: Marriage and Family, Property and Careers (2002) 2
Hardwick, Bess of *see* Talbot, Elizabeth Countess of Shrewsbury
Hartlepool, County Durham 238, 239
Hartlepool and Cleveland Junction Railway Company 238
harvest festival 198–9
harvesting 40
Haydon, Hannah (formerly Bashford *née* Swann), will of 258–9
haymaking 40
hearth taxes 23
heiresses 226, 263–4, 271
abduction of 100–26
Henry VIII 87
Heywood, Thomas 98
Hick, Bessy (Elizabeth) 237, 242, 243
Hipkiss, Maria 254–5
historical sources
account books 149–75
Books of Reference (Index Ledgers) 201, 206–25, 229–43
census data 226, 231
church and secular courts 33
innovative use of 271–2
landownership 22–5
primary and secondary sources 231
trade directories 252, 253
historiographies
abduction of heiresses 105
of female economic agency 244–6
landownership 228–9, 267–75
women and land 1–28
Hogg, Ann 235–6
Hogg, Thomas 235
Hood, Elizabeth (*née* Periam) 149, 150, **158**, 159–60
Hounsfield, John 236
household accounts 154
household goods, bequests of 262–4, 266
household heads 270
household reference persons (HRPs) 20
housework 33–8
housing crisis, in UK 3
housing developments 217, 219
Howard, George 109, 122–3
HRPs *see* household reference persons
Hume-Campbell, Amabel, 1st Countess de Grey 27, **158**, 165, 172
identity, and land/property ownership 25–8
illegitimate children, provision for in wills 257
improvement 85, 87–90, 159, 169–73
indentures **218**, **219**, 220, 258
Index Ledgers (Books of Reference)
property transaction data 201, 206–25
women's landownership 229–43
industrialisation 245
infant mortality 42
inheritance
by daughters 5, 52–4, 58–62, 204
Clifford estates, Westmorland 77–99
co-parceny 58, 61
eldest daughter preference 59, 61
gender inequalities 60
Islamic law 19
middle-classes 16, 206
partible inheritance 53, 206
primogeniture 5, 8–9, 19, 52, 58, 100, 205–6, 269, 271
second daughters 61
and voting rights 16–17
see also wills
inter-vivos transfers 56
interest-bearing lending 73, 76
investments 13–14, 233, 255
Islamic law 19
Isle of Wight, Hampshire 132, 142, 144
Italy 130
itinerant traders 35–6

James I 80, 81, 82
James II 93
James, Isabell 70
Jeffreys, Joyce
financial and agricultural business management 11
livestock holding 71
pasture land 67
will of 64–5, 66
jewellery, bequests of 263, 266
Johnson, John 103, 104
joint tenancies 53
jointures 9, 10, 93, 115
Jones, Elizabeth 113, 120
Jones, Norman 86–7
Jones, William 113, 120
Jonson, Ben 185–6

Kelly, James 102
'kindness' 116

King's Award, Clifford lands, Westmorland and Yorkshire 81, 82–3
'King's diseases' 97
Kinloss, Lord (Edward Bruce) 81
Knight, John, will of 61
Korda, Natasha 6–7

labourers, Elizabeth Montagu's use of 195–6, 198–9, 200
land, definition of 57
land agents 166
land metaphors 27
land purchases 66
Land Registry 19–20
land transfers 56–7, 107, 244–66
land values 3
landholding, landownership distinction 18
landownership
  gender inequalities 2–4, 17–21
  historical sources 22–5
  historiographies of 228–9, 267–75
  and identity 25–8
  intergenerational property transfers 244–66
  landholding distinction 18
  quantification of 22–5
  small-scale landholding 226–43
  spinsters 51–76, 235
  widows 235–6
landscape
  'natural' landscape 188
  pastoral landscape, construction of 176–200
  tourist engagement with 142–6, 147
  women's experience of 29–50
Langley Park 137
Lanhydrock estate **157**, **158**, 172
Lapidge, Samuel 180, 192
Latour, Bruno 90
laundry work 36
law
  1832 Reform Act 16
  abduction and capture 102, 112
  Chancery, Court of 8, 15, 111–12, 113, 121, 122
  European Court of Human Rights – 'Daughters' Rights Case' 27
  feme sole/*feme covert* 6, 224
  guardianship 112–13
  The Lawes Resolutions of Women's Rights (1632) 111
  and property ownership 4–10
  rape and abduction 103
  see also Court of Chancery; Court of Probate; legislation; litigation, women's use of
law of trusts 9
leaseholds 204
leases 56, 66–7
ledgers *see* account books; Books of Reference (Index Ledgers)
Leeds, West Yorkshire 249, 250
legislation
  County Council Act (1888) 16
  Married Women's Property Acts (1870, 1882 & 1893) 17, 205, 213, 226, 233, 234, 251, 252, 276
  Municipal Franchise Act (1869) 16
  Reform Acts (1832 & 1867) 16
  Statute of Rapes (1382) 102–3
Lemon, Ann 71
lending
  formal lending 73, 75
  interest-bearing lending 73, 76
Lincoln diocese
  formal lending with land 74
  land bequests 62, 66, 75
  landholding by spinsters 63, 64, *70*
  livestock holding *70*, 71, 73
  wills and probate inventories, spinsters' **55**, 56, 60
linen washing 36
Linthorpe, North Yorkshire **216**, 217
Lister, Anne 156, **158**, 173
litigation, women's use of 15, 107
  see also Court of Chancery; law
livestock holding
  by spinsters 69–76
  on common land 47
  decline of 72–3, 75–6
local histories 231
London
  market trade 45
  women plot owners **232**, 233, 240–2
Loseley Park estate **158**, 168, 170–1
Lowther, John 83, 94
'lunatic', definition of 104

Malay, Jessica 26
male line, failure of 106
Mallerstang, Westmoreland 89, 90
markets 44, 45–6
married women
  bequeathing right 205

business activities 12
childcare 36–7
'consent' to marriage 124
domestic violence 118–23
forced marriages 100–26
household accounts 154
land/property ownership 6–8, 226–7, 248–53
mortgages 218
property rights 54, 204–5
property transactions 202, 211–13, 224
prosecution for working on Sabbath 39
wills 205, **223**
women-to-women property transactions **221**

Married Women's Property Acts (1870, 1882 & 1893) 7, 17, 205, 213, 226, 233, 234, 251, 252, 276
Mason, George 189
Massey, Doreen 30
Massey, Hannah (Hannah Jackson) 256–7
Matlock, Derbyshire 144, 146
Mawmill, Thomas, will of 60
Meakin, Mary 70
meal preparation 34
memorandum books 154, 167, 168
men
agricultural work 38
childcare 37–8
property transaction data **207**, **211**, **216**
metaphors of land 27
micro-rentals 69
middle-classes
accounting skills 149
and inheritance 16, 206
women's sphere 15–16
Middlesbrough, North Yorkshire 214–15, **216**, 217
migration 273
milking work 47, 49
Mill, John Stuart 16
Miller, James, will of 260
Miller, Nicholas 111–12, 113
Mills, Sara 128
minimum wage 4
mining 152, 156, 165, 172–3, 186, 232
Mirror for Magistrates 98
Mitcham, County Durham 240
Molyneux, Jane More **158**, 167, 168, 169–71
money-lending 66, 67–8, 76
Monkey Island 137
Montagu, Elizabeth 26, 156, **158**, 165, 166, 176–200
and 'Capability' Brown 188–200
and labourers 195–6, 198–9, 200
moral responsibility of 196–7
Montagu, Frances, countess of Mar 104
Moore, Hannah 30
Morris, R. J. 205–6, 250, 261
Morris, Valentine 188, 189
mortgages 20, 68–9, 74, **218**, **219**, 220
mourning jewellery 263
Municipal Franchise Act (1869) 16

name, women's retention of 270
National Probate Calendar 231
'natural' landscape 188
neighbour disputes 39
network concept 90
Newdigate, Roger 133, 139, 141, 146
Newdigate, Sophia, travel journal of 26–7, 127–48
Norfolk diocese
formal lending with land 74
land bequests 66
landholding by spinsters *63*, *64*, *70*, *72*
livestock holding *70*, *72*, *73*
wills and probate inventories, spinsters' **55**
Normanby, North Yorkshire **216**
North Riding (Yorkshire), property transactions 201–25
Northallerton, North Yorkshire **216**, 217
Nottage, Margery 41
nuncupative testaments 56–7
Nuneham estate 197

occupations *see* work activities
Oliver, Margaret 234, 237, 242, 243
Ombersley, Worcestershire 53
operas 107
Osborne, Dorothy 47
Ovid 185, 189, 190
owner-occupiers 20
Oxford and Great Western Union Railway 235
Oxfordshire, women plot owners **232**, 233, 234–6

Page, Elizabeth 34–5
Paine, Edward 241–2
Paine, George 241
Paine, Georgiana 241–3

paintings 139–40
parish records 231
parks and gardens *see* gardens
parliamentary elections, Appleby by-election 94–6
partible inheritance 53, 206
the pastoral, construction of 176–200
pasture land, spinster landholders 67, 68
pasturing 69–71, 72
'patriarchal equilibrium' 273
patriarchy 32, 271, 273–4, 276
patronage networks 93, 96, 99
paupers 270
Payling, S. J. 115
Peak District, tourism 133, 143, 145–6
peerage 271, 275
Pendragon Castle 89
Percy, Elizabeth 136
Periam, John 159, 160
personal property, bequests of 262–4, 266
Peters, Christine 53
Philips, Fabian 78
Pickering, North Yorkshire **216**, 218
picturesque, the 142–3, 145
Piercefield (or Persefield) gardens 188
Pinchbeck, Ivy 244–5
plays 107
ploughing 38
pocket books 154
political power 16–17
poor women 48, 270, 272
Pope, Alexander 105
Portman Square, London 186
poverty, rural 196
Powys, Lybbe 136, 138
prenuptial agreements 9, 122
primogeniture 5, 8–9, 19, 52, 58, 100, 205–6, 269, 271
'private' trading 35
probate inventories **55**
probate records 231
  see also wills
property market/transactions, Deeds Registers data 201–25, 244–66
property ownership
  in early modern England 4–10
  gender inequalities 2–4, 17–21
  and identity 25–8
  and the law 4–10
  legal status of women 248–53
  married women 6–8, 202, 204–5, 211–13, 224, 226–7, 248–53
  spinsters 204, **212**, 213–14, **221**
  transfers of 56–7, 107, 244–66
  widows 204, **212**, 213, 220, 224
property prices 3
property reversion 65–6
property rights 9–10, 54, 204, 205, 227
provisions dealers 44–5
Prowse, Elizabeth (*née* Sharp) **158**, 160–4, *163*, 166, 167
Prowse, George 161
public houses (alehouses) 35
Purcell, Henry 107
purchasing of land 66

Quin, Matthew 164–5

railways
  Books of Reference (Index Ledgers) 229
  Durham Coast Railway 239
  Great Northern Railway 237
  Hartlepool and Cleveland Junction Railway Company 238
  investment in 234
  London 232, 240, 241
  Oxford and Great Western Union Railway 235
rambling 146
rape 48, 102–3, 105, 114, 124
'ravishment' 102, 105, 112, 113, 124
Rawson, Ann 71
re-conveyances **218**, **219**
Redcar, North Yorkshire **216**, 218
Reform Acts (1832 & 1867) 16
regional histories 231
Register of Deeds *see* Deeds Registers
Restoration period 107
reversion of property 65–6
revisionist history 15
Richmond, Surrey 241
Riley, Mary, will of 65
roads 46
Robinson, Thomas Tempest 254
royal courts 86
Royalists 106
Rubinstein, W. D. 229
rural businesses 12
rural land market 23
rural women, experiences 29–50
Russell, Anne 86
Russell, Margaret 78, 79, 80, 81

Sabbath observance 39

Sackville, Margaret 93, 95
Sackville, Richard 79–80, 82
St Croix (Caribbean) 261, 262
St John Mildmay, Jane **158**
Salmon, Frances, will of 65
Sandleford estate, Berkshire, pastoral landscape, construction of 176–200
Saville, John 5–6
Sayer, Elizabeth 47
Scarborough, North Yorkshire 214, 215–17
Seeliger, Sylvia 22–3
Segrave, Thomas, will of 57
sensibility, cult of 145–6
'separate spheres' theory 150, 245, 254, 269, 272, 273–4
separation, marital 256–7, 258
servants
  beneficiaries of wills 65
  childcare 37
  estate accounts 154, 156, 164, 166, 167
  household accounts 154
  livestock holding 70, 71
  mealtimes 34
  prosecution for working on Sabbath 39
  and spatial dynamics 29
sex 41, 48, 118
sexual assault 48, 102–3, 105, 114, 124
shares, investment in 13–14
Sharp, James 161, 162, *163*
Sharp, William 161
sheep 47, 72
Shepard, Alexandra 32
Shepard, Helene 71
shopkeepers 45
shopping, for food and drink 34–6
SIDA *see* Swedish International Development Cooperation Agency
silverware 262, 266
single women
  property ownership 248
  property rights 204
  wills of 223
  see also spinsters; widows
Skaife, Lancelot 83
Skelton, North Yorkshire **216**
Skinner sisters 219
Skipton Castle 87–8, 99
small-scale female landholding 226–43
smallholdings 9
Smelt, Leonard 181, 193–4
Smith, Richard 9
Smith, Susan 48
Smollett, Tobias 141–2
socage, rights of 112
social status 242–3
solicitors 166, 167
Somerset, Elizabeth, duchess of Beaufort **158**, 172
songs 41, 105
Sparrow, Olivia Bernard **157**, 166–7
spatial analysis, gender relations 29–50
Spence, Richard T. 78, 79, 96
Spicksley, Judith 8, 9, 23
spinning work 42–4, 46
spinsters
  formal lending with land 74
  gifts of land 65
  grazing rights 71
  inheritance of land 58–62
  landholding 51–76, 235
  livestock holding 69–74, 75–6
  money-lending 67–8, 76
  possession of land 62–9
  property transactions **212**, 213–14
  'spinster' term 55–6
  wills of 54–7, 62, 64–9, 209, **223**
  women-to-women property transactions **221**
  see also single women; widows
Spring, Eileen 5, 51, 109, 115, 125–6
Spufford, Margaret 52
Statute of Rapes (1382) 102–3
statute staple 69
Staves, Susan 54
stereotypes, cultural 274, 275
stewards 156, 164, 166, 167
Stobart, Jon 26–7
stock market 13
Stockton-on-Tees, North Yorkshire 217
Stonehenge 141
Stopes, Charlotte Carmichael 268
Stout, William 40
Stowe 138, 140
Stranton, County Durham 238–9
strict settlements 5–6, 9, 109
the sublime 143–4
Suffolk, spinning work 42, 43
suffrage, women's 16–17, 268, 276
sugar plantations 261, 262
surname, women's retention of 270
Swann, Thomas 259
Sweden 36
Swedish International Development Cooperation Agency (SIDA) 18

tableware 262
Tait, A. A. 205
Talbot, Elizabeth Countess of Shrewsbury 2
taste 137, 139, 244
  aesthetic gaze, the 145
  Edmund Burke, *A Philosophical Enquiry in the Origins of Our Ideas of the Sublime and Beautiful* (1757) 143
  romantic, the 143–4
  sensibility 146
  travel writing 136–7, 138
taxes, hearth 23
tenancies, joint 53
tenant–landowner relations 82–7, 88
textile industry 42
theft 39, 48–9, 166
Thompson, Frances 118
Thompson, Francis 109, 113, 116, 117, 118–20
Thompson, Richard 110, 111, 113
Thompson, Stephen 106, 113, 117
Thompson, William 101, 110, 111, 115–18, 120–2
Thompson, William, Jnr 121, 122, 123
Thornaby, North Yorkshire **216**, 217, 219
Tipping, Elizabeth 74
tithe disputes 40
topographical writing 131
tourism 127–48
  adventures and dangers 146
  ancient sites 133, 141
  art appreciation 139–40
  country house visits 127, 130, 131–2, 136–7, 147, 186, 187
  countryside 129
  culture 139–40
  garden visits 137
  Grand Tour 128, 130, 136, 141
  itineraries 130–5
  sensibility, cult of 145–6
town histories 140
towns, property transactions 215, 244–66
Townsende, Judith 45
trade
  cloth trade 42, 46
  dairy trade 44, 45
  grain trade 45–6
  itinerant traders 35–6
  provisions dealers 44–5
  women's involvement in 251–2
trade directories 252, 253
transfer of land/property 56–7, 107, 244–66
transfer of mortgages **218, 219**
travel, women's mobility 46
travel writing 127–48
  aesthetics 136–7, 142–8
  art appreciation 139–40
  ballroom measurement 140
  countryside 142
  domesticity theme 136
  state of the nation accounts 135
  topographical writing 131
  writing styles 133–5
tree felling/planting 170–1
Trotte, Peter, will of 72
trusts 234, 249–51, 253, 255, 257, 259, 260
  exploitation of 266
  law of trusts 9
  and married women's property rights 205, 206, 227
  validity of 227
Tufton, Nicholas 93
Tufton, Thomas 93–4
Tunstall, John 111, 112

Underway (Undercliffe), Isle of Wight 132
UNIFEM *see* United Nations Development Fund for Women
United Kingdom (UK)
  Extracted Probate Records 231
  housing crisis 3
  landownership 19–20
United Nations Development Fund for Women (UNIFEM) 19
United Nations Entity for Gender Equality and the Empowerment of Women (UN Women) 18
unmarried women *see* single women; spinsters; widows
Upton, Mary 241
urban economy, property transfers 244–66

Vesey, Elizabeth 183, 185, 186, 189, 190, 191
Vespond, Anne 66, 67
Vickery, Amanda 151–2, 154
violence
  abduction of heiresses 100–26
  against wood gatherers 49
  alehouse assaults 35
  domestic violence 118–23
  sexual assaults 48, 102–3, 105, 114, 124

Vitruvius Britannica (Campbell) 130–1
voting rights, women's 16–17, 268, 276

wages
 minimum wage 4
 spinners' 42–3
Wakefield, West Yorkshire 237
walking 146
Walter, John 32
Waltham Abbey 137
Wandle River 240
Wearing sisters 221–2
weavers 42
Webster, John 45–6
Webster, Joseph Lee 49
weddings 41
West Yorkshire, women plot owners **232**, 233, 236–7
Westmorland, Clifford estates 77–99
Wharton, Mary 103
Whitby, North Yorkshire **216**
Whitehaven, Cumberland 53
Whittle, Jane 23, 35
Wicken estate **158**, 160–4, 167
widows
 business owners/operators 254–5
 estate accounting/management 156, **157–8**, 161–4, 166–7, 168
 financial empowerment of 252–3
 landownership 235–6
 mortgages 218
 property rights 9–10, 204
 property transactions **212**, 213, 220, 224
 tithe disputes 40
 wills of **223**
 women-to-women property transactions **221**
 see also single women; spinsters
Wiesner, Merry 58
Williamson, Joseph 94, 95, 96
Willingham 52
wills 17, 22, 202, 222–3
 access to 231
 bequests to daughters/wives 59–62
 Birmingham sample 246–7, 254–66
 'death bias' 228
 domestic goods bequests 262–4, 266
 furniture bequests 262–3, 266
 household goods bequests 262–4, 266
 illegitimate children, provision for 257
 Index of Wills and Administration 231
 jewellery bequests 263, 266
 of married women 205, **223**
 nuncupative testaments 56–7
 personal property bequests 262–4, 266
 probate records **55**, 231
 servant beneficiaries 65
 of spinsters 54–7, 62, 64–9, 209, **223**
 spousal support provision 256–7
 under-representation of women in probate records 228
 values of male and female estates **264**
 'wealth bias' 228
 of widows **223**
 see also inheritance
Wilton, Wiltshire 138, 139
Winchester cathedral 139
Windsor, Berkshire 131–2
Wiskin, Christine 153
women
 account books 149–75
 correspondence 176–200
 diaries 77–99, 127–48, 272
 economic agency of 244–6
 economic disadvantages of 3–4
 mobility of 46
 and patriarchal dominance 274, 275–6
women-to-women property transactions 220–1
women's suffrage 268, 276
wood gathering 36, 49
Wood, Mary, will of 259–60
Woode, Anne, will of 70
Wooton Farm 140–1
work activities 11–17, 214–15, 267
 agricultural work 38–42, 46–9
 attitude to work 209
 business owners/operators 11–17, 24, 254–5
 childcare 36–8
 communal work 43
 cooking 34
 data sources 209, 210
 domestic work 33–8
 family firms 254–5
 housework 33–8
 laundry work 36
 milking work 47, 49
 money-lending 66, 67–8, 76
 provisions trade 44–5
 spinning 42–4, 46
 trade 44–5, 251–2
 wood gathering 36, 49
workplaces 29

World Conference of Women 18–19
Worthen, Hannah 8
Wrest Park, Bedfordshire 165
Wright, Margaret, will of 69
Wright, Nancy 4–5
Wyatt, James 178, 180–1, 191–2
Wyntor, Robert, will of 61

Yorkshire
  East Yorkshire gentry 105, 110
  Hotham, Sir John 105
  Humbleton estate 115
  partible inheritance 53
  property transactions 201–25
  women plot owners **232**, 233, 236–7

PEOPLE, MARKETS, GOODS: ECONOMIES AND SOCIETIES IN HISTORY

ISSN: 2051-7467

PREVIOUS TITLES

1. *Landlords and Tenants in Britain, 1440–1660: Tawney's* Agrarian Problem *Revisited*
edited by Jane Whittle, 2013

2. *Child Workers and Industrial Health in Britain, 1780–1850*
Peter Kirby, 2013

3. *Publishing Business in Eighteenth-Century England*
James Raven, 2014

4. *The First Century of Welfare: Poverty and Poor Relief in Lancashire, 1620–1730*
Jonathan Healey, 2014

5. *Population, Welfare and Economic Change in Britain 1290–1834*
edited by Chris Briggs, P. M. Kitson and S. J. Thompson, 2014

6. *Crises in Economic and Social History: A Comparative Perspective*
edited by A. T. Brown, Andy Burn and Rob Doherty, 2015

7. *Slavery Hinterland: Transatlantic Slavery and Continental Europe, 1680–1850*
edited by Felix Brahm and Eve Rosenhaft, 2016

8. *Almshouses in Early Modern England: Charitable Housing in the Mixed Economy of Welfare, 1550–1725*
Angela Nicholls, 2017

9. *People, Places and Business Cultures: Essays in Honour of Francesca Carnevali*
edited by Paolo Di Martino, Andrew Popp and Peter Scott, 2017

10. *Cameralism in Practice: State Administration and Economy in Early Modern Europe*
edited by Marten Seppel and Keith Tribe, 2017

11. *Servants in Rural Europe, 1400–1900*
edited by Jane Whittle, 2017

12. *The Age of Machinery: Engineering the Industrial Revolution, 1770–1850*
Gillian Cookson, 2018

13. *Shoplifting in Eighteenth-Century England*
Shelley Tickell, 2018

14. *Money and Markets: Essays in Honour of Martin Daunton*
edited by Julian Hoppit, Duncan Needham and Adrian Leonard, 2019